Empire of Dreams

D1500771

Empire of Dreams

The Science Fiction and Fantasy Films of Steven Spielberg

Andrew M. Gordon

ROWMAN & LITTLEFIELD PUBLISHERS, INC.
Lanham • Boulder • New York • Toronto • Plymouth, UK

ROWMAN & LITTLEFIELD PUBLISHERS, INC.

Published in the United States of America
by Rowman & Littlefield Publishers, Inc.
A wholly owned subsidiary of The Rowman & Littlefield Publishing Group, Inc.
4501 Forbes Boulevard, Suite 200, Lanham, Maryland 20706
www.rowmanlittlefield.com

Estover Road, Plymouth PL6 7PY, United Kingdom

British Library Cataloguing in Publication Information Available

Library of Congress Cataloging-in-Publication Data

Gordon, Andrew, 1945–
  Empire of dreams : the science fiction and fantasy films of Steven
Spielberg / Andrew M. Gordon.
       p. cm.
  Includes bibliographical references and index.
  ISBN-13: 978-0-7425-5577-8 (cloth : alk. paper)
  ISBN-10: 0-7425-5577-1 (cloth : alk. paper)
  ISBN-13: 978-0-7425-5578-5 (pbk. : alk. paper)
  ISBN-10: 0-7425-5578-X (pbk. : alk. paper)
  1. Spielberg, Steven, 1946– —Criticism and interpretation. I. Title.
PN1998.3.S65G67 2008
791.4302′33092—dc22

                              2007024397

Printed in the United States of America

♾™ The paper used in this publication meets the minimum requirements of
American National Standard for Information Sciences—Permanence of Paper for
Printed Library Materials, ANSI/NISO Z39.48-1992.

This book is dedicated to my son,
Daniel Taylor Gordon,
who at age three slept with an E.T. doll.

Contents

Acknowledgments ix

Introduction: "I dream for a living" 1

1 *Duel* (1971): Paranoid Style 13

2 *Jaws* (1975): Hydrophobia 29

3 *Close Encounters of the Third Kind* (1977; Rev. 1980):
Unidentified Flying Object Relations 55

4 *E.T.* (1982) as Fairy Tale 75

5 *Poltergeist* (1982): Divorce American Style 93

6 *Raiders of the Lost Ark* (1981): Totem and Taboo 109

7 *Indiana Jones and the Temple of Doom* (1984): Bad Medicine 125

8 *Indiana Jones and the Last Crusade* (1989):
Raiders of the Lost Father 137

9 *Always* (1989) and the Eternal Triangle 151

10 Short Films: "Kick the Can" (1983) and "The Mission" (1986) 169

11 *Hook* (1991): The Peter Pan Syndrome 183

12 *Jurassic Park* (1993) and *The Lost World: Jurassic Park* (1997):
Jaws on Land 203

13 *A.I.* (*Artificial Intelligence*) (2001): Separation Anxiety 227

14 *Minority Report* (2002): Oedipus Redux 243

15 *War of the Worlds* (2005) and Trauma Culture 253

Conclusion: Moving Toward the Light 267

Index 277

About the Author 291

Acknowledgments

Marleen Barr taught me a lot about science fiction; Brooks Landon and Vivian Sobchack, about science fiction film.

I am indebted to some colleagues at the University of Florida. The psychological insights of Norman Holland deeply influenced my writing about film. John Cech, Peter Rudnytsky, and Kenneth Kidd offered helpful suggestions about several chapters. BernaRowman 03 Fontsrd Paris and Hernán Vera did detailed readings of the entire manuscript.

My friend Craig Barish helped procure some of the illustrations in New York. I owe special thanks to the unflagging support and wisdom of my brother Phillip Gordon. And my fellow writer, the late, great David Walley, was a source of unfailing energy and encouragement for the forty-three years I knew him. He put a lot of time and energy into editing the book. He is sorely missed.

Various chapters were delivered as talks to the Group for the Application of Psychology at the University of Florida, the Science Fiction Research Association Conference, the Conference on the Fantastic in the Arts, the Eaton Conference on Science Fiction, and the International Conference on Literature and Psychology. I thank those organizations for allowing me to speak and the conferees for their input.

My students in an undergraduate course at the University of Florida on the cinema of Spielberg helped me hone my ideas. The University of Florida granted me a sabbatical to finish the book.

Thanks are also due to my editor at Rowman & Littlefield, Brenda Hadenfeldt, who believed in the book.

"Raiders of the Lost Ark: Totem and Taboo" originally appeared in *Extrapolation* 32.3 (Fall 1991): 256–67, and "*Duel*: Paranoid Style" appeared in

Compromise Formations: Current Directions in Psychoanalytic Criticism, ed. Vera Camden (Kent, OH: Kent State University Press, 1989), 199–213. Both are reprinted with permission of the Kent State University Press. *"Close Encounters:* Unidentified Flying Object Relations," appeared in *The Psychoanalytic Review* 82.5 (October 1995), 741–57, and is reprinted with permission of Guilford Press. *"Indiana Jones and the Temple of Doom:* Bad Medicine" appeared in *Foods of the Gods: Eating and the Eaten in Fantasy and Science Fiction*, ed. Gary Westfahl, George Slusser, and Eric S. Rabkin (Athens: University of Georgia Press, 1996), 76–85, and *"E.T.* as Fairy Tale" appeared in *Nursery Realms: Children in the Worlds of Science Fiction, Fantasy, and Horror*, eds. Gary Westfahl and George Slusser (Athens: University of Georgia Press, 1999), 11–27. Both are reprinted with permission of the University of Georgia Press.

For help obtaining stills, I would like to acknowledge Jerry Ohlinger's Movie Material Store.

Introduction

"I dream for a living"

Steven Spielberg, director of several of the biggest hits in Hollywood history as well as a producer and entertainment tycoon akin to Walt Disney, is probably the most popular and influential filmmaker in the world today. His films have become part of global consciousness and his cinematic style part of the visual vocabulary of world media.

There has been a great deal of resistance to taking Spielberg seriously, however, so that writing about his films tends to fall into the extremes of uncritical adulation or dismissive contempt. While most publications about Spielberg provide a fan's eye view of the man and his work, many academic critics dismiss his films as akin to animated cartoons or sentimental greeting cards.[1] I shall treat Spielberg with respect as a major filmmaker. So far, there has been no comprehensive study of all the science fiction (SF), fantasy, and horror films he has directed. I shall evaluate his achievement as one of the most significant American directors in these genres in the past thirty years and distinguish between his stronger and weaker films.

Spielberg's appeal as a storyteller is primarily visceral and emotional rather than intellectual. This accounts for a large measure of the critical resistance to his films, but appealing to the senses and bypassing the logical mind often enables him to reach levels of deep feeling. A director of tremendous technical proficiency and audiovisual flair, he has an extraordinary ability to tap into the fear and wonder of the child within himself and to evoke the responsive, emotional child in audiences everywhere.

Although Spielberg's films tend to be epics, they are usually warm and personal, even in part disguised autobiography. There is an intimate relation between the man and his work. "I dream for a living," Spielberg has said (Corliss 54). "I've never been through psychotherapy or psychoanalysis

1

. . . . I solve my problems with the movies I make" (Breskin 79).[2] He sees moviemaking as part of a process of collective or shared dreaming: "I interpret my dreams one way and make a movie out of them, and people see my movies and make them part of their dreams" (Breskin 79).

Because Spielberg's SF and fantasy films have a dreamlike quality and their central appeal is emotional, my approach to them is primarily—but not exclusively—psychological. I focus not only on the films and their relationship to their creator, but also on the reactions of critics and other audience members, including myself. I deal with such questions as: how does *Duel* evoke paranoia in the audience? Why did the opening of *Jaws* so terrify me when I first saw it that I wanted to leave the theater? How does Spielberg make me identify with an extraterrestrial in *E.T.* and with a robot in *A.I.*, so that *E.T.* makes me cry and *A.I.* makes me sad? And, by contrast, why do I find it so difficult to identify with the hero of *Close Encounters*, and why does the fantasy romance *Always* leave me cold?

The Spielberg I explore is the director of SF, fantasy, and horror films because these are the bulk of his work for over thirty years. Of the twenty-five theatrical features he directed from 1971 to 2005, sixteen are SF, fantasy, or horror, a coherent and impressive body of work that makes Spielberg one of the most prolific and important SF and fantasy filmmakers of his generation.[3] In versatility and range, Spielberg's achievement in contemporary American SF, fantasy, and horror film is perhaps comparable to that of Stephen King in contemporary American SF, fantasy, and horror fiction. Just as King helped to shift American horror in the 1970s from the gothic to the contemporary American small town, so Spielberg helped to domesticate the American SF and horror film, transposing it to the contemporary suburbs.

Granted, realism is a matter of convention, and even Spielberg's films in more "realistic" genres sometimes verge on the fantastic: for example, *1941* (1979) is a frenetic slapstick farce; *The Color Purple* (1985) is a Cinderella story; and *Empire of the Sun* (1987), with its sometimes surreal imagery, I have called "a boy's dream of war" (Gordon). Spielberg says, "I make movies that are a little bit above life, or below life, but not real life!" (Ebert and Siskel 71).

SPIELBERG AND LUCAS CHANGE AMERICAN SF AND FANTASY FILMS

According to Vivian Sobchack, American SF films released in the decade after Stanley Kubrick's *2001: A Space Odyssey*—that is, from 1968 to 1977—were "cool and detached in their vision, or cautionary and pessimistic in their tone" (Sobchak 226). Then George Lucas's *Star Wars* and Steven Spielberg's *Close Encounters of the Third Kind* were released in 1977 and sparked a renaissance in American SF and fantasy film. "Through some strange new transformation, technological wonder had become synonymous with domestic hope; space and time seemed to expand again, their experience and representation becoming what can only be called 'youthful'" (226).

This transformation is probably due to the fact that Lucas and Spielberg were both baby boomers—Lucas born in 1944, Spielberg in 1946—and among the first cineliterate, media-saturated generation to grow up with television and SF films. Lucas and Spielberg thrived in that post–World War II media sea, absorbed all those 1950s and 1960s television programs, SF and fantasy films, SF pulp magazines, cartoons, and comic books, and made that culture an integral part of their imaginations. Both also came of age in California during the late 1960s and the turn toward mysticism in the American counterculture. Thus Lucas and Spielberg and their films belong to what Christopher Lasch calls "the party of Narcissus," roughly corresponding to the New Left, New Age, feminists, and environmentalists, who glorify not rational man but natural man, "dreaming of a symbiotic reunion with nature" (Lasch 258). Lucas and Spielberg represented something new in SF film and in American culture: they were technocrats who called attention to "the dangers of 'instrumental reason' and industrial technology" and found an antidote in technologically innovative films that paradoxically affirmed "mysticism, spirituality, or the power of 'personhood'" (*Lasch* 253).

From 1975 to 1981, through the huge successes of *Jaws, Star Wars, Close Encounters,* and *Raiders of the Lost Ark,* they created a genre: the SF and fantasy adventure, special-effects blockbusters. As cultural landmarks in the 1970s and 1980s, the films of Lucas and Spielberg were imitated and parodied by many other movies and television programs in a wave of space opera, heroic fantasy, and sentimental fantasy.[4] Their works were part of a paradigm shift in the popular imagination, beginning in the late 1970s and continuing into the present, into a new age when SF and fantasy dominated and saturated popular culture, including comic books, video games and computer games, advertising, animated cartoons, music videos, and theme park rides, as well as film. Lucas and Spielberg became the Walt Disneys of their generation by domesticating myths and fairy tales for popular consumption and establishing their own leisure-time conglomerates. Like Disney, both have shown an uncanny ability as popular entertainers to plug into the desires of mass audiences, not simply in America but worldwide. While Lucas brought to SF film some of the epic sweep and romance of heroic myth, Spielberg brought some of the warmth of fairy tale.

For over thirty years, Spielberg has worked in the entire gamut of cinematic SF, fantasy, and horror: SF crossed with fantasy, with horror, or with film noir; heroic fantasy; children's fantasy; supernatural fantasy; and thrillers with touches of horror. His early SF films had little science and a lot of mysticism, and were driven largely by emotion, whereas his more recent SF films are more hard-edged, contain more science, and are driven by both emotions and ideas. Spielberg's work in SF, fantasy, and horror film shows an eclectic range of influences, including 1930s and 1940s cliffhanger serials, 1950s and 1960s SF film, as well as Disney cartoons, Chuck Jones cartoons, and television SF and fantasy. Spielberg also draws on literary sources: SF novelists including Richard Matheson, Michael Crichton, Brian Aldiss, Philip K. Dick; and H. G. Wells; and fairy tales like "Hansel and Gretel" and "The Frog King," along with the modern fairy tales *The Wizard of Oz*, *Pinocchio*, and *Peter Pan*.

In Spielberg's SF, fantasy, and horror films, the visual iconography, the plots, and the character types often bring us the sense of wonder, anxiety, and sentiment inherent in fairy tale. He called *E.T.* "a contemporary science-fiction fairy tale" (Crawley 114). Lester D. Friedman places Spielberg "squarely in the tradition of artists who sought to highlight the sublime in the everyday, the sense of wonder and awe amidst the dross of common experiences" (Friedman 117). In his suburban trilogy of *Close Encounters*, *E.T.*, and *Poltergeist*, I would argue that Spielberg became our wizard of the suburbs by transforming tract homes into fairy-tale cottages, bringing back some of the magic that had been leached out of mass-produced lives.

IN DEFENSE OF SF AND FANTASY FILM; IN DEFENSE OF SPIELBERG

Spielberg's enormous early success—a multimillionaire director before he was thirty—and the genres of SF, fantasy, and horror in which he worked, invited frequent critical dismissal of his early work as that of a slick popularizer who was canny at reading the market, spotting trends, and giving audiences what they want, a craftsman with great visual facility but little to say. His films were often put down as mawkish and manipulative, overdone, or too dependent on shock or sentimentality. He was charged with being a fuzzy-minded occultist, a *faux naif*, a case of arrested development, and he was blamed for infantilizing American culture during the age of Reagan (Britton). For a long time, the repeated complaints that Spielberg's films are childish or "politically incorrect" prevented him from receiving serious critical attention. I believe such criticism may fundamentally misunderstand not only Spielberg but also the value of SF, fantasy, and horror film.

A critical division about Spielberg's work has been evident since *Close Encounters*, his first SF film: on the one hand, some critics see his work as shallow, excessive, childish, manipulative kitsch; on the other hand, there are those who view it instead as visually powerful, sweeping, childlike in a positive sense, and often moving.

E.T.: Domesticating the fantastic: Suburban home as fairy-tale cottage. Universal, 1982.
Courtesy MovieStar News.

Lurking behind some of the hostile criticisms of Spielberg's early films may be an old prejudice against the genres of SF, fantasy, and horror. Many critics were upset that these previously marginalized genres became central and dominant in American film production after 1975, that is, after *Jaws*, *Star Wars*, and *Close Encounters*. It is a critical convention that certain film genres are read as "less fictional" (Westerns, gangster, or war films) and others as "more fictional" (the musical, horror, and fantasy). Stephen Neale writes, "It is no accident, therefore, that these genres [the musical, horror, and fantasy] have persistently been marginalized, relegated to the realms of escapism and utopia . . . or classified as suitable mainly for children and adolescents" (38).

We tend to forget that all narrative film is fantasy, whether we call it realistic or not. Westerns do not deal with a real West nor do private-eye movies depict the behavior of actual detectives. They are fantasies, based in turn on other fantasies, as popular fiction and film have evolved over the years, in conjunction with their audiences, shared public myths about the behavior and significance of "The Cowboy" or "The Private Eye." Says Will Wright, "As a social myth, the Western was always a fantasy" (124). "Realism" is a set of aesthetic conventions which change over time, and narrative films that pretend to present the world as it operates now or in the past are no less fantasies than films about the future. If fantasy is present to some extent in all narrative film genres, then there is little reason to marginalize genres which foreground the fantastic, such as SF, fantasy, and horror.

The easy dismissal of many of Spielberg's films as juvenile, escapist junk resembles the traditional attacks on SF and fantasy literature as second-rate genres suitable only for children. What about Dickens as a popular entertainer, writing novels that were in large part fairy tales and epic cartoons for grownups? "Part of Dickens's universal appeal must come . . . from his essentially 'comic strip' private imagination: the world of giants, demons, ogres, and beautiful princesses that had such a rapturous fascination for him . . . and for which he found counterparts in Victorian life" (Bayley 11). Indeed, there are many parallels between Dickens and Spielberg: their desire to touch the masses, their painting in broad strokes, their warmth and sentiment, their deep connection to childhood, and their expert invocation of the terror of facing "giants, demons, and ogres." The equivalents of Dickens's orphans—lost, cruelly abused, and endangered children—are all over Spielberg's films. In fact, in *Empire of the Sun* Basie and Jim resemble Fagin and Oliver, and in the film *The Color Purple* Celie reads aloud from *Oliver Twist*.

Some critics who dismiss Spielberg also assume a clear dichotomy between "mature" and "childish" art. The appeal of "the Lucas-Spielberg Syndrome," according to Robin Wood, is that of "the lost breast endlessly rediscovered" (163). And Robert Philip Kolker refers to "the nursery of the Spielberg world" (270). Such criticism ignores the regressive nature of the film medium itself. The semiotician Christian Metz has remarked that the act of viewing film puts one into a state of suggestibility akin to daydream or hypnotic trance (Metz 133). And Robert T. Eberwein compares viewing film to dreaming or temporarily returning to the condition of an infant. "Films in general seem both real and dreamlike because they appear to us in a way that activates the regressive experience of watching dreams on our psychic dream screens. The actual screen in the theater functions as a psychic prosthesis of our dream screen, a structure constituted by the mother and breast, or a surrogate for it, or by our own ego" (Eberwein 192). In other words, all narrative film could be said to offer the regressive appeal of "the lost breast endlessly rediscovered." One way to distinguish good film from bad is not whether the film is regressive, but the use it makes of controlled regression, what the psychoanalyst Ernst Kris called the "regression in the service of the ego" which is art (Kris 177). By that standard, *E.T.* is for me a great film, for it invites us to identify with a child as he develops.

Some of the resistance to the films of Spielberg, and to SF and fantasy film in general, may stem from a deep fear of losing our adult dignity and reverting to "childishness." We both desire to recapture what was valuable

Poltergeist: The TV as dream screen. MGM/UA, 1982.

about our earlier selves and we fiercely resist that desire. As has often been remarked, the "Golden Age" of SF is twelve, and the best SF appeals to the eternal, wondering child within us. According to the psychologist James Hillman:

> a restoration of the mythical, the imaginal and the archetypal implies a collapse into the infantile realm of the child. Our strong ego-centered consciousness fears nothing more than just such a collapse. The worst insult is to be called "childish," "infantile," "immature." So we have devised every sort of measure for defending ourselves against the child—and against archetypal fantasy. These defenses we call the consciousness of the strong, mature and developed ego (15).

Such rigid defenses may help to account for the many putdowns of the early Spielberg as a case of arrested development, along with the repeated demands that he "grow up." We might as well demand that Lewis Carroll "grow up," when the restoration of the child is what he does best. A Spielberg who was purely adult would not have been capable of creating films such as *E.T.* and *A.I.*

The fear of regression to childishness is reinforced by a particularly American disapproval and even fear of fantasy, which the SF and fantasy novelist Ursula Le Guin ascribes to "our Puritanism, our work ethic, our profit-mindedness, and even our sexual mores" (39). Le Guin says that Americans are taught "to repress their imagination, to reject it as something childish or effeminate, unprofitable, and probably sinful" (41–42).

Some attacks on the films of Spielberg therefore smack of neopuritan-
ism: entertainment is only good for us if it makes us *work*, and any cultural
phenomenon that is too pleasurable is suspect, a guilty pleasure. For Robin
Wood, for example, "The finer pleasures are those we have to work for"
(164). There may be different kinds of pleasure, but why is *pleasure* supposedly better as it approximates *work?* For Wood, "Fantasy, by and large, can
be used in two ways—as a means of escaping from contemporary reality
or as a means of illuminating it" (185). But the best fantasy provides both
escape and illumination, as, for example, does *Alice in Wonderland*. And
there are many different uses for fantasy besides escape or illumination,
including mental exercise and aesthetic delight. Most of all, fantasy is an
indispensable part of everyday reality: nobody gets through a day without
dreams, daydreams, or other imaginative devices.

The critical prejudice against SF, fantasy, and horror may derive not only
from a fear of childishness or of the "wrong" kinds of pleasure but also
from a fear of emotion and of the pleasure of feeling emotion. However,
success in fantasy films is measured by their capacity to evoke the requisite
feelings in the spectator: horror, anxiety, fear, or wonder (Neale 38). Writes
Spielberg's biographer Joseph McBride, "What Spielberg's harshest critics
may find most offensive about his style of filmmaking, in the last analysis,
is simply that he expresses deep emotion and does so without embarrassment" (McBride 376). His films are often unabashedly sentimental
or melodramatic in an old-fashioned way (including a return to the lush
symphonic scoring of classical Hollywood films), so that it is easy to dismiss them as corny, hokey, tearjerking, or manipulative. Charles Affron has
noted a fear of feeling in critical response to film:

> Art works that create an overtly emotional response in a wide readership are
> rated inferior to those that engage and inspire the refined critical, intellectual
> activities of a selective readership. . . .
>
> It is argued that blatantly emotional films cheapen and banalize emotion
> *because* they are blatant. Their promptness to elicit feeling offends those who
> consider being easily moved equivalent to being manipulated, victimized,
> deprived of critical distance. Art works are judged *bad* when . . . they attempt
> to convey deep feelings about the self, the family, love, commitment, ethics
> (1–2).

Deep feelings about "the self, the family, love, commitment, ethics" are
precisely the territory of Spielberg's films. Affron argues that all narrative
cinema speaks the language of feeling. Emotion is primary and ideas secondary in motion pictures; if a narrative film fails to move us through its
images and sound, then it has failed as cinema. Spielberg's films are too
often criticized on the very grounds for which they should be praised: that
they can move us.

Spielberg has noticed a defensive response to his films as "manipulative," which may occur even among viewers who enjoy them:

> People begin to get suspicious of your intentions when the films are so wildly popular . . . when it starts breaking records, some'll say, "Well, wait a second. I'm being tricked. There's some kind of evil seduction afoot. I don't trust that Spielberg. He's manipulating me now. I know, I enjoyed it, I saw it four times, but that little bastard manipulated me!" ("Dialogue on Film," 16)

All film is manipulative, and whether a film reaches an elite or a mass audience has little to do with whether it is good or bad art. Says Spielberg,

> Everything about movies is manipulative; when you walk into the theater, you're buying a ticket to manipulation! And all this accusation about how manipulative we are—perhaps more specifically I am—is nonsense. (Ebert 76).

Kolker, for example, dismisses Spielberg's works because of "their glibness and polish, their ability to excite the most accessible emotions" (237), not specifying what these emotions might be nor why they are "most accessible." He seems threatened by the emotional potential of Spielberg's films and analyzes them as if Spielberg were a dangerous cinematic tyrant, using phrases such as "the viewer will surrender," "power like this," "manipulates emotion," and "he tightens his film like a trap" (237–38). But why is emotional content in a film necessarily *bad*? Doesn't it take skill to move viewers? Didn't Chaplin, Ford, and Capra make audiences laugh and weep? Didn't Hitchcock "tighten his films like a trap"? Isn't this in large part why we treasure these directors?

I admit that sometimes my rational brain resists Spielberg while my heart gets swept away. In the final scene of *The Color Purple*, for example, it irks me that Celie's children, newly arrived in America from Africa, speak no English, even though they were raised by American missionaries—but I still have tears in my eyes from the emotional payoff, the mother-and-child reunion we have been awaiting since the beginning scene. Yet *The Color Purple* is not a film I care to revisit. By that standard, *E.T.* is one of Spielberg's masterpieces, a film which repays repeated viewings, a rich and satisfying film in which he is able through technical skill and visual power to evoke deep emotions that originate in childhood. If I came across it in a science-fiction magazine, I would never tolerate a story like *E.T.*, but on the screen it moves me every time: the poetic camera technique, the luminous images, and the tenderness of the director toward his characters help me to care about them.

Bruno Bettelheim wrote, "There is general agreement that myth and fairy tale speak to us in the language of symbols representing unconscious content" (36). Like fairy tales, Spielberg's SF, fantasy, and horror films "speak to us in the language of symbols representing unconscious content." As Dr. Hobby says to David in *A.I.*, referring to *Pinocchio*, "The Blue Fairy is part of the great human flaw: to wish for things that don't exist. Or to the greatest single human gift: the ability to chase down our dreams." Spielberg's SF, fantasy, and horror films, too, chase down dreams. In fact, they have become part of the dream life of the nation.

NOTES

1. Writes Nigel Morris, "Most books on Spielberg are uncritical popular hagiographies or highly critical personal biographies, while the films prompt enthusiastic but banal celebrations in cultish science fiction magazines. On the other hand, especially left-wing reviewers often sniffily dismiss the films on such grounds as conservative ideology, cuteness, racism, triviality and escapism" (Morris 4).

2. Elsewhere Spielberg admits he has been through psychotherapy. See my chapter on *Hook*.

3. I include *Poltergeist*, which is credited to Tobe Hooper as director, but Spielberg came up with the story, produced, and was on the set for most of the filming. *Poltergeist* has far more of Spielberg's directorial style and visual stamp than Hooper's.

4. For example, the movies *Starcrash* (1979), *Battle beyond the Stars* (1980), *Krull* (1983), and *Tron* (1982) are all influenced by *Star Wars*; *Mac and Me, Flight of the Navigator* (1986), and *Space Invaders* recycle the kid-and-alien-pal premise of *E.T.*; and *High Road to China* (1983) and *Romancing the Stone* (1984) emulate the cliffhanging derring-do of *Raiders*. *Airplane* (1980) and *Caddyshack* (1980) briefly parody *Jaws* (John Williams's famous shark theme music started showing up everywhere); *Spaceballs* (1987) spoofs *Star Wars*; *Ferris Bueller's Day Off* (1986) playfully uses the music from *Star Wars*; *UHF* (1990) mocks both the opening sequence of *Raiders* and the mashed potato scene of *Close Encounters*. On television, in the late 1970s *Battlestar Galactica* rips off *Star Wars*; in the 1980s, *ALF* puts an extraterrestrial in a suburban household for comic effect, as in *E.T.*, *Tales of the Gold Monkey* is yet another *Raiders* clone, and *Muppet Babies* parodies *Star Wars* and *Raiders* with Miss Piggy as Princess Leia and Kermit the Frog as Indiana Jones.

REFERENCES

Affron, Charles. *Cinema and Sentiment*. Chicago: University of Chicago, 1982.
Bayley, John. "Best and Worst." *New York Review of Books*, 1-19-89: 11.
Bettelheim, Bruno. *The Uses of Enchantment: The Meaning and Importance of Fairy Tales*. New York: Vintage, 1976.
Breskin, David. Interview with Spielberg, *Rolling Stone*, 10-24-85, 79.
Britton, Andrew. "Blissing Out: The Politics of Reaganite Entertainment." *Movie* 31/32 (Winter 1986): 1–42.

Corliss, Richard. "'I Dream for a Living,'" *Time*, 7-15-85, 54.

Crawley, Tony. *The Steven Spielberg Story*. New York: Quill, 1983.

"Dialogue on Film: Steven Spielberg." *American Film*, June 1988: 12–16.

Ebert, Roger and Gene Siskel. *The Future of the Movies: Interviews with Martin Scorsese, Steven Spielberg, and George Lucas*. Kansas City, MO: Andrews and McMeel, 1991.

Eberwein, Robert T. *Film and the Dream Screen: A Sleep and a Forgetting*. Princeton, NJ: Princeton University Press, 1984.

Friedman, Lester D. *Citizen Spielberg*. Urbana: University of Illinois, 2006.

Gordon, Andrew. "Steven Spielberg's *Empire of the Sun*: A Boy's Dream of War." *Literature/Film Quarterly* 19.4 (1991): 210–21.

Hillman, James. "Abandoning the Child." *Loose Ends: Primary Papers in Archetypal Psychology*. Irving, TX: Spring, 1978: 5–48.

Kolker, Robert Phillip. *A Cinema of Loneliness: Penn, Kubrick, Scorsese, Spielberg, Altman*. 2nd ed. New York: Oxford, 1988.

Kris, Ernst. *Psychoanalytic Explorations in Art*. 1952; rpt. New York: Shocken, 1964.

Lasch, Christopher. *The Minimal Self: Psychic Survival in Troubled Times*. New York: Norton, 1984.

Le Guin, Ursula K. "Why Are Americans Afraid of Dragons?" *The Language of the Night: Essays on Fantasy and Science Fiction*. Ed. Susan Wood. New York: Putnam's, 1979: 39-45.

McBride, Joseph. *Steven Spielberg: A Biography*. New York: Simon and Schuster, 1997.

Metz, Christian. *The Imaginary Signifier: Psychoanalysis and Cinema*. Trans. Celia Britton, Annwyl Williams, Ben Brewster, and Alfred Guzzetti. Bloomington: Indiana University Press, 1982.

Morris, Nigel. *The Cinema of Steven Spielberg: Empire of Light*. London: Wallflower, 2007.

Neale, Stephen. *Genre*. London: British Film Institute, 1980.

Sobchack, Vivian. *Screening Space: The American Science Fiction Film*. 2nd. Ed. New York: Ungar, 1987.

Wood, Robin. *Hollywood from Vietnam to Reagan*. New York: Columbia, 1986.

Wright, Will. "The Empire Bites the Dust." *Social Text* 6 (1982): 120–25.

1

Duel (1971)

Paranoid Style

What I was really striving for was a statement about American paranoia. *Duel* was an exercise in paranoia.

—Steven Spielberg (Taylor 78)

MAKING *DUEL*

Duel is a masterpiece of suspense, a simple, almost perfect movie: ninety minutes of road chase, a nightmare that barrels down the highway toward you with the inexorable power of a forty-ton truck. And it is as a kind of anxiety dream, a study in paranoia, that I wish to consider *Duel*. Although I recognize that there are many ways of viewing this primal confrontation of man and machine because the monster truck is a floating signifier as polysemous as the shark in *Jaws*, nevertheless, as Hitchcock taught us, any thriller that reaches us on more than a visceral level must have a psychological dimension, and Spielberg calls *Duel* "an exercise in paranoia."

Spielberg got his professional start from 1969 to 1973 at Universal Studios, directing television series and, eventually, three made-for-television movies: *Duel* (1971), *Something Evil* (1972), and *Savage* (1973).[1] *Duel* first aired as an ABC-TV movie of the week in 1971 and is considered one of the best movies ever made for television. The week after the movie aired on television, Spielberg received offers to direct feature films for various studios, but he was still under a seven-year contract to Universal. This may account for the in-joke in his film *1941* (1979): the prize offered at the big dance contest is a seven-year contract with a Hollywood studio. After *Duel*

13

won Special Mention at the twelfth Monte Carlo television festival, the film
was released in European theaters in 1973 with added footage—four additional scenes—to bring it to ninety minutes, and it won prizes at several European film festivals but was not released in American theaters until 1983.
It has since earned a cult following through cable showings and videotape.
So, although *Duel* was originally shot for television, it can be considered
Spielberg's first theatrical feature.

In 1971, the TV movie was a relatively new form, so there was room to ex-
periment. *Duel* was made for $450,000 and shot in two weeks on California
highways.[2] Spielberg created a giant mural, indicating every action sequence
along the route, and he filmed quickly, using two, three, and sometimes
four cameras at once: several positioned one hundred yards apart along the
roadside and one inside the car. Despite its low budget and tight shooting
schedule, *Duel* is a small masterpiece of camera technique, editing, and
suspense which wrings an audience dry.

The script by Richard Matheson is based on his story from *Playboy*, a
thriller about a timid businessman being chased down the highway by a
giant oil tanker truck. When Spielberg read the story, it triggered memories of highway phobia when he first drove the California freeways as a
teenager (Crawley 27). He says, "*Duel* was almost a once-in-a lifetime
story. . . . In all the years that I've been making movies, I have not found
anything as potentially fraught with suspense and tension as *Duel*" (Bianculli 23).

Like *Jaws* (1975), for which it is a kind of rehearsal, *Duel* partakes of elements of both the Hitchcock thriller and the horror film. Like most Spielberg films, *Duel* is a carefully calculated roller-coaster ride, programmed for
thrills—although it also has a certain psychological profundity. All the elements work together to involve the audience and allow us to identify with
the hero, an ordinary man forced beyond his limits when he is terrorized
by a huge truck in a highway duel to the death as ritualized as a bullfight,
suggesting that even insanity has its own nightmare logic. The film is filled
with surprises. The apparently psychopathic truck driver (or perhaps the
truck itself) toys with the hero David Mann in a sadistic cat-and-mouse
game, applying gradations of violence to initiate him into the code of the
duel, gradually stripping away his civilized restraints until he is ready to
kill or be killed. Similarly, Spielberg plays with his audience, tricking and
shocking by gradually building suspense, momentarily slackening it, fooling us when we are off guard, and then screwing the tension to an almost
unbearable level in the climax.

The merits of the film are in Richard Matheson's script (based on his
story), meticulous storyboarding, crisp editing and pacing, fluid and dynamic camera work, Billy Goldenberg's tense and eerie musical score (reminiscent of Bernard Herrmann's music for Hitchcock's *Psycho*) (Larson 243),

and Dennis Weaver's intense performance as the protagonist David Mann. Spielberg chose the actor because he had been impressed by Weaver's performance as a paranoid, twitchy character in Orson Welles's film *Touch of Evil* (1958).

It is the film of a young man—Spielberg was only twenty-four—who delights in showing what he can do with a camera to tell a story. For a car-chase movie, it has a rich variety of camera setups, angles, and lenses, as well as a sensuous menace in the lingering tracking shots along the sides of the huge moving truck or slow tilts down a truck driver's boots. It is an almost purely visual film. Spielberg wanted to make "a feature length silent movie" and cut most of the dialogue from the script, although the network executives made him restore some (McBride 204). The lack of dialogue emphasizes the hero's isolation in this paranoid thriller.

DUEL AND HITCHCOCK

Every thriller must be judged against Hitchcock's achievement, and *Duel*, like *Jaws*, demonstrates that Spielberg is an apt disciple of the master. The film follows many conventions of the Hitchcock formula: I think of films like *The Thirty-Nine Steps* (1935), *The Man Who Knew Too Much* (1934, 1955), or *North by Northwest* (1959). Although it is not a slavish imitation of any particular Hitchcock film, the elements are recognizable: The hero is an ordinary man who is suddenly plunged into trouble by sheer happenstance. Chaos and violence erupt, totally disrupting his complacent routine. Macabre and bizarre events take place in broad daylight. The hero's life is in danger, he is chased by a malevolent force, and the climax is a plunge over a cliff. Here is the cinematic return of the repressed, a paranoid nightmare with a happy ending. In *Duel*, as in the typical Hitchcock film, the hero is stripped of his secure, everyday identity and must prove his manhood by tapping hidden resources of endurance, resourcefulness, and courage. It may be low-budget Hitchcock, lacking some of his complex human interplay, depth of theme, and wit, but it is nonetheless a most effective thriller which successfully applies Hitchcock's essential method. "Spielberg follows the Master but, unlike pastiche Hitchcock thriller, adapts the techniques to his own sensibility" (Morris 29).

But unlike Hitchcock's thrillers, which take place in the "real world" (except for *The Birds*), *Duel* borders on the fantastic, which makes it that much more of an anxiety dream. A truck that large couldn't accelerate that fast. The hero's nemesis is a machine, not a man. The driver of the truck is a shadowy presence, glimpsed only momentarily, in fragments: a hand on the steering wheel, an arm signaling out the window, the bottom of some jeans and boots. He is never viewed whole and his face is never seen. As a result, the truck remains apparently driverless, and the hero seems pursued not by a human being but by a machine which embodies an irrational, demonic force. *Duel* fits Tzvetan Todorov's definition of the fantastic as a genre which involves the hesitation of the protagonist and the reader between two possible explanations, one natural and the other supernatural (Todorov 33). Richard Matheson, the author of the story and the script, is a writer of science fiction, fantasy, and horror who contributed to Rod Serling's *Twilight Zone* TV series, and *Duel* has been discussed as science fiction by the science-fiction novelist Brian Aldiss and as horror by the horror novelist Stephen King.

MAN VERSUS MACHINE

Critics have called *Duel* the apotheosis of the car-chase movie, ninety minutes of pure highway pursuit (Aldiss 175). But beneath that elemental structure is a primal confrontation of man versus truck that, somewhat akin to the archetypal confrontation of man versus whale in *Moby Dick*, lends itself to many different interpretations. It can be read as Man versus Machine, Suburban Man versus Rural American, Bourgeois Man versus Capitalism, or simply Man versus Thing.

First, the duel between the man and the truck could be seen, as Spielberg claims, as "an indictment of machines. And I determined very early on that everything about the film would be the complete disruption of our whole technological society. . . . And specially, where the truck was concerned, I wanted it to be the true, perfect, perpetual-motion machine" (Crawley 26). Like George Lucas's science-fiction film *THX 1138* (1971), the film expresses the technophobia of the late 1960s and early 1970s. But despite Spielberg's claim, *Duel* is not a clear indictment of machines; instead, it pits one giant machine run amok (the oil tanker) against a smaller machine (Mann's Plymouth Valiant). Spielberg criticizes not machines but the mechanization of life. He has said, "Dennis Weaver's whole life is very much like the truck's. . . . He's as regimented about his life style, about getting to work on time, as the truck is in waiting for people behind cul-de-sacs, ravines and canyons" (Crawley 26).

Second, Spielberg says that *Duel* is an indictment of suburbia. "The hero of *Duel* is typical of that lower middle-class American who's insulated by suburban modernization. . . . And a man like that *never* expects to be challenged by anything more than his television set breaking down and having to call the repair man" (Crawley 26). If so, *Duel* is a qualified indictment, for his suburban hero wins out in the end. In a sociological sense, David Mann is suburban man—a white-collar businessman in suit and tie, emasculated, passive, and harmless—challenged by a rural American, the truck driver—a blue-collar cowboy in boots and jeans, macho, aggressive, and deadly. When the truck first chases the Plymouth down the mountain, Mann's radio is tuned to a country music station. But the class conflict is posed in terms of the codes of the classic Western movie: the Easterner, a pale city fellow who lives by the rule of law, becomes a man only after winning a showdown with a Westerner, a rugged individualist and outlaw bred in the anarchy of the frontier. The Easterner must adopt the ruthless methods of the Westerner to defeat him, as in John Ford's The *Man Who Shot Liberty Valance* (1962). In *Duel*, truckers are "the personification of Western individualism, following their own rules" (Morris 26). According to two critics, before Mann's final confrontation with the truck, "he stalks toward it in the classic manner of a Western hero, and later snaps on his seat belt as though it were a six-shooter and gunbelt"(Pye and Myles 225). Spielberg says, "I felt very strongly that he should be a mild-mannered businessman of the hen-pecked variety, needing a major change in his life. His life needed changing, as they say in the Old West"(Crawley 26).

For that reason, among others, Spielberg was reluctant to agree with Italian critics who wanted to interpret the film as a Marxist allegory: "Surely, his fiendish truck represented the all-crushing forces of the capitalist Establishment? He refused to rise to the bait. He saw the truck, almost inevitably, as a train without tracks. As for the film, why that was *Godzilla vs. Bambi. . . .*" (Crawley 24).

Spielberg was referring to the short animated cartoon, *Bambi Meets Godzilla*, a brief parody in which Bambi the deer peacefully grazes in a clearing in the woods until a giant foot enters the frame from above and squashes Bambi flat, ending the film. His facetious reference points to the element of the fantastic in the film. Critics have also seen the influence of Chuck Jones's "Road Runner" cartoons in *Duel* (Mott and Saunders 20; Morris 26). As much as the film follows the patterns of the thriller or the Western, it is also based on the classic fairy-tale scenario of little man versus giant monster.

The monster of fantasy and horror—the truck in *Duel*—is a floating signifier which one can interpret as one wishes. Brian Aldiss emphasizes this multivalent nature of *Duel*: "The freedom it gives us—is that it is not, say, a Marxist tract, or a hymn of praise or hate about traffic on our roads. The ambiguities open up naturally when Mann moves from the safety and banality of the known to the challenge and beauty of the unknown" (Aldiss 175). Aldiss sees the film as fantasy, "an archetypal confrontation between Man and Thing" (174), and Thomas Lee Snyder sees the truck as Other, beast or monster: "This fear of the Outside, or fear of the Unknown, serves as the basis for the archetypal image of the monster, the primary archetype in many horror films" (Snyder 129).

Duel: The thriller allows us to see the world through paranoid eyes. Universal, 1971.

DUEL AND PARANOIA

Some critics hint at a psychological interpretation of *Duel*. For example, Aldiss mentions that the film opens "with the car swinging out of one of those little suburban villas where The Family develops all its classic manias" (Aldiss 175) and Snyder claims that "the evil truck is really an attack from within, and David Mann's paranoia is really a fear of the savagery that lurks within us all" (Snyder 131). Friedman says that, "As in many monster movies, Mann confronts two competing sides of himself," the civilized versus the violent and irrational (Friedman 130). Pye and Myles write that "it would be amusing to read the film as a parable of a man denying his sexuality and its implacable force; perhaps even a man denying his homosexuality. . . ." But they admit that the hero's problems are not simply sexual:

> The whole giant weight of trivial problems is rolled together in one homicidal machine. We know Mann is anxious about a contract and worried about his job; we see the fragility of his relationship with his wife; there are hints of economic anxiety and overprotectiveness about possessions like his car. Under such pressure a man's identity becomes uncertain; he can be forgiven the paranoid fantasy that the truck represents. (Pye and Myles 225–26)

All thrillers have "paranoid" elements, and Snyder and Pye and Myles mention David Mann's "paranoia." As Jerry Palmer writes, "the world that the thriller portrays is a paranoid world . . . what it does is propose to the reader that he too should see the world through paranoid eyes" (Palmer 86–87). *Duel* is not only a chase story but also a psychological fable in the form of a paranoid nightmare for both hero and audience. *Duel* is "an attack on the spectator" (Morris 21). The film begins like an anxiety dream in which you are prevented from getting to an important meeting by a series of frustrating delays. Then it turns into a real nightmare: you forget about the meeting because now you are fleeing from some implacable, unstoppable evil which is chasing you and wants to kill you for no apparent reason. Through Mann's experiences, we can safely go crazy, participate vicariously in a paranoid state, confront the most monstrous evil imaginable, and emerge victorious. For those benefits, we are willing to undergo the director's controlled sadism.

Paranoids are alone with their fear: "The thriller hero is always, intrinsically, isolated" (Palmer 29). Throughout *Duel*, Mann becomes progressively more isolated in his battle with the truck. The roads are unnaturally empty, there are no police visible, the one time he tries to phone for help, the truck rams the phone booth, and the driver he asks to call the police doesn't want to get involved. By the climax of the film, Mann realizes that he is on his own; no one is going to help him.

His most persistent difficulty is in persuading anyone that he is indeed being persecuted, that his life is in danger, and that he is not, in fact, crazy, "like a Hitchcock hero who, in trying to point out a mad villain, himself appears mad" (Brode 35). He even comes at times to doubt his own perceptions and wonders if he is losing his grip. An old farmer who sees Mann crash into a fence is skeptical and amused when Mann claims that a truck was chasing him and tried to kill him. The crowd in a restaurant laughs at him, and when a man there whom he mistakenly believes to be the driver of the truck tells him, "You need help," Mann attacks him, is beaten, and is told to leave.

Impotence and humiliation are the order of the day for Mann; the film gives him the full treatment, enough to confirm his feeling that everyone is against him. He is first humiliated in front of an old man who watches him stagger into the restaurant and then in front of the crowd in the restaurant who witness his bizarre behavior and enjoy his defeat in the fight. When Mann tries to push a stalled school bus, the children jeer him: "You can't do it!" one child mocks. And he can't; his bumper gets stuck under the bus. He grows so hysterical as the truck approaches that one kid announces, "You must be outta your brain!" When he tries to persuade the bus driver that the truck driver is crazy, the bus driver says, "If I had to vote on who's crazy around here it would have to be you." To the outside world, Mann exhibits all the symptoms of a man suffering from classic delusions of persecution (Mott and Saunders 21). Their laughter at him only increases his feeling of being persecuted, of receiving no respect as a man.

Mann's seemingly crazy behavior is justified by the plot; the threat he faces is real. Someone is out to get him; he just doesn't know who it is. As they say: even paranoids can have real enemies. Yet on another level he *is* deluded and frequently acts on mistaken premises because he begins to sense threat everywhere: he attacks the wrong man in the restaurant, and he assumes the truck will harm the school bus when it actually turns around to help. The threat may be real, yet, in another sense, the truck is symptomatic of the eruption of his deepest fears. Mann is predisposed to paranoia.

The most "paranoid" scene in the film is the unnerving episode in Chuck's Café. Mann goes to the men's room in this truck stop to recover from a narrow escape after his first pursuit by the truck. He reassures himself, "All right, boy, it was a nightmare, but it's over now. It's all over." Yet when he looks out the front window of the restaurant, the truck is parked outside, evidently awaiting him. The nightmare will continue. He tries to rationalize the presence of the truck ("He probably eats here all the time") but grows increasingly disturbed. The probing, subjective camera, the close-ups, and the eerie music emphasize his mental distress and heighten the suspense in this scene. Mann sits isolated in a booth, trying to hide his face behind a hand as he nervously scans a solid phalanx of the enemy: truck drivers seated at a counter, most wearing the boots and jeans that are the only identifying marks of the driver of the killer truck. That driver knows Mann's face, but Mann doesn't know his. Almost any man in the café could be his nemesis. All the faces seem to glare at him in hostile close-ups. The tension builds until Mann provokes an assault by a driver. But when the lethal truck suddenly pulls away, we realize that none of the men in the café could have been its driver. Spielberg has played a cruel and clever trick on both hero and audience, raising false expectations, enabling us to participate in Mann's unhinged state, and plunging us into the condition of paranoia where the ordinary becomes treacherous and we scan the environment for menacing clues. The deliberately restricted vision of the scene—restricted to what Mann sees and imagines, "conveys paranoia" (Morris 27). We become like Mann, victims of our heightened awareness of danger, unable to trust our perceptions, subject to delusions.

Spielberg treats his hero and his audience with the same sadistic glee, subjecting us to such cruel teases at other points in the film: when the sleeping Mann is jolted awake by the blast of a horn which he (and we) take to be the truck's but proves instead to be a train's, or when Mann, with the truck in hot pursuit, pulls off to the side of the road toward what looks like a police car but turns out to be a company car painted black and white. A close viewing reveals that the company is a pest control service named "Grebleips"—Spielberg spelled backwards (Morris 30). Once the director induces paranoia in the hero and the audience, he can play such tricks at will.

PARANOIA AND REPRESSED HOMOSEXUALITY

Of the many psychoanalytic explanations of paranoia, the best-known (though by no means universally accepted) theory is Freud's, for whom paranoia represents a defense, through projection and denial, against a homosexual fantasy (Freud 33). Pye and Myles speculate that Mann may be "denying his homosexuality, since truckers, boots, and cruel game-playing have a disproportionate importance in the commercial American gay culture" (Pye and Myles 225). In Chuck's Café, when Mann nervously sidles up to a trucker, it could be read as either confrontation or come-on. There is also an unexplained detail in that scene: while Mann eyes the truckers, a man in a blue work shirt plays pool with a buxom blonde in a short red dress. We see the woman in some other shots, too: she seems to be a loose woman associated with the truckers. We could read the male pool player symbolically as Mann's antagonist, and the woman in the red dress becomes associated with Mann's red car (the color red is used sparingly in the film, so that we notice it) or with Mann himself.

Positing an unacknowledged homosexual conflict is one way to explain the symbolism of a little car being pursued all over the California highways by a giant oil tanker bent on ramming it from behind. Mann continually scans the mirror, afraid of an imminent assault from the rear. He even expresses a perverse admiration for the truck and its driver, sarcastically exclaiming, "O boy, you're beautiful!" And when the truck plunges over the cliff along with the little car at the climax of the film, it is a *liebestod*, a "death-locked embrace" (Crawley 27).

THE HERO'S PROBLEMS WITH WOMEN

But even if we posit repressed homosexuality in Mann, the opening of the film suggests that his problems lie elsewhere and are rooted in a fear and hatred of women. It is not that he is attracted to men but that he feels like less than a man because he is dominated by women.

The film opens in darkness, with the sound of a car starting up, and then we see a garage and the street and realize that we are following a character's point of view as he drives. The subjective camera at the beginning helps us merge with the hero's viewpoint and continues through the opening credits. Aldiss calls the hero's home a "nursery middle-class environment" (Aldiss 175); if we agree, we could then interpret the opening as Mann's leaving the womb and entering the world. But it is a dangerous world; as we note, "The first shot that is not from the driver's viewpoint is framed, menacingly, by strands of barbed wire" (Pye and Myles 224).

After the first close-ups of the driver, the soundtrack on the radio changes. At first it consisted of traffic reports and ads, emphasizing the routine ("Things seem to be pretty normal on our southbound freeways"), a standard Spielberg tactic of making the fantastic more believable by grounding it in the everyday. Now it changes to a talk show and the first suggestion of the abnormal. A beleaguered middle-aged man with a fruity voice calls in, wondering if he can check the box on the government census form identifying himself as "head of the family." He says he hates "the rat race," so his wife works and he stays home and does housework. He wears a house dress and slippers and worries that the neighbors will find out; "it's so embarrassing." His ambiguous gender status bothers him: "I'm not really the head of the family, and yet I'm the man of the family, although there are people in the neighborhood who would question that. . . ." Then he launches into a misogynistic tirade against his feared and hated wife, the longest stretch of dialogue in the film:

> Well, quite frankly, the day I married that woman that, unfortunately, I've been married to for the last twenty-five years. . . . Well, it's true, I lost the position as head of the family. . . . You know how women are before you marry them. They're so nice. Suddenly, they become so aggressive. I mean, she became so *aggressive* after. Just took over everything. I'm afraid of her. I've been wanting to divorce her. . . . She doesn't know I'm calling. But that woman just *drives me* up the wall and over the other side. (Emphasis added.)

Later, we see that, despite his amusement at the radio caller, Mann resembles this pathetic wimp, and that he, too, has problems containing his anger at his wife and himself, so the duel becomes a way to release his rage about his emasculation.

As the radio caller's complaint concludes, we first glimpse the aggressive oil truck that will become Mann's antagonist. The protagonist, who is not so much driver as driven, becomes identified with the henpecked man and the truck with his wife—or, by the logic of misogyny, with all women.

That Mann's difficulties are with both male and female authority figures (though more with women) is emphasized in an early scene at a gas station. As Mann pulls up to a pump, the truck pulls in also, dwarfing his car. The truck looms ominously throughout the scene, many of the shots favoring it, and twice it impatiently blats its horn for service. The service-station attendant is a short, skinny, servile man who lisps and limps, perhaps a reflection of the hero's shrunken self-image. Mann tells him, "Fill it with ethyl," and the attendant replies with a tired pun, "If Ethel don't mind," and says, "You're the boss," but Mann replies bitterly, "Not in my house, I'm not." Mann is under a woman's heel and can only do things "if Ethel don't mind." Meanwhile, we see shots of the trucker's boots and jeans as he paces behind the truck; here is a man clearly accustomed to being the boss.

Mann then calls his wife from a laundromat, revealing his anxiety and anger. He begins by apologizing to her "about last night," but her replies quickly anger him:

> "You think I should go out and call Steve Henderson and challenge him to a fist fight or something?"

> "No, of course not. But, honey, I think you could have at least said something to the man last night. I mean, after all . . . practically trying to rape me in front of that whole party."

She drops the subject, only to start badgering him about getting home on time, to which he replies:

> "If Forbes lets me go in time."

> "Is it that important that you see him?"

> "Huh! He's leaving for Hawaii in the morning. The way he's been griping to the front office, if I don't reach him today, I could lose the account."

She continues to browbeat him about not being home in time for dinner: "It's your mother. God knows she's not coming to see me." Twice he says "there probably won't be a problem," but he is irritated, and when she hangs up, he looks whipped and unsettled. The call, which began as his apology, has only worsened things.

Throughout this scene, Mann is further diminished and trapped visually, framed in a long shot in a narrow space between the telephone on the wall and a table. He props his leg against the table but has to remove it to let a fat lady pass to get her clothes from a dryer in the foreground. For much of the shot, Mann is further framed within the circle of the open dryer window, which makes him look like a specimen under glass (Mott and Saunders 20). "Mann literally is viewed through a female lens" (Morris 24). In the background looms the truck, and in the foreground, the arm of the fat lady intrudes as she extracts her clothes, coinciding with the line "It's your mother." Dialogue and images combine to emphasize Mann's entrapment by the domestic. The fat lady and the dryer, the wife on the phone, and the mother coming to visit: these make up the world of women which imprisons him. And looming above him is the image of the truck. According to one psychoanalyst, "One finds in certain paranoids that the father . . . has paradoxically posed less of a threat to the patient's integrity in childhood than the first source of woe—a mother intensely intrusive, suffocating, destructive of her child's bid for autonomy and independence" (Greenberg 76). That seems true of the protagonist of *Duel*.

The phone call suggests that his duel with the truck replaces the fist fight with Henderson, the meeting with Forbes, and the dinner with wife and mother, all of which he cannot carry out. The truck is, in fact, as over-bearing, griping, and demanding as his wife and Forbes, as intrusive as his mother, as aggressive as Henderson, and as oppressive and elusive as Forbes. The enormous bulk of the truck—emphasized by slow and low traveling shots, shots with it filling the screen or driving aggressively toward us, or numerous shots where it dwarfs the car—suggests the size of the threat Mann is avoiding.

The situation in the laundromat is repeated in the restaurant when Mann meets a kindly, grey-haired waitress old enough to be his mother. She seems maternally sympathetic when he requests an aspirin: "Oh, your head aches." But both aurally and visually she is presented as threatening to Mann. We hear her before we see her, through the rattle of the silverware she flings onto the table, which startles the nervous, distracted Mann and the viewer. He is indecisive as she stands and looks down on him, awaiting his order. In one shot, her arm dangles into the right-hand side of the frame, reminding us of the fat lady in the laundromat. And in another shot, we see the truck through the window, in the background behind her; the waitress is another woman or mother figure associated with that malevolent truck.

Another ambiguous woman is the "snake lady," an old woman who runs a gas station and "Snakerama" where Mann stops to try to telephone the police. Like the waitress, she is grey-haired and friendly, and we pity her when the truck smashes her snake tanks. But the scene is touched with macabre humor: Mann brushes a tarantula off his pants, and we last see the lady with a snake in her hands, a parody of a distraught mother holding a sick child.[3] This "snake mother" also contributes to the undercurrent of sexual ambivalence in the film, with its feminized males and aggressive women.

The final woman Mann encounters is the worst of all. Mann flags down a car driven by an old man and his wife to ask them to call the police. They look like kindly grandparents, but the old man is reluctant to get involved. As Mann desperately begs for help, the woman panics and orders her husband to drive off, repeating the pattern of the weak man and the domineering woman. The couple resemble Mann and his wife; on another level, however, they are the bad parents. Their refusal emphasizes Mann's physical and psychological isolation in his paranoid nightmare. Once they leave, he finally realizes that no one is going to rescue him, and he heads back to his car for the climactic showdown.

Duel does not seem to fit Freud's theory of paranoia as much as it does Melanie Klein's. Klein posited an infantile position of fear and suspicion she called "the paranoid-schizoid position." While Freud writes of the persecuting homosexual love object (symbolically, the father), Klein claims paranoid persecution has its basis in infantile imagoes of both parents.[4] If the problem of the hero of *Duel* is his uncertain male identity, then the figure who pursues him (the truck) is also sexually ambivalent, especially if we assume it is his own projection. The truck combines the internalized persecuting imagoes of both sexes and both parents: it is both persecuting phallus and smothering breast.

One interesting aspect of his duel with the truck is that he seems to wish it. First, he deliberately provokes the truck, responding to its dangerous highway games by playing stupid passing games of his own. Next, at many points he could have driven to a police station, stopped his journey entirely, or turned around and gone home. He doesn't have to accept the truck's challenge, but he really seems to welcome it, and his efforts to seek help are belated and halfhearted. All this suggests that the truck represents his own psychic projection, and that the threat it symbolizes has a peculiar personal urgency for Mann.

PARANOIA AND ANAL SADISM

I have suggested that the truck may symbolize for the hero the persecuting parents. But it also seems to embody the hero's own hostile impulses against love objects turned against himself; that is one way to preserve the objects and disavow one's aggressive or ambivalent feelings toward them. There are yet more possible levels of meaning associated with the persecuting force in paranoia. Some psychoanalysts claim that the symbolism of the persecuting object is strongly colored by the "anal sadistic" phase of development.[5] Because the persecuting object represents whatever the person disavows or rejects in himself—such as homosexual or aggressive impulses—unconsciously it becomes associated with waste products.

Mann shows certain traits one might call "anal retentive": he worries about being on time for his appointment or for dinner at home, and he is fastidious about his dress (he wears a tie even while driving) and his car. Before the day is over, however, he will be reduced to a sweaty, bloodstained wreck, and his car will be dirtied, bashed, scratched, pounded, dented, and finally totally demolished. When he first sees the truck, it offends him: he is in his clean, shiny car, stuck behind a large, dirty tanker spewing exhaust fumes from its stack (Mott and Saunders 19). The smoke invades his car, and he coughs and mutters, "Talk about pollution!" Later, try as he might, he can't escape the truck: it keeps hounding him from the rear. Spielberg made the truck as dirty as possible: "I put dead bugs all over the windshield so you'd have a tough time seeing the driver. Dead grasshoppers in the grille. And I gave the truck a bubble bath of motor oil and chunky-black and crud-brown paint" (McBride 203). When the truck topples over a cliff at the end, the revenge is psychologically appropriate; one might say that Mann has eliminated the persecuting object by excreting it.

THE TRUCK AS CHARACTER

The film engages our interest not only because of the vulnerable hero but also because of the fascinating, mysterious villain, with its motiveless malignancy. Truck and unseen driver seem to be a single unit, a blend of machine and man. The truck is a horror movie monster with some human dimension (albeit psychopathic). Spielberg deliberately chose a truck "that had a great snout. I thought that with some remodeling we could really get it to look human. I had the art director add two tanks to both sides of the door. . . . They were like the ears of the truck" (McBride 203). The death throes of the truck are given monumental significance through its slow-motion fall down a cliff. Through shots of the still spinning wheels and oil dripping like blood, we are invited to observe the destroyed truck as though it were a dying creature. Says Spielberg, "I thought it would be more interesting to show the truck expiring, slowly ticking away—the truck's a nasty guy, you want to see him twisting slowly, a cruel death" (McBride 205). As much as it is anthropomorphized, the truck is also turned into a savage beast with "a great snout." Nightmares and phobias are closely connected to paranoid states, and, according to a psychoanalyst, "The content of nightmare experience itself would seem to be reflective of the level of regression to which the dream is drawn. . . . Generally, the introjects prior to the age of two are represented as threatening aspects of other persons or as menacing machines and animals" (Meissner 592). Critics have compared the menacing machine in *Duel* to wild animals such as a wolf, shark, or dinosaur.[6] The truck stalks Mann like a wolf tracking its prey, and it charges like a bull or rhino; its horn sounds like the cry of an enraged bull elephant, and it spouts smoke like a fire-breathing dragon. As the truck plunges over the cliff in a slow-motion fall, we hear its "death cry," which Stephen King aptly describes as "a series of chilling roars . . . the sound, we think, a tyrannosaurus rex would make going slowly down into a tar pit" (King 163).[7] As monstrous beast, the truck thus prefigures the shark in *Jaws* and the dinosaurs in *Jurassic Park* and *The Lost World*.

CONCLUSION: FREE-FLOATING ANXIETY

In sum, the monster truck can be read as homosexual persecutor, as the bad parents, as Mann's aggression turned against himself, or as a savage beast. All this possible symbolism is not contradictory but mutually reinforcing; it enriches the symbolic suggestiveness of the evil truck through layers of overdetermined meaning. "The film benefits from these uncertainties . . . consequently appealing to a wide audience" (Morris 21). The movie may be carefully programmed, but it affords us a great deal of imaginative latitude.

We project onto the truck our own nightmare fears and battle alongside Mann against our worst private demons. *Duel* offers the pleasures of suspense and of mastering anxiety. For example, the film may seem misogynistic on the surface, but its terrors are so free-floating that any viewer, male or female, can translate them into personal terms. One woman viewer told me she assumed the unseen truck driver was a woman. She rooted for the truck, perhaps seeing it as a projection of her own desire for revenge against men. But I assume most viewers will root for the hero to stop being a wimp, for in his assertion of manhood lies our hope to defeat our personal demons.

Duel is a nightmare assaulting us in broad daylight. Spielberg may not be as intellectually challenging a filmmaker as Hitchcock, but he is an extremely skillful craftsman who knows which buttons to push to engage the audience on a primal level. He must be very well acquainted with the territory of phobias, nightmares, and paranoid anxiety to have made a film as riveting as *Duel*.

NOTES

1. The made-for-TV movie differs from the Hollywood feature by usually having a lower budget, less preproduction, shooting, and postproduction time, lower-paid stars (normally television rather than movie actors), more closeups for the smaller screen, and an episodic structure building to numerous dramatic climaxes to allow for commercial breaks. Because of advertisements, it is also usually shorter than a Hollywood movie.

2. Spielberg says he shot *Duel* in sixteen days (Tuchman 46). Elsewhere he says fourteen days ("Dialogue on Film"). Richard Corliss says twelve days.

3. Snyder interprets these snakes, like the leaking radiator hose in Mann's car, as "phallic metaphors," symbolizing "Mann's loss of masculinity and fear of castration," and mentions that they prefigure the snakes in *Raiders of the Lost Ark* (Snyder 131).

4. "These two dangerous objects—the bad breast and the bad penis—are the prototypes of internal and external persecutors" (Klein, *Envy* 32). It is also not surprising that the internalized images of the "bad parents" should be conflated into a single image. As Karl Abraham says about paranoia, "Another point to be noted in regard to the part of the body that has been introjected is that the penis is regularly assimilated to the female breast . . ." (Abraham 490).

5. "To a paranoiac . . . the love object is equivalent to faeces which he cannot get rid of" (Fenichel 429). "Among the organs projected onto the persecutor, feces and buttocks play a predominant role" (Abraham 490). Klein believed that in the unconscious, the "bad penis" was "equated with these dangerous faeces" (Klein, *Love* 412).

6. See Pye and Myles 23; Aldiss 174; and Snyder 130.

7. Actually, a sound editor distorted the roar of the prehistoric Gill-Man from the horror movie *The Creature from the Black Lagoon* (1954) (McBride 205).

REFERENCES

Abraham, Karl. *Selected Papers of Karl Abraham*. Rpt. 1979, New York: Brunner/Mazel, 1927.

Aldiss, Brian. "Spielberg: When the Mundane Breaks Down." *This World and Nearer Ones: Essays on Exploring the Familiar*. Kent, OH: Kent State University Press, 1979: 173–80.

Bianculli, David. Interview with Steven Spielberg. *Starlog*, January 1986, 13-18, 23.

Brode, Douglas. *The Films of Steven Spielberg*. New York: Citadel Press, 1995.

Corliss, Richard. Review of *E.T. Time*, May 31, 1982, 58.

Crawley, Tony. *The Steven Spielberg Story*. New York: Quill, 1983.

"Dialogue on Film." *American Film*, June 1988, 15.

Fenichel, Otto. *The Psychoanalytic Theory of Neurosis*. New York: Norton, 1945.

Friedman, Lester D. *Citizen Spielberg*. Urbana: University of Illinois, 2006.

Freud, Sigmund. "On the Mechanism of Paranoia." *General Psychological Theory: Papers on Metapsychology*. Ed. Philip Rieff. New York: Collier, 1963.

Greenberg, Harvey R. *The Movies on Your Mind*. New York: Dutton, 1975.

King, Stephen. *Danse Macabre*. New York: Everest House, 1981.

Klein, Melanie. *Envy and Gratitude and Other Works, 1946–1963*. New York: Delacorte, 1975.

———. *Love, Guilt and Reparation and Other Works, 1921–1945*. New York: Delacorte, 1975.

Larson, Randall D. *Musique Fantastique: A Survey of Film Music in the Fantastic Cinema*. Metuchen, NJ: Scarecrow Press, 1985.

McBride, Joseph. *Steven Spielberg: A Biography*. New York: Simon and Schuster, 1997.

Meissner, W. W. *The Paranoid Process*. New York: Jason Aronson, 1978.

Morris, Nigel. *The Cinema of Steven Spielberg: Empire of Light*. London: Wallflower, 2007.

Mott, Donald R. and Cheryl McAllister Saunders. *Steven Spielberg*. Boston, MA: Twayne, 1986.

Palmer, Jerry. *Thrillers: Genesis and Structure of a Popular Genre*. New York: St. Martin's Press, 1979.

Pye, Michael and Lynda Myles. *The Movie Brats: How the Film Generation Took Over Hollywood*. New York: Holt, 1979.

Snyder, Thomas Lee. *Sacred Encounters: The Myth of the Hero in the Horror, Science Fiction, Fantasy Films of George Lucas and Steven Spielberg*. Ph.D. dissertation, Northwestern, 1984.

Taylor, Philip. *Steven Spielberg: The Man, His Movies and Their Meaning*. 3rd edition. New York: Continuum, 1999.

Tuchman, Mitch. "Close Encounters with Steven Spielberg." *Steven Spielberg Interviews*. Ed. Lester D. Friedman and Brent Notbohm. Jackson: University of Mississippi Press, 2000: 37–54.

Todorov, Tzvetan. *The Fantastic: A Structural Approach to a Literary Genre*. Ithaca, New York: Cornell University, 1975.

2

Jaws (1975)

Hydrophobia

> The film hit a nerve somewhere. Maybe because it's basically Freudian.
>
> —Steven Spielberg (Crawley 50)

THE CRITICS ON *JAWS*

Jaws (1975) reflects the increasing self-reflexivity and diversity of American horror movies in the 1970s and 1980s. Horror in those decades was becoming aware of its own tradition and often paid homage to or parodied its predecessors even as it incorporated elements of other movie genres, including adventure films, Westerns, family dramas, and science fiction (Sobchack). Thus *Jaws* has been discussed by critics not only as a horror movie but also as part of the 1970s cycle of "disaster" films (Yacowar) or as a Howard Hawksian male adventure film (Derry 80–81; Auty 278). Moreover, as a fable of man versus sea monster it has mythic overtones in a tradition going back to the Bible (Leviathan, Jonah and the whale), *Beowulf*, and *Moby Dick*. *Jaws* has also been interpreted as yet another version of "The American monomyth," in which an Edenic community is disrupted by evil and corruption until it is rescued by a selfless and pure heroic redeemer (Jewett and Lawrence 142–68). In particular, *Jaws* has interested ideological critics as a test case of a contemporary American film inculcating white male, bourgeois, patriarchal values. As these critics see it, the hero of *Jaws* is "the paternal savior," restoring family and community in the wake of Vietnam and Watergate (Kolker 287).

I accept the validity of these various approaches: the shark in *Jaws* is "a symbolic vehicle . . . essentially polysemous" (Jameson 142). But I want to

29

Jaws: Spielberg directs Dreyfuss and Scheider. Universal, 1975.

suggest ways in which *Jaws* might also be usefully approached in terms of depth psychology. Most Hollywood horror movies, like other Hollywood genres, are conservative, but filmgoers do not select horror films primarily for ideological reassurance but for deeper psychological reasons. As Spielberg says, "The film hit a nerve somewhere. Maybe because it's basically Freudian."

WHY WATCH HORROR MOVIES?

I don't go to many horror movies. When I first saw *Jaws* in 1975, I was so scared by the opening sequence that I wanted to race out of the theater in a panic. I hadn't been so terrified by a film since the shower scene in *Psycho* (1960). Yet I stayed till the end of *Jaws*. Why did I stay? This leads to some larger questions: What brings us to horror movies in the first place? How do they make us feel? What shocks us and what defends us as we view them?

Horror is the only genre named for an *emotion*; horror is measured by the visceral response of the viewer. One way to consider horror movies is to say that they provide safe nightmares. Horror temporarily concentrates and vents the viewer's latent aggression and anxiety. As Philip Brophy says, "The gratification of the contemporary horror film is based upon tension, fear, anxiety, sadism, and masochism—a disposition that is overall both tasteless and morbid. The pleasure of the text is, in fact, getting the shit scared out of you—and loving it; an exchange mediated by adrenalin" (Brophy 5). Horror films are like roller-coaster rides: they give you a safe, controlled scare, a series of carefully programmed shocks and surprises, taking you to the limit and back home again. They are designed to make you want to repeat the experience. The screams of a horror film audience and of roller-coaster riders are as much shrieks of delight as they are of fear.

Horror films release repressed and forbidden material while carefully defending against that material. The paradox of horror movies is that they seem to produce pleasure through anxiety. Perhaps anxiety is central to the pleasure of the viewing because we want to pay for indulging repressed desires, or perhaps it is because the physiological responses to fear are similar to those for sexual arousal. For some viewers, the line between pleasure and unpleasure stretches so thin that the material of the film becomes too raw to manage, the anxiety too close to the real thing to bear. But a successful horror film enables most viewers to master the anxieties it unleashes. According to Noel Carroll, because of the psychological appeal of horror, psychoanalysis "is more or less the *lingua franca* of the horror film and thus the privileged critical tool for discussing the genre" (Carroll 16).

JAWS: THE OPENING SEQUENCE

Jaws opens with a moving camera showing the ocean floor, accompanied by the ominous bass notes of John Williams' shark theme building to a crescendo. My tension and expectancy build with the music. I am underwater, or is it in the territory of the unconscious? I see what the shark sees as it restlessly swims in search of food; the movement of the camera is a stalking rhythm. Spielberg also uses subjective camera at the beginning of *Duel* and *E.T.*, but only in *Jaws* does the opening shot come from the point of view of the unseen *antagonist*. By being given a shark's-eye view, I am implicated along with the shark, momentarily identifying with the aggressor. (There is precedent for this device in horror films such as *Creature from the Black Lagoon* [1954] and *Psycho* [1960].) At the same time, I am denied knowledge of the shark because I cannot see it. The shark is in a position of power: it sees, but itself remains unseen.

As the shark theme peaks, the music ceases, and the location abruptly changes from the cold underwater world to a warm beach scene: a group of young men and women enjoying a party at night around a campfire. The camera pans across them as they talk, laugh, sing, and enjoy oral pleasures, such as kissing and drinking. The pan stops at one young man who is facing away from the group, gazing at something offscreen. He too is engaged in oral activity, alternately drinking beer and smoking a cigarette (or is it a joint?). He is eyeing a woman who sits apart from the rest; from his point of view, she smiles back at him. I see her through his gaze, as the shark sees its victims. I begin to wonder if the young man is another shark cruising for prey. (But the real shark proves more potent and gets the girl instead?) He walks toward her, but we don't hear their dialogue, so we remain protectively detached (Morris 58).

After the opening shark's-eye view, I am temporarily relaxed by the warm light of the campfire, the music, the festive atmosphere, and the race down the beach for an inviting skinny dip by moonlight. There is also disarming comedy: the woman (Chrissie) laughs as she strips; the man (Tom) is so drunk he topples head over heels, laughing at himself. I see her nude silhouette and anticipate sexual pleasure.

But from the opening scene, I know more than they do: that the water is dangerous. It is night, and they are alone, drunk, too far from the group, and that water is very dark, so I am tensed for something awful to happen (I want it yet I don't want it—can I stand to see it?) and I get it. The man is temporarily helpless from drink; the woman races ahead, outstripping him in more than one sense, and he stumbles behind, too drunk to undress. He collapses near the water and soon falls asleep. "Cutting between the two zones creates omniscient narration, for we know more than Tom and Chrissie. The difference between the two zones—the frenzied activity in the water, the calmness surrounding Tom—creates a heightened suspense concerning Chrissie's plight: will she be saved or killed?" (Buckland 88).

But the first man we meet in the film cannot perform: he cannot keep up with the woman, enter the water, rescue her, or make love to her. This failure seems to affect all the men in *Jaws*. When the young man collapses, he lies flat on his back, one leg raised, a sexual posture traditionally read as "feminine." His repeated cry, which punctuates the scene, is ironic: "I'm coming! I'm definitely coming!" The only one "coming" in this scene is the shark. The novel *Jaws* by Peter Benchley had sex scenes, but the only sex in the film is enacted by the shark.

Soon my senses are assaulted by shocking violence: symbolic rape, dismemberment, and death. The scene seems sexually sadistic. Instead of passion, I get pain. Is the woman being punished for her sexual liberation, for her foolishness in swimming alone, or for her poor choice of a partner? Is the audience being punished?

In this opening sequence, as in *Duel*, Spielberg is inspired by Hitchcock. We have many of the same elements as the shower scene in *Psycho*: the sexual frisson of the beautiful naked blonde, mixed with suspense and terror at her vulnerability, and the killer, announced by a point-of-view shot. In both scenes, pleasure, relaxation, and sensuality are transformed into pain, terror, and violent death. Hitchcock and Spielberg turn us into voyeurs and implicate us in a violent attack which is equated with a sexual act.

The pattern of building suspense and then releasing it through a climax of incredible violence could also be said to mimic sexual arousal and orgasm. Both films had a tremendous influence on the public by making an ordinary activity suddenly seem terrifying: just as *Psycho* made people afraid to take showers, so *Jaws* made them afraid to swim in the ocean. *Jaws* increases the violence over *Psycho*, since the shower murder takes place well into the movie, whereas *Jaws* opens with the attack.

Spielberg learned from Hitchcock some of the techniques for grabbing an audience viscerally and teaching it not to relax. Like the shower scene in *Psycho*, the opening of *Jaws* instills a sense of tension and dread so that I constantly anticipate danger. Hitchcock says of *Psycho*, "The showing of a violent murder at the beginning was intended purely to instill into the minds of the audience a certain degree of fear of what is to come. Actually, in the film, as it goes on, there's less and less violence because it has been transferred to the minds of the audience" (Samuels 480).

Spielberg says of *Jaws*, "I . . . wanted to do it [the movie] for hostile reasons. I read it [the novel] and felt I'd been attacked. It terrified me and I wanted to strike back" (Crawley 42). He also says, "I chose to make a movie that would reach audiences on two levels. The first level was a blow to the solar plexus, and the second was an uppercut, just under the nose; it was really a one-two you're out combination. I never intended anything deeper than that. . . . And I really said, I'm going to make a primal scream movie. . . . *Jaws* is almost like I'm directing the audience with an electric cattle prod" (Combs 113).

Spielberg certainly succeeded in shocking me with his electric cattle prod. When I first saw *Jaws*, the opening scene, as I said, appalled me. It was not only the visual impact of the attack but the cries for help and screams of pain of the young woman that affected me: I felt helpless. The impulse is to rush to aid a screaming person; even if you are watching a play or a movie, you want someone to stop the pain. But here I knew no one would. Only a quick death would bring relief, but this scene was thrusting the agony at me, close up, and prolonging it. I wondered why I was subjecting myself to this and if I was going to be able to tolerate the rest of the movie, given an opening this shocking.

But I would have felt foolish walking out on a movie that had just started. I had come with friends, the theater was filled, and millions of people had already enjoyed this movie. It was a socially approved experience; it was critically acclaimed. "It's only a movie," I told myself. I could always avert my eyes or cover my face during the shocking parts, as I had done as a kid. And after such an opening, what would happen next? So I stayed. Spielberg gives interludes of calm so that the audience can recover, and he carefully spaces out the shocks. Thus nothing else in the film was as painful as the opening scene (although the gruesome death of Quint came close).

The psychiatrist Harvey Greenberg discusses the trend toward "cruel" horror movies, initiated by *Psycho* and continued by such movies as *Jaws* and *Alien* (1979). Cruel horror, he claims, is an ordeal designed to test "the viewer's capacity to endure psychic pain"(Greenberg 89). People attend these movies repeatedly out of a desire to master their fears. Most horror movies since *Jaws* are far more grisly. *Alien*, which transposed *Jaws* to outer space with a female protagonist, upped the ante in violence with its shocking "chestbuster" scene. It was many years before I saw *Jaws* again; the initial shock was greatly diminished by time and familiarity. *Jaws* now seems relatively tame compared to the explicit gore of such series as the *Nightmare on Elm Street* and *Friday the Thirteenth* movies. But perhaps to overcome my initial fear, I have viewed it repeatedly and studied it carefully to understand how it scared me so much.

A close look at the opening scene of *Jaws* reveals the difference between Spielberg's style and Hitchcock's in the shower scene in *Psycho*. Hitchcock works by indirection: rapid, shock cutting gives only fragmented images through which we are allowed to imagine the attack. We never see the killer clearly or the knife actually striking the victim. Spielberg does not rely on rapid cutting to fragment the action; instead, he uses relatively long takes. The camera moves very little; rather, the victim is dragged back and forth across the screen, and we get intimate closeups of her violent movement and her agonized face.

Before the attack begins, its imminence is signaled by increasingly closer shots of the body and legs of the young woman seen from below, from the shark's point of view. The emotions invoked in the viewer are multiple: as a heterosexual male, I read the provocative shots of her torso as sexual invitation, but I know the shark reads it as another kind of provocation, an invitation to attack. I become apprehensive, not only about the imminent attack, but also about my own male responses, which are voyeuristically indulged and simultaneously condemned by implication as sharklike and carnivorous. The shark's-eye point-of-view, in other words, is the view from the primitive, ravening id, from dangerous desires.

Once the attack commences, the viewer sees only what is happening above the water. *Jaws* cinematographer Bill Butler invented a water box to float the camera exactly at water level to film the attack (Buckland 89). The scene is horrifying not only because of the woman's agonized facial expressions, cries for help, and screams of pain but also because of the gruesome things I cannot see and *imagine* happening underwater. The unnatural movement of the woman across the screen is terrifying. Her torso is rapidly propelled, several times, back and forth across the surface of the water in a way no human body could move on its own. The effect of this rapid movement across the frame would have been vitiated had Spielberg used rapid cutting or a moving camera. As the camera setups graphically demonstrate, she is in the grip of some huge force which is moving her like a puppet, but we cannot see the monstrous puppeteer. The film critics Mott and Saunders write that this scene "exemplifies Spielberg's strong sense of visual style. Without gimmicks, or obvious special effects, he carefully applies the principles of terror" (Mott and Saunders 39).

In the opening scene, Spielberg, like Hitchcock in the shower scene in *Psycho*, plays upon the viewer's wish to know and yet not to know the monstrous, to see and yet not to see. Not only is the attacker invisible, but so are the underwater effects of its attack. Even before the attack, when the woman first begins swimming, there is a provocative shot of her leg rising above the water as her body disappears below it. This is a teasing shot in many senses: it is meant to tease her male companion; it also teases heterosexual male viewers in the audience; and we know that she is unintentionally tempting the shark. Now you see her, now you don't; I wonder if the attack has already begun. And once the shark arrives, Spielberg continues to tease with the presence and absence of the victim, who is snatched underwater or pulled offscreen, out of our sight, several times before she disappears permanently beneath the surface.

The shark displays all the characteristics Harvey Greenberg lists for a successful horror film creature. It is violent, ruthless and implacable in its assaults in an inhuman way, ungraspable (unseen or only glimpsed briefly, in fragments), lewd (it is a voyeur and a rapist), and yet strangely beautiful (Greenberg 93). The shark's monstrous beauty becomes apparent later, in the photographs of sharks and their awesome jaws, and in images of its sleek body gliding silently and powerfully through the water. Hooper describes the shark as "a perfect engine." Although the horror movie creature is inhuman, it is also better than human, somehow admirable in its perfection. As the robot Ash says in *Alien* (1979), describing the alien creature in words that could also describe the shark: "A perfect organism. Its structural perfection is matched only by its hostility. . . . I admire its purity. A survivor. Unencumbered by conscience, emotions, or delusions of morality."

The qualities of the shark as monster also include its enormous size (sheer size can be terrifying, especially when combined with animal ferocity, as in *King Kong*), and its apparently preternatural cunning and malevolent designs against its human pursuers (like *Moby Dick*). Unstoppable and seemingly unkillable, it terrorizes an entire town and outwits many shark hunters. It comes to seem omniscient and omnipresent beneath the water, and we never know where or when it will strike next.

In its first attack, we cannot see the shark, only evidence of its ruthless implacability and inhuman power. The attack is agonizingly prolonged. In the first phase, the woman is dragged across the water. She reaches the bell buoy and clings to it for a respite; we hope the attack is over. But a second phase commences, which does not end until she is pulled under for the

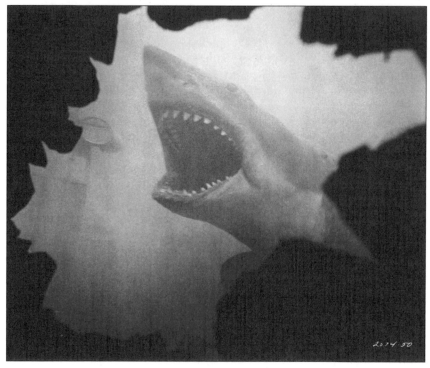

Jaws: All-devouring, a perfect organism. Universal, 1975.

last time. Abruptly, all the screaming, music, and violent, churning motion cease. We hear only the distant clanging of the bell and see only the placid surface of the water. But this unruffled calm is now charged with the menace of the unseen.

It seems to me that *Jaws* triggers many different primitive fears and fantasies in the viewer; thus there are a number of different yet mutually compatible ways of considering the opening sequence. For example, according to Dennis Giles, horror cinema reveals the monster or horrifying object but also defends us against it through concealment. There is pleasure in seeing but also "pleasure in *not seeing*—the delayed, blocked or partial vision which seems so central to the strategy of horror cinema" (Giles 41). Stephen Heath discusses the "drama of vision" in film: "*Jaws* . . . with its play on the unseen and the unforeseeable, the hidden shark and the moments of violent irruption" (Heath 514). *Jaws* teases us with glimpses of a horrible, taboo violence which we want to see but at the same time do not really want to see or acknowledge desiring to see.

As a fantasy about oral incorporation, the opening sequence seems to enact what Bertram D. Lewin calls "the oral triad": memories of being fed at the breast lead to unconsciously connected fantasies and anxieties about devouring, being devoured, and falling asleep (Lewin, *Psychoanalysis of Elation* 103–04). The opening shot, from the shark's point of view, seems to make us identify with a ravening beast, but the campfire scene on the beach counters that with positive, passive oral pleasures; the drunken young man is particularly infantile. The shark attack leads to fantasies and fears about sex as being devoured. And the sequence ends with an image of falling asleep: the young man's drunken stupor mimics postcoital bliss or the peace of a slumbering infant.

It is also possible to interpret the opening sequence of *Jaws* in Kleinian terms. According to Melanie Klein, very young children have sadistic fantasies about copulation between the parents as a mutual oral devouring. The child imagines the mother as somehow devouring the penis and retaining it inside her, where it persists as a destructive force. This destroyer is as much a projection of the child's aggression as it is a representation of the phallus. The child wants to see for itself what is happening inside the mother. In a male, oedipal scenario, he penetrates inside her to rescue her and slay the destroyer. This fantastic scenario is one possible way to read *Jaws*, seeing the shark as a floating, destructive penis, an oral devourer within the body of the mother (the ocean).

Spielberg's comments in interviews suggest that *Jaws* activated in him fantasies and fears about oral sadism and regression to the womb, and he conjured up images of a cannibalistic human fetus, a shark swimming in the womb: "Then there's the theory of its relationship to our pre-natal hours, because people are like sharks at one point. They know how to survive in the water" (Crawley 150). He also says:

> When I first got involved in the project, the thing that terrified me most was the idea that there's something else out there, that has a digestive system with intake; and the whole idea of being on somebody else's menu was just utterly horrifying. It was a horrifying thought to be part of the food chain. *Jaws* is a raw nerve movie, it's just baring your nerves and saying this is about the birth sac, you swim around in yourself. (Combs 112)

Thus, on one level, the film is about ourselves, or our fantasies about our most primitive, sharklike selves: the fetus in the womb or the infant at the breast.

That is Spielberg's response, but there is bound to be a great deal of variation in individual responses to *Jaws*, depending upon how the viewer reads the shark, that floating signifier, and how he or she defends against the fantasies and anxieties that the film brings into play, and attempts to make the experience of horror tolerable and aesthetically pleasurable.

The opening attack in some ways seems to me more horrible than the murder in *Psycho* because the killer is inhuman: the victim is not only mutilated or killed; she is also *devoured*. Yet in other ways, we are well defended by the opening of *Jaws*. First, the scene is bloodless. Second, the touches of comedy are amusing and disarming. Third, we are detached and can even perversely enjoy the killing. We know the victim well in *Psycho*—she is the heroine of the film—and Hitchcock spends considerable time making us sympathize with her before she is suddenly stabbed to death in the shower. But Chrissie is dispatched right after she is introduced; she is a stranger to us and also to her drunken companion. As David Thomson remarks, "The opening sequence of *Jaws* is one of the most captivating rapes ever filmed, and since the girl is only a nameless figure, no one we know, there is a part of us that exults in the rapturous power of the attack. No girl in any American love scene cries out with such honest amazement" (Thomson 179). Thomson chooses a sadistic stance toward the opening sequence, forgetting that the girl has a name: she tells the young man she is called Chrissie. Peter Biskind says that the close-ups on the woman's face seemed to him "a diabolical parody of all those Hollywood bedroom scenes in which the camera registers celluloid ecstasy by discretely holding on a face," while the body is never shown (Biskind 1). In contrast to Thomson, Biskind detaches himself from the violence intellectually and aesthetically.

There are sexual cues throughout the scene, but in the context of horror, they become turned into a "diabolical parody," into sadomasochistic sex. Just as the shots split the scene into killer below the water, young woman above the water, and young man on the beach, so we may shift between shark, victim, and detached bystander (the drunken, helpless young man becomes a stand-in for the immobile audience). Out of the three, any viewer can construct a defensive stance toward the scene, which may be sadistic, masochistic, or detached, or some mix of these elements.

MALE FANTASY AND PHOBIA

I dwelled at length on the opening scene because it is so intense. There is no gradual buildup, as there is in *Duel*. Instead, the shock effect of the opening immediately initiates the viewer, suggests the rules of the game Spielberg is playing, and introduces the psychological elements that will be developed in the rest of the movie.

Many critics have asserted that *Jaws* is a violent fantasy that plays on castration anxiety.[2] The film is centrally concerned with male fears and desires, especially the masculine desire to prove one's potency, and with male initiation rituals, territoriality, rivalry, and bonding. This is not surprising for a film based on a novel by a man (Peter Benchley), with a screenplay by a group of men (Benchley, Carl Gottlieb, Howard Sackler, and John Milius, among others), produced by two men (Richard Zanuck and David Brown), and directed by a man (Steven Spielberg). There is only one leading lady (Ellen Brody), and in the last half of the film, there are no women at all, just the trio of heroes (Brody, Hooper, and Quint) and the shark. So I intend to look at the film as a masculine one, although in certain ways (as in the relationship between Quint and Hooper) the film mocks machismo.

But to see *Jaws* solely as a white male fantasy does not fully explain its popularity with a huge audience, both young and old, male and female. I have suggested that *Jaws* may trigger in some viewers sadistic fantasies about copulation as oral devouring. Such fantasies are not exclusively male or female in origin. Moreover, *Jaws* plays on phobia, a nearly universal human phenomenon, in which one can become paralyzed by excessive and irrational anxiety, torn between desire and fear, or between desire and the fear of knowing one's desire. The hero of *Jaws*, Police Chief Brody, is hydrophobic (afraid of getting in the water). Just as *Duel* plays on paranoia, *Jaws* seems to induce a temporary phobic state in the viewer ("Don't go near the water!").

BRODY'S INITIATION

Jaws concerns Brody's initiation into manhood. Carl Gottleib, the chief scriptwriter for *Jaws*, summarizes the filmmakers' conception of Brody's character and development:

> Though only one of the trio of stars in the picture [the others are Richard Dreyfuss as the icthyologist and shark expert Matt Hooper and Robert Shaw as the shark hunter Quint], he would be the one who is on-screen almost throughout the story, and his character was the most complex. He would have to begin as a man who lets others shape his decisions, even to the point where those decisions cost people their lives; he would have to discover his flaw, struggle to correct it, and emerge at the end of the picture as a man who has faced up to the demons inside him and conquered them while at the same time subjecting himself to the gruesomest sort of physical danger. (Gottleib 69)

Brody is presented from the outset as having a problem with his masculine identity. Almost until the very end, Brody is passive, reluctant, inept, and ill-equipped to be a hero. Like David Mann in *Duel*, Brody is a wimp pushed to the limits by a superhuman threat until, in the final showdown, he is deprived of all aid and must confront the menace alone and prove his manhood by killing or being killed.[3]

Brody left his job as a New York City policeman because he felt helpless in the face of overwhelming violence. He couldn't even protect his family:

The crime rate in New York will kill you. There's so many problems you never feel like you're accomplishing anything: violence, ripoffs, muggings. Kids can't leave the house, you got to walk them to school.

So he retreated to Amity, a New England summer resort town on an island:

But in Amity, one man can make a difference. In 25 years, there's never been a shooting or a murder in this town.

Ironically, Amity is no safe haven; instead, it proves to be a kind of Wild West. Like the sheriff in *High Noon* (1952), Brody is the only lawman in town, and he discovers he can expect no help from the craven Mayor or the panicked townspeople. *Jaws*, like *Duel*, borrows from the situations and codes of the Western.[4]

The first half of the film is a series of slaps in the face to Brody, attacks on his manhood. In Amity, he is made to feel even more helpless than in New York. He can't protect the community or his family against the shark threat; the Mayor and town council won't let him close the beaches, and he witnesses a boy, Alex Kintner, being attacked and devoured by the shark; he is publicly slapped by the boy's grieving mother; and he sees his elder son threatened by the shark, as if to pay for the death of Alex.

As a passive watcher, subjected to scenes of horrible violence, but paralyzed into inaction, Brody is a stand-in for the audience at a horror movie. He is like the dreamer in a nightmare who cannot move although terrible danger threatens. The movie makes us want him to overcome his paralysis. Brody fails to act because he is a newcomer to Amity and his job is insecure, because he has a phobia about water, but primarily because he typically responds to stress with passivity, withdrawal, depression, and drinking. He withdrew from New York, and when he feels guilty about the boy's death, he withdraws again. Hooper finds Brody at home, deadening his guilt with whiskey. Later, after his elder son is hospitalized for shock from a shark encounter, Brody hands his sleepy younger son to his wife:

BRODY: Want to take him home?

MRS. BRODY: Back to New York?

BRODY: No, home here.

This is a turning point: Brody will no longer retreat from danger, even if it means facing his worst fear by going to sea to kill the shark.

Although our sympathies are with the underdog Brody, because he is so passive or inept he is overshadowed for much of the film by the more forceful Hooper and Quint. Hooper snaps him out of his depression and self-pity, forces him to overcome his fear of the sea and to act, and allies with him in the battle against the Mayor and the hunt for the shark. Only at the very end, when Quint is dead, Hooper is underwater in his scuba gear, the boat is sinking, and Brody is alone, does Brody show his heroic potential.

As Gottleib says, Brody at the end "has faced up to the demons inside him and conquered them." This makes explicit the link between Brody and the shark: the shark is not simply a external menace but also a representation of an internal menace. We can consider the shark, in a sense, as a product of Brody's nightmare, just as the truck in *Duel* may be considered, in a sense, as a projection of David Mann's irrational side. All of Brody's fears are concentrated into the single figure of the shark. It is his personal demon, a "floating signifier" which embodies his (or our) unleashed aggression and ravenous oral desires.

The phobia about water which paralyzes Brody could be defensive and represent the side of the character (or of the viewer) which does not really want to know his own desire. Thus the persistent teasing maneuver in the film between the desire to know and not to know, to see and not to see, between the surface of the water and what lies beneath.

BRODY INTRODUCED

Once the antagonist, the shark, is introduced in the opening sequence and claims his first victim, we meet the protagonist, Chief Brody. After the attack, from the long shot of the bell buoy and the calm surface of the sea, the camera pans slightly right and there is a dissolve to the same seascape in daylight. "The graphic match betwen Brody's view of the sea and Chrissie's death in the sea the previous night serves implicitly to link them . . ." (Buckland 91). A large black object fills most of the frame and temporarily blocks our view. We are momentarily disoriented until the object resolves into the silhouette of a head and shoulders framed against the sea. It is Brody looking out his bedroom window as he arises in the morning. This striking introduction to Brody makes him loom large against the sea, which now is charged with menace. Brody's silhouette also connects him to the couple on the beach, who were also silhouetted.

The previous scene ended with the young man falling asleep against the background of the sea, and this one begins with Brody waking up against the sea. It is also possible to read the first, nighttime scene as Brody's nightmare; now, the morning after, he is waking up after a bad dream. However, we soon see that his nightmare is just beginning. After the initial nighttime horror comes a daytime scene of comforting domesticity: Brody gets up groggily and converses with his wife, who lies in bed, a dog perched on her blanket. This establishes the structuring pattern of the first half of the film,

Jaws: The terrifying alternates with the domestic. Universal, 1975.

in which the terrifying alternates with the domestic, until the horror comes to intrude upon and dominate the home. (Grounding the fantastic in the familiar and domestic is a favorite device of Spielberg's films.) We go from the couple on the beach to Brody and his wife; the narrative link suggests that the Brodys are also potential victims of the shark. But the male and female positions of the first scene are reversed: now the woman is lying down and the man is active, suggesting that he is the one more at risk.

Troubling details intrude on this pleasant domestic scene: the couple express concern for their two sons, and the older boy, Michael, enters with his hand bleeding ("I got cut—I got hit by a vampire"), reminding us of the previous scene and foreshadowing the later shark attack on him. Then, as Brody receives a call about the missing woman, in the background Michael asks his mother if he can go swimming. As Brody leaves, his wife warns him to be careful, but he laughs it off: "In this town?" Amity has lulled him into calm, but we know better. Our initial impression of the Brodys is of a close, loving family, but already we fear for their safety.

Spielberg and the scriptwriters make the family central to increase our sympathy with Brody, involve a family audience, and raise the issue of Brody's manhood because he is shown at first as powerless to protect either the community or his family. For example, unlike the novel, Brody and his family are present when Alex Kinter is killed, Mrs. Kintner publicly slaps Brody, and Brody's own son is attacked by the shark (but unhurt). Thus, in his struggle with the shark, Brody's manhood is at stake, his authority not only as police chief but also as husband and father. He is made both more sympathetic and vulnerable than in the novel as well as more heroic at the end.

In the beginning, Brody is isolated and outnumbered by the Mayor and his cronies, who do everything possible to deny the shark threat and to keep the beaches open. The Mayor keeps cramping Brody, upstaging and coun-termanding him. Hooper talks about the shark's territoriality: it reserves for itself a certain area where the feeding is good. The Mayor too is eager to maintain his territory. As Brody strides through the town (to the tune of a marching band in an onscreen parade), about to close the beach, he is fol-lowed hard on his heels by the Mayor and the newspaper editor, who want the beach open. The coroner, who phoned Brody to verify that the young woman was the victim of a shark attack, has also contacted his friends, the town leaders.

As Brody is about to board the ferry to warn some swimming Boy Scouts, he is overtaken by the Mayor, the newspaper editor, and the coroner. There is a motif in this film of men hunting in packs: the Mayor's hunting party, the comic armada of shark fishermen in overloaded boats, and finally the trio of Quint, Hooper, and Brody. As Lionel Tiger has written about male bonding, "There is a close relationship between maleness, politics, and ter-ritory" (Tiger 80). Aboard the ferry, the Mayor and his group gang up on Brody, three against one, and he is pinned to the extreme left in a tightly framed shot. Intimidated, Brody capitulates.

Later, in the town council meeting, the Mayor is again surrounded by his male cronies, the selectmen. Brody is physically apart from this group, and his isolation is emphasized by showing him in one-shots. In the town meeting, the Mayor puts Brody on the spot by making him the bearer of the bad news about closing the beaches. The Mayor himself then announces the good news: the closing will only be for twenty-four hours. Thus he makes Brody the fall guy, undercutting and betraying him. Brody never agreed to only a one-day closing, but there is nothing he can do after the Mayor's pub-lic announcement in a place where he is protected by all his male cronies.

QUINT INTRODUCED

In the town meeting, the vulnerable Brody is overshadowed and upstaged by two more confident men: first the Mayor, and then Quint, who takes over the chaotic meeting, instantly commanding attention by scraping his fingernails across the blackboard. (The universal revulsion at blackboard screech may derive from animal instinct: the sound resembles the warning cries of macaque monkeys.)[5] With that blackboard stunt, Quint enters the film like a classroom bully. Quint issues a warning and a challenge to the crowd, although an ambiguous warning, as much against himself and the danger he represents as against the shark. He sits alone, deliberately apart from the crowd, in the back of the hall, and he takes them by surprise, just as the shark takes his victims. He is also set apart by his rudeness, his thick New England accent, and his macho, seaman's swagger in this tame tourist village. Quint wants a lot and wants it all for himself: "I don't want no volunteers. I don't want no mates. There's too many captains on this island. Ten thousand dollars for me by myself." Quint hunts sharks and is himself sharklike: a loner and a greedy devourer. Even as he talks with relish about the feeding habits of the shark—"This shark swallow you whole. A little sinking, a little tenderizing, down you go"—he is energetically crunching food in his mouth. Later we find that, like the shark, Quint is missing a tooth. From his first scene, Quint is identified with the shark; in his final, gruesome death scene, it is as if Quint so identifies with the shark that he *merges* with it.

Brody must battle not only the shark and his own fears but also these two men: the Mayor on land in the first half of the film and Quint at sea in the second half. The Mayor and Quint could even be considered different versions of the same figure, the "bad father" who wants to destroy his children. The Mayor is so obsessed with getting summer dollars for the town that he causes the death of several people, including a child, and endangers his own children and Brody's son. Quint is like Captain Ahab, so obsessed with his vendetta against the shark that he risks his boat, his life, and the lives of his crew. Brody later finds himself caught between the threat of the shark and the threat of Quint. In one scene, he flees the pulpit of the boat because of its proximity to the shark, only to almost run into the tip of Quint's harpoon.

Quint takes charge of Brody's initiation by cutting him off from his family and the everyday, domestic world. Quint takes Brody away from his wife, out to sea, and intrudes on Brody's farewell to his wife by mocking her with dirty sea chanteys. He frightens her, and she exits the film running away from the harbor. Later, Quint won't allow Brody to talk to his wife, and when he crazily smashes the radio, he could be said to be finally cutting Brody's umbilical cord.

Brody must gain his manhood by confronting and destroying three versions of the "bad father": first the Mayor, then Quint, and finally the shark. Thus, in his final scene, the Mayor has a nervous breakdown, babbling to himself, and out of focus in the shot while Brody is in sharp focus. The broken Mayor signs the paper that Brody thrusts in front of him. Brody has finally overpowered him, so the Mayor exits the film. Quint now replaces the Mayor as father figure and as an obstacle. In the next scene, Brody must confront Quint in Quint's territory. Hooper also argues with Quint, echoing the earlier scene in which Hooper became angry at the Mayor.

In the film's most gruesome scene, we see the shark's enormous jaws swallow whole the still living Quint. As the film switches from implicit to explicit horror, the scene has great effect because of the earlier tease between seeing and not-seeing. The death of Quint combines symbolic overtones of sexual intercourse, the primal scene, and castration. It is the doom Quint had predicted for himself in his chilling speech, the longest in the film, about his survival in World War II of the sinking of the Indianapolis, most of whose crew were eaten by sharks. His mate Herbie Robinson was "bitten in half below the waist." Robert Phillip Kolker writes, "His [Quint's] death—in the film's most grisly scene—is the death of the old father" (Kolker 281). That *Jaws* is concerned on some unconscious level with imagining the death of fathers is also suggested by the critic David Thomson's comment: "I have sat next to a child so distressed by one moment in *Jaws* that he cried out, as if he had dreamed the death of his father"(Thomson 173).

BRODY, HOOPER, AND QUINT

If Quint is the old, tyrannical father who must be overthrown, then Brody and Hooper are the sons in what Freud called "the primal horde," the brothers who band together to overpower the father (Freud, *Totem and Taboo* 141–46). Many critics called *Jaws* a variant on the "buddy" film featuring two male comrades, so popular in the late 1960s and early 1970s; the film ends with Brody and Hooper swimming together to shore (Kolker 286; Biskind 26).

The bonding between Brody and Hooper is consummated through drinking and hunting: the two share a bottle of wine, then, as Brody watches, Hooper conducts an autopsy on a shark, and Hooper and Brody go out on Hooper's boat on a night pursuit of the shark. The bonding of the trio—Quint, Hooper, and Brody—takes place aboard Quint's boat. Again, the context is drinking and hunting, combined with a comic matching of scars between Quint and Hooper, and climaxed by a song. Lionel Tiger claims that male bonding came about through hunting activities. Certain violent activities of groups of men, such as hunting, fishing, or warfare, lead to bonding which can break down traditional hierarchies and create a camaraderie with perhaps a homoerotic tinge. Drink helps to consummate the bond (Tiger 70, 234). After they cooperate in their first encounter with the shark, the three men celebrate, and the class-based hostility between Quint and Hooper temporarily disappears. Their bonding has begun with

Jaws: Male bonding of Quint, Brody, and Hooper. Universal, 1975.
Courtesy MovieStar News.

hunting and is sealed with drink, the comic contest of masculine prowess, and song.

Nevertheless, the alliance among the three is only temporary; Quint, Hooper, and Brody form an unstable triangle. Brody and Hooper were friends before meeting Quint and saw each other as the forces of sanity battling madness: not simply the shark, but the irrational behavior of the Mayor and the townspeople. Hooper warns Brody, "You're going to be the only rational man left on this island after I leave tomorrow." Later, both struggle against what Brody calls Quint's "certifiable" lunacy.

Although Brody and Hooper appear sane by comparison with such characters as the Mayor and Quint, they are not free of mental quirks. Brody has his phobia about the water, and Hooper is a self-proclaimed shark lover, ever since a shark nearly ate him when he was a boy. Hooper describes his boat as "a floating asylum for shark fanatics"; Hooper is similar to Quint, another traumatophile so fascinated by sharks that he has made a career out of them. Peter Biskind claims that Hooper is "more interested in shark fucking then shark hunting. He even goes so far as to offer himself as bait in the cage (shark teasing) . . ." (Biskind 26). Quint accuses Hooper of having "soft hands." Some critics sensed something effeminate about Hooper: he is a "curiously sexless schoolboy"(Britton 32), he is "cast in a rather 'feminine' role, almost as a midwife in the scene where he guts a shark," and he "is threatened with rape . . . attacked by the shark from below, much like the woman in the opening minutes" (Auty 278). In one scene, Hooper puts on a homosexual voice: as Brody and Quint bicker, Hooper calls out archly, "O, boys, I think he's [the shark] back for his noon feeding."

The homosexual undertones in the portrayal of Hooper may serve as a way of deflecting suspicion from the passive Brody. Films about male comrades or male bonding must also defend against the suggestion of the homoerotic. At first, Brody and Hooper appear to be best buddies. But once they are aboard Quint's boat, Brody becomes "the domesticated husband excluded from a latent love affair between Quint and Hooper" (Biskind 26). If we conceive of Brody and Hooper as symbolic brothers, then on Quint's boat they become his opponents and rivals for his love; they are reunited only after Quint dies. Quint, who wants total control, initially sees Hooper as a threat. Quint plays tyrannical, bullying father to Hooper's rebellious teenage son. In another sense, if Quint is schoolyard bully, then Hooper is class clown, mocking Quint and mugging behind his back. Brody, the landlubber, Quint treats with paternal contempt.

JAWS AND PHOBIA

If Duel could be said to induce temporary paranoia in the viewer, then Jaws induces phobia. There is a similarity between the paranoia of David Mann in Duel and the phobia of Chief Brody in Jaws: both conditions are manifestations of excessive anxiety, except that in paranoia the fear is provoked by people whereas in phobia the fear is a reaction to a specific situation. Both Duel and Jaws justify the hero's fears by grounding them in real dangers. Mann is being pursued by a killer truck and Brody has good reason to be afraid of the water because of the shark. Nevertheless, Mann was profoundly insecure before the encounter with the truck, and Brody's hydrophobia preceded the arrival of the shark. The two men are fearful not so much because of the menace; instead, the menace is tailor-made to fit their fears. The truck could be said to erupt out of Mann's unconscious, just as the shark erupts out of Brody's; in a sense, each film can be considered as the anxiety dream of its hero (through, of course, it also functions in different ways as an anxiety dream for its creators and for its audience).

There are two comparable scenes in Duel and Jaws: the scene in Chuck's Café in Duel epitomizes Mann's paranoia, just as the attack on the Kintner boy in Jaws represents Brody's phobia. In both scenes, the hero scans an environment where danger seems everywhere and is helpless against the threat. In Chuck's Café, Mann does not know which truck driver is his antagonist, and so all become suspect, and on the beach, Brody does not

know where or when the shark might attack, so that it becomes omnipresent, and every movement he sees in the water, however innocent, becomes
ominous. Both scenes throw in false clues to mislead us as they build tension to a climax. Above all, both help us to identify with the hero's anxiety
through subjective camera.

In *Jaws*, Brody has just been ordered by the Mayor not to close the
beaches. Now Brody sits on the beach, ostensibly out for a day of relaxation with his wife and kids, but actually there because of his nervous fear
of what may happen. Because of his phobia, the jittery Brody is unable to
enter the water, and because of the official coverup, he is unable to warn
anyone of the danger. It is an impossible situation because, caught in an
approach-avoidance bind, there is nothing Brody can do except watch helplessly. Suspense builds for him and the viewer as we wonder who will be
the shark's next victim. The camera singles out a series of figures: will it be
the fat lady? the dog? the frolicking couple? the boy on the raft? or one of
the other kids?

As Brody watches, once again we are teased by what we can and cannot
see. Brody's view, which becomes ours, is intermittently blocked by passers
by and people who come up to talk to him and interrupt his vigil. Along
with him, we strain to see, and the partial and blocked vision causes him
and us to misread: what we take to be a shark fin turns out to be a grey bathing cap, and a shrieking woman (an echo of the opening scene) is merely
being lifted in the water by her playful boyfriend. Everything becomes ominous and threatening.

At the climax of the scene, as Brody's horror-struck face registers the
shark attack on the boy, the camera executes a trick maneuver, simultaneously zooming in while tracking out. Brody's face seems to move forward
while the background recedes. Spielberg borrowed this dizzying shot from
Hitchcock's *Vertigo* (1958), another film about a hero who must overcome a
crippling phobia (in *Vertigo* it is fear of heights).[6] The shot is the cinematic
equivalent of a phobic effect, psychologically appropriate for Brody. Even as
Brody is temporarily paralyzed, rooted to his chair with shock and disbelief,
the shot thrusts him forward, as if pushing him into the water he fears so
much (Derry 80). The shot expresses both his physical paralysis and his
emotional dizziness. Spielberg wanted the effect "for suspense, shock and
environmental distortion. . . . Almost as an afterthought, he agreed that
such a shot could also cause sea-sickness in an audience" (Crawley 46).
To Robert P. Kolker, "The movement is expressive both of his [Brody's] response and the viewer's own reaction to the long delayed event, an interesting visual representation of panic. With such an effect, Spielberg charges the
spaces of the shot itself with fear and desire" (Kolker 276).

This confluence of terms—"panic," "fear," and "desire"—well describes
the paradoxical condition of phobia, which comes from the Greek "pho-

bos," meaning "fear," "terror," "panic," or "flight." Phobia has been defined as "a special form of fear which 1) is out of proportion to the demands of the situation, 2) cannot be explained or reasoned away, 3) is beyond voluntary control, and 4) leads to the avoidance of the feared situation" (Marks 3). Phobic anxiety creates an involuntary physiological response, like that evoked by any strong fear, which can include rapid breathing, dry mouth, dizziness, faintness, inability to move, and a sensation of impending death. Brody suffers from phobic paralysis, and Hooper (who sometimes seems to be an extension of Brody) often suffers from heavy breathing and dry mouth. In defense, the afflicted person tries to avoid the phobic situation whenever possible (Mavissakalian and Barlow 2).

Brody seems to have deliberately put himself in harm's way by living on a small island, for he is so afraid of the sea that he hates boats, prefers to stay in his car during ferry rides, and never goes swimming. Moreover, whenever anyone mentions his phobia, he becomes so uncomfortable that he quickly changes the subject.

Freud believed that phobia was a symbolic disguise, akin to dreaming (Freud, *Introductory Lectures* 411). The ego flees a desire it believes dangerous, the repressed desire is converted into anxiety, and the anxiety is connected with some external danger (410). For example, Freud's patient little Hans was phobic about horses, and Freud decided that the boy was really afraid of his father, but it was easier to avoid horses than to avoid the father (Freud, "Analysis of a Phobia"). Since we are never told the origin of Brody's phobia, we cannot say what it means for him, but we can speculate about what it may represent for the audience. Brody claims to be afraid of drowning, but the film does not play on that fear; instead, it induces an irrational fear of sea bathing out of the extremely remote possibility of being eaten by a shark. Does this represent castration anxiety, or, as Chris Auty claims, a more generalized fear of "dissolution, not only in the body but in the body politic of the town . . . a general sense of lost control"(Auty 278)? Or is it a fear of our own oral sadism?

According to the psychiatrist Bertram D. Lewin, the manifest anxiety of phobias "could be overdetermined and fed by more than one latent source, so that besides castration anxiety, it would contain contributions from the anxieties of pregenital and preoedipal times"(Lewin, "Phobic Symptoms" 300). That is, regression to oral sadism could lead to a fear of oral punishment, as in *Jaws*.

Moreover, the sea is commonly considered feminine, a mother symbol. The fear of the water could also mask anxiety about a desire to merge with the mother or to return to the womb. In the first half of the film, woman are punished: Chrissie Watkins, Mrs. Kintner, and Mrs. Brody. In the second half, women are absent but might be said to be there all the more eloquently for their absence, as Michael Ryan and Douglas Kellner argue. The all-male adventure "doesn't make sense except as a confirmation of manhood, that is, as the ability to perform with women. Woman is always there, in other words, as threatening perhaps as the shark" (Ryan and Kellner 64). Hooper jokes that the tattoo Quint had erased read "MOTHER." The critic Jane E. Caputi argues that the shark represents the archetype of the Terrible Mother which must be ritualistically killed by the men.

Yet if the sea is feminine, one could argue that the shark seems masculine, not a "vagina dentata" but a sort of penis with teeth. Aside from representing the infant in the oral sadistic phase, it may also represent a fantastic image of the avenging father. Bertram D. Lewin claims, "In many dreams and phobias, the biting or ravenous animal has this connotation: it is the greedy and jealous father, intruding with his claims, as the child thinks, for his full share of the oral enjoyment" (Lewin, "Phobic Symptoms" 308).

The theories of Melanie Klein allow us to combine these two fantasy images: the shark as infant in the womb and the shark as father. According to Klein, the boy's "fear of his parents combined in copulation and forming an inseparable unit hostile to himself . . . brings on danger-situations which I consider as the deepest sources of sexual impotence."

> These specific danger-situations arise from the boy's fear of being castrated by his father's penis inside his mother—that is, of being castrated by his combined, "bad" parents—and his fear, often strongly evinced, of having his own penis prevented from retreating and of its being shut inside his mother's body. This fear has a bearing, I think, on various forms of claustrophobia. It seems certain that claustrophobia goes back to the fear of being shut up inside the mother's dangerous body. (Klein 242)

Klein's theory may help explain the film's most gruesome scene, in which Quint is swallowed whole by the shark. This climactic scene, in which Brody is once again a terrified and helpless witness, unable to move, as he was during the attack on the Kintner boy, seems to combine all the paralyzing, phobic anxieties at work in the film: fear of sexuality as oral devouring, fear of being shut up inside the mother's body, and fear of being attacked and castrated by the father. These fears have paralyzed Brody. Once he witnesses Quint's death—the father receiving the revenge the son fears—he is suddenly freed from his paralysis and becomes active and potent.

CONCLUSION: *JAWS* SWALLOWS US WHOLE

Although *Jaws* appears to be an exclusively male adventure film, it plays upon fears which appeal to a wide popular audience, both young and old, male and female. These include not only castration anxiety but also a more generalized fear of damage to the body, as well as oral sadistic fantasies, fears relating to sexuality, and fears and desires about returning to the womb. The "floating signifier" of the shark and Brody's phobia about water focus these diffuse anxieties. In the first half of the film, we may get a certain guilty pleasure in watching victim after victim devoured; the second half expunges our guilt through the sea adventure and the final destruction of the monster. In the first half, the shark is a mysterious, unseen presence; in the second half, it is gradually revealed, and we come to fear it less. Our identification with Brody, who overcomes his phobia through aversion therapy and kills the sadistic monster through a symbolically appropriate revenge (he shoots it in the mouth), enables us to triumph vicariously over our own fears, as in *Duel.*

The psychological power of *Jaws* is that it is both about *being* the shark and *defeating* the shark. As Spielberg says, "It was a horrifying thought to be part of the food chain. *Jaws* is a raw nerve movie, it's just baring your nerves and saying this is about the birth sac, you swim around in yourself"(Combs 112). *Jaws* swallows us whole, and we love it.

NOTES

1. Ideological critics of *Jaws* include Britton, Biskind, Heath, Jameson, Kolker, and Ryan and Kellner.

2. "*Jaws* is the perfect movie for anyone with a larger-than-life castration complex" (Sharp). "Film and poster together imply that some of the film's success lies in its use of castration anxiety and men's fear of woman" (Pye and Myles 238). But Auty objects to the reductive interpretation of *Jaws* as a "simple fantasy of rape or castration" (Auty 277–78).

3. "The policeman, like Mann in *Duel*, is a man with deadened responses and uncertain resources who is pushed into an extraordinary situation" (Pye and Myles 237).

4. Jonathan Lemkin interprets *Jaws* as a continuation of the Puritan tradition, the American "collision between wilderness and community," with the sea as wilderness. But Spielberg would be most familiar with the opposition between wilderness and community from Western films. And the climactic confrontation—lone man with a rifle in a showdown with the villain—is a classic Western scene.

5. See "Blackboard Screech." Researchers at Northwestern University, led by psychologist Randolph Blake, found that the "voiceprint" of blackboard screech closely resembles the warning cries of macaque monkeys, and speculate that we may have inherited the aversion to the sound from our primate ancestors.

6. Among critics who mention the influence of *Vertigo* on this shot, see Crawley 46–48; Monaco 177; Derry 80; and Kolker 275.

REFERENCES

Auty, Chris. "The Complete Spielberg." *Sight and Sound* (Autumn 1982): 278.
Biskind, Peter. "Between the Teeth." *Jump Cut* 9 (1975): 1 and 26.
"Blackboard Screech." *Omni*, June 1987, 36.
Britton, Andrew. "*Jaws.*" *Movie* 23 (Winter 1976-1977): 27.
Brophy, Philip. "Horrality—The Textuality of Contemporary Horror Films." *Screen* 27.1 (Jan.–Feb. 1986), 5.
Buckland, Warren. *Directed by Steven Spielberg: Poetics of the Contemporary Hollywood Blockbuster*. New York: Continuum, 2006.
Caputi, Jane E. "*Jaws* as Patriarchal Myth," *Journal of Popular Film* 6 (1978): 305–26.
Carroll, Noel. "Nightmare and the Horror Film: The Symbolic Biology of Fantastic Beings." *Film Quarterly* 34 (1981): 16.
Combs, Richard. "Primal Screen: An Interview with Steven Spielberg." *Sight and Sound* (Spring 1977): 111–13.
Crawley, Tony. *The Steven Spielberg Story*. New York: Quill, 1983.
Derry, Charles. *Dark Dreams: A Psychological History of the Modern Horror Film*. South Brunswick, NJ: A. S. Barnes, 1977.
Freud, Sigmund. "Analysis of a Phobia in a Five-year-old boy" (1909). *The Standard Edition of the Complete Psychological Works of Sigmund Freud*, Vol. X. Trans. and ed. James Strachey. London: Hogarth, 1955, 3–149.
———. *Introductory Lectures on Psychoanalysis* (1915–1917). *The Standard Edition of the Complete Psychological Works of Sigmund Freud*, Vol. XVI. Trans. and ed. James Strachey. London: Hogarth, 1955.
———. *Totem and Taboo. The Standard Edition of the Complete Psychological Works of Sigmund Freud*, Vol. XIII. Trans. and ed. James Strachey. London: Hogarth, 1955.
Giles, Dennis. "Conditions of Pleasure in Horror Cinema." In *Planks of Reason: Essays on the Horror Film*, ed. Barry Keith Grant. Metuchen, NJ: Scarecrow, 1983, 38–52.
Gottleib, Carl. *The Jaws Log*. New York: Dell, 1975.
Greenberg, Harvey. "Reimagining the Gargoyle: Psychoanalytic Notes on *Alien.*" *Camera Obscura* 15 (1986): 87–108.
Heath, Stephen. "*Jaws*, Ideology, and Film Theory." *Movies and Methods*, Vol. II. Ed. Bill Nichols. Berkeley: University of California Press, 1985, 509–14.
Jameson, Fredric. "Reification and Utopia in Mass Culture." *Social Text* 1 (Winter 1979): 130–48.
Jewett, Robert and John Shelton Lawrence. "Apocalyptic Jaws and Retributive Ecstasy." *The American Monomyth*. Garden City, New York: Doubleday, 1977, 142–68.
Klein, Melanie. *The Psychoanalysis of Children*. Trans. Alix Strachey. 1921; rpt. New York: Delacorte, 1975.
Kolker, Robert Phillip. *A Cinema of Loneliness: Penn, Kubrick, Scorsese, Spielberg, Altman*, 2nd ed. New York: Oxford University Press, 1988.
Lemkin, Jonathan. "Archetypal Landscapes and *Jaws.*" *Planks of Reason: Essays on the Horror Film*. Ed. Barry Keith Grant. Metuchen, NJ: Scarecrow, 1984, 278–87.
Lewin, Bertram D. "Phobic Symptoms and Dream Interpretation," *Psychoanalytic Quarterly* 21 (1952): 300.

———. *The Psychoanalysis of Elation.* London: Hogarth, 1951.

Marks, Isaac M. *Fears and Phobias.* New York: Academic Press, 1969.

Mavissakalian, Matig and David H. Barlow, eds. *Phobia: Psychological and Pharmacological Treatment.* New York: Guilford, 1981.

Monaco, James. *American Film Now: The People, the Power, the Money, the Movies.* New York: Oxford University Press, 1979.

Morris, Nigel. *The Cinema of Steven Spielberg: Empire of Light.* London: Wallflower, 2007.

Mott, Donald R. and Cheryl McAllister Saunders. *Steven Spielberg.* Boston: Twayne, 1986.

Pye, Michael and Lynda Myles. *The Movie Brats: How the Film Generation Took Over Hollywood.* New York: Holt, 1979.

Ryan, Michael and Douglas Kellner. *Camera Politica: The Politics and Ideology of Contemporary Hollywood Film.* Bloomington: Indiana University Press, 1988.

Samuels, Charles Thomas. "Hitchcock." *Great Film Directors: A Critical Anthology.* Eds. Leo Braudy and Morris Dickstein. New York: Oxford, 1978, 479–90.

Sharp, Christopher. Review of *Jaws. Women's Wear Daily,* June 16, 1975.

Sobchack, Vivian. "Child/Alien/Father: Patriarchal Crisis and Generic Exchange." *Camera Obscura* 15 (Fall 1986): 7–34.

Thomson, David. *Overexposures: The Crisis in American Filmmaking.* New York: Morrow, 1981.

Tiger, Lionel. *Men in Groups.* New York: Vintage/Random, 1970.

Yacowar, Maurice. "The Bug in the Rug: Notes on the Disaster Genre." *Film Genre Reader,* ed. Barry Keith Grant. Austin: University of Texas, 1986, 217–35.

3

Close Encounters of the Third Kind (1977; Rev. 1980)

Unidentified Flying Object Relations

SPIELBERG'S SUBURBAN TRILOGY AND THE UNCANNY

After I viewed *Close Encounters* (1977; revised 1980), *E.T.* (1982), and *Poltergeist* (1982) in succession, the three began to blend together in my mind, and I hallucinated the following film, which might be entitled *Close Encounters with an Extraterrestrial of the Poltergeist Kind*:

Halloween night: three a.m. Strange creatures are abroad in suburbia.

In the valley, a network of tract homes glows like jewels under an infinite black night sky sprinkled with stars. The wind rises. Multicolored clouds boil in from the east, lightning brewing inside them.

All the parents have fallen into an exhausted sleep in front of live TV sets which cast hypnotic flickers across the room.

As strange creatures trouble the town, only one person is awake: a child (little Stevie Spielberg). The curtains of his bedroom flutter. He feels a breathless expectation. Outside the window, tree branches thrash, throwing shadows across a toy-cluttered floor. Something is loose out there, calling him. His fear and wonder grow.

He hears the sound of something downstairs raiding the refrigerator, and he's sure it's not his parents. Now there is something in his room: looming on a Darth Vader poster on the wall . . . rolling across the floor in a toy police car . . . speaking to him from the toy record player. . . .

Steven Spielberg's "suburban trilogy" consists of *Close Encounters, E.T.,* and *Poltergeist.* I group the three films together because they are closely linked in subject matter—contemporary American suburban families under stress, kidnaped children, and paranormal phenomena—in emotional tone—a mix of mystery, suspense, fear, comedy, warmth, breathless anticipation, and wonder—in technique—awing the viewer by the power of light, sound, spectacle, and special effects—and in their underlying psychological concerns with separation anxiety, the fear of death, and the return of repressed material in the fantastic form of aliens or ghosts. In all three films, recognizable contemporary middle-class American families are shattered by strange forces erupting from outer or inner space. This is a trilogy of domestic fantasies, cinematic fairy tales about loss, separation, and abandonment, culminating in mother-and-child reunions. They are Spielberg's signature films, in which he forged his characteristic style and subject matter, becoming our wizard of the suburbs, transforming contemporary tract homes into fairy-tale cottages.

In certain ways, *Close Encounters, E.T.,* and *Poltergeist* are so closely linked that they might almost be considered versions of the same film. In all three, Spielberg seems to be working out similar preoedipal concerns, although *Close Encounters* and *E.T.* are benign and *Poltergeist* transforms similar material into nightmare. Of the three, *Close Encounters* is the most epic, grandiose, and hysterical, *E.T.* the most tender and lyrical, and *Poltergeist* the most horrific. But all three have moments of operatic spectacle, tenderness, and terror.

The protagonists in the three films are children or child-men. *Close Encounters, E.T.,* and *Poltergeist* seem to be saying, "A monster has stolen my baby!" but they are also saying, "My parents have turned into monsters!" These are films about divorce and separation anxiety, and, in a way, they all re-create Spielberg's boyhood home in suburbia and attempt to overcome the destruction of that idyllic existence.

In 1965, shortly after the family moved to California, his parents separated, the most traumatic event of his young life. Spielberg was then eighteen, but he and his three younger sisters had known for years that their parents were unhappy. "I used film, I think, to escape into a world of fantasy. Away from my parents. . . . They weren't getting along and there was a lot of noise in the house at night." "Sound traveled from bedroom to bedroom, and the word [divorce] came seeping through the heating ducts. My sisters and I would stay up at night, listening to our parents argue, hiding from that word. And when it traveled into our room, absolute panic set in. My sisters would burst into tears, and we would all hold one another" (Spielberg 63).

The home was no longer safe; it had been invaded by hostile, alien forces. Scenes of homes and bedrooms being invaded are the stuff of Spielberg's suburban trilogy: the parents quarreling in front of the children; the aliens snatching the boy from his home in *Close Encounters* (significantly, they try to enter through the heating ducts); the men in spacesuits invading Elliott's home in *E.T.*; and the children cowering in terror in their bedroom in *Poltergeist* (a film in which there is also "a lot of noise in the house at night").

In Spielberg's recollection of the breakup of his boyhood home, the children are separated from the parents, huddled together for protection, yet the parents are present through the sound of their bitter argument. The children listen, unable to sleep, fascinated but terrified to hear the awful, forbidden word "divorce" spoken by the parents.

According to Freud, the German "heimlich" (homelike) is an ambiguous word which shades over into its opposite, "unheimlich" (uncanny): "on the one hand, it means that which is familiar and congenial, and on the other that which is concealed and kept out of sight" (Freud 129). The eerie effect of the uncanny comes when the familiar slides into the strange. Everything is uncanny "that ought to have remained hidden and secret, and yet comes to light" (130). For Spielberg, divorce is an uncanny event. In his memory, the children are at home with their parents, who are "familiar and congenial" and yet at the same time "concealed and kept out of sight." The children overhear words "that ought to have remained hidden and secret, and yet come to light."

In Spielberg's film trilogy, we are in the realm of the uncanny. This emotion is created by a momentary regression to a primitive or preoedipal stage where the boundaries between reality and fantasy, the living and the dead, the animate and the inanimate, the self and the not-self are fluid. Freud writes, "Our analysis of instances of the uncanny has led us back to the old, archaic conception of the universe, which was characterized by the idea that the world was peopled with the spirits of human beings, and by the narcissistic overestimation of subjective mental processes (such as the belief in the omnipotence of thoughts)" (147). Animism, superstition, and belief in the omnipotence of thoughts also characterize Spielberg's trilogy.

He anchors his fantasies in reality by setting them in the present, usually in an easily recognizable American suburb. For example, Muncie, Indiana, the famous "Middletown," is the primary location in *Close Encounters*, and the hero Roy Neary is Joe Average, a technician for the local power company. Spielberg fills the scene with prominently featured brand names and logos—McDonald's, Shell, Baskin-Robbins, and Budweiser—which are not just product plugs but add credibility to the fantasy. He also saturates his films with allusions to familiar items of American mass culture. Television sets frequently play in the background (in his films, families never turn the television off), featuring bits of real programs which act as subliminal commentary on the action: in *Close Encounters* this includes *Police Woman*, *Days of Our Lives*, the movie *The Ten Commandments*, a Daffy Duck cartoon, and the ABC News with Howard K. Smith (fictitious news but the real broadcaster). We hear part of a Johnny Mathis record, and the hero refers to Disney's animated film *Pinocchio*.

In *E.T.*, there are numerous references to *Star Wars*, Space Invaders, Dungeons and Dragons, and *Star Trek*. "Papa Oo Mau Mau" plays on the radio and clips from *This Island Earth, The Quiet Man*, a Tom and Jerry cartoon, and a telephone ad are on the television. E.T. learns English from a Speak and Spell toy, a Buck Rogers comic strip, and *Sesame Street.*

Poltergeist opens with the National Anthem playing on television at the close of the broadcast day. Later we see on the televison a football game and Mr. Rogers. More "homelike" you cannot get.

Nevertheless, in *Close Encounters, E.T.,* and *Poltergeist,* home is no longer home, the parents are no longer the parents, and the children have been captured by strange creatures. Toys move by themselves or float in midair; clown dolls, trees, and vacuum cleaners attack their owners; aliens and ghosts have come out of the closet or the television set; and Dad sits at the dinner table, playing with his mashed potatoes. "You've probably noticed something a little funny about Dad. Don't worry. I'm still Dad," says Roy Neary in *Close Encounters.* Sorry, Dad, but you're not: you've turned into an alien. And the children too have been taken over by aliens or ghosts. All this reflects the topsy turvy effects of divorce on the stability of the American home.

In *Close Encounters,* household objects also become uncanny, charged with eerie, hidden significance: a glob of shaving cream, a child's mudpile, that heap of mashed potatoes. "Damn it, I know this!" Neary exclaims. "I know what this is. This means something. This is important." His obsession leads him on a quest, a religious pilgrimage in which he abandons job, home, wife, children—everything—for another encounter with the mysterious aliens.

The uncanny in Spielberg's trilogy is usually imbued with an aura of mysticism, of religious awe. *Close Encounters,* for example, plays on the sorts of emotions evoked by religious miracles: confusion, amazement, fear, wonder, and awe. Just as *E.T.* functions as a kind of Christ figure, so the spirits in *Poltergeist* are diabolic. The films place the protagonist (and allow the audience to place itself) in a childlike frame of mind and gain our credence through realistic background detail and, presumably, our faith through overwhelming spectacle. And the aliens or poltergeists combine the attributes of children—they are capricious and playful—with those of parents—they are powerful and can be nurturing or terrifying. The alien or ghosts are uncanny figures, totally other and yet eerily familiar, a whisper from our earliest experience, long forgotten or repressed. Spielberg's suburban trilogy is not so much about unidentified flying objects as about unidentified flying *object relations.*

RELIGION IN CLOSE ENCOUNTERS

Early in *Close Encounters,* Roy Neary's children are watching *The Ten Commandments* (1956), the last film of director Cecil B. DeMille, on television. *Close*

Encounters itself is, in many ways, indebted to the films of the fifties—not only the flying saucer subgenre of science fiction but also the Biblical spectaculars. As critics have noted, the movie is a religious epic, with the aliens as gods or angels[1] : they are omniscient and omnipresent, telepathic, able to defy gravity, to overcome the limitations of time and space, and associated always with blinding light. Like St. Paul, the hero Roy Neary experiences a revelation at a crossroads and is born again. He abandons his previous life in an all-consuming quest for the godhead, contact with the aliens. Although he is mocked and scorned, driven nearly insane, and loses his job and his wife and children, he persists in his single-minded devotion. One critic says, "Like Moses, Neary has to reach his Mount Sinai . . . the Devil's Tower" (Williams 27). Like Christ at his crucifixion, Neary is thirty-three. And Neary is the chosen one: among the twelve civilians who reach the mountain, he is the only one to ascend into the heavens in the mothership, the chariot of the gods.

SPECIAL AFFECT

As in the Biblical epics of the 1950s, in *Close Encounters* Spielberg attempts to impress through the power of light, sound, and special effects and to induce in both the characters and the audience the emotions associated with religious miracles: confusion, amazement, fear, wonder, and awe. Whereas the Biblical spectaculars relied on the power of conventional religious mythology, Spielberg draws on the power of contemporary pop mythology, the persistent belief in UFOs and alien visitation. He tries to gain our credence through realistic contemporary detail and our faith through overwhelming spectacle, giving the audience "the same awestruck feeling reported by those who claim to have experienced close encounters" (McBride 285). As two critics say, *Close Encounters* "is to UFOlogy what *The Sign of the Cross* was to the Christian religion" (Pohl 262).

According to Vivian Sobchack, in American science fiction films starting with *Star Wars* and *Close Encounters*, "special effect" equals "special affect." She claims that the emotion expressed in contemporary science fiction film often tends to be a free-floating euphoria created by technological display. *Close Encounters* "initiates a new iconography of beatific human wonder, editorially linking affect to effect. Heads tilted, eyes gazing upward with childish openness and unfearful expectancy—this is the human face of transcendence whose emotion is enacted by what it sees" (Sobchack, *Screening Space* 284). The faces staring up at the alien mothership in the final sequence of that film have always reminded me of blissed-out Moonies.[2]

My concern here is with the exact nature and possible psychological origin of the "special affect" evoked in the characters and perhaps as well in much of the mass audience of *Close Encounters*.

Close Encounters: Blinded by the light: a transformational moment. Columbia, 1980.

THE TRANSFORMATIONAL OBJECT

The psychoanalyst Christopher Bollas speaks of "the transformational object": a memory from early object relations, when the mother "continually transforms the infant's internal and external environment." In later life, we may "search for an object that is identified with the metamorphosis of the self." In aesthetic experiences, for example, we may feel "an uncanny fusion with the object" which derives from the return of something strangely familiar, "something never cognitively apprehended but existentially known" (Bollas 16). Bollas claims this is a recollection of fusion with the maternal "transformational object."

Many adults search fanatically for a total transformation which they imagine will come about through religious or ideological experience. This obsessive craving can be understood as "a kind of psychic prayer for the arrival of the transformational object: a secular second coming of an object relation experienced in the earliest period of life" (17).

Roy Neary's obsessive search for the UFO can be considered a quest for the transformational object, a pilgrimage that goes backwards from adulthood to infancy. Stephen Farber calls the film "a hymn to regression and emotional retardation" (McBride 283). *Close Encounters* regresses to a primitive or preoedipal stage where the boundaries between reality and fantasy, the animate and the inanimate, mother and child, self and not-self are fluid. This breakdown of boundaries is experienced by the hero as a feeling of oceanic bliss akin to religious ecstasy: "a secular second coming." That is why the film has all the overtones of a Biblical epic: throughout it, both hero and audience are awaiting the second coming. The payoff comes in the phantasmagoria of light and sound in the conclusion: the aliens return to pick up Roy and lift him into the heavens; similarly, the movie picks us up and sweeps us toward the fulfillment of a fantasy. And just as the aliens function as Roy's transformational object, so I would suggest that Spielberg as director of the film functions as ours.

Although Roy Neary has much in common with earlier Spielberg heroes—David Mann in *Duel* and Brody in *Jaws*, characters who need to find their identity and to assert their manhood by leaving behind wives and children and going out into a dangerous world—paradoxically, Roy finds his identity and manhood by continuously regressing. He begins as a child-man and ends in a state of infantile bliss as he enters the spectacular womb of the mothership. The dazzling, brightly lit carrousel of a ship, claims Sobchack, "resolves Roy Neary's intense and incompatible desire both to regain his patriarchal power and become a born-again child" (Sobchack, *Screening Space* 284).

THE OPENING SCENE OF *CLOSE ENCOUNTERS*

The film opens with a transformational moment which suggests both the Biblical instant of creation and the birth trauma. Spielberg as director plays God, opening his movie by announcing, "Let there be light!" He relies brilliantly and suggestively on the fundamental powers of the cinema, painting with light and sound. Out of blackness and silence an eerie musical sound slowly builds until it climaxes with a shattering chord and a sudden flash of light that fills the screen. This opening shot establishes the pattern throughout the film of abrupt switches from darkness, stillness, and silence to blinding light, rapid movement, and loud noise. Spielberg repeatedly lulls and then jolts the audience, keeping us alert by inducing the startle reflex. He places the viewer in a position similar to that of an infant subjected to sudden and bewildering transformations in its environment, with no control over the abrupt alterations in stimuli.

But by the end of the film the dangerous, intrusive alien light has been transformed into a reassuring maternal light. Writes Robert Phillip Kolker, "Threat and protection, fear and security are the opposing poles of Spielberg's thematic. The light piercing through his films plays on both violating the viewer's safe distance from the narratives by demanding attention, forcing the gaze, hiding objects and then revealing those objects, surrounding them with a protective glow" (Kolker 271).

In this opening shot, Spielberg not only startles but also visually disorients us. Out of the whiteness, two lights approach, accompanied by a howling noise and the sound of machinery. We don't know where we are or what the lights are; they could even be the lights of a flying saucer. Only as they approach are they revealed as the headlights of a jeep seen through the obscuring clouds of a desert sandstorm (this may be a homage to the desert scenes in the 1950s science-fiction films *It Came from Outer Space* [1953] and *Them* [1954], or to *Lawrence of Arabia* [1962]). Spielberg exploits the same visual uncertainty for comedy, mystery, or suspense in later scenes, when neither the characters nor the audience can tell at first the difference between the lights of a car or a helicopter and those of a UFO.

Along with the visual disorientation goes a deliberate confusion of sound. The opening scene is a babble of voices speaking English, Spanish, and French, further confused by overlapping dialogue and lines shouted against the howling sandstorm. The welter of sound, along with rapid movement and quick cutting, add to the tension of the opening, which is a scene of mystery and high excitement, a moment of uncanny discovery. By the end of the film, the characters have essentially moved beyond (or regressed away from) the need for the confusions of language, communicating almost entirely through light, musical tones, and gestures.

The first closeup in the film is of the face of Laughlin, the English-French interpreter, who interprets for the audience as well, asking questions necessary for the exposition: "Where's the pilot? Where's the crew? How the hell did it get here?" and most important, "What the hell is happening here?" (Buckland 118). He is a short man who is repeatedly dwarfed during the opening scene by high angle shots. In the final shot, he takes a few nervous steps backward and looks up fearfully at the sky. Laughlin's bewilderment, wonder, and fear cue the audience; the opening is meant to induce in us the kinds of emotions appropriate to the witnesses of a religious miracle.

The aliens are established in this opening scene as mysterious, godlike, unseen presences who come out of the heavens and perform miracles. The airplanes that they leave in the desert are totems which represent their power (airplanes function as holy objects in many Spielberg films, especially *1941*, "The Mission," *Empire of the Sun*, and *Always*). The aliens are also symbolized by blinding light and a haunting tune. "Una luz muy bonita pero muy espantosa," says the Mexican policeman, expressing his emotional ambivalence: "A very beautiful but a very frightening light." Like the mother seen by an infant, the alien mothership appears suddenly and vanishes unpredictably, totally altering the environment. The innocent, the crazy, or the childlike fall under its spell. "El sol salió anoche y me cantó," says the crazy old Mexican: "The sun came out last night and sang to me." One imagines the mother crooning a lullaby.

The aliens are not that different, however, from Spielberg the unseen director, who startles us at the opening of his film with a flash of light and a blast of music. In his relation to the audience, Spielberg functions as the aliens do toward the hero Roy Neary: as magician and miracle maker, as transformational object.

THE CHARACTER OF ROY NEARY

We first meet Roy as he is playing in his living room with electric trains. Their typical American, middle-class suburban household is cluttered and claustrophobic (as opposed to the wide-open spaces of the conclusion) (Williams 27). It is not a scene of domestic tranquility: Roy lacks a good rapport with his children and his wife, and the tension foreshadows his later alienation from his family. Superficially, they resemble a television sitcom family, complete with hapless dad, domineering mom, and three fractious kids. There is some comedy in their introductory bickering and in Roy's later crazy antics, but the Nearys grow progressively less amusing, and their problems are not resolved easily and sentimentally as in a television comedy; they only get worse. In the background in the Nearys' first scene, the younger son, Toby, who is five or six years old, smashes a doll against a playpen. In a later scene Toby pounds the piano keys as his parents argue: his discord reflects the family's disintegration. This is not a happy family, so it is not surprising that it eventually breaks up.

Roy's elder son, eight-year-old Brad, is baffled by his father's attempt to explain fractions, and all three kids are unimpressed with his choice of a film for family viewing. The kids want to play miniature golf, but Roy is determined to take them to *Pinocchio* because he enjoyed its "furry animals and magic" when he was a boy. Brad says contemptuously, "Who wants to go see a dumb cartoon, rated G for kids?" Roy is the real child in the family (later Brad calls him a "crybaby").

Like David Mann in *Duel*, Roy seems henpecked. Although Roy is happy playing with his trains, his wife Ronnie shows her unhappiness by criticizing and belittling him; she is the most unsympathetic wife in Spielberg's films (the nagging wife in *Duel* is also unpleasant, but she only has a cameo appearance). In her opening lines, Ronnie reminds Roy of his promise to take them to a movie and thrusts the paper in front of him so he cannot ignore her request. Then she complains bitterly about his hobby materials cluttering her breakfast table, sits in a chair and glares at him, and criticizes him in front of the children about his methods of parenting. On the phone, she tells his supervisor that "Roy can't drive at night without me." She condescendingly calls him "Jiminy Cricket" because of his preference for *Pinocchio*. In other words, Ronnie treats Roy as if he were her fourth child, the problem child, and tries to get her way by criticizing, belittling, manipulating, and sulking. In contrast, Roy seems like a big kid trying to jolly the family along but always overruled by Ronnie. Ronnie is not only his wife but also his bad mother.

In later scenes, Ronnie proves to be far more conventional and closed-minded than Roy. She doesn't believe in UFOs and censors the newspaper so Roy won't find anymore articles about them to feed his obsession. She is overly concerned about what the neighbors will think and unsympathetic to her husband's nervous breakdown, treating it as the bad behavior of a wayward child, something he is doing deliberately to upset her and wreck the family. The characters in this film divide along questions of *belief*: grownups like Ronnie who treat the saucers as childishness, nonsense, or insanity, versus those who are children at heart, like Roy, and believe in magic. One critic says that *Close Encounters* "establishes a two-class system: the childlike and the nonchildlike" (Neustadter 234); the same is also true of *E.T.*, "Kick the Can," and *Hook*.

Roy's family is negatively characterized so that we will not be bothered later when Ronnie takes the children and leaves him. In fact, we are glad to see them go. Freed of the burden of dreary domesticity, Roy can now ascend totally into the realm of the fantastic, finally boarding a spaceship and abandoning his wife and children, perhaps forever, in favor of a space family.

Like Pinocchio, Roy hungers to become a real live boy, and he gets his wish upon a star granted because he never loses faith, so that the good fairy ultimately returns to him. What this child really needs is a good mother, not the evil wife-mother Ronnie.

As Roy drives his truck that night on business for the power company, he loses his way in the dark and cries out, "Help, I'm lost!" What happens next suggests that the aliens are responding to his cry and helping him to find himself, or at least to find the magic he secretly desires. An extreme long shot shows the truck as tiny, overshadowed by the enormous night sky; we sense that Roy is driving into something cosmic and mysterious. When the alien light strikes his truck at the crossroads, all hell breaks loose: disturbances in electricity and gravity, and objects moving by themselves. He gasps and twitches, overwhelmed. (Ironically, the same kind of disturbances in *Poltergeist* are perceived as evil, and the characters have no desire to repeat them.) Roy has been chosen, blinded by the light and seized by the power; the aliens leave their mark on him externally, through sunburn, and internally, through a telepathically implanted obsession. Call it religious conversion, mystical transformation, or nervous breakdown, but from that moment Roy's life is ruled by the compulsion to repeat the experience and merge with the aliens. As he races after them in his truck, the ship passes overhead; symbolically, Roy is cast into the shadow of the object. What is this huge object that overwhelms both physically and psychically, an object with which one desires to merge, but a symbolic representation of the mother as perceived by the infant?

For Roy, the desire to fuse with the aliens is a consummation beyond the sexual. Later that night, he takes his wife to the Echo Summit, hoping to show her the return of the ships, and she tries to neck with him to distract him from what she sees as his unhealthy obsession. "They kiss, but Neary's eyes are skyward, choosing to remain in the world of pre-puberty" (Williams 24). (In *Jaws*, Ellen Brody also uses sex to try to distract her husband from his obsession with the shark.) The world of adult sexual relationships is excluded from the film: even the possible romance between Roy and Jillian is never fulfilled because that would prevent him from sailing off to the stars. Roy's sexuality gets sublimated into playing with his mashed potatoes (or with clay) and into looking, as when he and Jillian spy on the landing site at Devil's Tower, like children spying on the primal scene.

Roy's story is paralleled by that of four-year-old Barry Guiler, who also abandons home and mother to chase aliens. "Barry lives alone with his mother, Jillian, in [a] fatherless pre-Oedipal paradise" (Torry 194). Both Roy and Barry love mechanical toys, and both seek only to return to the bliss of the womb, represented by the gigantic mothership. From his first encounter with the aliens, Barry is unafraid and accepting. To him, the aliens are a giggle, ideal playmates: "toys" and "ice cream," he calls them, the good mother and none of the bad. When Barry is pulled through the cat door by the aliens, it is a birth scene run backward.

ALIEN AS BREAST

It is interesting how often in *Close Encounters* the aliens are associated with food: both Roy and Barry call the ships ice cream cones; Ronnie asks if they resemble tacos or "those Sara Lee moon-shaped cookies"; the alien visitors raid the family refrigerator (as the extraterrestrial does in *E.T.*); the trucks going to meet the aliens are falsely labeled Piggly Wiggly, Coca Cola, and Baskin Robbins (ice cream again); and Roy tries to sculpt the tower out of mashed potatoes.

Significantly, two early drafts of the script of *Close Encounters* directly associate the aliens with breasts. In a second draft screenplay (dated September 2, 1975), Ronnie has consulted a psychiatrist who might help Roy and quotes him to Roy about "Isakower's phenomenon," in which "the brain retains information from infancy long before your memory is able to recall it. The large circular thing you saw getting closer and closer probably represents your mother's breast with its promise of food" ("Close Encounters," 1975 screenplay, 55–56). Roy angrily rejects Ronnie's psychologizing.

In a draft dated May 10, 1976, the reference persists, but now it is downgraded to something Ronnie read in *Cosmopolitan*:

> RONNIE: The fact that these things come closer and closer represents your mother's breast with its promise of food. When satisfied, you, the infant, lose interest in the breast which goes away, getting smaller. The shape of the female breast is . . .
>
> ROY: Ronnie, I did not see my mother's tits coming in low over the Mt. Pleasant foothills! ("Close Encounters," 1976 screenplay, 52–53).

Nevertheless, despite Roy's dismissal of her psychologizing, both drafts contain a scene in which Roy becomes fixated on Ronnie's breasts, reminding us of the shape he keeps obsessively sculpting:

> A new and curious mood colors over him. He has leveled his vision on Ronnie's healthy breasts. But strangely, not in any way sexual. . . . Ronnie hunkers down between the sheets so that her breasts silhouette against a shaft in the moonlight on the beige dresser. GREENHOUSE [Neary's name in early drafts] WATCHES THE SILHOUETTE AND IS MYSTERIOUSLY TRANSFIXED BY IT. ("Close Encounters," 1975 screenplay, 37)

> Roy slides down to her breasts and . . . fixates. Almost immediately his anxiety flows out of him. He cocks his head to the side and stares at her silhouetted breast. ("Close Encounters," 1976 screenplay, 66C).

Roy's responses here would have to be called infantile: like a baby, he does not perceive the breast as sexual, and the sight of it eases his anxiety. These scenes were omitted from the film, probably because Spielberg considered them too psychologically and sexually explicit; nevertheless, their persistence through several drafts suggests that Spielberg (or the writers he hired) was aware of the psychosexual undercurrents of the fantasy he was creating. Douglas Trumbull, who was in charge of visual effects for *Close Encounters*, says, "My first concept was the mother ship underbelly—this big thing that hung down from there—should look like a giant breast with a nipple" (McBride 278).

Of course, it is too simple to say that what Roy and Barry seek is the bliss of the womb or the maternal breast. These objects are associated with the transformational object, which, as Bollas notes, represents a memory trace of an early relationship: the infant's experience of fusion with the mother and of the mother's power to transform the environment.

THE CHARACTERIZATION OF THE ALIENS

What is unique about the transformational object in this film is not so much the omnipotence of the aliens, which one would expect, but their asexuality, their childishness, their lack of language, and their prankishness. The asexuality and childishness render them innocent and appealing and cancel the threat of their power. They are naked as cherubs, carry no instruments or weapons, and have no visible sexual organs. Like E.T., whom they resemble, they represent the paradox of impotent omnipotence, the powerful figure of the parent crossed with a child's imaginary companion, who remains on the child's own level. Their lack of verbal language (they communicate through music) links them to the preverbal infant's perception of the mother; at that stage, all language is music, meaningful only as emotional tones. The film itself largely dispenses with dialogue in its closing minutes, using light, gesture, and music, the language of pure emotion.[3]

The irrational behavior of the aliens is another matter. They have godlike powers but behave like imps or elves. These merry pranksters lead policemen on a high-speed chase, nearly collide with a passenger plane, cause blackouts over entire cities, plunk a missing ship in the middle of a desert, and kidnap many people, including a child, apparently just for the hell of it. This is scarcely appropriate behavior for envoys from another world out to win friends on planet Earth. Instead, they seem to delight in wreaking havoc for no reason, although, as in *Poltergeist*, no one is seriously harmed by their antics, only shaken up. They are impractical jokers, benign mischief makers. All is presumably made right in the end when they return the missing people (which overlooks the problem of the time lost in captivity). But their irrational behavior keeps us in suspense, making us wonder for most of the film if these aliens are good or evil. One critic notes, "several of their initial actions have seemed capricious, even cruel . . . the aliens have been associated with loss and the threat of loss, as they will be again in the abduction of Barry" (Torry 193).

Close Encounters is built around many of the trappings of a horror movie, and the aliens in some ways behave like monsters, so that Spielberg could easily recycle this same material in *Poltergeist*. But at the same time, *Close Encounters* employs some of the conventions of a romantic film: these aliens are playing with and even wooing the earthlings. A good illustration of this generic blending is the kidnaping of Barry: it is the scariest scene in the movie, but there is a striking difference between the response of the mother and that of the child. Although Jillian is terrified as the aliens penetrate her home to seize her son, Barry is totally accepting. He knows they have come to play, and he invites them to slide down the chimney as if he were expecting Santa Claus. The scene enacts an ambivalent response to the transformational object, which, as the Mexican said, is both very beautiful and very frightening. (There is a similar ambivalence in an early scene in *Poltergeist*: after Diane demonstrates the spooky goings-on in her kitchen, she jumps for joy like a cheerleader while her husband's eyes go wide with fear and her little daughter yawns.) Here, as Jillian cowers in terror because extraterrestrials threaten to invade her house, the phonograph, in ironic counterpoint, plays a Johnny Mathis love song: "Chances are, if I wear a silly grin/ The moment you come into view. . . ."

So the terror of loss or separation anxiety is countered by the promise of love: horror movie crosses with the romance of boy and alien. The prankishness of the aliens in this scene has two possible connotations, one malevolent and the other benign, reflecting a split in the attitude toward the maternal object: on the one hand, it is seen as a monster callously toying with human beings; on the other, it is a lover playing with its beloved. Horror movie crosses with romance. And Roy Neary's story is also a love story: boy meets UFO; boy loses UFO; boy gets UFO.

SPIELBERG AS MERRY PRANKSTER

Many of Spielberg's films aside from *Close Encounters* deal with pranksters or monsters on a spree or rampage for little or no apparent reason, including *Duel, Sugarland Express, Jaws, 1941, Poltergeist, Jurassic Park*, and even *Schindler's List*. Sometimes these characters are evil, but in other films they mean no harm. Spielberg himself is a prankster, and cinema offers him free rein, like the aliens, to play god or devil, to wreak havoc while harming no one. In particular, Spielberg likes to startle and surprise the audience with tricks, jokes, and sight gags. He wants to shock the audience but then to hug them; the hug undoes the harm and sets you up for the next shock or surprise. This is also how he tormented his three younger sisters when they were growing up. And while filming *Raiders of the Lost Ark*, he would unexpectedly drop live snakes or tarantulas on actor Karen Allen to elicit real screams on camera. "But I always kissed her, gently, after every take" (Crawley 95). (I wonder if he would have dared pull this stunt on Harrison Ford!)

Spielberg is great at playing cinematic tricks, and they impress and entertain vast audiences. It is possible that he has simply endowed the aliens in *Close Encounters* and the ghosts in *Poltergeist* with some of his own personality traits. But if we consider the aliens as the transformational object, their prankishness may also reflect erratic or capricious maternal care. I imagine an infant who is alternately scared and reassured. Roy Neary pleads with his wife, "Ronnie, I'm really scared. I want you to help. . . . Just hold me. Just put your arms around me." But Ronnie, representing the bad mother, violently rejects him. Spielberg's aliens seem to partake of both aspects of the maternal object: they are a source of bliss but they are also elusive jokers who can drive you crazy. So Spielberg may in part be doing to audiences what was done to him, or the way that he experienced the relationship with the mother in childhood. That long, beatific closing sequence of *Close Encounters* may be necessary in part to relieve both the characters' and the audience's frustration.

DEPARTURE AND REUNION, SEPARATION AND FUSION

The film could be said to be patterned by an opposition between departure and reunion, separation and fusion. Barry twice wanders off from his mother and twice is reunited with her. Roy stays home, but his family leaves him. In a poignant moment, the lonely Roy looks out from behind the curtains at his neighbors in their backyards; he is forever separated from them and their everyday lives. Roy and Jillian are dramatically reunited just as she is about to depart from the train station in Wyoming, then they are separated when they are arrested, reunited on the helicopter, and finally part with a kiss at the alien landing site. Roy's climactic departure combines both separation and fusion: he is leaving the earth but joining the aliens in the mothership.

A similar opposition in the film occurs between the creation of boundaries and the breaking down of boundaries. Ronnie is concerned with territoriality: she resents Roy's stuff on her breakfast table. As their marriage disintegrates, Roy locks himself in the bathroom, and then Ronnie too locks the door against him. The authorities erect barriers to keep people away from Devil's Tower; Roy ignores their obstacles, driving against the traffic or crashing through the roadblocks. He is inspired or compelled by the aliens, who represent the exhilarating dissolution of all boundaries: At the state line between Indiana and Ohio, they fly through the toll booths without stopping. Time and distance mean nothing to them, as in the way they treat the stolen planes and the ship. They even break down the barriers between minds through telepathy. "Indeed, the film is about breaking down barriers—national, linguistic, physical, and bureaucratic. . . . When the barriers are broken, it culminates in an event which is world-changing" (Engel 376).

Close Encounters plays on these oppositions between separation and fusion, barriers and the dissolution of barriers because the goal of the hero and the film seems to be to overcome separation anxiety, to break down all boundaries and achieve the bliss of total fusion with the transformational object. In this film, many are called, but only Roy is chosen, and he seems to be picked by Lacombe and the aliens through the pure omnipotence of wishful thinking—certainly not through anything that he says. His fusion with the aliens is suggested by penetrating beams of light and telepathic communion, culminating in his final entry into the mothership and the liftoff into outer space.

Robert Phillip Kolker suggests how Spielberg uses camera movement as well to help the viewer overcome separation anxiety as the film ends:

> there are a series of low angle tracks moving *away* from the wondering humans, releasing tension, preparing the viewer not only for the departure of the space-craft, but for his or her own separation from the narrative—though the final separation is not complete until the viewer is further subdued and excited by the massive forms of the ship and the overwhelming soundtrack. (278)

Close Encounters and *E.T.* have prolonged, operatic conclusions which are heavily weighted, deeply emotional scenes of farewell. There is no dialogue in the final minutes of *Close Encounters* except for little Barry, as a sort of stand-in for the viewer, saying "Bye" to the departing mothership. Both Roy and the viewer have recuperated the transformational object, and now we must be prepared to separate from it: thus the protracted close.

OEDIPAL CONFLICT IN *CLOSE ENCOUNTERS*

Is the film, however, entirely about the infant-mother dyad? What has happened to oedipal conflict? What is the function then of such apparent father figures as Lacombe? One critic sees the film as symbolically expressing an oedipal conflict: "Neary's experience of loss, his fear of losing his mind (a symbolic castration), and . . . the insistent image of the Devil's Tower involve him in a strategic reenactment of the Oedipal drama. . . . Neary must undergo a symbolic 're-Oedipalization' the effect of which is a renewed faith in the ultimate beneficence of paternal authority" (Torry 194).

I would argue, however, that although there may be an oedipal conflict underlying the action, the film is fundamentally regressive: it defends against oedipal anxiety by a flight into an earlier stage. Roy's avoidance of adult sexuality, his irresponsibility, and his preference for play all imply this regression. The Devil's Tower may appear to evoke the "role of the paternal phallus" (Torry 194), but as I have suggested, in this film it also serves as a symbolic breast. And the mothership is a spectacular floating breast.

In *Close Encounters* (and in *E.T.* as well), fathers and male authorities are generally absent or untrustworthy. Barry has no father—it is never explained why Gillian is a single parent—and Roy abdicates his parental responsibility, although he gains a new space family at the end in which he can be simultaneously parent and child. "Surrounded by the little and curious aliens, bathed in light, Roy Neary is a figure beatifically re-solved as powerful patriarch, loving father, and lovable child" (Sobchack, "Child/

Alien/Father" 21). Government officials are bad fathers who cover up the existence of the UFOS, lying to the public (this combines the conspiracy theories of UFOlogists with post-Watergate paranoia), and Roy is angry with them and rebels against them.

The exception, the only good father figure in the film, is Lacombe, who resembles Keys in *E.T.*: a scientist who shares the hero's faith in miracles and magic, a benign, permissive father who is really a child at heart. Spielberg says he wanted Truffaut for the part after seeing the famous director act in his films *L'Enfant Sauvage* (*The Wild Child*) (1970) and *La Nuit Americaine* (*Day for Night*) (1973): "He was a man-child in those films. Ingenuous and wise, a father-figure with this very wild-eyed, young outlook on life. I didn't want the stoic with the white hair and the pipe. . . . He [Truffaut] was the best possible choice. Such a *mensch*. So human" (Crawley 63). These remarks suggest that Truffaut, a fellow director, functioned for Spielberg as a reflection of his own ego ideal or idealized self-image as a wise man-child, forever young, similar to the function of the director Richard Attenborough in *Jurassic Park*. The fact that he resorts to the Yiddish of his parents to describe him may imply that Truffaut is as well a substitute parent for Spielberg: not a stoic like Spielberg's father but warm and young at heart like Spielberg's mother. In other words, Truffaut/Lacombe unites the aspects Spielberg prefers in child, father, and mother into a single idealized figure, a self-representation. Moreover, as a Frenchman who barely speaks English, Lacombe is an authority but also an outsider. Like the extraterrestrials, he is simultaneously child, adult, and alien (Sobchack, "Child/Alien/Father" 21). The matching gestures and smiles of Lacombe and the space creature at the end suggest their similarity.

CONCLUSION: SEE NO EVIL

To combine child, father, and mother into a single figure—Neary, Lacombe, or the alien—I see as Spielberg's (probably unconscious) strategy in *Close Encounters*, a way to evade or neutralize oedipal conflict. It is a strategic retreat or regression.

In its invitation to regress and its benign view of the universe, *Close Encounters* is very appealing and comforting. Regression, after all, can be fun. Roy Neary moves from depression into mania; the end of the film is visually and emotionally euphoric both for the hero and the audience. A temporary manic high, too, can be lots of fun. And viewed as *son et lumière*, a spectacle meant to induce awe and wonder, it is a dazzling, seductive film. The images are rich, suggestive, and, for many, deeply moving. "Even an unbeliever cannot see that great final ship approach without a tingle of excited delight" (Pohl 262).

Close Encounters: *Son et lumière*: The euphoria of the encounter. Columbia, 1980.

But the rational or skeptical side of me resists its sweet and sunny appeal and sees it as a potentially cultist or occultist movie; that's why the ecstatic faces staring upward at the aliens in the conclusion remind me of blissed-out Moonies. *Close Encounters*, some critics complained, "obviously plays to the sort of religious revivalism rampant in the mid and late seventies" (Ryan and Kellner 260). I think of what Christopher Evans wrote in *Cults of Unreason*: "With the old Gods dying, if not dead, and the world menaced by threat of total destruction as never before in its history, men are turning to the skies to seek their redeemers there"(164). In 1978, shortly after *Close Encounters* was first released, a student of mine said she was so impressed by the movie she was seriously thinking of dropping out of school to investigate reports of saucer sightings. I agreed that it was a lovely movie but advised her not to waste her time.

Perhaps I resist *Close Encounters* because the solutions it offers are too easy. A woman told me, "The really courageous thing for Roy would have been not to walk into the mothership but to go home and clean up the mess he left in the living room!" That's the adult in us reacting against the seductively childlike appeal of this film.

I referred to the quote from *The Ten Commandments*, but *Close Encounters* is not really Biblical parable: There is no harsh God here who forces the Israelites to wander forty years in the desert. It is more like fairy tale, a softened version of "Pinocchio" or "Hansel and Gretel." Like Pinocchio, Roy gets his wish to be transformed by the good fairy. At the end of the film, says Spielberg, "Roy becomes a real person. He loses his string, his wooden joints . . ." (McBride 283). But there is no Monstro, the terrible whale that swallows boys alive (and no giant shark either!); instead there is a benevolent mothership that welcomes the hero inside. Alternately, we can see Roy and Barry as orphans who get lost in the woods and discover a gingerbread house. But once they enter the enchanted cottage, they find no witch who wants to fatten them up for the kill, only friendly aliens who want to play. "Everybody in this movie is so bloody *benign*—and the good feeling is contagious" (Corliss 80). "Conflict is not so much *re*solved as *dis*solved" (Morris 18). For me, that's the problem with *Close Encounters*: even Oz had wicked witches, and *Duel* and *Jaws* had a mad truck and a crazed shark. But in the world of the transformational object, there is no evil to overcome.

NOTES

1. For views of *Close Encounters* as a religious film, see for example the articles by Corliss, Fairchild, Gardner, Henning, Kael, Kauffmann, and Torry. Entman and Seymour argue that the film has religious form but no religious content: "Religions have theologies, duties, parables, and worldly institutions, all of which provide some rational reason to have faith and some guidance in living in accordance with that faith. The aliens provide none of this" (4). Friedman says that Spielberg's films have spirituality but no deity, that his faith resides in human potential.

2. For my reading of *Close Encounters* as an occultist film, see Gordon, "*Close Encounters*: The Gospel According to Steven Spielberg."

3. On the theme of communication in *Close Encounters*, see Engel.

REFERENCES

Bollas, Christopher. *The Shadow of the Object: Psychoanalysis of the Unthought Known.* New York: Columbia, 1987.

Buckland, Warren. *Directed by Steven Spielberg: Poetics of the Contemporary Hollywood Blockbuster.* New York: Continuum, 2006.

"Close Encounters of the Third Kind." 2nd Draft Screenplay by "Sam Irvin." September 2, 1975.

"Close Encounters of the Third Kind." Revised Draft Screenplay by Steven Spielberg. May 14, 1976 (includes revisions dated April 22, 1976, and May 10, 12, and 14, 1976).

Close Encounters of the Third Kind: The Special Edition. Columbia, 1980. Producers: Julia Phillips and Michael Phillips. Story: Steven Spielberg. Screenplay: Steven Spielberg. Director: Steven Spielberg. Visual Effects: Douglas Trumbull. Director of Photography: Vilmos Zsigmond. Additional Photography: William A.

Fraker, Douglas Slocombe, John Alonzo, Laszlo Kovacs. Production Design: Joe Alves. Editing: Michael Kahn. Music: John Williams. Cast: Richard Dreyfuss (Roy Neary); Teri Garr (Ronnie Neary); Melinda Dillon (Jillian Guiler); Cary Guffey (Barry Guiler); Bob Balaban (David Laughlin), Francois Truffaut (Lacombe).

Corliss, Richard. "An Encounter of the Best Kind." *New Times*, December 9, 1977, 76 and 80.

Crawley, Tony. *The Steven Spielberg Story*. New York: Quill, 1983.

Engel, Charlene. "Language and the Music of the Spheres: Steven Spielberg's *Close Encounters*." *Literature/Film Quarterly* 24.4 (1996): 376–82.

Entman, Robert and Francie Seymour. "Close Encounters with the Third Reich." *Jump Cut* 18 (1978): 3–6.

Evans, Christopher. *Cults of Unreason*. New York: Dell, 1975.

Fairchild, B. H. "An Event Sociologique: *Close Encounters*." *Journal of Popular Film* 6.4 (1978): 324–49.

Freud, Sigmund. "The Uncanny." *On Creativity and the Unconscious: Papers on the Psychology of Art, Literature, Love, and Religion*. Ed. Benjamin Nelson. 1919; rpt. New York: Harper and Row, 1958, 122–61.

Friedman, Lester D. *Citizen Spielberg*. Urbana: University of Illinois Press, 2006.

Gardner, Martin. "The Third Coming." *New York Review of Books*, January 26, 1978, 22.

Gordon, Andrew. "*Close Encounters*: The Gospel According to Steven Spielberg." *Literature/Film Quarterly* 8.3 (1980): 156–64.

Henning, Clara Maria. "*Star Wars* and *Close Encounters*." *Theology Today* 35.2 (1978): 202–6.

Kael, Pauline. "The Greening of the Solar System." *New Yorker*, November 28, 1977, 174–81.

Kauffmann, Stanley. "Epiphany." *New Republic*, December 10, 1977, 20–22.

Kolker, Robert Phillip. *A Cinema of Loneliness: Penn, Kubrick, Scorsese, Spielberg, Altman*. 2nd Ed. New York: Oxford, 1988.

McBride, Joseph. *Steven Spielberg: A Biography*. New York: Simon and Schuster, 1997.

Morris, Nigel. *The Cinema of Steven Spielberg: Empire of Light*. London: Wallflower, 2007.

Neustadter, Roger. "Phone Home: From Childhood Amnesia to the Catcher in Sci-Fi—The Transformation of Childhood in Contemporary American Science Fiction Films." *Youth and Society* 20.3 (1989): 227–40.

Pohl, Frederik and Frederik Pohl IV. *Science Fiction: Studies in Film*. New York: Ace, 1981.

Ryan, Michael and Douglas Kellner. *Camera Politica: The Politics and Ideology of Contemporary Hollywood Film*. Bloomington: Indiana University Press, 1988.

Sobchack, Vivian. "Child/Alien/Father: Patriarchal Crisis and Generic Exchange." *Camera Obscura* 15 (1986): 7–34.

———. *Screening Space: The American Science Fiction Film*. 2nd. ed. New York: Ungar, 1987.

Spielberg, Steven. "The Autobiography of Peter Pan." *Time*, July 15, 1985, 62–63.

Torry, Robert L. "Politics and Parousia in *Close Encounters of the Third Kind*." *Literature/Film Quarterly* 19.3 (1991): 188–196.

Williams, Tony. "Close Encounters of the Authoritarian Kind." *Wide Angle* 4.5 (1983): 23–29.

4

E.T. (1982) as Fairy Tale

A friend of mine took a family of Cambodian refugees to see their first movie in America: *E.T.* (1982). Toward the end of the movie, tears were running down the cheeks of their seven-year-old son. Yet he didn't understand a word of English. That's cinematic power: a movie that doesn't really need language to communicate, that's as strong as a silent by Griffith or Chaplin. E.T.'s death scene may be the contemporary equivalent of the death of Dickens's Little Nell: millions weep.

Spielberg poured a lot of his childhood feelings into *E.T.*, which he calls "a very personal story . . . about the divorce of my parents, how I felt when my parents broke up." The figure of E.T. was based on the imaginary companions he conjured up out of his boyhood loneliness: "When I was a kid, I used to imagine strange creatures lurking outside my bedroom window, and I'd wish they'd come into my life and magically change it" (McBride 327–28). "My wish list included having a friend who could be both the brother I never had and the father I didn't feel I had anymore" (72). Because of the artistry with which he evokes these deep personal feelings, *E.T.* is the best of Spielberg's suburban trilogy—*Close Encounters* (1977, 1980), *Poltergeist* (1982), and *E.T.*—and may well be his masterpiece; lyrical, warm, and tender, it can bring tears to the eyes of both children and adults. When my son was three, an E.T. doll was his favorite teddy bear. Although I have viewed the film perhaps a dozen times, I can never see it all the way through without my eyes misting over.

Yet *E.T.* is similar to *Close Encounters*, which I have argued is a cult movie, a wet dream of a "UFO-ologist," with paper-thin characters in a tissue-thin plot of mysterious appearances and disappearances and massive government coverups, concluding with an inspiring light show and the ascent into heaven of the chosen one in a chariot of the gods (Gordon). On the surface, some of these things are also true of *E.T.* (1982): the heroes are the childlike and pure of heart, the villains are scientists, and the good fairies are extraterrestrials who possess not science but paranormal powers and a technology so mysterious that it is inseparable from magic. Both movies gloss over too many holes in their plots and end in a warm bath of wish fulfillment about gods from outer space. Spielberg appropriates the iconography of science fiction (spaceships and alien beings) but fashions plots closer to fantasy and fairy tale. Writes John Baxter, "No serious science fiction writer would have given house-room to the tale Spielberg told in *E.T.* . . . The story is sentimental and trite" (Baxter 245).

Given the similarities between the two movies, why do I love *E.T.* despite myself? Why am I willing to excuse the same faults—mysticism and sentimentality—that I deplore in *Close Encounters*? Why does *Close Encounters* leave me unmoved while *E.T.* makes me cry? I can think of four reasons. First, it may be because the characters in *Close Encounters* are sketchy and difficult to care about, while those in *E.T.* are more complete human beings—with the alien, oddly, the most human of them all. Second, where *Close Encounters* is often solemn and mawkish, the sentimentality of *E.T.* is balanced by a nice sense of humor: few scenes in modern cinema are as touching and as funny as Elliott trying to explain his toys to a wide-eyed, uncomprehending E.T. Third, although *Close Encounters* has skillful cinematography, Spielberg in *E.T.* views the world through the visionary eyes of a child and childlike alien, thereby poeticizing the ordinary. Scene after scene has a warmth, intimacy, and sense of wonder created through careful lighting and camera placement: Elliott doing the dishes at the kitchen sink, wreathed in rising clouds of steam, gazing up out the window; or Elliott moving hesitantly in the darkness under a crescent moon, away from the safe light of the house toward the strangely glowing backyard shed—a scene with "a sacramental feel, like the discovery of the grail or the manger" (Joannides). Fourth, the fundamental reason why *E.T.* works for me is the child's-eye view of the film, consistently maintained through waist-level shots. To watch thirty-year-old Richard Dreyfuss play with his mashed potatoes is appalling; to watch ten-year-old Henry Thomas drop his pizza is appealing. *E.T.* is children's literature, whereas *Close Encounters* is childish.

Spielberg is not only an expert director of children but also an expert storyteller for children. He and scriptwriter Melissa Mathison (who also wrote *The Black Stallion* [1979], a similar movie about a boy inseparable from his horse) fashioned a contemporary fairy tale with an intuitive grasp of child psychology and added a new figure to pop mythology. E.T. lives in the popular psyche as surely as Peter Pan—a comparison Spielberg makes inevitable by including a reading from J. M. Barrie's story in the movie.

Like Peter Pan, E.T. is a sprite who never grows up, who descends on a household of children, makes them believe in fairies, and teaches them to fly, themes Spielberg returned to (with less success) in *Hook* (1991). The scientist "Keys" and his ominous band tracking down E.T. and the children are equivalent to Captain Hook and his pirates, adult villains who intrude on a blissful Neverland.[1]

Melissa Mathison wept when Spielberg first told her the story. "I was immediately sold on the story, but not on any sort of sci-fi level. It was the idea of an alien creature who was benevolent, tender, emotional, and sweet that appealed to me. And the idea of the creature's striking up a relationship with a child who came from a broken home was very affecting." She turned to fairy tales for inspiration for the screenplay because "in fairy tales, adults are not present. This gives the kids a chance to solve their own problems and to have their own existence. Also, this means that E.T. becomes a father figure, in a way, to Elliott" (Wuntch).

E.T. AS FROG KING

Spielberg's "extraterrestrials" in both *Close Encounters* and *E.T.* are really updated versions of the trolls, dwarfs, elves, leprechauns, and other enchanted creatures who populate folklore and fairy tales (Eisenstein). In the Grimm brothers' fairy tale "The Frog-King," a princess goes into the forest and, while playing with a golden ball, drops it into a well. An ugly frog promises to return the ball if she takes him home: "if you will love me and let me be your companion and play-fellow . . . and sleep in your little bed" ("Frog King" 18). In the end, we all know, the frog is transformed through contact with the princess into a handsome prince who marries her. In *E.T.*, an alien visitor who looks like a frog appears suddenly out of the forest. When Elliott tosses a ball into his backyard shed, E.T. returns it to him, symbolically binding the two of them together. Later, Elliott takes E.T. into his bedroom as his "companion and play-fellow." The parallel with the Grimms' tale is reinforced when Elliott releases the school laboratory frogs because they resemble E.T., his frog prince.

E.T., however, is not transformed into a human being by the boy's touch; he remains an alien. Instead, the boy is transformed by E.T.'s magical touch into a more loving, mature, and whole human being than he was before—a sort of "handsome prince." Richard Corliss writes that E.T. "eventually proves as beautiful as an enchanted frog," but he first must be rescued by a child "whose Galahad strength only E.T. and the moviegoer can immediately discover" (Corliss).

For Bruno Bettelheim, fairy tales are not simply wish fulfillment but embody psychological truths: "a fairy tale enlightens him [the child] about himself, and fosters his personality development" (Bettelheim 12). The fairy tale symbolizes inner conflicts, suggests how they may be resolved, and thus "reassures, gives hope for the future, and holds out the promise of a happy ending" (26). *E.T.* is the best of Spielberg's three "suburban" fantasies because it is both the closest to the classic fairy-tale pattern and the most profound psychologically, affirming our human potential, our emotional resources, our power to love, and the possibility of healing and growth. In *Close Encounters*, the gods from outer space come down and rescue Roy Neary; in *E.T.*, a god from outer space and a boy become friends and rescue each other. *Close Encounters* features not the child hero of the fairy tale but an adult who behaves like a child and loses our sympathy, and *Poltergeist* entirely lacks psychological growth; any reassurance or hope for the future offered by these two films is superficial. "*Close Encounters* was lauded as a film about hope, but what it promotes is the hope that a man could escape the responsibilities of his family and job" (Sheehan 58). As for *Poltergeist*, Pauline Kael notes, "What's lacking is what *E.T.* has—the emotional roots of the fantasy, and what it means to the children" (Kael 124). *E.T.* is a meaningful fairy tale about a boy's psychological maturation.[2]

Bettelheim categorizes "The Frog-King" as a fairy tale that "center[s] on the shock of recognition when that which seemed animal suddenly reveals itself as the source of human happiness" (Bettelheim 286). This shock of recognition is also central to the appeal of *E.T.* Spielberg made his space creature deliberately ugly: "He's fat and he's not pretty. I really wanted E.T. to sneak up on you—not in the easy way of an F.A.O. Schwarz doll on the shelf. The story is the beauty of his character" (Michener and Ames 64). When E.T. reveals tender emotions and other human characteristics, he makes what we usually reject—what we consider animal or alien within us—seem suddenly human and acceptable. E.T. is within us; he is part of all of us. As Vivian Sobchack puts it, "Aliens R Us." (Sobchack, *Screening Space* 293).

Like all good fantasies, Spielberg's film transforms not only the strange into the familiar but also the familiar into the strange. The extraterrestrial E.T. is more "human" than the really alien intruders in the film: the faceless scientists in NASA spacesuits, the moon men who invade Elliott's home. A detailed look at the opening scene of the film demonstrates how Spielberg's technique creates that reversal of expected values and fosters in the audience a strong identification with the alien creature.

E.T.: THE OPENING SCENE

The lyrical opening of *E.T.* represents Spielberg working at the height of his powers as a poet with a movie camera. Fusing light, sound, music, camera angles, movement, and editing rhythms to involve the audience and tell a story without words, he domesticates the fantastic and creates sympathy for the alien.

It begins with credits flashed in purple on a black screen. The title, *E.T.: The Extraterrestrial*, and the eerie music lead us to expect something unusual. There is a dissolve into an establishing shot of a starry night sky and then a slow tilt down to reveal some treetops, the silhouette of a redwood forest. The serene pastoral setting, the music (now soft and traditional), and the smooth movement downward into familiar territory are reassuring. But the opening night sky reminds us of the vast, unknown universe beyond our world, and the movement downward suggests the path of a spaceship as it lands (Jameson 11). The music grows louder in the next shot: as if we were perched high in the trees, we look down on a brilliantly lit spaceship sitting in a forest clearing. We begin *in medias res*; the aliens have already landed. A spaceship in a forest is extraordinary, but this is not the overwhelming, cathedral-sized mothership of *Close Encounters*. It is simpler, scaled down, not awe inspiring but soothing, familiar despite its unfamiliarity: round and lit up like a jack-o'-lantern or a Christmas tree ornament (Jameson 11).

Now we cut to a slow pan, close to ground level, of the ramp of the ship glimpsed through branches. The pan continues across the clearing and there are several dissolves, suggesting a time lapse, and we see the silhouettes of strange creatures moving in the clearing. In the first close-up in the film, long, thin alien fingers reach up to caress a tree branch. The gesture is framed against a circle of light from the ship in the background, foreshadowing the famous shot of the boy pedaling his bicycle across the full moon, with E.T. in a basket on the handlebars.

These opening shots display many of Spielberg's characteristic techniques. He uses a traditional opening sequence of establishing shot, long shot, then progressively closer shots; at the same time, he moves downward from sky to treetops to ground level. The conventional cutting, smooth, slow camera movements, and soft music put us at ease. The shots are clear-cut and carefully framed, with lighting used to pinpoint certain elements within the frame.

Yet while he is employing these traditional devices, Spielberg does something uncommon (in 1982) for a science-fiction film: he presents the aliens first. There are no humans in that clearing, and we see the creatures through the eye of the camera, not the eyes of characters in the film. We glimpse them first at a distance, as if we are spying on them from behind some trees. The night, the distance, the obscuring branches, and the silhouetting effect of the backlighting keep them indistinct. They are extraterrestrial, extraordinary, mysterious, but also sympathetic: through those traditional film techniques, Spielberg domesticates the aliens, predisposing us to like them despite their strangeness. They are elves in the forest primeval, fairy-tale creatures. They immediately make themselves at home in nature: those fingertips tenderly touching the tree branch show a reverence for the environment.

Since we are not yet allowed to see the aliens clearly, we are next shown the interior of the ship to suggest how truly alien they are. There is a slow pan across alien vegetation: glowing mushrooms and strange, glistening and steaming cones. Crediting his audience with some intelligence, Spielberg never explains anything about the aliens; oddities, such as the vegetation, are simply presented, and we must make sense of them for ourselves, deducing that they are botanists. For example, when an owl hoots, the aliens seem startled and their chests glow red; then they relax and the glow fades. We deduce that they are timid creatures who give off this red heartlight when they are frightened; it suggests blushing (we find out later that it is also associated with happiness). Later in the scene the frightened E.T. gives himself away when his chest begins to glow.

The gentleness and timidity of the aliens is also suggested when a rabbit is untroubled by the presence of E.T. in the forest. We hear little E.T. coo as he cradles a seedling tree. He walks meditatively through the forest, dwarfed by giant redwoods, which we see in a low-angle shot, making them resemble enormous columns in a cathedral. The religious calm of the scene and the gradual shift to subjective camera favoring E.T.'s point of view win us over. An unnatural creature has been made to seem natural, even saintly. E.T. is shown in the opening scene to love not only nature but also the things of man; he sits to admire the lovely glow of the town, a jewel-like network of lights in the valley below. In fact, his attraction to things terrestrial and human causes him to stray too far from the ship and leads to his being stranded.

The calm, meditative mood is now shattered by the arrival of a human search team. "A fierce animal roar accompanies the irruption of scientists' off-road vehicles" (Morris 86). The music changes to a loud, fast, and tense chase motif. We see the arriving trucks from E.T.'s point of view: huge and glaring, driving aggressively forward to fill the frame in a kind of phallic invasion, a technique Spielberg mastered filming the truck in *Duel*. Spielberg facetiously called *Duel* "Bambi Meets Godzilla" (Crawley 24), and the opening of *E.T.* also evokes *Bambi*, with E.T. as a terrified animal, a loveable and helpless creature fleeing for his life from hunters in the forest. In fact, adult males are the true aliens in this film, scary creatures usually shown at waist level, from a child's or alien's point of view. For most of the film, they are faceless. The leader of the search is identified, like a jailer, by the huge key ring on his belt. Unlike the aliens, the men show no respect for the environment; they tromp through the forest, and poisonous fumes belch from their truck tailpipes. Their light is not the comforting glow of the spacecraft or heartlight, or even the warm gleam of the suburbs, but the glaring, probing light of flashlights or truck headlights.

The opening scene of *E.T.* thus effects a clever reversal of traditional values. With tremendous economy of means, employing deceptively reassuring techniques and not a single word, Spielberg turns the alien into the standard of the human and the humane, making the audience identify strongly with the alien creature while converting adult human males into the real, terrifying Other. The paranoia aroused in many 1950s American science fiction films about creepy "alien invaders" with menacing technology is here displaced onto male scientists and their intrusive machinery.

MOTHER AND CHILD IN *E.T.*

If the opening discredits men, then it also implicitly validates the maternal and childlike. In the next scene, Elliott's mother tells the children, as they investigate a backyard disturbance, "Put those knives back!" and later, again the sole woman in the scene, she pleads with the government agents, "No guns! They're children!" "Put away your weapons" is one of the messages of *E.T.*: the extraterrestrial is naked and carries no weapons (and no visible sex organs). In the opening scene, the human invaders are associated with such phallic imagery as trucks, keys, and flashlights. In contrast, E.T. is associated with the maternal: the egg-shaped ship and gardening.

The night in the opening scene is also maternal. In the suburban trilogy, creatures typically emerge at night, as if erupting out of the unconscious. But the night in *E.T.* is neither as mysterious as in *Close Encounters* nor as scary as in *Poltergeist*; instead, from the beginning it seems warm and embracing. Elliott twice sleeps outdoors, something none of the characters in *Close Encounters* or *Poltergeist* could safely attempt. When an interviewer mentioned the reassuring, "mothering feeling" one gets from the night in *E.T.*, Spielberg replied:

> Yeah, it is Mother Night. Remember in *Fantasia* Mother Night flying over with her cape, covering a daylight sky? I used to think, when I was a kid, that that's what night really looked like. The Disney Mother Night was a beautiful woman with flowing, blue-black hair, and arms extended outward, twenty miles in either direction. And behind her was a very inviting cloak. (Sragow 26)

Clearly the image of the maternal night, repeated at the end of *Close Encounters* and *Always*, has a powerful emotional meaning for Spielberg that dates back to his childhood, a feeling he is able to evoke in the viewer as well.

Even as E.T. is associated with the maternal, he is also childlike. The opening can be considered a symbolic birth, with E.T. the infant born out of the egg-shaped mothership. He is small and wobbles like a toddler. When he strays from home, his curiosity puts him in danger: he is the little child

lost who figures in many Spielberg films. His terrifying encounter with the
search party represents a sudden, violent rupture of the mother-infant dyad
by the intrusion of the father. These hunters are fairy-tale giants concocted
out of a small child's fear of grownups.

Thus the opening scene presents a fantasy of separation, with E.T. as
fairy-tale child or Bambi: a baby animal abandoned by its parents and at
the mercy of the dark forest and ruthless hunters. To enjoy the story, we
must sympathize with the creature by drawing upon the frightened child
or the nurturing mother within ourselves. Or rather, since E.T. combines
mother and child in a single figure, we must move between these two positions in our response to the alien. As we identify with the alien, we love
ourselves.

THE PROBLEMATIC FATHER

The position that remains problematic for both characters and audience
for most of the film, however, is that of the father. Until almost the end,
men are either absent (Elliott's missing father) or are giant, initially faceless
menaces seen only at waist level (the hunters, the biology teacher, a policeman)—though I will argue later that E.T. also functions as an idealized,
childlike, sexually unthreatening father.

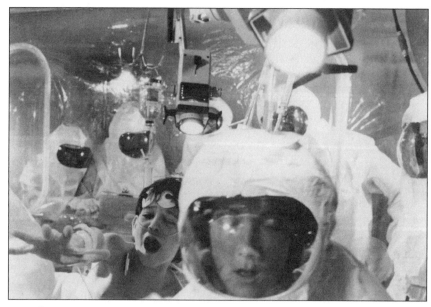

E.T.: Elliott cries out at losing E.T. Science is harsh and cold, and adult males are aliens.

Men represent science, and science is the enemy in this film, with its authority, rationality, and insensitivity. Elliott must keep E.T. from falling into their hands because "They'll give it a lobotomy or do experiments on it." The critic Roger Neustadter writes, "As science and scientists are portrayed as alienated from nature in such films as *Close Encounters of the Third Kind*, *2001*, *E.T.*, and *Flight of the Navigator*, the child is shown to be the incarnation of simplicity, naturalness, and innocence" (Neustadter 238). In *Close Encounters* and *E.T.*, alien science is like the aliens—magical, emotional, childlike, benevolent, and asexual—but human science is like grown men: rational, unemotional, adult, malevolent, and threateningly phallic.

Except for the reconciliation with Keys at the end, the film presents a pre-Oedipal view of adult males as intrusive, overpowering, and ominous. That is why audiences cheer when Elliott disrupts the science teacher's lesson by liberating the frogs and when Elliott and Michael steal the van from the officials. In the film's vision, men are evil spies who intrude on domestic bliss with phallic machinery. One shot epitomizes this idea: right after Elliott announces to his brother and sister that he's keeping E.T., we look down on the homes from the hilltop; a large black camera intrudes into the frame from the left and rapidly snaps a series of pictures. Normally one expects children to spy on the world of adults; here, men spy on children.

E.T. reverses the traditional Oedipal resolution in which the boy identifies with the father; instead, at the end Keys the scientist, as substitute father, identifies with the child Elliott (just as the scientist Lacombe in *Close Encounters* comes to identify with the childlike Roy Neary). The adult male viewer of *E.T.* must effect the same identification to transact this fantasy successfully and accept at the end the children's triumph over the world of men.

E.T. AS CHILD GOD

Until well into the picture, we don't know exactly what E.T. looks like; kept in suspense, we see him only partially or in silhouette. We first glimpse E.T.'s face the same moment that Elliott does, and our shock is tempered by humor since both human and alien respond in the same appalled manner. E.T.'s fright is expressed through telekinesis: garbage cans topple and roll, and swings oscillate wildly. The chaotic movement could equally well express Elliott's psychic upheaval at coming face to face with the "monster" who later proves to be his double.

Despite his initially repellent appearance, E.T. looks strangely familiar: with dwarfish body and wizened face (large eyes, tiny nose, reptilian appearance), he resembles a fetus not yet fully formed in the womb. Like a baby, he waddles clumsily as he walks, pokes everything within reach, tastes and tries to eat inedible objects. He is prone to upset things and cause messes. He is also easily frightened, and his moods are intense but mercurial. These characteristics endear him to us, as if he were that most sensitive of creatures, a human infant.

E.T. grows up rapidly before our eyes, progressing from gestures to sounds, words, and phrases. Finally he masters his environment by constructing a communicator to "phone home" (this Rube Goldberg device is a child's dream of a slapdash invention, concocted out of parts from a children's toy and household items). Elliott sometimes thinks of E.T. as a fellow child: when he tries to persuade him to stay, he says, "We could grow up together, E.T." Although the creature is like a child, he is also a repository of ancient, mystic wisdom, like the Jedi master Yoda in *The Empire Strikes Back* (1980): in the Halloween parade, E.T. strays from the children to follow a trick-or-treater dressed as Yoda.

As much as he is child or wise old man, E.T. is also a divine being. As child god, he is small and helpless yet paradoxically enormously powerful. Like a god, he descends to Earth from the heavens and mingles with the sons of men, risking his life to aid them. Elliott discovers him in a backyard shed that resembles a manger. E.T. is misunderstood, hunted, captured, tormented, dies, and is reborn. His coming is, as Keys tells Elliott, "a miracle." Associated with his divinity are his inexplicable psychic powers, such as telepathic empathy with Elliott and others, psychokinesis (the ability to move and levitate objects by mental energy), the "healing touch" of his magic finger, and, most awesome of all, the Christ-like power of resurrection: he brings dead flowers and then himself back to life. Moreover, like a deity, E.T. has an instinctive rapport with children, and adults must become as little children to understand and love him. With his heartlight and his magic finger, E.T. represents the divinity as creator and healer. By the end, he has healed Elliott's broken home, united the children of a fragmented suburban development in their crusade to save him, and united scientist and layperson, adult and child, in common awe of a miraculous creature beyond their understanding. The film thus blends fairy tale with religious fable.[3]

Except for the spoken words "miracle" and "believe," the religious undertones are conveyed visually, iconographically: E.T. clad in a white robe, heartlight glowing, resembling a Christ figure. One advertisement emphasized his long, glowing finger, reaching like the hand of God touching Adam in Michelangelo's painting. *E.T.*, says the critic Hugh Ruppersberg, gives us "the image of the good-hearted, kind, loving alien, the cosmic incarnation of Christian myth and doctrine. The film succeeds by stimulating religious emotions in camouflaged form and by

E.T.: The religious connotations of the film are suggested iconographically.
Universal, 1982.

its vision of a cosmos where the individual has a cosy and secure place"
(Ruppersberg 36).

E.T. AND ELLIOTT

The religious qualities of E.T. as child god do not exhaust his significance,
as he is what psychoanalysts would call an "overdetermined" figure. E.T. is
filled with psychological meaning for both Elliott and the audience—which
further accounts for the film's profound emotional impact.

Elliott is a neglected, friendless boy, abandoned by his father, and with a
mother too distracted by her own grief to be of much help. He is a middle
child squeezed between an older brother who relates mostly to his peers
(who disdain Elliott) and a little sister too young to understand the family
problems. He also lacks friends his own age. For Elliott, E.T. functions like
an "imaginary companion" who substitutes for an entire family: father,
mother, sibling, and pet rolled into one. If E.T. is the fairy-tale elf, then
Elliott is the fairy-tale child: lonely, ignored, ridiculed, clumsy, but still possessing hidden powers of intelligence, resourcefulness, bravery, and love,
qualities that will be revealed at the proper time. The coming of E.T. liber-
ates Elliott's heroic potential.

Talking about the genesis of the film, Spielberg says:

> I remember wishing one night that I had a friend. It was like, when you were
> a kid and had grown out of dolls or Teddy bears or Winnie the Pooh, you just
> wanted a little voice in your mind to talk to. . . . To me, Elliott was always the
> Nowhere Man from the Beatles song. I was drawing from my own feelings
> when I was a kid and didn't have that many friends. . . . (Sragow 26)

"Transitional objects" such as the Teddy bear Spielberg mentions mediate
between the infantile self and the mother; they are neither self nor nonself,
but something in between, transitional in the creation of a self (Winnicott).
Imaginary companions are more sophisticated; they are created at a later,
Oedipal stage of development: Linus's blanket in *Peanuts* is a transitional
object, while Calvin's tiger friend, Hobbes, in *Calvin and Hobbes* is an imaginary companion.

The psychologist Jerome Singer, commenting on the appeal of E.T.,
mentions that children often need imaginary playmates to "help them
make sense in their switch from their parents to the outside world" (Nelson). Many psychiatric commentators see the imaginary companion as a
precursor to the ego-ideal or superego—that is, to the psychic function
that approximates the role of the parents (Fraiberg; Sperling; Nagera;
Bach). The psychiatrist Wayne A. Myers found that imaginary companions are created in response to "narcissistic blows" such as "abandonment by one or both parents" (Myers 513), which is the case with Elliott
(and also with his creator, Spielberg). By splitting the self, one creates a
double, compensating for loss. Anna Freud claimed that an imaginary
animal companion helps its creator to avoid painful realities by denial:
"Thus the 'evil' father becomes in phantasy a protective animal, while
the helpless child becomes the master of powerful father-substitutes"
(A. Freud 85). S. Bach sees the imaginary companion as "an envied and
idealized [introjected paternal] phallus . . . used defensively to perpetu-
ate a regressive, narcissistic solution of the oedipus conflict" (Bach 160).
Myers agrees that the companion serves "as an idealized phallic self-
representation" for a child who thinks of himself as lacking the phallus
(Myers 313).

The notion of E.T. as imaginary companion helps to explain some of
his complex and sometimes contradictory functions: as Elliott's double, as
father substitute, and as walking phallus. First, as doubles, their names are
similar (E.T. and Elliott), and they seem part of the same character, working together like an inseparable pair linked by telepathic empathy: "a little
voice in your mind to talk to," as Spielberg says. E.T. is a magical double
who completes the boy, which is why the separation of the two at the end is
so wrenching for the audience. E.T. represents the part of himself Elliott has
split off or disavowed: the pain, loneliness, and feeling of being abandoned

he has been suppressing since his father left. As the psychologist John F. McDermott Jr. puts it:

> E.T. looks like Elliott feels. He seems to express Elliott's own bottled-up lone-liness as he gradually succumbs to the trauma of separation from a familiar milieu. E.T. is Elliott's alter ego. E.T. and Elliott are really one. They simply split into rescuer and victim as we move back and forth between them. (McDermott 14)

Elliott is able to project his own problems onto E.T., a creature who needs rescuing even more than Elliott does (Drezner 271).

As his double or alter ego, E.T. also represents the previously repressed, animal side of Elliott and helps him grow up by liberating his libido. (We tend to forget the lascivious nature of Pan, the goat-footed demigod from whom Peter Pan derives his name.) Pauline Kael notes that "the telepathic communication he develops with E.T. eases his cautious, locked-up worries, and he begins to act on his impulses" (Kael 119). When E.T. gets drunk, Elliott starts acting silly in the classroom, frees the laboratory frogs, and emulates John Wayne in *The Quiet Man* (1952) by sweeping a pretty girl into a rapturous embrace. This liberation is part of Spielberg's strategy: "How many kids, in their Walter Mitty imaginations, would love to save the frogs or kiss the prettiest girl in class? That's every boy's childhood fantasy" (Sragow 26).

Besides being the boy's double, as an imaginary animal companion E.T. is also a powerful father-substitute the boy can master. As the critic Paul Joannides notes, *E.T.* is a "fantasy of maturation" which "plays on the child's dream of omnipotence—the friend who is equipped with superhuman powers, but who remains dependent" (Joannides). Even as Elliott fathers E.T., so E.T. replaces the missing father. Another critic, Marina Heung, claims that "Elliott and E.T. offer each other the solace of a surrogate family to replace the one each has lost." When E.T. dresses in a bathrobe, drinks beer, and watches TV, he stands in for the missing father, and when he listens in with Elliott as the mother reads a bedtime story to Gertie, he completes the family circle (Heung 84). Phyllis Deutsch, a feminist critic, writes, "When E.T. is not a clinging infant, making mothers of us all, he is the flipside of the fantasy: the ultimate patriarch who has come to mend the fractured family and restore order in the kingdom" (Deutsch 13). Nevertheless, as a childlike, asexual alien, E.T. is an unthreatening authority figure, a patriarch who needs fathering, the father without the phallus.

Paradoxically, E.T. does not need the phallus because his entire body is a phallic symbol. The asexual, childlike qualities of E.T. defend against the sexuality he unconsciously represents. The imaginary companion, after all, has been considered as an idealized phallic self-representation, a way of overcoming fears of emasculation. In Bettelheim's interpretation, the frog king (a kind of imaginary animal companion to a girl) expresses the child's changing attitudes toward sexuality: at first the frog (the phallus) looks repugnant, but then it is transformed into a handsome prince (Bettelheim 290). Like a frog, E.T. is small, wrinkled, and ugly. But when he is excited, his neck extends in a kind of erection. Sobchack mentions that in the figure of E.T., "all problematic patriarchal . . . power [is] displaced . . . in the sensuosuly warm glow at the tip of an 'innocently' elongated (and phallic) finger" (Sobchack, "Child/Alien/Father" 25). Elliott hides him in his bedroom, keeping him a secret from his mother but bragging about him to his siblings and peers. He called his older brother Michael "penis breath," suggesting, perhaps, Elliott's sense of weakness in relation to older males, but once he gains possession of E.T., he tells Michael, "I have absolute power." E.T. inspires the boy to intoxicating feats of virility. And there is no need to mention how Freud would interpret dreams of flying.

If E.T. is Elliott's budding manhood, then the latter part of the film could be interpreted as a nightmare of castration anxiety: male authorities pursue him, circling ever closer, and finally invade his home to sever Elliott from his E.T. But Elliott outsmarts them and finds a satisfactory resolution of the Oedipal crisis. E.T. plays dead and then comes back to life, but Elliott returns him to the womb of the mothership, where he will be safe from harm.

E.T. ends, like *Close Encounters*, with a retreat from the dangers of masculine assertion, back to the womb of mothership and Mother Night. Yet *E.T.* does not seem as narcissistic and regressive in its resolution as *Close Encounters*, perhaps because of *E.T.*'s child hero and also because of the successful splitting the film enacts through its double hero. Even as E.T. is being returned to the womb, Elliott escapes from one: he walks out of the plastic sheath that encloses his house, and when he pulls the pins on the plastic tunnel trailing behind the truck, he symbolically cuts the cord. In contrast, at the end of *Close Encounters*, Barry is reunited with his mother while Roy fuses ecstatically with the alien mothership. *Poltergeist* reverses the end of *Close Encounters*, emphasizing the potentially terrifying consequences of that retreat, the fear of being reabsorbed by a monster mother. As Andrew Sarris notes, "the most harrowing effects in *Poltergeist* tend to be return-to-the-womb rather than phallocentric" (Sarris 59).

CONCLUSION: WE ARE E.T.

Sarah Harwood argues that E.T. is "a confused, and often contradictory film" whose conclusion is "deeply ambivalent" (Harwood 172). I would argue instead that *E.T.* is so popular because it is a rich and psychologically nuanced tale which is capable of different readings and successfully addresses many different audiences.

E.T. operates through the powerfully emotive, irrational imagery of childhood, dreams, and fairy tales. From the beginning its visual style encourages us to identify strongly, first with the alien as underdog, and then with the boy, who are representatives of our best qualities: innocence, resourcefulness, bravery, and love. This identification is more profound than that effected by other Spielberg films because it is not undercut by irony or distancing (think, for example, of how we are distanced from the mysterious unseen aliens for most of *Close Encounters*). The bond between Elliott and E.T. is so strong that we become enmeshed in it. E.T. is such a positive creation and a suggestive figure on so many possible levels, both conscious and unconscious—as loving mother, innocent child, Christ figure, the child's double or imaginary companion, kindly father, best friend, brother, or even beloved pet (*E.T.* is modeled in part on such emotionally stirring boy-and-animal films as *The Yearling* [1946], *Old Yeller* [1957], and *The Black Stallion* [1979])—that viewers will almost certainly respond deeply to one or more of these.

And at the most fundamental level, the film arouses and successfully overcomes the universal human anxiety over separation, offering tremendous reassurance. Growing up, Spielberg felt rootless because his family moved so often: "And it would always be that inevitable good-bye scene. . . . Where all my friends would be there and we'd say good-bye to each other and I would leave. This happened to me four major times in my life. And the older I got the harder it got. *E.T.* reflects a lot of that" (McBride 47). He created the film out of memories of his own childhood loneliness and of the effects of his parents' divorce and suffused it "with a poignant Freudian sense of loss" (Baxter 245). After E.T. dies and is reborn, we are willing to release him, for the creature wants only what we all want: to go back home. And he will remain behind in Elliott's mind, which he touches, saying, "I'll be right here." We can take this as the promise of the parent whose memory will remain to guide us or as the promise of the god who will never abandon us (his ship leaves behind the rainbow sign). Douglas Brode says the ending of *E.T.* reminds one of classic Disney movies such as *Snow White* and *Cinderella*, with "the sweet sorrow of parting as necessary as it is difficult" (Brode 122).

None of the interpretations I have suggested is complete or entirely exhausts the possible meanings of *E.T.* Like a fairy tale, it is a maturational fantasy that recapitulates certain stages of human psychological development, encompassing both our past and our present and suggesting clues about our future. Richard Stoves, a psychiatrist who interviewed children aged eight to twelve immediately after they saw the film, reports that "*E.T.* is a fairy tale for the preadolescent child" (Nelson). But clearly the film, one of the most popular in movie history, appeals to a far broader audience. Interview a sample audience of a different age and you will come up with different answers. With its lovable, abandoned alien who is both omnipotent and dependent, its double hero, its wise children who triumph over the adults, its thrilling rescue and happy ending, this space-age fairy tale appeals on many different levels. Says Nigel Morris, "Central to *E.T.*'s popularity is . . . differential audience address: to adults and children, cineastes and casual moviegoers" (Morris 89). Each viewer will resonate on a slightly different psychological chord to this rich and reassuring fantasy. For children, *E.T.* is a voyage of emotional discovery; for adults, a rediscovery of feelings we thought we had lost or outgrown. A five-year-old of my acquaintance summed it up very well: "It's a story about love." Like another cinematic fairy tale, *The Wizard of Oz*, *E.T.* shows the extraordinary journey we all must take to return to the place at our heart's core: "Home."

So why do millions weep at the death of E.T.? Why does it move me every time I see it? Why did the little Cambodian boy cry even though he didn't understand a word of the dialogue? As the novelist Martin Amis says, "We were crying for our lost selves. This is the primal genius of Spielberg" (Baxter 245).

NOTES

1. Among the critics who mention the E.T.–Peter Pan connection, see Sarris; Michener and Ames 63; and Corliss.

2. Amid the chorus of superlatives for *E.T.*, Andrew Sarris sounds a dissenting note which is worth considering: "Spielberg (and Lucas) may be creating fairy tales that serve not so much as rites of passage as pleas for a permanent childhood." And Richard Grenier, a right-wing critic, objects to "the message of *E.T.* . . . that except for us [Americans], it is a benign universe."

3. Although the alien Klaatu in the science fiction film *The Day the Earth Stood Still* (1951) looks and sounds human, so that he blends into society, E.T. has some similarities to Klaatu as messiah or Christ figure. Here are some of the parallels between *E.T.* and *The Day the Earth Stood Still*: Klaatu comes to Earth on a peaceful mission (to save mankind from destroying itself with nuclear weapons) but is misunderstood and feared so that he has to hide among ordinary people. Klaatu possesses super-science which is inexplicable and magical, appears much younger than his years (he looks thirty-seven but is twice that age), opens locked doors just by touching them, and has amazing powers of self-healing. Klaatu's best friend is a little boy whose father is gone (in this case, killed in World War II). He also meets a sympathetic scientist, Dr. Barnhardt, who understands his message of peace. He uses Earth technology (a flashlight) to communicate with his spaceship. Finally, he is hunted down and caught by the authorities, dies, but is resurrected and flies home in his ship at the end.

REFERENCES

Bach, S. "Notes on Some Imaginary Companions." *The Psychoanalytic Study of the Child*, Vol. 26. New York: Quadrangle Books, 1971, 159–71.

Baxter, John. *Steven Spielberg: The Unauthorised Biography*. London: HarperCollins, 1996.

Bettelheim, Bruno. *The Uses of Enchantment: The Meaning and Importance of Fairy Tales*. New York: Knopf, 1977.

Brode, Douglas. *The Films of Steven Spielberg*. New York: Citadel Press, 1995.

Corliss, Richard. "Steve's Summer Magic." *Time*, May 31, 1982, 56.

Crawley, Tony. *The Steven Spielberg Story*. New York: Quill, 1983.

Deutsch, Phyllis. "E.T.: The Ultimate Patriarch." *Jump Cut* 28 (1983): 12–13.

Drezner, Jeffrey. "E.T.: An Odyssey of Loss." *The Psychoanalytic Review* 70 (1983): 269–75.

Eisenstein, Alex. "The Forerunners of CE3K." *Fantastic Films*, April 1978, 28.

Fraiberg, Selma. *The Magic Years*. New York: Scribner's, 1959.

Freud, Anna. *The Ego and the Mechanisms of Defense*. New York: International Universities Press, 1946.

"The Frog-King, or Iron Henry." *The Complete Grimm's Fairy Tales*. New York: Pantheon, 1972.

Gordon, Andrew. "*Close Encounters*: The Gospel According to Steven Spielberg." *Literature/Film Quarterly* 8.3 (1980): 156–64.

Grenier, Richard. *Commentary*, August 1982, 66.

Harwood, Sarah. *Family Fictions: Representations of the Family in 1980s Hollywood Cinema*. New York: St. Martin's Press, 1997.

Heung, Marina. "Why E.T. Must Go Home: The New Family in American Cinema." *Journal of Popular Film and Television* 11.2 (1983): 79–85.

Jameson, Richard T. Review of *E.T. Film Comment*, February 1982, 11–14.

Joannides, Paul. "Luminous/Numinous." *London Review of Books*, 20 Jan.–3 Feb. 1982, 16.

Kael, Pauline. "The Pure and the Impure." *New Yorker*, June 14, 1982, 119–22.

McBride, Joseph. *Steven Spielberg: A Biography*. New York: Simon and Schuster, 1997.

McDermott, John F., Jr. "E.T.: A Story of Separation." Unpublished essay.

Michener, Charles and Katrine Ames. "A Summer Double Punch." *Newsweek*, May 31, 1982, 64.

Morris, Nigel. *The Cinema of Steven Spielberg: Empire of Light*. London: Wallflower, 2007.

Myers, Wayne A. "Imaginary Companions, Fantasy Twins, Mirror Dreams and Depersonalization." *Psychoanalytic Quarterly* 45 (1976): 503–24.

Nagera, Humberto. "The Imaginary Companion: Its Significance for Ego Development and Conflict Solution." *The Psychoanalytic Study of the Child*, Vol. 24. New York: International Universities Press, 1969, 165–96.

Nelson, Bryce. "E.T. Speaks to Children—but Not Via Telephone." *New York Times* News Service, *Gainesville* [FL] *Sun*, Dec. 21, 1982, 6B.

Neustadter, Roger. "Phone Home: The Transformation of Childhood in Contemporary Science Fiction Films." *Youth and Society* 20.3 (March 1989), 227–40.

Ruppersburg, Hugh. "The Alien Messiah in Recent Science Fiction Films." *Journal of Popular Film and Television* 14.4 (1987): 159–66.

Sarris, Andrew. "Spielberg's Sand Castles." *Village Voice*, June 15, 1982, 59.

Sheehan, Henry. "The Panning of Steven Spielberg." *Film Comment* 28.2 (May–June 1992): 54–60.

Sobchack, Vivian. "Child/Father/Alien: Patriarchal Crisis and Generic Exchange." *Camera Obscura* 15 (Fall 1986): 7–34.

———. *Screening Space: The American Science-Fiction Film*. New York: Ungar, 1987.

Sperling, O. F. "An Imaginary Companion Representing a Pre-stage of the Super-geo." *The Psychoanalytic Study of the Child*, Vol 9. New York: International Universities Press, 1984, 252–58.

Sragow, Michael. "A Conversation with Steven Spielberg." *Rolling Stone*, July 22, 1982, 25–28.

Winnicott, D. W. *Playing and Reality*. London: Tavistock, 1971.

Wuntch, Philip. "Henry and Melissa and Stephen and E.T." *Dallas Morning News*; rpt. *Gainesville Sun*, July 9, 1982, B2.

5

Poltergeist (1982)

Divorce American Style

MAKING *POLTERGEIST*: E.T.'S EVIL TWIN

Since its release, there has been continuing disagreement over whether *Poltergeist* can be considered a Spielberg film because it was supposedly directed by Tobe Hooper. This is one of those unresolved issues in the history of American science fiction and fantasy film, like the debate over whether *The Thing from Another World* (1951) should be credited to producer Howard Hawks or director Christian Nyby (Warren 48). For example, in 2002 David Thomson argued that "It is pretty well agreed now that *Poltergeist* deserves to be read as a Spielberg work" (Thomson), yet in 2006 Warren Buckland did a statistical style analysis of *Poltergeist*, comparing its first thirty minutes in terms of factors including shot duration, camera angle, and camera movement, with the first thirty minutes of other films by Spielberg and by Hooper, and concluded that *Poltergeist* was directed by Hooper (Buckland 154–67).

Yet Spielberg came up with the story for *Poltergeist*, hired two writers to do the screenplay, and then rewrote it himself. He picked the cast and crew, storyboarded the film with an artist, and served as line producer with Frank Marshall. Spielberg was on the set all day for all but three days of filming, and he supervised all post-production, including sound, visual effects, promotion, and advertising. Spielberg chose Tobe Hooper, best known for the cult horror movie *The Texas Chainsaw Massacre* (1974), as director only because Spielberg was directing *E.T.* and it was illegal to direct two movies at the same time. Hooper was placed in an uncomfortable situation because of Spielberg's need to control all aspects of production. Hooper delivered the first cut and Spielberg made the final cut. Rumors

Poltergeist: Who directed: Spielberg (left) or Hooper (holding Coke)? MGM, 1982.

flew that Spielberg, not Hooper, was the real director, to the point that Spielberg had to publish an open letter in *Variety* congratulating Hooper on his contribution to *Poltergeist.* He says he will never again make the mistake of letting someone else direct a Spielberg screenplay (McBride 340).

Although the issue of who actually "directed" *Poltergeist* may never be resolved, I would argue that it is undeniably a Spielberg film because it has all the earmarks of one. It helps to place the film in his canon so that it can be compared to the rest of his films. *Poltergeist* is the last of Spielberg's suburban trilogy, which begins with *Close Encounters* and includes *E.T.*, all comforting movies which have so many similarities in subject matter and theme that they might be considered three different versions of the same movie, one that is harrowing yet also spiritual and warm: the invasion of average, middle-class households by strange forces and the kidnaping of children. All three end with reunion or transcendence; they are fairy tales in which the pure of heart win out.

Spielberg says that *E.T.* and *Poltergeist* "both erupted at about the same time, while I was directing *Raiders*" (Chase 52). Their simultaneous "eruption" suggests that the films are unconsciously linked. While he was on the set of *Raiders*, he was also thinking back to *Close Encounters*: "I've got to get back to the tranquility, or at least the spirituality, of *Close Encounters*, because I miss it, I miss the warmth of that as opposed to just the high adventure of *Raiders*" (McCarthy 54). *Poltergeist* is inspired in part by *Close Encounters*: "I

Poltergeist: Hooper and Spielberg on the set. MGM, 1982.

always wanted to make a ghost movie, ever since I was a kid. . . . So I kind of blended a little bit of the kidnaping of the child in *Close Encounters* with the research I had done about poltergeists . . ." (Royal 87).

To put it another way, *Close Encounters* gave birth to the twins *E.T.* and *Poltergeist,* the good twin and the evil one:

> *Poltergeist* is what I fear and *E.T.* is what I love. . . . One is about suburban evil and the other is about suburban good. . . . *Poltergeist* is the darker side of my nature—it's me when I was scaring my sisters half to death when we were growing up—and *E.T.* is my optimism about the future and my optimism about what it was like to grow up. . . ." (Kakutani)

> *E.T.* is my personal resurrection, and *Poltergeist* is my personal nightmare. A lot of things in both movies came from my growing up. *Poltergeist* is about my fears—of a clown doll, of a closet, of what was under the bed, of the tree in New Jersey that. . .scared me with its long, twiggy fingers." (Sragow 113)

The division between the two movies—love story with monster in *E.T.* and horror story with monster in *Poltergeist*—is not clearcut. As Neil Sinyard notes, "*E.T.* has something of the appearance of a horror film in which all the conventions have been reversed," with a sympathetic monster (Sinyard 78). And despite its being a horror film, Spielberg says of *Poltergeist*, "I think it's very spiritual; I think the film is very tender in places" (McCarthy 55)—remarks that could apply equally well to *E.T.*

Poltergeist might usefully be compared as well to earlier Spielberg horror movies, which also concern average suburbanites terrorized by monsters. Like *Something Evil*, his made-for-television movie, it concerns a family living in a haunted house and a mother who rescues her child from the spirits of the dead. Like *Duel*, the hero is isolated (in *Poltergeist* the family is the collective hero). And, like *Jaws*, greedy developers endanger an ordinary, happy community. But in *Poltergeist* evil is not embodied in a single object like a truck or a shark: it is abstract and diffused and takes many different forms.

Aside from its close connections with *Close Encounters* and *E.T.*, *Poltergeist* was influenced by two Richard Matheson horror stories, "Through Channels" and "Little Girl Lost" (Crawley 145). "Little Girl Lost," Matheson's 1953 short story, he turned into a teleplay for *The Twilight Zone* in 1962. Spielberg requested a videotape of "Little Girl Lost" before making *Poltergeist* (McBride 337). Matheson's story concerns a couple awakened one night by the sound of their six-year-old daughter crying; they can hear her but can't find her anywhere in the apartment. A physicist friend theorizes that she has fallen through a hole into another dimension. Then the dog disappears as well. The father steps through the hole to recover his daughter and the dog, and the friend pulls out all three. Spielberg creates a similar little girl lost but turns the hole into another dimension into the spirit world, changing the story from science fiction to fantasy. Having the little girl kidnaped by ghosts makes it more dramatic and threatening rather than simply accidental. He also "feminizes" Matheson's story by making the mother rather than the father into the rescuer and replacing the male physicist with two women, a parapsychologist and a medium.

Poltergeist cost more than *E.T.* because it had over a hundred special effects to *E.T.*'s forty. But the two films are similar in look. *Poltergeist*, says Spielberg, is "very much like *E.T.* in that it has a 'normal,' hard-key look. But when the normalcy of the family is being double-exposed with the horror of these intruders, the style becomes darker, eerier, with more shadows and less fill light" (Chase 59). Spielberg's twin movies were delivered simultaneously in May of 1982 to enormous media attention and popular acclaim; between them, they dominated the box office that summer and that year. But it was *E.T.* that would become the classic.

Reviewers liked the warmth of the family in *Poltergeist* and the quality of the acting. But some objected that the plot of *Poltergeist* was confused or nonsensical and full of weak devices such as the hoary notion that the house was built over a graveyard or the stock horror-movie premise of the family's spending yet another night in the haunted house after their daughter is rescued (Benson; Auty; Asahina). The long monologues on matters occult were dismissed as "metaphysical gibberish" (Denby) or "mumbo jumbo" (Keneas). Reviewers liked some of the effects, but thought others feeble or overdone. One reviewer called the movie "a muddled affair which uncontrollably throws in just about every horrific effect in the satanic book" (Coleman), including bending spoons, furniture that moves by itself, flickering lights, spectral presences, hallucinations, haunted closets, trees and dolls that come to life, levitation, ghosts, goblins, and skeletons. And, as the effects escalated, there was no logic to the proceedings: "You are never exactly sure what the ground rules are" (Benson).

POLTERGEIST AS OPTIMISTIC HORROR

Despite the fact that it throws at the audience "just about every horrific effect in the satanic book," *Poltergeist* is a curiously optimistic horror movie.

Poltergeist: A normal, happy American family. MGM, 1982.

Poltergeist: A broken home. MGM, 1982. Courtesy MovieStar News.

A friend of mine, a baby boomer who grew up in the suburbs in southern California, says that sometimes when she is feeling down she plays videotapes of *Close Encounters* or *Poltergeist*. These movies show families like hers in backgrounds she is familiar with. I told her I could understand the comforting appeal of *Close Encounters*, but to turn to a horror movie like *Poltergeist* for reassurance, to overcome depression? She said it was because the family sticks together. In the climax, a mother enters the mouth of hell to rescue her child. As David Sterritt writes, "There's a sense of warmth and security running through *Poltergeist* that takes a lot of the edge off the explosive scenes . . . not a single character is killed or even harmed, despite a lot of harrowing close calls. . . . Watching goodness and normality triumph over the forces of darkness and disarray, it's natural to recall that Spielberg had his origins as a filmmaker while he was still at a fairy-tale age" (Sterritt).

As I have argued, one way of viewing Spielberg's suburban trilogy is as three movies about divorce and separation anxiety: in *Close Encounters*, that anxiety is overcome through union with a space family which functions as a transformational object, and in *E.T.*, the alien becomes substitute father, mother, and child to heal a fractured family. Although it might seem odd to discuss *Poltergeist* in these terms since it features the only intact family in the trilogy, nevertheless I would argue that its unspoken subject is divorce.

On the surface, *Poltergeist* seems to be not about divorce but about the fear of death, of what lies beyond the grave. But death is "the undiscovered country from whose bourn/no traveler returns," as Hamlet says in Shakespeare's play. Because death is the great tabula rasa, we fill in the blank, inscribing it with fears with which we are already familiar: fears of the dark, of sleep or unconsciousness, of bodily injury, of age or decay, or of whatever most terrifies the particular individual. In Spielberg's case, these appear to be fears of separation from the parents, of a family torn asunder. He creates the happy Freeling family only to scare them out of their wits and give them a terrible battering: first the son is almost killed and then the younger daughter is kidnaped. Their house turns against them; it becomes haunted, unsafe, and uncanny. In the end it is destroyed: it is, literally, a broken home. As Douglas Kellner remarks, "The scenes of separation throughout the movie express fear of impending disintegration of the family and fear of separation from the haven of the family" (Kellner 125). Spielberg arouses these fears in order to overcome them; like *E.T.*, the film is part of his rehearsal for marriage and parenthood.

One way of explaining *Poltergeist* is that Spielberg seems to recapitulate certain early conflicts over separation or fusion with the mother, conflicts which in his case were perhaps repeated in his adolescence due to the trauma of his parents' divorce. He says, "*Poltergeist* is what I fear and *E.T.* is what I love. . . . One is about suburban evil and the other about suburban good . . ." (Kakutani 30). The suburbs consist of isolated nuclear families: mothers and fathers with their children, each family in its own house. What Spielberg loves, what is good about the suburbs is family closeness; what he fears, what is evil, is the breakup of the home. He writes:

> I was about 16 when our family moved from Phoenix to Northern California, and soon after, our parents separated. They hung in there to protect us until we were old enough. But I don't think they were aware of how acutely we were aware of their unhappiness—not violence, just a pervading unhappiness you could cut with a fork or a spoon at dinner every night. For years I thought the word "divorce" was the ugliest in the English language. Sound traveled from bedroom to bedroom, and the word came seeping through the heating ducts. My sisters and I would stay up at night, listening to our parents argue, hiding from that word. And when it traveled into our room, absolute abject panic set in. My sisters would burst into tears, and we would all hold one another. And when the separation finally came, we were no better off for having waited six years for it to occur. (Spielberg 63)

In *Close Encounters*, the aliens try to invade the home and kidnap a child through the heating ducts. And in *Poltergeist*, Spielberg restages that anxiety over divorce in scenes of the children terrified by strange noises at night, clinging together in a panic over "ghosts." He seems to split object representations into good and bad: the idealized Freeling family, with good mother and father and children (and even a kindly surrogate grandmother in the parapsychologist Dr. Lesh), is attacked by a poltergeist Manson family which is really their bad, distorted mirror image.

That is the weakness of the film as I see it. *Poltergeist* is too well defended, disguising its real subject: the flaws in ourselves or in the people we love which break families apart. That is the real "suburban evil." The Freeling family is too nice, which makes the film too reassuring and superficial. We get the Spielberg warmth, comedy, and wonder, along with plenty of thrills, chills, suspense, and beautiful or gruesome special effects, but it lacks *psychological* horror.

Since the parents in *Poltergeist*, Diane and Steve Freeling (he is given Spielberg's first name), are such good parents and sympathetic people, the bad parents are symbolically represented by the ghosts. These ghosts first manifest themselves through the television set; the movie opens and closes with images of a television. Spielberg says that when he was growing up, "my step-parent was the TV set" (Crawley 12). In *Poltergeist*, TV plays the role of the evil step-parent, seducing and swallowing children; it functions like the witch who entices Hansel and Gretel with a gingerbread house so she can eat them or the wicked queen who offers her stepdaughter Snow White a shiny poisoned apple.

THE OPENING SCENE OF *POLTERGEIST*

The disturbing opening shot of *Poltergeist* shows an abstract pattern of wavering black and white dots to the sound of "The Star-Spangled Banner." The visual disorientation continues until the camera pulls back, as the National Anthem ends, to reveal the statue of the Marines raising the flag at Iwo Jima; it is a television station signing off at the end of the broadcasting day. Like Hitchcock, Spielberg upsets the audience by temporarily subverting a familiar national icon (Canby). Similarly, the sacred institution of the American family will be assaulted in the film by the uncanny. After the station goes off the air, what is left is eerie black-and-white static and white noise. The camera pulls back further to reveal the father, Steve Freeling, asleep in his chair, bathed in the flickering rays of the set. We first meet the family when it is at its most vulnerable, asleep, and the forces of chaos and the void are loose in the home. As the first draft of the screenplay says, "Transmission ends and a BLAST of disturbing static rules the airwaves" ("Poltergeist" 1), and later, "Transmission ceases and the soft roar of dead air fills the room as the static white snow colors the walls, making shadows flicker and warp" ("Poltergeist" 14). The static is an evil, roaring beast which emerges at night out of "dead air" to rule the household. The static could represent the force of the unconscious or the repressed, the anarchy which reigns when ordinary, daytime mental "transmission" ceases and we sleep. One of the parapsychologists later suggests the television may be receiving messages from "inner space."

In contrast to the evil beast of the television set is the friendly family dog, who trots upstairs and through the bedrooms, searching for food. As the camera tracks the dog, we are introduced to the other sleeping members of the family: the mother Diane (a memo pad on her nightstand is, significantly, heart-shaped), sixteen-year-old daughter Dana, eight-year-old Robbie, and finally five-year-old Carol Anne. There is something creepy about this opening camera movement: the camera seems to emerge out of the TV and prowl the house while the occupants are asleep, and it knows what's going to happen (the camera also does this in several later scenes when the family is asleep). The omniscient camera is another force at large in the Freeling home, one which seems to have more in common with "the TV people" than with the family dog.

Little Carol Anne senses something; she wakes up and walks downstairs, as if hypnotized or sleepwalking, into the flickering light of the TV, summoned by voices only she can hear. As in *Close Encounters* and *E.T.*, the children's sleep is disturbed by strange spirits (Denby 71). Carol Anne talks to the TV as if it were a person, but we hear only her side of the dialogue. She kneels before the screen and touches it as if praying at an altar. (In *Close Encounters*, Roy and Jillian also touch the screens of their TVs, but in that film the set is a benign totem whereas here it is evil.) The rest of the family, which by now has also woken up, is baffled and upset as they watch her. Later in the film, ghosts emerge from the static and pull Carol Anne through to "the other side," so that she can only communicate with her parents as a faint voice out of the TV set.

POLTERGEISTS AND ORAL AGGRESSION

In contemporary American culture, viewing television is often denigrated in terms suggesting oral passivity: "boob tube" or "couch potato." The flip side of those fears is the notion not only that we feed off television images but also that TV will swallow us. Many American parents are afraid that their children have become hypnotized, consumed by the TV set; *Poltergeist* literalizes those anxieties (Kellner 127). Television here becomes the bad breast which does not nourish but devours.

In both *Close Encounters* and *E.T.*, the aliens are associated with sweets: ice cream and cookies in *Close Encounters* and candy (Reese's Pieces) in *E.T.* But in *Poltergeist*, the supernatural creatures prevent the characters from eating: they disrupt a breakfast by shattering a glass and bending the silverware, and they disrupt a dinner by turning the meat rotten and maggotty. Another way of putting it is that the extraterrestrials are orally gratifying or nourishing figures whereas the ghosts are orally sadistic, akin to the shark in *Jaws*: Diane teases Carol Anne that if you overfeed goldfish they turn into sharks, and in the first draft screenplay, Robbie says, "This place's got jaws" ("Poltergeist" 56).

There are numerous examples of the poltergeists' oral aggression: Carol Anne and everything in the children's bedroom gets sucked into the closet; Marty, one of the parapsychologists, is bitten when he tries to enter the bedroom; and in the climax, the closet develops a giant mouth which threatens to devour the children and Diane (it looks like the Sarlaac in *Return of the Jedi*). In the script, the effect is described as "a living mouth, all gums and blinding light and at the very back, a pale yellow esophagus that spirals to abysmal depths" ("Poltergeist" 112). Alternately, this image can be read as vaginal; Andrew Sarris says "the most harrowing effects in *Poltergeist* tend to be return-to-the-womb" (Sarris 59). If the aliens in *Close Encounters* function for the hero as the good mother or the good breast, then the ghosts in *Poltergeist* are the reverse.

POLTERGEISTS AS CHILDREN

Nevertheless, even if the ghosts suggest the bad mother, they are also in a sense children like the aliens and E.T. According to Freud, ghosts are simply the child's (or the neurotic's) imago of the bad side of the parents (Freud 65). As expressions of the child's imagination, they are themselves childlike. The psychic Tangina tells the parents, "To her [Carol Anne], it simply *is* another child. To us, it is The Beast."

"Poltergeist" means "bratty ghost." Right after the opening there is a comic scene in which a group of bratty children play a mischievous prank on a grownup. A hefty man holding a case of beer laboriously pedals a too-small child's bike. Kids sitting on the curb send their remote-control toy cars after him, causing him to fall off the bike and drop the beer, which sprays in all directions. The farce continues in the same scene when Steve Freeling engages his fat, obnoxious neighbor in a battle of duelling remote controls; again, the television sets seem to have minds of their own. Ironically, on the television the macho aggression of a football game battles with the gentle Mr. Rogers, who sings, "Please, won't you be my neighbor?" We see a series of connected motifs: bratty children, or adults who behave like children

(Synder 150), and remote-control devices used to play practical jokes at a distance. The poltergeists too begin with these sort of playful, juvenile stunts, although their pranks gradually escalate into the truly vicious.

A similar mixture is at work in the Spielberg-produced *Gremlins* (1984): the gremlins begin with malicious mischief and build to total carnage; like the poltergeists, the gremlins can be likened both to playful children and to unleashed aggression from the id. *Poltergeist*, however, wants to be a horror film whereas *Gremlins* plays it mostly for laughs.

Poltergeist expresses not only Spielberg's boyhood fears but also his aggressive way of overcoming those fears by playing scary tricks on his sisters: "*Poltergeist* is the darker side of my nature—it's me when I was scaring my younger sisters half to death when we were growing up . . ." (Kakutani 1). All those jokes via remote control in the film could serve as a metaphor for the power of the filmmaker to play pranks on an audience through technology that operates at a distance: it's Spielberg the "bratty ghost" trying to scare us.

POLTERGEISTS AS ALIENS

As pranksters and powerful spirits—both children and adults at the same time—the poltergeists are similar to the aliens in *Close Encounters*. Both have psychic powers, behave irrationally, play tricks, and never speak. The scene in *Close Encounters* in which the aliens kidnap little Barry Guiler from his home resembles the kidnaping of Carol Anne from her bedroom in *Poltergeist*: both involve penetrating beams of light and self-animating objects. The poltergeists are the aliens turned nightmarish rather than benign.

Nevertheless, the characters respond to the poltergeists with the same mix of emotions with which the characters in *Close Encounters* respond to the aliens: terror but sometimes also wonder and delight. One reviewer even complained that Spielberg "treats the title spirits as if they were extraterrestrials. The film's tone is more one of wonder and awe—fine for an outer space film—than of thrills and chills" (Chanko 430). For example, when the characters in *Poltergeist* watch the parade of ghosts down the staircase, they are awestruck, like witnesses to a religious miracle, much like the characters at the end of *Close Encounters* and *E.T.* The emotion is more appropriate when directed toward the benign aliens than toward these demons and lost souls. Such inappropriate affect again suggests that the creatures in all three films have a similar unconscious origin, although in *Poltergeist* Spielberg has reversed their polarity from good to bad. According to Chris Auty, "Suburbia for Spielberg is like the libido—a lake of contradictory wishes and impulses which can be expressed in forms either beatific or horrific" (205).

POLTERGEIST INVASION AS SEXUAL ASSAULT

The beatific aliens in *Close Encounters* and *E.T.* significantly lack one aspect of the libido: sexuality. His extraterrestrials are neuter, asexual or presexual, like children before they develop awareness of gender. In Spielberg's films, adult sexuality is often scary. As the ghosts of adults, the poltergeists are sexual beings, and that is part of what makes them so horrible.

The movie hints that the poltergeist attacks are disguised sexual assaults, directed primarily against women. When Carol Anne begins sleepwalking, the worried Diane recalls an incident from her own childhood. When she was ten, she strayed outside her home while sleepwalking and wound up asleep in a strange man's car. Fearing the worst, her father had her examined "for bruises and hickeys." Although she laughs now about this incident, it was obviously traumatic then, and she seems to fear Carol Anne may be molested. In the climax of the film, when the teenage daughter Dana returns home from an evening with friends, hickeys are visible on her neck.

Through match cutting, the poltergeists are associated with a team of male construction workers who invade the home and harass the women. When the ghosts first emerge from the TV, Carol Anne ominously announces to the family, "They're here!"; immediately, there is a cut to a tractor gouging out the earth in the backyard for a swimming pool, a kind of phallic invasion. (This hole in the ground later becomes a place of terror, like an open grave.) Diane catches one of the construction workers sticking his hand through the kitchen window to steal a taste of the sauce from her cooking pot; the sexual symbolism here hardly needs elaboration! Later, another construction worker makes crude remarks to the adolescent daughter Dana, who gives him the finger.

Still later we see Diane take a bath: shots of her removing her clothes, lingering shots of her luxuriating in the tub, and closeups of the drain seem to allude to the shower scene in *Psycho* (1960). The suspense is prolonged until she is stretched out on her bed. What follows is one of the most erotically suggestive scenes in a Spielberg film, as Diane, clad only in panties and a nightshirt, is bounced on the bed by unseen forces. As she thrashes up and down, it suggests rape by an invisible assailant. The first draft screenplay is even more explicit: "The nightgown is suddenly torn away revealing her breasts. They are kneaded and flattened. Hulking finger impressions can be seen sinking deeply into her" ("Poltergeist" 110). As in *Close Encounters*, Spielberg toned down both the language and the amount of skin shown to preserve a PG rating.

Poltergeist has a great deal of what could be called "primal scene" imagery: the one time Steve and Diane are about to have sex, Robbie barges in on them, and the rest of the movie is about horrible things that go on behind closed doors, about strange noises and things that go bump in the night. The attack of the poltergeists, then, may represent in part a child's distorted version of violent adult sexuality.

This may seem contradictory: how can poltergeists symbolize simultaneously the bad mother—bad breast or devouring womb—aggressive children, and the bad, sexually assaulting father? The contradiction, however, is only an apparent one. Inside every unconscious mind, there is an entire family constellation of object representations: ourselves as children, along with the ways we internalized our relationships with mother, father, and siblings. Often these objects battle it out against one another, repeating the conflicts of childhood.

THE CLIMAX OF *POLTERGEIST*

The climax of *Poltergeist* combines imagery of separation anxiety, divorce, death, and rebirth—all the central concerns of the film, and for that matter, the concerns as well of *E.T.* The climax occurs when the mother enters her children's closet (a true anxiety closet!) to rescue her kidnaped daughter from the poltergeists. Passing through the doorway represents transit into the spirit world, a descent into the unknown, into limbo or the inferno. They tie a rope around her waist, and her husband promises not to let go of the rope, so that she can retrieve Carol Anne and return safely. But he panics and releases it prematurely. In a sense, the rope equals their marriage, the ties that bind. His premature release of the rope represents the fear of divorce, which here becomes equivalent to death.

Diane tumbles down the rope and lands on the living room floor, clinging to Carol Anne. We don't know if they are alive or dead. In a graphic rebirth scene, mother and child, both covered with red slime, are rushed into a water-filled tub and told to breathe. They revive. The rope has now changed symbolically from the bonds of matrimony to the birth cord. The father's failure has imperiled both mother and child, who descend into death but return. Like E.T., they appear to die and then are reborn.

But even this climax is insufficient to resolve the anxiety about divorce which is behind the plot, so Spielberg gives us a second, grand climax which repeats the first: Steve leaves the house and Diane and the children are again in danger of being kidnaped or killed by the evil spirits. Once more, the mother rescues them. The father returns at the last minute to get his family away as the entire house collapses. Talk about broken homes! In real life, Spielberg's mother remained with the children but his father left for good. In the movies, Spielberg can replay the trauma of divorce as horror yet still give it a happy ending.

CONCLUSION: *POLTERGEIST* LACKS INTERNAL STRUGGLE

The weakness of *Poltergeist* is that its conflicts are too external. The truck in *Duel* or the shark in *Jaws* are powerful symbols that seem to emerge from the unconscious because the heroes are *already* paranoid or phobic. Similarly, in *E.T.*, the alien appears when the family is fractured and the child is alienated. In contrast, in *Poltergeist* there is no internal struggle because the family is too normal; the horror doesn't reflect any problems in their character or in their relationships, so the poltergeists lack psychological power. And since we don't find out the cause of the disturbances—the desecration of the cemetery—until very late, for most of the movie the events have no apparent reason for happening. Pauline Kael writes, "What's lacking is what *E.T.* has—the emotional roots of the fantasy and what it means to the children. There is nothing about Diane and Steve and their kids that relates in any way to what happens to them. The parents show their love for Carol Anne, but it was never in doubt" (353). Tom Genelli and Lyn Davis Genelli believe *Poltergeist* lacks "true eeriness." In *Dead of Night* (1946), another horror film about the transit into an afterlife, transit "is the experience of the unravelling of our own minds into their primordial components. *Poltergeist* fundamentally portrays transit a something that *happens* to people because of things beyond their control" (111).

Poltergeist might be usefully compared to another, truly disturbing horror film with a similar premise, which preceded it by two years: Stanley Kubrick's *The Shining* (1980). Based on the novel by Stephen King, *The Shining* is also about a family living in a haunted house (in this case, a hotel) constructed over a cemetery, an innocent child with psychic sensitivity who makes the first contact with the evil spirits of the dead, and a courageous mother who rescues her child. But whereas the family in *Poltergeist* begins as utterly normal, the family in *The Shining* is dysfunctional to begin with. The father is abusive and, under the evil influence of the hotel, becomes a crazed killer. *Poltergeist* lacks the disturbing power of *The Shining*, in which the terror comes from a father bent on murdering his wife and child.

The best horror presents us with a mirror in which we may glimpse our worst selves. Instead of a mirror, *Poltergeist* gives us a television set. *Poltergeist* hides its true subject, the terror of divorce, a subject Spielberg deals with more openly in *Close Encounters* and *E.T.* Compared to a horror movie such as *The Shining*, *Poltergeist* looks like the story of an average American family assaulted by special effects.

REFERENCES

Asahina, Robert. Review of *Poltergeist*. *New Leader*, July 12–26, 1982, 19.
Auty, Chris. Review of *Poltergeist*. *Monthly Film Bulletin*, September 1982, 205.

Benson, Sheila. Review of *Poltergeist*. *Los Angeles Times*, June 4, 1982, Calendar 1.

Buckland, Warren. *Directed by Steven Spielberg: Poetics of the Contemporary Hollywood Blockbuster*. New York: Continuum, 2006.

Canby, Vincent. "Vivid Angry Spirits." *New York Times*, June 4, 1982, C 16: 2.

Chanko, Kenneth M. Review of *Poltergeist*. *Films in Review*, August 9, 1982, 430.

Chase, David. "An Interview with Steven Spielberg." *Millimeter*, July 1982, 52–62.

Coleman, John. Review of *Poltergeist*. *New Statesman*, September 17, 1982, 26.

Crawley, Tony. *The Steven Spielberg Story*. New York: Quill, 1983.

Denby, David. Review of *Poltergeist*. *New Yorker*, June 7, 1982, 71.

Freud, Sigmund. *Totem and Taboo* (1912–1913). *The Standard Edition of the Complete Psychological Works of Sigmund Freud*, Vol. XIII (1913–1914). Trans. and Ed. James Strachey. London: Hogarth, 1955.

Genelli, Tom and Lyn Davis Genelli. "Between Two Worlds: Some Thoughts beyond the 'Film Blanc.'" *Journal of Popular Film and Television* 12, 3 (Fall 1984): 100–11.

Kael, Pauline. Review of *Poltergeist*. *Taking It All In*. New York: Holt, 1984, 351–53.

Kakutani, Michiko. "The Two Faces of Spielberg: Horror vs. Hope." *New York Times*, May 30, 1982, II: 1, 30.

Kellner, Douglas. "Fear and Trembling in the Age of Reagan: Notes on *Poltergeist*." *Socialist Review* 69 (May–June 1983): 121–31.

Keneas, Alex. Review of *Poltergeist*. *Newsday*, June 4, 1982, Part II, 7.

McBride, Joseph. *Steven Spielberg: A Biography*. New York: Simon and Schuster, 1997.

McCarthy, Todd. "Sand Castles." *Film Comment*, May–June 1982, 53–59.

Poltergeist. MGM/UA, 1982. A Steven Spielberg Production. Producer: Steven Spielberg and Frank Marshall. Associate Producer: Kathleen Kennedy. Director: Tobe Hooper. Story: Steven Spielberg. Screenplay: Steven Spielberg, Michael Grais, and Mark Victor. Director of Photography: Matthew F. Leonetti. Visual effects Supervisor: Richard Edlund. Music: Jerry Goldsmith. Starring: Craig T. Nelson (Steve Freeling); JoBeth Williams (Diane Freeling); Beatrice Straight (Dr. Lesh); Dominique Dunne (Dana Freeling); Oliver Robins (Robbie Freeling); Heather O'Rourke (Carol Anne Freeling); Zelda Rubinstein (Tangina).

"Poltergeist." Draft of the Screenplay by Steven Spielberg, Mark Victor, and Michael Grais. Dated June 19, 1981 but includes revisions dated 3/23/81, 3/27/81, 4/10/81, 5/8/81, and 7/7/81.

Royal, Susan. "Steven Spielberg in His Adventures on Earth." *Steven Spielberg Interviews*. Eds. Lester D. Friedman and Brent Notbohm. Jackson: University Press of Mississippi, 2000: 84–106.

Sarris, Andrew. Review of *Poltergeist*. *Village Voice*, June 15, 1982, 59.

Sinyard, Neil. *The Films of Steven Spielberg*. London: Bison Books, 1986.

Snyder, Thomas Lee. *Sacred Encounters: The Myth of the Hero in the Horror, Science Fiction, Fantasy Films of George Lucas and Steven Spielberg*. Diss. Northwestern University, 1984. 8423307. Ann Arbor: University of Michigan, 1984.

Spielberg, Steven. "The Autobiography of Peter Pan." *Time*, July 15, 1985, 62–63.

Sragow, Michael. "A Conversation with Steven Spielberg." *Steven Spielberg Interviews*. Eds. Lester D. Friedman and Brent Notbohm. Jackson: University Press of Mississippi, 2000: 107–19.

Sterritt, David. Review of *Poltergeist*. *Christian Science Monitor*, June 17, 1982, 18.

Thomson, David. "Alien Resurrection," *The Guardian*, March 15, 2002. www .guardian.co.uk/Archive/Article/0,4273,4374066,00.html

Warren, Bill. *Keep Watching the Skies! American Science Fiction Movies of the Fifties*, Volume I, 1950–1957. Jefferson, NC: McFarland, 1982.

6

Raiders of the Lost Ark (1981)

Totem and Taboo

RAIDERS AND THE SERIALS

In the three *Indiana Jones* films (1981, 1984, and 1989), Spielberg collaborated with George Lucas, who originated the concept, contributed ideas to all the stories along with Spielberg, and served as executive producer while Spielberg directed. I will argue that whereas Spielberg's science fiction and fantasy films often resemble fairy tales, the *Indiana Jones* series, like Lucas's *Star Wars* saga, are structured as myths. The difference is that *Star Wars* is an epic saga in six acts with a hero who evolves from film to film, but the *Indiana Jones* series repeats much the same mythic pattern in each film.

Like the *Star Wars* films, *Raiders of the Lost Ark* (1981) is also a pastiche of and homage to an outdated Hollywood genre: *Star Wars* was inspired in part by the *Flash Gordon* serials, and *Raiders* attempts to re-create the genre of Saturday matinee adventure serials, the cliffhangers of the 1930s and 1940s.[1] Spielberg recalled going as a child to the Saturday matinees and seeing such serials as *Tailspin Tommy, Masked Marvel, Commander Cody*, and *Spy Smasher*. But when he and Lucas screened all fifteen episodes of *Don Winslow of the Navy*, "we were bored out of our minds." They agreed that the serials may have impressed them as youngsters in the 1950s but didn't hold up twenty-five years later. So they decided, "we won't really base it on the serials, but we will certainly tip our hats in that direction, because that's where the inspiration first struck. . . ." (McCarthy 59).

Like the serials, it is set in the 1930s and is episodic, with a quest plot which displays a brazen disregard for narrative logic but serves as the framework for a succession of action set pieces and elaborate stunts. Nevertheless, *Raiders* does not merely imitate the tacky thrills of the old cliffhangers, which were low-budget filler. It tells the story not in short weekly episodes but in a single feature-length film, and makes use of an enormously larger budget and much better, more "realistic" production values, including location shooting, state-of-the-art special effects, wide-screen color, and Dolby stereophonic sound. The action is almost nonstop, barely allowing the audience time to catch its breath before the next cliffhanger, but executive producer Lucas, screenwriter Lawrence Kasdan, and director Spielberg have also spiced the story with constant touches of visual style and humor. The visuals resemble as well the slam-bang illustration of today's action comic books. Spielberg says, "within each shot I substituted content for coverage. Packed as much action and style and humor into each set-up as I possibly could" (McCarthy 57). The sophisticated composition, camera movement, and editing of *Raiders* also distinguish it from the cheaply made serials.

So what we have is not simply a revival of the serials (the economic conditions and the particular audience for that form no longer exist) but, like *Star Wars*, a new kind of adventure fantasy, an elaborate entertainment which attempts to allow a more sophisticated, demanding audience to experience the feeling and original impact the serials had on naive young viewers decades ago.[2] Noel Carroll writes that *Raiders* is based on "the loving evocation through imitation and exaggeration of the way genres were" (Carroll 248). According to Spielberg, "it puts people in the same place that made me want to make movies as a child, which is wanting to enthrall, entertain, take people out of their seats to get them involved . . ." (McCarthy 58). Harrison Ford summed up the movie: "*Raiders* is really about movies more than it's about anything else. It's intricately designed as a real tribute to the craft" (Crawley 99). According to Omar Calabrese, there are supposedly 350 references to other films in *Raiders* (Calabrese 173).

The success of *Raiders*, the biggest hit movie of 1981, spawned two more *Indiana Jones* movies and other imitative high-adventure movies (such as a remake of *King Solomon's Mines* [1985]) and television series (*Tales of the Gold Monkey*) in its wake. Along with Rambo in the *Rambo* series (1982, 1985, 1988), John McClane in the *Die Hard* series (1988, 1990, 1995), and Martin Riggs in the *Lethal Weapon* series (1987, 1989, 1992, 1998), Indiana Jones became the characteristic 1980s Hollywood action hero.

Lester D. Friedman claims that the three Indiana Jones movies constitute a single integrated narrative, "an evolutionary bildungsroman with Indiana Jones at its core" (Friedman 76–77). That is questionable because there is no indication the filmmakers had a coherent, three-act sequence in mind; in fact, the second movie in the series, *Temple of Doom*, is actually set earlier in time than the first. The movies are rather a series, like the James Bond movies, which repeats the elements of a successful formula over and over. Indy learns something in each film, but it is the same moral lesson—to value people over sacred objects—each time: that is repetition rather than growth. Each film, however, does possess an internal coherence because each follows a similar mythic pattern.

RAIDERS AS MONOMYTH

Apart from its formal differences from the old serials, *Raiders of the Lost Ark* transcends the pulpish thrills of the genre to which it pays homage by being deliberately structured as a monomyth, like *Star Wars* (Gordon). Once again, this reflects the influence of George Lucas. As one critic writes, "*Raiders* is a timeless story about the heroic quest for a sacred object and the conflict between good and evil" (Roth 13). Another notes that *Raiders* follows "the epic mode of classical myth, the oedipal trajectory of primitive initiatory rituals, and the religious quests of legend and holy writ. . . . Indiana Jones, the putative hero of *Raiders*, follows the classical narrative trajectory of the mythological hero as outlined by Joseph Campbell in *The Hero with a Thousand Faces*" (Tomasulo 331–32).

The monomythic structure of the film is clear: it follows the pattern of departure, initiation, and return and adheres closely to the various stages of the adventure that Campbell enumerates. Indy receives the call to adventure and leaves his everyday world—in which he is a professor of archaeology—and sets off on a quest to some of the most exotic locations on the globe in search of an ancient religious treasure of mysterious and awesome powers, the Lost Ark of the Covenant. (The subsequent two pictures in the series, *Indiana Jones and the Temple of Doom* [1984] and *Indiana Jones and the Last Crusade* [1989], follow the same mythic formula, substituting the lost Sankara stones or the Holy Grail for the supernatural power of the Ark.) On his quest for this legendary prize, he battles the forces of pure evil (the Nazis), descends into the underworld (the Well of Souls), and risks his life repeatedly until he returns with the Ark, having saved the world. The pattern is similar to the adventures of Luke Skywalker in the *Star Wars* saga.

What interests me in the pop culture monomyth that Lucas and Spielberg and their collaborators have created in *Raiders* is the central object of the quest, the Ark itself. Like the statue in John Huston's *The Maltese Falcon* (1941), the Ark is the focus of all the passions and violence unleashed in the plot. The Ark is a mysterious, legendary object, holy and hidden. Men will kill for it, for it is imbued with strange powers, a kind of superweapon which can level cities and kill multitudes, like a nuclear bomb. As one character says, "An army which carries the Ark before it is invincible." In this respect, it resembles the Death Star in *Star Wars*. Yet the Ark is also imbued with an aura of the sacred and the forbidden, which can best be explained by reference to Freud's *Totem and Taboo*. Freud claims that objects become taboo because of ambivalent oedipal desires, and that the purpose of taboo is to allay guilt and effect a reconciliation with the father (Freud 32–35).[3]

I would suggest that the dual quest of Indiana Jones—for the Ark and for his old love Marion Ravenwood—can be understood on one level as an oedipal quest which enacts ambivalent desires both to rebel against the father and to be reconciled with him. I do not mean by this to imply that Indiana Jones could be said to possess an "unconscious"—he is a fictional construct, a superhero in a fantasy action adventure—but that he becomes the vehicle through which the story plays out an oedipal scenario similar to the one enacted in the *Star Wars* trilogy (*Indiana Jones and the Last Crusade*, with its father-son conflict, reaffirms the oedipal struggle which underlies *Raiders* and all of Lucas's films). Thus Indy resembles both Luke Skywalker and Han Solo, Marion is the spunky heroine like Princess Leia; Belloq equals Darth Vader, the Nazis are the Imperial Stormtroopers; and the Ark has both the evil aura of the Death Star and the power of "the Force."

THE OPENING OF *RAIDERS*

The opening sequence seems at first to be a separate, self-contained adventure, unrelated to the rest of the picture. It serves as a trailer or teaser for what follows, a movie in miniature compressing into a few minutes enough breathtaking action, thrills, chills, and hair's-breadth escapes from death for an entire feature. *Raiders* begins *in medias res*, like *Star Wars*, as if this were chapter Four of a continuing serial. Spielberg said the idea of the opening was "to grab the audience immediately, to show almost the third-act climax of a movie . . . in the first twelve minutes" (Crawley 91). But the opening sequence also foreshadows the conflict to come, demonstrating the horrible consequences of violating a taboo object (Roth 14). Says Spielberg, "It is really the end of the *Raiders* that preceded *Raiders of the Lost Ark* . . . *Raiders of the Lost Fertility Goddess!*" (Crawley 91).

We first encounter Indy as he is near the end of a laborious trek through a South American jungle with two ragged helpers and some native bearers on a quest for some yet unspecified treasure. The natives flee in terror when bats fly out of the mouth of a stone idol. Already, we are in the nightmare realm of the tropical, the exotic, the proscribed, and the taboo. Immediately, death threatens: they find a poison dart stuck to the trunk of a tree, a sign that the dangerous Hovido tribe is near, guarding sacred territory. Then, in the movie's first of a long string of surprises, one of the seedy helpers betrays Indy, pulling a gun to shoot him in the back.

Even this early, any viewer already knows a lot about the hero: he is the strong, silent type, for he has said nothing yet; he is commanding, for he always goes first; he is determined, for he has gotten this far; he acts quickly and decisively; and he is resourceful, intrepid, and apparently fear-less. Nothing seems to faze him: neither the stone idol and the bats which panic the superstitious natives, nor the poisoned dart which alarms his assistants, nor the attempt on his life. He anticipates the dangers and is confident that he can overcome all obstacles. Thus far, our hero is simply a compendium of heroic cliches, and everything in the film is deliberately presented in a bravura, hyperbolic style to make the character larger than life. He is a figure out of a boy's fantasy; James Bond, with his hyperactive sex drive, is a hero perhaps more suited to the adolescent male imagination. The cowardly helpers are foils to create further obstacles to the prize and to accentuate the protagonist's potency and heroism. This is a throwback to 1930s stereotypes: the heroic white American versus the superstitious, craven, or treacherous natives.

But Indy is more than your standard hero; he also has a mythical dimen-sion. He is seen at first only from the back, from the shoulders down, or in shadow. The concealment adds an aura of mystery, just as Spielberg aroused curiosity by concealing the truck driver in *Duel*, the shark in *Jaws*, and the alien and his pursuers in *E.T.* In one of the most dramatic introductions in recent cinema, we first glimpse Indy's face the moment he turns and, crack-ing his bullwhip, flicks the gun out of the hand of the man about to shoot him. The face is stern, impervious; he speaks with his whip. Superhuman, he seems to have eyes in the back of his head: He senses danger behind him and reacts faster than the man with his finger on the trigger. Characteristi-cally, his first act, flicking the bullwhip, is one of phallic assertion.

Later we find that, like Superman, Indiana Jones has a dual identity: the mild-mannered professor of archaeology versus the bold treasure hunter. Again, like Superman in the 1979 movie, he is a contemporary superhero, fallible (afraid of snakes), sometimes bumbling, and ironically self-aware ("I'm just making this up as I go along," he says at one point).

Along with his mythical and superhuman qualities, there is a moral ambiguity about Indy, as his introduction in the shadows suggests. In his quest and in his costume, he resembles Fred C. Dobbs, the prospector for gold played by Humphrey Bogart in John Huston's *The Treasure of the Sierra Madre* (1948): the fedora, the leather jacket, the dust, sweat, and stubble. Both Dobbs and Indy lust after gold, to the point of fanaticism, obsession, and paranoia. The difference is that Indy's treasure hunt is legitimized by his doctorate in archaeology, and his paranoia is justified since he lives in a world where booby traps, betrayal, and instant death lurk around every cor-ner. So Indy has the heightened senses and ruthless survival instinct of the paranoid. Whereas Dobbs's mental and moral deterioration was contrasted with the rectitude of his two partners, Indy in the opening sequence seems a positively heroic paranoid compared to his sleazy, treacherous compan-ions. The only moral of the opening sequence seems to be: Never go searching for gold with men dressed in rags. Nevertheless, if Indy is a mythic hero, there is still something at times harsh and brutal about him. Spielberg says of Indy as played by Harrison Ford, "He's a remarkable combination . . . of Errol Flynn from *The Adventures of Don Juan* [1948] and Humphrey Bogart with Fred C. Dobbs in *The Treasure of the Sierra Madre.* . . . Harrison can be villainous and romantic all at once" (Crawley 93).

The film seems to be trying to have it both ways about Indy: he is a James Bond-style superhero yet also a sweaty, grubby soldier of fortune, a shadowy, mercenary figure unlike Bond.[4] Why the complexity? It seems to me that one reason Indiana Jones is presented as morally ambiguous in *Raiders* is that the activity in which he is involved is always portrayed as sacrilege; he is a graverobber. Indy tampers with the taboo, and in movie morality such behavior is suspect and carries a price. In the primitive morality of so many American horror and science-fiction films through the 1950s, there were always things "man was not meant to know."

Indy transgresses boundaries. First, in the opening sequence he violates a sacred temple and steals a holy object, a golden idol, defying all the warning signs. Second, in the main plot, he again ignores the many warnings and braves death to steal another golden idol, the Ark. The first raid is symbolically an assault against a mother figure (he penetrates a cave to steal a fertility goddess), the second an assault against a father figure (the

Raiders of the Lost Ark: The price of breaking taboo. Paramount, 1981.

Ark is associated with Moses and the Ten Commandments). Indy's trials, his many brushes with death, can be considered the price for violating taboo. And neither raid is really successful, for in both cases the sacred objects are taken out of his hands by more powerful forces: Belloq in the opening sequence; the U.S. government in the closing one. In the end, it is safer not to possess the dangerous totem: the Ark ends up crated up in a government warehouse, as lost to the world as it was in the Egyptian tomb. The same pattern is repeated in the three *Indiana Jones* films: the holy object is stolen and the taboo violated, but in the end the object is safely hidden again in obscurity or returned to its rightful place, so the taboo is reinstated.

The guardians and booby traps and many forms of sudden death which surround the holy icon in the opening sequence of *Raiders* testify to the power of taboo. The cave scene rapidly triggers an avalanche of primal fears and phobias. If one does not get to you, then the next will: fears of the dark and the unseen; fears of being buried alive; fears of cobwebs, dust, and bugs; fears of the body being penetrated, violated, or crushed—bitten by tarantulas, punctured by arrows, impaled on stakes, or crushed by a collapsing ceiling, a descending stone wall, or a giant rolling boulder; fears of falling into a bottomless pit; and fears of the dead—decaying corpses, mummified bodies, and skeletons. The filmmakers seemed to delight in the excess and proliferation of these horrors, which caused me (and, I suspect, many other viewers as well) to react not with horror but with admiration and amusement, similar to the thrill evoked by a quick ride through an especially inventive House of Horrors. Although *Raiders* uses some of the elements of a horror movie, it aims more to thrill with perilous adventures than to shock with overwhelming horror. Nevertheless, I noted that the scenes of greatest horror coincided with the violation of a sacred, taboo object in the Temple, in the Well of Souls, and in the climactic scene when the Nazis open the Ark.

As Freud mentions, the idea of taboo expresses an ambivalent pairing of emotional attitudes: "on the one hand, 'sacred,' 'consecrated,' and on the other, 'uncanny,' 'dangerous,' 'forbidden,' 'unclean'" (18). He explains the prohibitions of taboo as stemming from emotional ambivalence: the desire to commit the oedipal crime yet the fear of doing so. Thus the taboo combines "veneration and horror" (25). The golden idol in the South American temple is an object of worship, yet it is also horrendous, made almost unreachable through a series of elaborate, lethal booby traps. It is a holy object contained in an unclean place: a sort of tomb, a dark cavern filled with cobwebs, bugs, and corpses. Similarly, the Ark, hidden away in the dark Well of Souls, is surrounded by terrifying giant statues, deadly asps and cobras, and piles of skeletons.

Taboo also "closely resembles the neurotic's fear of touching, his 'touching phobia'" (Freud 73). Thus in the opening sequence, when Indy finally reaches the glowing, golden idol, he longs to seize it but knows he must move cautiously, for touching it may mean his death. To avoid triggering another alarm, he must instantly replace the idol with a bag weighted with sand. His hands approach carefully, and simultaneously his helper's fingers twitch in anticipation, heightening the suspense (such gestural mimicry is characteristically Spielbergian—recall the mimicry between boy and alien in *E.T.*). After he grabs the statue, Indy's brief elation turns to panic when the altar stone begins to sink and all hell breaks loose: the ceiling caves in as arrows fly out from slots in the walls. To grasp the taboo object means to risk death. Before he got to the idol, Indy anticipated all the perils: don't step in the light and don't tread on the wrong stones. But once he touches the idol, the risks increase and accelerate, and he doesn't foresee the collapsing cave, the treacherous helper, the falling wall, or the giant rolling boulder. The idol is a hot potato that endangers or kills everyone who touches it; it passes from hand to hand, and no one can hold it for long. This pattern is later repeated with the Ark, which is stolen by Indy and restolen many times by Belloq and the Nazis. Almost everyone who comes in contact with the taboo object is killed.

INDY AND BELLOQ

The French archaeologist Belloq, as critics have noted, is not only the hero's rival in the quest to possess taboo objects, but also his doppelganger or shadow (Snyder 209; Roth 19–20). Indy is American, straightforward and physical; Belloq is European, devious and cerebral. Indy is grubby; Belloq is impeccably dressed in white. Indy relies on labor and sweat to attain his goals; Belloq lets him take the physical risks, then outwits him and steals the prize. Indy is laconic; Belloq eloquent. Indy speaks only English (at least in this movie), whereas Belloq is master of many tongues (French, English, Hovido, German, and Hebrew). Indy is made to seem crude in contrast to the suave, sophisticated Belloq, who twice refers to the need to "behave like civilized people." The film plays on American stereotypes of the simple, virtuous American versus the cultivated, corrupt European, since Belloq has allied with Nazis and will stop at nothing to get the Ark.

Despite the opposite characteristics of the rivals, Indy and Belloq are similar in their moral ambiguity. Belloq recognizes that they are both self-serving and obsessed with obtaining the treasure no matter the cost:

> Where shall I find a new adversary so close to my own level? You and I are very much alike. Archaeology is our religion. Yet we have both fallen from the pure faith. Our methods have not differed as much as you pretend. I am only a shadowy reflection of you. It would take only a nudge to make you like me. To push you out of the light.

Ironically, even as Belloq says the above lines to Indy, Belloq is in the light, and Indy, who is ready to murder him in retaliation for Marion's apparent death, is in shadow on the left of the frame. In its imagery of a light and dark side, representing good and evil, *Raiders* is like the *Star Wars* trilogy, and Belloq plays a role similar to Darth Vader's.

Belloq, like Vader, represents both the hero's potential evil which the hero refuses to acknowledge and the father figure in an Oedipal rivalry. The first time we see Belloq, he looms above Indy as he steals the golden idol, saying, "Dr. Jones. Again we see there is nothing you can possess which I cannot take away." The same positioning—Belloq above, Indy below as Belloq steals the prize—is repeated in the Well of Souls. There, Belloq echoes his opening line: "So once again, Jones, what was briefly yours is now mine." As Indy's rival and evil double, Belloq goes beyond Indy in violating taboo. He is a megalomaniac who covets the godlike powers of the Ark for himself: "It is a radio for speaking to God." (In *Indiana Jones and the Last Crusade*, the suave American millionaire Donovan, who craves immortality through possessing the Holy Grail, plays the same role as Belloq.) In the finale, Belloq commits sacrilege by staging a travesty of an ancient ritual. He dresses like a rabbi of Old Testament times, chants in Hebrew (the language for speaking to God), and dares to tamper with the holy Ark by opening it. When Belloq goes up in flames, he is dying in Indy's place (Snyder 211).

MARION AND THE ARK

Just as Indy and Belloq are symbolically paired, so are the prizes for which they compete: the Ark and Marion Ravenwood. Marion, Indy's former girlfriend, is linked with the Ark from the beginning of the quest. To locate the Ark, he must first locate her. Abner Ravenwood, Indy's former mentor, owned the headpiece to the staff of Ra, key to the location of the Ark. But ten years before, Indy had an affair with Marion, Ravenwood's daughter, who was then a teenager, causing a falling out between the teacher and his prize pupil. Indy has seen neither since. Before he begins his quest, Indy has the following conversation with his friend and boss, the archaeologist Marcus Brody:

INDY: Suppose she [Marion]'ll still be with him [Ravenwood]?

BRODY: Possibly. Marion's the least of your worries right now. . . . I mean that for nearly 3,000 years man has been searching for the lost Ark. It's not something to be taken lightly. No one knows its secrets. It's like nothing you've gone after before.

INDY: Marcus, what are you trying to do, scare me? You sound like my mother. . . . I don't believe in magic, a lot of superstitious hocus pocus. I'm

Raiders of the Lost Ark: "Do you know what you did to me? To my life?"
Paramount, 1981.

going after a find of incredible historical significance. You're talking about the
boogeyman.

Indy here sounds like Han Solo in *Star Wars*: the man who believes only
in his gun and not in "the power of the Force" but who will later learn
otherwise. What particularly interests me in their conversation, however,
is the conjunction of several anxiety-provoking topics: Abner Ravenwood,
Marion, the Ark, Indy's mother, and the boogeyman. Later, Marion tells
Indy that the late Abner "loved you like a son." What alienated Abner was
Indy's seduction and abandonment of Marion, who says, "I was a child! I
was in love! It was wrong and you knew it! . . . Do you know what you did
to me? To my life?" Marion, like the Ark, is a prize "not to be taken lightly"
and surrounded by taboo ("It was wrong and you knew it"). Seducing the
daughter of a man who was like a father to him could be considered symbolic incest.

Significantly, Indy is warned against the Ark by two good father figures:
first Brody and then Indy's Egyptian friend Sallah (father to an enormous
brood of children). Like Brody, Sallah warns of the danger of violating taboo: "It was something man was not meant to disturb. Death has always
surrounded it. It is not of this earth."

Marion is so closely associated with the Ark that the two are almost interchangeable: they are both treated as valuable prizes, objects of barter, constantly stolen and recaptured, passing from the hands of one man to another. Marion's fate is linked with the Ark's. Like the Ark, she is surrounded by danger and hidden in a remote location (Indy finds her running a bar in the mountains of Nepal); she wears around her neck the headpiece that is the key to the Ark's location; she comes along with the headpiece to Egypt. The scene in which Indy unseals the Ark in the Well of Souls is crosscut with Belloq's attempted seduction of Marion (she too is "unsealed"; Belloq watches in a mirror as she undresses): as a religious taboo is being broken, so is a sexual one. After the Nazis lift the Ark out of the Well, they throw Marion into it, as if she were its replacement. When they take the Ark off Katanga's ship, they also take Marion. Later, Indy threatens to blow up the Ark unless Marion is freed; again, the two are treated as equivalent. Belloq tells Marion, "You are beautiful" and says the same thing later about the apparition of a woman who appears out of the opened Ark: "It's beautiful!" Significantly, the beautiful ghost changes into a death's head. When the Nazis break open the box, all hell breaks loose; the Ark is female, a "Pandora's box."

Indy's dual quest—for the Ark and for Marion—is a way of repeating his original Oedipal crime and at the same time undoing it. He is both protecting the Ark and violating it, in the same way that he is constantly rescuing Marion and yet putting her in grave danger by associating with her. Says one critic, "Poor Marion suffers a great deal of pain in the film (she is bound and gagged repeatedly, slapped around, threatened with a fiery poker). I first thought the filmmakers were indulging some kind of weird SM fantasy" (Asahina 19).

Indy originally violated taboo by seducing Marion; symbolically, he also killed Ravenwood. Now he will break a taboo once again: gaining the Ark will reunite him with Marion and make amends to her and her father for the injury he did them; he will also complete the unfinished quest of his dead mentor. In Freud's theory, one way to see the totem object is as "a surrogate father." In their relation to it, the tribe attempts "to bring about a kind of reconciliation with the father" (Freud 144).

It might seem confusing that the Ark is connected both with the father (Abner Ravenwood, Moses, the Ten Commandments, the power of God, and the boogeyman) and the mother (Marion and Indy's mother). Yet the totem is really symbolic of both parents: the ambivalent emotions surrounding taboo combine veneration of the parents with the horror associated with incest. The refusals to touch the totem or to violate the taboo are intended to reassure the father that the mother will remain sacrosanct.

Indy's violation of taboo is thus ostensibly an act of obedience: he will rescue the totemic object from the hands of evil (Nazi) fathers and deliver it into the hands of good (American) fathers. Yet his deepest anger in the film is directed toward father figures, and the Nazis and Belloq provide a convenient focus for his rage. At one point, Indy becomes deeply depressed and starts drinking alone, believing he has unintentionally caused Marion's death. His depression turns to murderous rage when he confronts Belloq, whom he blames for what happened to Marion, and he is ready to die so long as he can take Belloq with him. And at the end of the film, he rages against the "bureaucratic fools" in Army Intelligence who take the Ark away from him. His repeated anger suggests that the action of the totemic plot, which according to *Totem and Taboo* is intended to bring about a reconciliation with the father, has not entirely worked out an underlying resentment of authority figures. According to Douglas Brode, "Throughout the trilogy, he [Indy] will emerge as a man in search of a proper father figure. . . ." Indy felt so betrayed "by the father who was not there during childhood" that he betrays other father figures (Brode 95). It is only in the third film in the series, *Last Crusade*, that the hero atones with his father.

THE ARK, LIGHT, AND FIRE

As a taboo object, the Ark is viewed with ambivalence, as both divine and demonic. It is associated with light and fire—a dangerous light human beings were not meant to look upon and a scourging, destructive fire (similarly, the Grail in *Last Crusade* brings healing or eternal life to the faithful but instant death to the unrighteous). The Ark is first seen in an illustration in an old book: from it emanate rays of light that Indy describes as "lightning, fire, power of God." Men struck by the rays writhe in death agonies, foreshadowing the climactic destruction of the Nazis. Later, when Marion holds up the shining medallion, the headpiece to the staff of Ra, it is juxtaposed in the image with a candle flame. The medallion lies in the fire that consumes Marion's bar and becomes so hot that its pattern is branded into the palm of the Nazi who grabs it (again suggesting the taboo against touching). He screams in pain after grasping the headpiece, just as he screams later in the climactic scene when the Ark is opened and the Nazis burst into flames. When an Egyptian examines the medallion and says its markings mean "honor the Hebrew God whose Ark this is," the lighted lamps on his ceiling mysteriously begin to sway. In the Map Room, when sunlight hits the crystal on the headpiece, blinding beams of light shoot out, like the rays in the illustration of the Ark. The night that Indy and his helpers open the Well of Souls to reveal the Ark, lightning crackles in the sky. Indy fights with flaming torches the snakes who guard the Ark. The Ark itself is golden, glowing with an apparently sacred light. When it is crated up, heat from within burns the swastika off the crate. And in the climax, a scourging fire melts and incinerates the Nazis. Only Indy and Marion survive because they refuse to look upon God's holy fire.

The fire connected with the Ark suggests the idea of sinners in the hands of an angry God and of fire as ritual sacrifice, which occurs in *Temple of Doom* as well. The fiery, climactic scene of *Raiders*, a ritual at an altar, resembles a human sacrifice to avenge a wrathful God. As Freud writes, "the portion of the sacrifice allotted to the god was originally regarded as being literally his food . . . fire, which caused the flesh of the sacrifice upon the altar to rise in smoke, afforded a method of dealing with human food more appropriate to the divine nature" (33–34). The fiery sacrifice is meant to atone for the violation of taboo.

CONCLUSION

Thus I would argue that *Raiders* is not as lighthearted a romp as an initial viewing might suggest. It transcends the old action serials because it is deliberately structured as a coherent myth which taps into the power of religious awe, the occult, and things repressed, unconscious, and taboo. The object of the quest, the Ark, is not merely a "MacGuffin" (Hitchcock's term for the excuse for the action) but a holy icon which the film imbues with a genuinely spooky aura. *Raiders* has some of the chilling power of the uncanny, and all its humor and adventure help us to accept the breaking of taboo.

NOTES

1. Among the 1930s and 1940s serials which inspired *Raiders* are *Lash LaRue, Tim Tyler's Luck, Tailspin Tommy, Masked Marvel, Spy Smasher, Don Winslow of the Navy, Commander Cody, Blackhawk, Zorro's Fighting Legion, Zorro Rides Again, Secret Service in Darkest Africa,* and *Nyoka and the Tigermen.* On the sources of *Raiders*, see Ansen 60; Crawley 90–91; Scapperotti 49; Buckland 132–36, and Sullivan. The quest for a valuable or mythical artifact is central to many serials; for example, *Adventures of Captain Marvel* (1941) features a quest for a golden scorpion. Indy's whipcracking comes from *Lash LaRue* and the many *Zorro* serials. Harmon and Glut describe an incident in the Republic serial *Zorro's Fighting Legion* (1939) which sounds like one in *Raiders*: in "The Descending Doom," a huge skip-drum rolls down a mine shaft about to crush the hero (Harmon and Glut 297). A boyhood friend of Spielberg says Indy's jump from a horse onto a speeding truck comes from *Zorro Rides Again* (1937) (McBride 81).

Greil Marcus claims that *Raiders* was profoundly influenced by comic books. Specifically, he argues that "the opening sequence was stolen from Carl Barks's 'The Seven Cities of Cibola,' *Uncle Scrooge* 7, September 1954" and the ending from "the end of

Barks's 'The Golden Fleecing,' *Uncle Scrooge* 12, December 1956" (Marcus 64). This is possible, since Spielberg loved Disney comics when he was a boy (McBride 61).

John Baxter points instead to the influence on *Raiders* of 1950s adventure movies like *Journey to the Center of the Earth* (1959) and *King Solomon's Mines* (1950) (Baxter 194), and Douglas Brode mentions *20,000 Leagues under the Sea* (1954) (Brode 92). The list can be extended to other movies of the 1930s and 1940s: as many critics note, Marion is a Howard Hawks heroine, and there are also touches from *Casablanca* (1941), an action scene borrowed from John Ford's *Stagecoach* (1939), and a nod in the ending to Welles's *Citizen Kane* (1941). Buckland mentions *Secret of the Incas* (1954). Spielberg and Lucas are steeped in Hollywood history and love old movies and adventure stories of all kinds, including those in old comic books. Nevertheless, the core of *Raiders* comes from old serials.

2. Jameson 116–17 discusses the "nostalgia film" such as *Star Wars* or *Raiders* which children and adolescents can take straight, while adults can respond to it nostalgically as a return to the aesthetic objects of an earlier period. On one level, *Raiders* is "*about* the '30s and '40s, but in reality it too conveys that period metonymically through its own characteristic adventure stories (which are no longer ours)."

3. There is also an anthropological interpretation of taboo as a violation of the boundaries between such categories as male/female, human/animal, or self/world. See Douglas, *Purity and Danger*. Nevertheless, I find Freud's psychoanalytic explanation of taboo better able to explain certain aspects of *Raiders*.

4. During the 1970s, Spielberg had been turned down as a director for a James Bond film. Lucas pitched *Raiders* to him as "better than Bond" (Crawley 90).

REFERENCES

Ansen, David. Review of *Raiders of the Lost Ark*. *Newsweek*, June 15, 1981, 60.

Asahina, Robert. Review of *Raiders of the Lost Ark*. *New Leader*, June 29, 1981, 19.

Baxter, John. *Steven Spielberg: The Unauthorised Biography*. London: HarperCollins, 1996.

Brode, Douglas. *The Films of Steven Spielberg*. New York: Citadel Press, 1995.

Buckland, Warren. *Directed by Steven Spielberg: Poetics of the Contemporary Hollywood Blockbuster*. New York: Continuum, 2006.

Calabrese, Omar. *Neo-Baroque: A Sign of the Times*. Trans. Charles Lambert. Princeton, NJ: Princeton University Press, 1992.

Carroll, Noel. *Interpreting the Moving Image*. New York: Cambridge University Press, 1998.

Crawley, Tony. *The Steven Spielberg Story*. New York: Quill, 1982.

Douglas, Mary. *Purity and Danger: An Analysis of the Concepts of Pollution and Taboo*. Boston: Ark, 1966.

Friedman, Lester D. *Citizen Spielberg*. Urbana: University of Illinois Press, 2006.

Freud, Sigmund. *Totem and Taboo and Other Works. The Standard Edition of the Complete Psychological Works of Sigmund Freud*, Vol. 13 (1913–14). Trans. and ed. James Strachey. London: Hogarth, 1955.

Gordon, Andrew. "*Star Wars*: A Myth for Our Time." *Literature/Film Quarterly* 6.4 (Fall 1978): 314–26.

Harmon, Jim and Donald F. Glut. *The Great Movie Serials: Their Sound and Fury.* Garden City, NY: Doubleday, 1972.

Jameson, Frederic. "Postmodernism and Consumer Society." *The Anti-Aesthetic: Essays on Postmodern Culture.* Ed. Hal Foster. Port Townsend, WA: Bay, 1983, 111–25.

Marcus, Greil. "Eighties." *Film Comment,* November–December 1989, 61–64.

McBride, Joseph, *Steven Spielberg: A Biography.* New York: Simon and Schuster, 1997.

McCarthy, Todd. "Sand Castles." *Film Comment,* May–June 1982, 53–59.

Raiders of the Lost Ark. Paramount, 1981. Story: George Lucas and Philip Kaufman. Screenplay: Lawrence Kasdan. Executive Producers: George Lucas and Howard Kazanjian. Director: Steven Spielberg. Music: John Williams. Director of Photography: Douglas Slocombe. Starring: Harrison Ford (Indiana Jones), Karen Allen (Marion), Paul Freeman (Belloq), Ronald Lacey (Toht), John Rhys-Davies (Sallah), Denholm Elliot (Brody). Running Time: 113 minutes.

Roth, Lane. "Raiders of the Lost Archetype: The Quest and the Shadow." *Studies in the Humanities* 10.1 (June 1983): 13–21.

Scapperotti, Dan. "Lucas and Spielberg Revive Slam-Bang, Saturday Matinee Thrills," *Cinefantastique* 11.3 (September 1981): 49.

Snyder, Thomas Lee. *Sacred Encounters: The Myth of the Hero in the Horror, Science Fiction, Fantasy Films of George Lucas and Steven Spielberg.* Diss. Northwestern University, 1984. Ann Arbor, MI: University Microfilms 8423307.

Sterritt, David. Review of *Raiders of the Lost Ark. Christian Science Monitor,* June 18, 1981, 18.

Sullivan, Peter. "Raiders of the Movie Serials." *Starlog* 49 (August 1981): 52–53.

Tomasulo, Frank P. "Mr. Jones Goes to Washington: Myth and Religion in *Raiders of the Lost Ark,*" *Quarterly Review of Film Studies* 7.4 (Fall 1982): 331–40.

7

Indiana Jones and the Temple of Doom (1984)

Bad Medicine

> I thought archaeologists were always funny little men searching for their mommies.
>
> —Willie Scott in *Indiana Jones and the Temple of Doom*

Bruno Bettelheim once said that how you relate to food reveals how you feel about your mother (Barnes 16). If that's so, then *Indiana Jones and the Temple of Doom* seems to be saying something awful about somebody`s mother, for the plot revolves to a remarkable degree around ingesting substances that are vile, unspeakably disgusting, or poisonous. In the opening scene, Indiana Jones swallows poison; later, he and his friends are offered unpleasant-looking food by starving Indian villagers. In one of the film's most notorious scenes, the characters are served a banquet featuring a series of increasingly disgusting menu items; in another, a man is lowered alive into a pit of flaming lava as a sacrifice of "flesh and blood" to the goddess Kali; and Indy is forced to swallow "the black blood of Kali," which turns him into a zombie slave of the Thuggee cult! The poor guy doesn't even get a spoonful of sugar to help the medicine go down. The film, says Spielberg's biographer Joseph McBride, bullies the audience and stirs "little emotional involvement other than a frequent sense of disgust" (McBride 354). *Doom* is a carnival of bad taste that appears to me to be centrally concerned with primitive, sadomasochistic fantasies involving fears of being poisoned or swallowed alive (to the unconscious mind, there's little difference between eating and being eaten).

I say "somebody's mother" because it's difficult to know to whom to ascribe the gruesome oral fantasies in this collaborative effort: To writer and producer George Lucas? To screenwriters Willard Huyck and Gloria Katz? To director Steven Spielberg? Or to the collective imagination of all of them? Lucas, after all, gave us the gluttonous Jabba the Hutt swallowing live bait in *Return of the Jedi* (1983); Huyck and Katz scripted Lucas's *American Graffiti* (1973), featuring a teenager who gets drunk and vomits; and Spielberg directed *Jaws* (1975), in which the shark wants to eat everyone, and *Jurassic Park* (1991) and its sequel, *The Lost World* (1997), in which the dinosaurs want to eat everyone. Spielberg also came up with the story for *The Goonies* (1985), in which the juvenile heroes are grossed out in underground caverns as in *Doom*. Lucas says, "It [*Doom*] was meant to be a little darker, then we sort of got carried away. I was going through a divorce and was not in a very good mood, so it turned out a lot darker than it probably should have" (Matloff 76). McBride says "the film's unusually gruesome and disturbing imagery . . . gives cause to wonder what was going on in Spielberg's subconscious"(McBride 353). Yet Spielberg says that, unlike Lucas, "I was not going through a divorce; I had just come off a huge success with *E.T.* and I was in a good mood" (Matloff 76).

Interestingly, as he was promoting *Doom* when it was released in 1984, Spielberg described the film in orally positive terms, calling it "a sort of banquet, a visual feast" (Elkins 52). He said, "It's a popcorn adventure, with a lot of butter" (Elkins 51). Yet years later, he distanced himself from the film because of its bad reputation, this time using orally negative imagery: "in those days, that kind of stuff wasn't on my diet" (Matloff 76). He also says that he directed the third *Indiana Jones* movie "just to clear my palate of the bad taste from the second" (Matloff 80).

Moviegoing, of course, is commonly associated with consuming popcorn, soda, and candy. But it's surprising how often reviewers resorted to images of food to describe their reactions to *Doom*. Those who thought it great good fun said, "It should do wonders for the popcorn business" (Reed 30) or should "whet one's appetite for the inevitable successor" (Buckley 426). One reviewer who found it shallow compared it to "the proverbial Chinese meal, where heaps of fun can still leave one hungry shortly thereafter" (*Variety* 26). Finally, those who hated the film compared it to disgusting food: "They're going to have to scrape youngsters out from under seats like old chewing gum with this one" (Benson 1); and "Spielberg himself may be turning into an evil wizard casting spells, and like the victims of the Thuggees, who drink black blood and lose their souls, we may all need to get away from him . . . " (Denby 12). In other words, *Doom* seems to trigger oral fantasies—some pleasant and some downright nightmarish—in many viewers.

SEXIST AND RACIST ELEMENTS OF *DOOM*

Many critics simply dismiss the film because of its sexist and racist fantasies. For example, Moishe Postone and Elisabeth Traube read the film as a series of misogynistic fantasies revealing "a deeply rooted fear of female sexuality" (13) and see Indy's adventures underground as "a nightmarish anxiety dream" about a sexual encounter (14). Like most critics of the film, they point to the heroine Willie Scott, a stereotypical dumb blonde gold digger out of a 1930s movie, but they also point to the fact that the Thuggees, the villains, have sinned by betraying the masculine god Shiva in order to worship the destructive power of the goddess Kali.

The film is inarguably sexist; despite the fact that one of the screenwriters is a woman, it's a throwback to old Hollywood clichés about women. Because it was inspired by the film *Gunga Din* (1939), it is also racist in the style of 1930s American popular media: the foreigners are villains, children, loyal servants, or dependent on the great white hero Indy to rescue them. *Doom* is the most reactionary product of either Lucas or Spielberg, a movie about which they were first enthusiastic, then, after the critical onslaught, defensive, and finally apologetic.[1] In adopting the conventions of certain 1930s Hollywood film genres, they also imported wholesale the cultural assumptions of these old movies.

Nevertheless, I question whether most viewers read the underground horrors of *Doom* as an attack on women, as do Postone and Traube. First, Western viewers know nothing of Indian gods and would be unaware that Shiva is masculine and Kali feminine; the film does not tell us that. Second, the fantasies here constitute an "archaeological" return to an exceedingly primitive psychic level; even if Indy's quest could be said to express a flight from sexuality, that escape is into a preoedipal realm of oral terrors. Fears of being swallowed alive are neither exclusively masculine nor feminine but are the stuff of fairy tales and horror movies, as witness the popularity of *Jaws, Jurassic Park* and its sequel, and this movie.

A KLEINIAN READING OF *DOOM*

An alternative reading of the morbid fantasies circulating in *Doom* can be provided through the theories of the child psychiatrist Melanie Klein. Klein posited what she called a "paranoid-schizoid position" as the earliest phase of development. The infantile ego, she claimed, first sees the world as omnipotent and destructive and itself in constant danger of being destroyed. This is the paranoid world of *Doom*, in which the characters are constantly threatened by the environment or by powerful villains and evil magicians: in the opening sequence alone, Indy and his companions are endangered by gunfire, poison, falling from a tall building, a car chase, jumping from a plane without a parachute, sledding down a mountainside, falling off a cliff, and rafting down a wild river. According to Klein, the earliest mental defenses against the fear of destruction of the ego are projection, introjection, and splitting:

From the beginning the ego introjects objects "good" and "bad," for both of which the mother's breast is the prototype—for good objects when the child obtains it and for bad when it fails him. But it is because the baby projects its own aggression on to these objects that it feels them to be "bad" and not only in that they frustrate its desires: the child conceives of them as actually dangerous— persecutors who it fears will devour it, scoop out the inside of its body, cut it to pieces, poison it—in short, compassing its destruction by all the means which sadism can devise. These imagoes . . . are installed by it not only in the outside world but, by the process of introjection, also within the ego . . . the ego marshals against the persecutors inside the body the same forces as it employs against those in the outside world. These anxiety contents and defence-mechanisms form the basis of paranoia. In the infantile dread of magicians, witches, evil beasts, etc., we detect something of this same anxiety. . . . (Klein 40–41)

In other words, viewed from a Kleinian perspective, *Doom* is a paranoid fairy tale/horror movie about an internal conflict between "good" and "bad" object representations.

The chief way in which the film makes its menu of horrors acceptable—more "palatable," if you will—is through comedy. As Pauline Kael noted, "Grownups who are upset by the menu at the banquet must be forgetting how cheerfully kids have traditionally sung such macabre ditties as 'The worms crawl in, The worms crawl out, The worms play pinochle on your snout . . .' and 'Great green gobs of greasy grimy gophers' guts. . . . And I forgot my spoon. . . .'" Kael quotes these verses at greater length and with obvious delight—another instance of the grotesque food fantasies this movie seems to activate in viewers (Kael 180).

THE OPENING OF *DOOM*

The playful note is established in the opening sequence, an imitation 1930s, Busby Berkeley-style dance spectacle in which nightclub singer Willie Scott belts out Cole Porter's "Anything Goes" in Chinese. As Nigel Morris notes, *Temple of Doom* is a film which does not demand to be taken seriously (Morris 109). Interestingly, Willie first emerges out of red smoke from the mouth of a dragon, anticipating the later red-tinged Temple sequences and the many other images of hellmouths in the film, including a spike chamber, caverns, a boiling lava pit, an ore crusher, and the jaws of alligators. The opening song-and-dance routine reassures the audience that the dangers in the film are really fake, staged.[2] The phony dragon, in and out of whose mouth Willie steps so casually, implies that, whatever perils the heroes will later face, they will not be eaten alive. The filmmakers are playing with cinematic conventions in order to arouse audience fears in a safe, protected context.

After the dance number, the nightclub sequence (at Club "Obi Wan," an in-joke from filmmakers to audience that again suggests the movie is only a lark) quickly turns into carefully orchestrated chaos involving gangsters, gunplay, and mass hysteria, the kind of scene Spielberg excels at staging. Despite the death of two characters in the melee (one good guy, one bad), Spielberg maintains a tone of high-spirited farce, so that the sequence resembles the frenetic slapstick of the dancehall scene in *1941* (1979). Significantly, the chaos has elements of a food fight, with ice cubes spilled across the floor and a gunman skewered with a flaming shiskabob spear. And in one revealing moment, Indy is poised to stab Willie in the breast with a fork!

During this scene, Indy is poisoned by a drink provided by Chinese gangsters. As he searches desperately across the dance floor for the missing vial containing the antidote, Willie hides it in the top of her dress. When Indy roughly sticks his hand down the front of her dress to seize the antidote, she protests she's not "that kind of girl," interpreting his maneuver as a sexual assault. This early incident establishes the conflict between the "bad breast" containing poison and the "good breast" offering the antidote. It also sets the tone of the comedy in the film, a playful, cheerful sadomasochism with which the filmmakers treat the conflict (except for the lapse into lurid horror in the Temple sequence).

FEAST AND FAMINE

The next reference to food occurs when Indy and his companions are offered a meal by poor Indian villagers. The food looks unappetizing to Willie, but Indy forces her: "That's more food than these people eat in a week. They're starving. . . . You're insulting them and you're embarrassing me. Eat it." Much of the film concerns knowing the right from the wrong thing to eat (is it a coincidence that Spielberg's mother runs a kosher deli?). What Willie rejects as the poisonous, "bad breast," Indy correctly interprets as nourishing food and a generous gift.

The village is suffering from famine. As their shaman explains and Indy translates, "When the sacred stone was stolen, the village wells dried up and the river turned to sand. The crops were swallowed up by the earth and the animals lay down and turned to dust. Then one night there was a fire in the fields. . . ." Along with the terror that the "bad breast" will poison one goes the fear that it will deny one all nourishment.

In contrast to the famine in the village is the feast in the palace; in fact, the former is caused by the latter. But the bounty at the palace is noxious, representative of the "bad breast": first, "Snake Surprise," consisting of a giant baked snake, which, sliced open, disgorges live, slithering eels; next, cooked beetles and a steaming soup with floating eyeballs; and, climaxing the repast, a dessert of chilled monkey brains spooned out of the open skull. All these disgusting delicacies are eagerly devoured by fat, gluttonous rajahs. The filmmakers must have had tremendous fun dreaming up the menu, and

Indiana Jones and the Temple of Doom: The gross-out banquet. Paramount, 1984.

Spielberg serves it up with aplomb. His perfect timing delivers both shock and humor.

Nevertheless, the humor masks the horror of the scene, a horror based on fears from Klein's paranoid phase when the child imagines persecutors "will devour it, scoop out the inside of its body" (41). As the meal is served, Indy asks about rumors of "human sacrifice." The assault on the body is suggested by the snake slit open (the eels are like intestines), the detached eyeballs, and the brains scooped out of the skull (eating monkey seems close to cannibalism since monkeys resemble human beings). The assault continues later, no longer masked by humor, when Mola Ram, the Thuggee high priest, rips the living heart out of a man (through black magic, the victim survives to be sacrificed to fire).

The banquet scene again suggests the difficulty in this film of knowing good breast from bad. Evil hides behind a beautiful facade, like the beautiful Pankot palace which conceals the underground horrors of the Temple. Willie rejects the good food from the peasants but looks forward to the lavish banquet at the palace, which makes her sick. Perhaps the confusion between good and evil originates in the defense of splitting: the infant cannot tolerate ambivalence, loving and hating the same object, so it splits the mother in two, into a good breast which satisfies and a bad breast which frustrates or poisons. The benevolent shaman of the village (who first appears mysterious and menacing because of the ominous music and low camera angle with which he is introduced) and the evil Mola Ram are really different aspects of the same object. In the same way, Indy often seems to be at war with Willie, as when he holds a fork at her breast or lowers her into the lava pit: Is he good or evil? Does he love Willie or want to kill her?

The sequence after the banquet is the most emblematic in the film of the conflict between good and bad objects. Indy wins over the starving Willie with fruit (in an interesting reversal, he tempts her with an apple) and they seem about to have a love scene. But the loveplay is interrupted, first by their mutual egotism and then by a Thuggee strangler. As Indy searches for the Thuggee hideout, he pushes against the stone breasts of a statue to open a hidden passageway. Meanwhile, Willie, thinking Indy is perversely neglecting her charms, points to her live bosom: "Hey, I'm right here!" Symbolically, Indy is rejecting the good breast in order to do battle against the bad one.

IN THE UNDERGROUND

References to devouring or to terrible food proliferate in the underground passageways and the Temple sequence. In the dark, Indy and his sidekick, the Chinese orphan boy Short Round, crunch something underfoot which sounds to them like "fortune cookies" but the light reveals to be a carpet of live bugs. Next they are almost killed in a spike chamber that resembles devouring jaws, and they pass through a cavern whose stalagmites and stalactites suggest a large red mouth. In the Temple itself, Spielberg said, "I wanted the entryway into what we called the whipping chamber to look like a demon with a mouth wide open" (Elkins 57). And the heroes witness a man being lowered alive into a flaming pit via a device Pauline Kael says "looks like a deep-fat fryer" (Kael 180); he is a human sacrifice to Kali, Indy later explains, "an offering of flesh and blood." Kali here is the bad mother who does not nourish but devours her offspring, like the witch in the Grimms' "Hansel and Gretel" or the ogress in Perrault's "Sleeping Beauty."

The devouring of children is also suggested by child labor: all the children of the poor village have been kidnaped to provide slave labor for the mine. To use exclusively children rather than adults as slave laborers makes no sense, except to intensify the evil of the cultists. But psychologically, it fits: these children have been literally torn away from the good breast and enslaved to the bad one.[3]

The underground passageways and mine tunnels have been variously interpreted as the inferno or the vagina (Postone and Traube 12; Hoberman 1). But they can also be seen as symbolizing the inside of the body or the unconscious mind. According to Klein, to the infantile imagination, the bad object is not only outside, but introjected, also persecutes one inside. The ego then "marshals against the persecutors inside the body the same forces as it employs against those in the outside world" (Klein 41). The characters (and the audience) are symbolically descending into their own depths, traveling inside the body, where psychic forces threaten bodily integrity: Indy and his companions watch as the heart is torn out of a living man by an evil wizard.

The ingestion of the bad breast occurs when Indy is forced to drink the "black blood," a scene that suggested to Pauline Kael "a child's fear of a dose of medicine" (Kael 181). At first, Indy spits out the bad medicine, but then they hold him so he has to swallow. The poisoning in the opening scene was only a foretaste of this. Now that he has internalized the bad breast, he loses ego integrity. He goes into convulsions and emerges in a trance as a servant of the evil mother, ready to sacrifice the good breast (Willie) at the behest of Kali. The conflict between these split versions of the maternal object is resolved when Indy is restored to his old self, rescues Willie, and sends the villains to their doom: appropriately, they are eaten by alligators.

FATHER-SON RELATIONSHIPS IN *DOOM*

Is the fantasy content of the film as narrow as this, concerned solely with eating or being eaten, fixated on the oral, on the mother-infant bond? *Doom* does go beyond the mother-child dyad to develop some strong father-son relationships as well. Chief among these is that of Indy and Short Round, his sidekick and child double but also, in a sense, his adopted son. Their relationship is diabolically parodied by that of the gangster Lao Che and his maniacal, tommy-gun-wielding son, and by Mola Ram and the boy Maharajah. The evil father figures include not only Lao Che and Mola Ram, but also Chattar Lal (the Maharajah's minister, who is a Thuggee priest) and the chief guard who whips the children. In contrast stand Indy, the shaman and the chieftain of the village, and the British Captain who rescues Indy at the end. Thus the movie could certainly also be said to be patriarchal, involving a struggle between good and evil father figures for possession of the son. Joseph McBride argues that, "like so many other irresponsible father figures in Spielberg's works, Indiana Jones in *Temple of Doom* must exorcise his adult weaknesses and undergo a purifying test of character in order to be worthy of his fatherly responsibilities" (McBride 357). Indiana Jones, who in *Raiders of the Lost Ark* was a loner, here becomes a liberator of children.

The movie tries to turn Indiana Jones into a family man with the addition of a woman and a child, and in the final scene Indy and Willie are surrounded by the happy Indian children he has freed. But Short Round expresses some jealousy. As Indy and Willie embrace, he sits astride an elephant and laughs as the beast squirts the pair with water from his trunk: "Very funny!" The film thus ends with a joke that could be read as phallic defiance of the parents (Biskind 132).

Indiana Jones and the Temple of Doom: Family reunion. Paramount, 1984.

CONCLUSION

Nevertheless, in that final scene, the kidnaped children return home to a joyous mass reunion of parents and children, with the emphasis on the mothers. This is characteristic Spielberg territory: the mother and child reunion. Separation anxiety—the fear of being torn away from the good mother and given over to the power of the bad mother—underlies the plots of many Spielberg films, including *Sugarland Express* (1974), *Poltergeist* (1982), *Empire of the Sun* (1987), *A.I.* (2001), and *Indiana Jones and the Temple of Doom* as well. As Willie tells Indy, "I thought archaeologists were always funny little men searching for their mommies." According to Douglas Brode, Indy is "a Spielbergian hero whose main problem has to do with separation from the mother" (Brode 141). Lucas is more interested in father-son reunions. So perhaps the oedipal concerns of the three *Indiana Jones* movies can be ascribed primarily to Lucas, who originated the idea for the series and always foregrounds such conflicts in his movies, as in the *Star Wars* series. The oral fantasies may then be largely Spielberg's contribution, as a way of retreating or regressing from the oedipal conflict.

Whoever was responsible for the gruesome fantasies of *Indiana Jones and the Temple of Doom*, they do not recur in the next film of the series, *Indiana Jones and the Last Crusade* (1989). No one pauses to eat in that film, and the only nourishment they seek is a drink with father or a sip from the Holy Grail, the cup of the ultimate Father. Mothers are absent; instead we get Indy as son desperate for reconciliation with his dad in a movie that might be termed *Raiders of the Lost Father*.

NOTES

1. Spielberg later distanced himself from *Temple of Doom*: "I wasn't happy with the second film at all. It was too dark, too subterranean, and much too horrific. I thought it out-poltered *Poltergeist*. There's not an ounce of my own personal feeling in *Temple of Doom*" (McBride 355).

2. The opening dance routine "is not only very funny but acts as an immediate dislocation of reality—Berkeley's routines cannot work on a stage since they require an audience looking straight down on the dancers. It at once sets the action in a special time (in the Thirties) and in a specific locale: the same universe as MGM musicals inhabited . . ." (Walker 99). Busby Berkeley's routines are fantasy: they may begin on the confined space of a theater stage but they soon expand in a fantastic, dreamlike way into enormous spectacles on a sound stage, choreographed for the camera, not for a theater audience. In following these conventions, *Doom* announces at the opening that it is a film fantasy playing affectionately with old generic expectations.

3. McBride says that *Doom* trivializes Spielberg's personal obsessions: "one need only compare the glibly picturesque treatment of child slavery in *Temple of Doom* with the angry passion that suffuses every frame of the forced-labor camp scenes in *Schindler's List*" (354–55).

REFERENCES

Barnes, Julian. "Night for Day." *New York Review of Books*, October 11, 1990, 14 and 16.

Benson, Sheila. Review of *Temple of Doom*. *Los Angeles Times*, May 23, 1984, *Calendar*, 1.

Biskind, Peter. "Blockbuster: The Last Crusade." *Seeing through Movies*, Ed. Mark Crispin Miller. New York: Pantheon, 1990, 112-49.

Brode, Douglas. *The Films of Steven Spielberg*. New York: Citadel Press, 1995.

Buckley, Michael. Review of *Temple of Doom*. *Films in Review*, August 9, 1984, 426.

Denby, David. Review of *Temple of Doom*. *New York*, June 4, 1984, 72.

Elkins, Merry, ed. "Steven Spielberg on *Indiana Jones and the Temple of Doom*." *American Cinematographer*, July 1984, 51–60.

Hoberman, J. Review of *Temple of Doom*. *Village Voice*, June 5, 1984, 1.

Indiana Jones and the Temple of Doom. Paramount, 1984. Executive Producer: George Lucas and Frank Marshall. Producer: Robert Watts. Director: Steven Spielberg. Story: George Lucas. Screenplay: Willard Huyck and Gloria Katz. Director of Photography: Douglas Slocombe. Editor: Michael Kahn. Music: John Williams. Running Time: 118 minutes. Starring: Harrison Ford (Indiana Jones), Kate Capshaw (Willie Scott), Ke Huy Quan (Short Round), Amrish Puri (Mola Ram).

Kael, Pauline. "A Breeze, a Bawd, a Bounty." *State of the Art*. New York: Dutton, 1985, 175–82.

Klein, Melanie. "A Contribution to the Psychogenesis of Manic-Depressive States." *Essential Papers on Object Relations*. Ed. Peter Buckley. New York: New York University, 1986, 40–70.

Matloff, Jason. "Serial Thrillers." *Premiere*, October 2003, 72–80, 104.

McBride, Joseph. *Steven Spielberg: A Biography*. New York: Simon and Schuster, 1997.

Morris, Nigel. *The Cinema of Steven Spielberg: Empire of Light*. London: Wallflower Press, 2007.

Postone, Moishe and Elisabeth Traube. "*Indiana Jones and the Temple of Doom*: The return of the repressed." *Jump Cut* 30 (1985), 12–14.

Reed, Rex. Review of *Temple of Doom*. *New York Post*, May 23, 1984, 30.

Variety. Review of *Temple of Doom*. May 16, 1984, 26.

Walker, John. Review of *Temple of Doom*. *The Film Yearbook: 1985*. Ed. Al Clark. New York: Grove, 1986, 98–99.

8

Indiana Jones and
The Last Crusade (1989)

Raiders of the Lost Father

MAKING *THE LAST CRUSADE*:
GRADUATING FROM CLIFFHANGER U.

In *Temple of Doom*, archaeologists are "funny little men searching for their mommies." But in *The Last Crusade* they are searching instead for their daddies.

Spielberg had agreed with Lucas to direct three *Indiana Jones* films. Although *Temple of Doom* grossed over $100 million, Spielberg was upset by its critical reception. So one reason for making the third film, besides honoring his agreement, was "to apologize for the second one." They had difficulty coming up with a storyline that would satisfy both of them and discarded several ideas. "It wasn't until we maneuvered into the Grail myth, this father-son thing, that it became exciting to everybody," says Lucas (Woodward 16).

As in all the *Indiana Jones* collaborations, it is hard to know whom to credit with specific ideas such as the search for the father. One journalist says the notion originated with Lucas and screenwriter Jeffrey Boam (Griffin 89–90), but another says it came from Spielberg (Fong-Torres 31). Father-son relationships are central to the *Star Wars* saga, and Lucas conceived of Indiana Jones as rebelling against his father, much as Luke does in *Star Wars*. Lucas says, "Indiana Jones has always loved adventure, and at some point, in college or whenever, that side took over. It's obvious that it had to have been a rebellion against his father" (Woodward 16). Jeffrey Boam says, "I think maybe George has his own father fixation. . . . Steven knows these are George's movies. . . . He approaches them as what John Ford used to call 'a job of work'" (McBride 401). Nevertheless, as Nancy Griffin writes, "It is not a coincidence that Spielberg, Ford, and Lucas have all recently become fathers.

Or that Spielberg, whose relationship with his own father has never been warm, could effect a fictional rapprochement more satisfying than anything real life has brought. But he adds hastily, 'My dad's nothing like Sean Connery'" (Griffin 90). Lucas, who researched Grail lore, says, "The real issue in the Grail legends is finding inner happiness, eternal satisfaction. The film is about a father and son finding one another, rather than going after some specific thing. They find the Grail in each other" (Woodward 16).

Lucas originally envisioned the father as resembling his own guru, scholar Joseph Campbell (Woodward 16). Spielberg disagreed. He says, "Who better than the original James Bond to have given birth to this archaeologist adventurer and rogue?" (Griffin 90). "I think George saw the role played by an anonymous, English character actor. I wanted another star. He thought Sean was too powerful. I said that Harrison would wipe the floor with him, or they'd wipe the floor with each other" (Woodward 16). Evidently Spielberg wants to find a strong father, but Lucas seems afraid that the strong father might overwhelm him (as Darth Vader threatened to do to Luke).

Harrison Ford, who, like Spielberg and Lucas, had a young son at the time the film was made, says, "A lot of it is based on real feelings, real stations in the parent-child relationship. . . . It develops through the son's dependence on the father, to a kind of evenness between the two of them to, finally, the father's dependence on the son. It's what goes on between sons and fathers. Having been both, I find it truthful" (Strauss 17).

Spielberg knew going in that this would be the last of the series. He says, "It feels like the end of an era, and the end of a quest." He was happy to make the film but happy as well to say good-bye to his "popcorn days" (Griffin 89). "I've learned more about movie craft from making the Indiana Jones films than I did from *E.T.* or *Jaws*. And now I feel as if I've graduated from the college of Cliffhanger U" (Corliss 83).

Reviewers were generally ecstatic, praising the return to the good form of *Raiders*, and also the action, the humor, and the acting of Connery.[1]

THE SEARCH FOR THE FATHER

All three *Indiana Jones* movies deal with male rites of passage, but the third of the series, *The Last Crusade* (1989) makes explicit the oedipal conflict which underlies all the movies. Like the *Star Wars* saga, *Crusade* concerns the hero's search for manhood through confrontation and reconciliation with a lost father. The missing father here becomes identified with the Holy Grail ("Find the man and you will find the Grail," one character tells Indiana Jones); the quest for the Grail becomes a pretext for Indy's quest for his father. As in *Star Wars*, the mother is eliminated so that the plot becomes a contest between two men; the "Power of the Force" turns into the divine power of the Grail, and Jedi Knight becomes Grail Knight. But unlike the somber conflict between Darth Vader and Luke Skywalker, the father-son conflict of Dr. Henry Jones and Dr. Jones, Jr. is not so much oedipal myth as oedipal comedy.

Even as Indiana Jones searches for his father, Lucas and Spielberg search for their cinematic forefathers by resurrecting and recombining elements of old Hollywood formulas, including 1930s and 1940s cliffhangers, Westerns (*Crusade* begins in Monument Valley, like a John Ford movie, and ends as the heroes ride on horseback into the sunset), World War II adventures, spy movies, 1950s Biblical epics, and even buddy comedies. Appropriately, the father that Harrison Ford recovers is Sean Connery, for Ford as Indiana Jones played a role in the 1980s similar to that played by Connery as James Bond in the 1960s.

THE OPENING SEQUENCE

The opening sequence returns us to the past (Utah 1912) and Indiana Jones's adolescence, when he is a daring, idealistic Boy Scout out of Frank Merriwell or the Hardy Boys (Spielberg himself was an Eagle Scout). We see the establishment of the hero's identity as an adolescent through a myth of origins, an adventure which quickly and cleverly explains his preference for archaeological derring-do, and accounts as well for his trademark whip and costume of leather jacket and fedora, as well as his facial scar and fear of snakes. We also see the crucial imbalance in his identity caused by his father's emotional absence.

The theme of the opening is Indy's abandonment or betrayal by authority figures (which foreshadows his later betrayal by Elsa and Donovan), leaving him on his own. The critic Charles D. Leayman writes, "In contrast to the 'buddy-buddy' films of the 1970s, the strictly '80s character of Indiana Jones has always seemed chronically self-absorbed, paranoid, alone, alienated . . . even, apparently, from his father" (Leayman 99). Like Rambo, another popular 1980s film hero, Indy often functions as a one-man army who has separated from the chain of command. In the opening, Indy is part of a troop of Boy Scouts (which at first is made to appear like a troop of mounted cavalry)[2] but quickly strikes off on his own. When Indy needs help, the Scout leader is nowhere to be found, the first male authority to let him down.

Indy steals the priceless "Cross of Coronado" from a gang of mercenary, cave-robbing scoundrels (reminiscent of *Tom Sawyer*—one of the robbers even resembles Injun Joe). The gang is in the employ of a limping man with a cane who wears a white linen suit with a red carnation and a panama hat. "Panama Hat" is the first of a series of stereotypical bad father figures in the

film, including Indy's father, the American millionaire Donovan, the Nazi
Colonel Vogel, and Hitler, the archetypal evil father. Panama Hat's limp and
cane could symbolize his emasculation, or the son's fear projected onto the
bad father. Later, the evil gang is replaced by the Nazis: the shot of Indy
spying on the cave robbers is paralleled by the shot of Indy looking down
on the Nazis inside the Castle Grunwald. Peter Biskind likens the scenes of
Indy spying, both here and in *Temple of Doom*, to the child's discovery of
the "primal scene," "redolent of forbidden voyeurism of taboo activities"
(Biskind 133). Panama Hat is later replaced by the Nazi sympathizer Donovan, another looter of Christian treasures; Panama Hat wants the Cross for
himself, just as Donovan wants the Grail to gain immortality. The image of
Indy on horseback, chased across the Utah desert by robbers in a truck and
car, is also repeated later in the scene of Indy on horseback, pursued across
the African desert by a Nazi tank.

During Indy's struggle against the gang on the circus train, dangerous
phallic symbols proliferate: snakes, lions, whips, knives, and, comically,
a rhinoceros horn which erupts between his legs. The Cross of Coronado,
which Indy thrusts into his pants, represents the power of the father: it
was given to Coronado in 1520 by Cortez, so it goes back to the Spanish
conquistadors. Indy as archaeological swashbuckler becomes part of that
imperial, patriarchal lineage. Peter Biskind notes, "The suggestive proximity
of Cross, snake, and private part makes explicit what the two previous films
had only implied: the power of the coveted object of the quest, be it Ark,
Ankara Stone [sic], Cross of Coronado, or Holy Grail, is the power of the
phallus, or, better yet, dad's phallus" (Biskind 134).

The most significant betrayal of Indy by a male authority in the opening
sequence is that by his father. When the boy races home, excited to tell his
father about his discovery, Dr. Jones is so absorbed in copying an illuminated manuscript in his lifelong religious quest for the Grail that he does
not even give his son a glance, telling him to count to twenty—in Greek.
The illustration later turns up in a stained glass window in Venice, and his
line, "May he who illuminated this manuscript illuminate me," is fulfilled
in his final "illumination" through the Grail. But his face is hidden in his
first appearance, suggesting his emotional absence from his son. This absence is repeated later by his physical disappearance; the delay in showing
him arouses curiosity, like the delay in showing the shark in *Jaws* or the
alien in *E.T.* The father is established in the opening as an aloof pedant
with no apparent interest in his son. Years later, the adult Indy rebukes
him, "What you taught me was that I was less important to you than people
who'd been dead five hundred years in another country. And I learned it so
well that we've hardly spoken for twenty years."

The family dog looks up when Indy enters, but Dr. Jones does not. In the
movie's last scene, "Junior" says he renamed himself "Indiana" after the dog

since he got more affection from the animal than from his father. (George Lucas is actually George Lucas, Jr., after his father, and Lucas named his hero Indiana after his dog.) His repudiation of the name of the father becomes a sticking point. His father will only refer to him as "Junior," a name Indy despises since it suggests diminution and living in his father's shadow. Not until the end of the film does Dr. Jones acknowledge his son's separate identity by calling him "Indiana."

After his father fails him, Indy is betrayed by yet another untrustworthy older man, the sheriff who turns the Cross over to the villains. The message of the sequence, claims Peter Biskind, is "the *echt* lesson of the sixties: don't trust adults, particularly those in authority" (Biskind 112). But the lesson is softened by the parting gift of the head looter "Fedora," who wears a leather jacket and Stetson hat, and resembles the grown Indy or a cross between Harrison Ford and Steven Spielberg (White 10). Fedora admires the boy's courage and gives him the approval he craves, saying, "You lost today, kid, but that doesn't mean you have to like it," as he crowns Indy by placing his hat on Indy's head. In a striking match cut, the hat comes up to reveal the grown Indy twenty-six years later, still bloody but unbowed as he attempts once again to steal the Cross from Panama Hat. He has assumed the identity of the man he admired, along with his fedora and leather jacket. Critics call Fedora "an amoral alternative role model" (White 10); a "good-bad-guy ideal" (Kael 103); and "Indy's adult alter ego and displaced father-figure" (Leayman 98).

There is much play in the opening sequence on *hats* and on *loss*; Fedora's remark ("You lost today, kid") links the two. When Indy can't find the scoutmaster, he says, "Everyone's lost but me." During the chase, he loses his scout hat, as if losing his boyhood innocence, but Fedora replaces it with the hat which will become part of his adult identity. When Indy retrieves the Cross in 1938, all that is finally left of the villain is his panama hat floating in the water.

In fact, within the *Indiana Jones* series, Indy becomes identified with his stetson; he is the man with the hat, and the man who never loses his hat. Sometimes he even risks his life to retrieve it. Loss of hat becomes equated with loss of identity, loss of manhood, or even death. Later in *Crusade*, Indy's hat falls off just as a Nazi tank is about to topple over a cliff. We fear for a moment that he has fallen to his death on the tank, but he returns, and the wind blows the hat back to him.

The loss that is so feared in the film is not so much the loss of a hat, a Cross, or even a father, but of manhood. The word "lost," in all its senses —failure, loss of direction, and object loss—is repeated throughout the film: "You lost today, kid"; Brody once "got lost in his own museum"; and Dr. Jones laments when he thinks Indy is dead, "I've lost him." Not the Grail but the father is the film's main lost object, and when Indy declares

"Everyone's lost but me" or says of his father, "He's lost and I'm not," he is denying the loss of masculinity. The film moves toward a final acceptance of the inevitability of loss, when his father tells Indy, who is still reaching for the Grail, to "let it go."[3]

INDY'S SPLIT IDENTITY

Indy's adult identity is split between that of the rogue and that of his father: we first see him as an adventurer dressed in the fedora and leather jacket, yet in the next scene he is an anthropology professor lecturing a class, dressed in a three-piece suit and bow tie, which is really the uniform of Dr. Jones, Sr. The stuffy professorial role feels false, his father speaking through Indy, and the rest of the film contradicts his stern lecture about anthropology as dull library research rather than adventures in the field. Trapped in his office, with a mob of students outside, Indy escapes out the window, quickly abandoning the campus for the world of adventure, and we never again see him as Professor.

Yet Indy's inability to relinquish entirely the scholarly identity shows that, as much as he is the rogue adventurer, he still imitates and even tries to best his father. For one thing, he fancies himself a better teacher than Dr. Jones, Sr., whom he calls acidly "a teacher of medieval literature—the one the students hope they don't get" and "Atilla the professor." But the similarity of father and son is comically highlighted when a Nazi holds a gun on them and says, "Dr. Jones" and they put up their hands simultaneously and answer "Yes" in unison. Elsa mentions the resemblance between father and son, even though Indy persistently denies it. When they first meet, she says, "You have your father's eyes," and he counters, "And my mother's ears." Later she says, "You don't disappoint, Dr. Jones. You're a great deal like your father." He replies, "Except he's lost and I'm not." When they discover the knight's tomb, she tells him he's "Just like your father—giddy as a schoolboy." Indy says of his father, "He never would have made it past the rats. He hates rats—he's scared to death of them," neglecting to mention his own phobia about snakes. He keeps anxiously trying to distinguish himself from his father and to prove that he's more of a man than him.

Indy also prides himself on being more skeptical than his father, who is a devout Christian and a firm believer in Grail lore. At first, Indy dismisses the Grail myth as a "bedtime story" and "an old man's dream," fit only for gullible children and the credulous elderly, not for *real* men like Indy. And he tells his students, "We cannot afford to take mythology at face value." He complains to his father that Dr. Jones's lifelong search for the Grail is an "obsession," adding, "I never understood it. Neither did Mom." Despite his complaint, Indy shows the same stubborn, obsessive desire to possess antiquities as his father; both are more passionate about ancient objects than about people. Indy blames his father's faith in the Grail for his neglect of wife and child, leading to his mother's death and his own alienation.

THE QUEST OF THE KNIGHT OF FAITH

Crusade, like most films by Lucas or Spielberg, comes down to a question of *belief*: you must cease resisting with your rational mind and believe, like a child, in the fantastic. On another level, the religion that both Lucas and Spielberg propose is really a faith in the power of the ultimate fantasy— Hollywood movies. Luke Skywalker must learn to "Trust the Force"; Roy Neary must believe in the aliens even though he thinks he's going crazy; Elliott must believe in E.T. to keep the creature alive. And Indy must be converted to his father's faith in the Grail. For all his skepticism, Indy asks Brody, "Do you believe, Marcus? Do you believe the Grail actually exists?" Kazim, the "Knight of the Cruciform Sword," is ready to die for his belief and tells Indy, "My soul is prepared. How is yours?" Indy denies that he is looking for the Grail; he says he's searching for his father, when in fact, he's looking for both. Within the film, the Grail becomes identified with and equivalent to the father, just as in *Raiders* the Ark becomes equivalent to Marian.

The equivalency of father and Grail is shown when Donovan shoots Indy's father to force Indy to recover the Grail. Donovan tells Indy, "It's time to ask yourself what you believe." In *Crusade*, belief becomes a question of accepting the faith of your fathers, or more directly, of accepting your father. Indy must take a literal "leap of faith" or his father will die.

Like the *Star Wars* saga, the three *Indiana Jones* movies are religious quests, and the elements of fantasy in each have to do with religious mysticism. In each film there is a Manichean struggle between good and evil. Repeated descents into the underworld—underground temples, caves, or catacombs—are followed by a return from the place of death and darkness into the world of the living. There are repeated references in *Crusade* to the "holy" versus the "unholy." The library in Venice is a converted church, and Elsa says, "We're on holy ground." Yet just beneath its surface lie the dark, filthy catacombs, a place of rats and skeletons. When they visit Berlin, Dr. Jones says, "We're pilgrims in an unholy land." Berlin is hell, an inferno lit with burning books, a prelude to the conflagration of the war. There Indy is thrust face to face with Hitler, the prince of darkness, who autographs his father's Grail diary. This meeting with the evil father is countered later by the meeting with the Grail Knight in his holy sanctuary.

AMBIVALENCE TOWARD THE FATHER

In the *Star Wars* trilogy, both good and evil are embodied in the father, Darth Vader. Dr. Jones is no Vader, but he is both a deeply religious man and a neglectful father. The other father figures in the film, good or evil, are like split-off fragments of Dr. Jones. The Grail diary is his life's work; when he mails it to Indy, he is placing his life in his son's hands. Indy handles the diary with reverence, as though it were his father's body or a Bible. But when Hitler inscribes it, he becomes symbolically its coauthor, the "Dark Side" of the father.

Crusade, like *Return of the Jedi*, is a rescue fantasy in which the son tries to prove his love by rescuing the father. In both films, in the end the father returns that love by rescuing the son. In such fantasies, when the son holds the power of life or death over his father, the wish that the father live is so strong because it defends against the equally powerful wish that he die.

We see Indy's lifelong anger at his father, for example, when he guns down the Nazis while yelling at his father—"I told you—don't call me Junior!"—a comic displacement of his rage. In contrast, when Donovan shoots Dr. Jones in cold blood, it is the most shocking moment in the movie or in the entire *Indiana Jones* series: the gunshot reverberates as if in an echo chamber. The camera pans quickly from right to left as Dr. Jones turns in shock to his son; then there is a straight cut to a reverse pan, from left to right, as Indy turns to face him. This rapid camera movement is deliberately dizzying. The moment until he falls is drawn out, and reaction shots register the pain on their faces. The shock is so strong, I believe, because Donovan is acting out Indy's rage against his father. When Indy brings the holy water in the Grail and heals his father, he miraculously undoes the effects of the evil wish, as in a fairy tale. And Donovan must be destroyed in the movie's most gruesome scene.

Indy's hostility toward his father is matched by his father's hostility toward him: in his first scene he is emotionally aloof; later he mistakes his son for a Nazi and smashes a vase over his head, afterwards showing more concern for the vase than for his son; and he slaps Indy's face when Indy swears "Jesus Christ."

ELSA AND THE OEDIPAL TRIANGLE

What hurts Indy more than the slap, however, is the revelation that his father slept with Elsa before he did. She was initially attracted to Indy because she saw his father in him. "Spielberg had to overcome his own qualms about having Indy and his father sleep with the same woman, an obvious Freudian stand-in for Mom (in an even darker twist, the film also suggests that the

Indiana Jones and the Last Crusade:
Elsa dominates both father and son. Paramount, 1989.

treacherous Elsa has slept with Adolf Hitler)" (McBride 402). The film copes with its blatantly oedipal implications by playing them for laughs.

Some critics see Elsa as a sterotypical "Nazi bitch" and the most sexist portrayal in the series (Leayman 99; Klawans 862), but others consider her Indy's equal and the strongest woman in the series(White 11; Corliss 83). Peter Biskind reads Elsa as a combination of the amoral, seductive archae-ologist Belloq in *Raiders* (who also allied with the Nazis to get the prize) along with Marion from the same film: "in her themes of power and sexual-ity converge" (Biskind 134). Elsa is thus not only Indy's lover but also, like Belloq, his shadow double and his rival; she too is a doctor of archaeology. Moreover, she disturbs the bond between father and son and wants to pos-sess the Grail.

There is nevertheless an ambiguity about Elsa. On the one hand, she is a misogynistic fantasy: a femme fatale and scheming Nazi bitch, unscrupulous, greedy, self-serving, and nymphomaniacal. On the other hand, she shows pity when Kazim dies and shock when Dr. Jones is shot. Although she uses and betrays them, she seems genuinely fond of Dr. Jones and in love with Indy. Even when she turns Indy over to the Nazis, she doesn't want to lose his affection, saying, "I'm sorry," and telling him, "Don't look at me like that. We both wanted the Grail. I would have done anything to get it. So would you." Later, she protests, "I believe in the Grail, not the swastika." And when Indy shouts, "Who cares what you think?" she replies, "You do!" When he has his hand on her throat, ready to throttle her, he relents. At the end, she betrays Donovan so that she and Indy can have the Grail. As he tries to hold onto her hand to keep her from falling into a chasm, he calls her "honey."

Some of the ambiguity in the portrayal of Elsa as Nazi slut and loving woman arises because she embodies both bad and good mother in the oedipal conflict. As Peter Biskind notes, "After two installments of *coitus interruptus*, Indy actually has sex with the female lead. . . . As we might suspect, both he and she have to be taught a lesson" (Biskind 134). Indy has violated taboo by stealing his father's woman. As she stands over father and son, who are tied together back to back in two chairs, and whispers lovingly in Indy's ear, "I can't forget how wonderful it was," the vain Dr. Jones takes her message as meant for him, until Elsa aggressively kisses Indy. In this psychoerotic tableau, father and son are helplessly bound together as the dominatrix towers over them. In the opening sequence, father betrayed son; now the bad mother betrays both of them. Son cuckolds father, but the guilt is transferred to the woman. He can't be blamed because, like Oedipus, he wasn't aware that she first slept with his father, and now, he is helpless as she kisses him.

As soon as Elsa departs, the Nazi Colonel stands in the same position, above the bound Indy, but instead of kissing him, he punches him in the face, the evil father punishing him. The scene is a bondage fantasy demonstrating the sadomasochistic connection between pleasure and pain, sex and punishment.

Elsa must be punished for having slept with both father and son, sacrificed to the reunion of father and son. She dies so that Dr. Jones and Indy may live. "Woman removed from the equation, male competition is purged" (Morris 156). Beneath the "flip surfaces" of the *Indiana Jones* series, Charles D. Leayman sees "the attempted retrieval of masculine certitude in a feminist age of radical doubt" (Leayman 99). In the movie, along with the wish to kill the father circulates the desire to eliminate the mother. Dr. Jones accuses Donovan, "You would sell your own mother for an Etruscan vase." Nevertheless, Dr. Jones is not that different, since Indy blames his mother's death on his father's Grail obsession.

LAST CRUSADE AS BUDDY COMEDY

In *Star Wars*, Luke Skywalker was another motherless boy who needed to be reconciled with his father; both series end with this process of atonement. Nevertheless, *Crusade* has none of the somber oedipal overtones of the *Star Wars* trilogy because the situation is played as sex farce: Harrison Ford's double takes and Sean Connery's satisfied smirks, the physical comedy, and the witty repartee (DR. JONES: "I'm as human as the next man." INDY: "I *was* the next man!"). Father and son are literally bound together despite their mutual distaste and bound also by their attraction to the same woman. Although Dr. Jones is crotchety and self-absorbed and creates as many problems as he solves, Indy comes to admire the old man's faith, wisdom, and ingenuity. Likewise, despite Dr. Jones's initial repugnance at Indy's violence, he later takes up a gun, telling Brody, "This is war!" As they repeatedly save each other's lives, they come to recognize in each other the same stubbornness and daring. Moreover, each becomes more like the other (Friedman 98). Through their forced association and growing teamwork, they learn from each other and are bonded through mutual respect and even love, in one of the oldest Hollywood comic formulas: the buddy movie.

CONCLUSION

Indiana Jones and the Last Crusade is not as lurid and gruesome as *Temple of Doom*, and it excels in its action sequences and in the humorous interplay between Indy and his father, who is a complex, amusing character. But *Crusade* lacks the freshness of *Raiders of the Lost Ark*. By the third film, we have already seen many of these perils and these nasty Nazis.

The film is weakest in its shallow spiritualizing; the sequence with the Grail Knight embarrassingly resembles a 1950s Hollywood biblical epic. As Pauline Kael notes, Spielberg "invokes pop Christian symbolism without any apparent awareness that this may be offensive" (Kael 104). Kael had been complaining for several pictures that Spielberg had gone soft:

> The tone deafness that has been afflicting Spielberg's work ever since he became a consciously inspirational director. . . . Directors who made big commercial hits used to feel guiltless, but Spielberg is too anxious, too well intentioned. He thinks it isn't enough to give the audience pleasure. Trying to give it what he feels he owes it (wisdom), he softens and sentimentalizes the action. . . . Spielberg, who was perhaps the greatest of all pure, escapist movie directors, is being acclaimed for turning into a spiritual simp. (103–05)

The sentimentality and spirituality had been in his work since *Close Encounters* (1977), but at least *Close Encounters* and *E.T.* do not attempt to point any morals, whereas most of his films beginning with "Kick the Can" do, and "The Mission" and *Last Crusade* are both weakened by blatant Christian symbolism.

Kael is correct about Spielberg's straining for significance, although in her enthusiasm for Spielberg as "pure, escapist" action director, she negates everything else of value in his films. I agree with Vincent Canby, who in his review of *Last Crusade* says that Spielberg's are among the rare children's films "so full of wit and intelligence and even genuine feeling" that adults enjoy them as well. "He is working in a limited field, but he is trying to enlarge it . . . it is clear his movies are growing up" (Canby). And, as Joseph McBride notes, in *Last Crusade, Always* (1989), and *Hook* (1991), Spielberg "bent traditional genres to express his own style and feelings, like the studio directors he admired from Hollywood's Golden Age." Because of the changes taking place in Spielberg's life in the late 1980s, including marriage, fatherhood, and divorce, "the most interesting and unusual thematic elements in *Last Crusade, Always,* and *Hook* revolve around troubled relationships between fathers and sons or father-son surrogates" (McBride 399).

NOTES

1. Novak's review was typical: "you're not likely to see many manmade objects come this close to perfection. . . . an adventure film that is fast, muscular, playful, warmhearted and sheer pleasure." Travers wrote that Spielberg's tricks "are executed in grand style. . . . It's Spielberg's wide-eyed enthusiasm that turns *The Last Crusade* into the wildest and wittiest Indy of them all," and Corliss noted that "Spielberg's camera style never misses a trick." On the negative side, Ansen, Klawans, and Kael thought that without Connery's presence, *Last Crusade* would be virtually indistinguishable from *Raiders*.

2. Critics differ on how to read this opening visual joke (cavalry turns into Boy Scouts). Armond White calls it "brilliantly clever revisionism" of standard patriotic fare such as John Ford Westerns, proving that "American action in the primeval West is, essentially, child's play" (White 10). But Peter Biskind considers it an allusion to "the dangers of growing up" (Biskind 133).

3. White reads the film as a critique of Western imperialism, since the Joneses show the wisdom to leave the Grail where it belongs and not return it to a Western museum. But the film turned out to be, unintentionally, eerily prophetic of the Gulf War which followed it a year later: two Englishman and an Arab are led by an American on a holy crusade in an Arab desert where they battle against the forces of Hitler (George Bush compared Saddam Hussein to Hitler). They kill a lot of troops and easily capture the rest. And they save the world and preserve the Holy Grail (oil?). Perhaps "Operation Desert Storm" could have been entitled *Indiana Bush and the Last Crusade*.

REFERENCES

Ansen, David. Review of *Indiana Jones and the Last Crusade. Newsweek* 5-29-89, 69).
Biskind, Peter. "Blockbuster: The Last Crusade." *Seeing through Movies.* Ed. Mark Crispin Miller. New York: Pantheon, 1990, 112–49.
Canby, Vincent. Review of *Indiana Jones and the Last Crusade. New York Times,* 6-18-89, 15.

Corliss, Richard. "What's Old Is Gold: A Triumph for *Indy 3*." *Time*, May 29, 1989, 82–84.

Fong-Torres, Ben. "Connery. Sean Connery." *American Film*. May 1989, 28–33.

Friedman, Lester D. *Citizen Spielberg*. Urbana: University of Illinois Press, 2006.

Griffin, Nancy. "Manchild in the Promised Land." *Premiere*, June 1989, 86, 89–90, 93–94.

Indiana Jones and the Last Crusade. Paramount, 1989. Story: George Lucas and Menno Meyjes. Screenplay: Jeffrey Boam. Producer: Robert Watts. Director: Steven Spielberg. Starring: Harrison Ford (Indiana Jones), Sean Connery (Dr. Henry Jones), Denholm Elliott (Marcus Brody), Alison Doody (Dr. Elsa Schneider), John Rhys-Davies (Sallah), Julian Glover (Walter Donovan), River Phoenix (Young Indy), Michael Byrne (Vogel), Kevork Malikyan (Kazim), Robert Eddison (Grail Knight), Richard Young (Fedora), Paul Maxwell (Panama Hat).

Kael, Pauline. "Hiccup." *New Yorker*, June 12, 1989, 103–05.

Klawans, Stuart. Review of *Indiana Jones and the Last Crusade*. *The Nation*, June 19, 1989, 862.

Leayman, Charles D. Review of *Indiana Jones and the Last Crusade*. *Cinefantastique*, 1989, 98–99, 118.

McBride, Joseph. *Steven Spielberg: A Biography*. New York: Simon and Schuster, 1997.

Morris, Nigel. *The Cinema of Steven Spielberg: Empire of Light*. London: Wallflower Press, 2007.

Novak, Ralph. Review of *Indiana Jones and the Last Crusade*. *People*, 6-5-89, 13.

Strauss, Bob. "A Finale for Indy." *Los Angeles Times*; rpt. *Gainesville Sun, Scene Magazine*, May 26, 1989, 17.

Travers, Peter. Review of *Indiana Jones and the Last Crusade*. *Rolling Stone* 6-15-89, 31.

White, Armond. "Keeping Up with the Joneses." *Film Comment*, July–August 1989, 9–11.

Woodward, Richard D. "Meanwhile, Back at Skywalker Ranch." *New York Times*, May 21, 1989, 1, 16 H.

9

Always (1989) and the Eternal Triangle

WHY DID SPIELBERG REMAKE *A GUY NAMED JOE?*

For years, Spielberg was determined to remake Victor Fleming's melodrama *A Guy Named Joe* (1943), a wartime fantasy about a flier who dies in combat and returns as a ghost to guide a novice pilot who becomes his romantic rival. As early as *Jaws* (1975), Spielberg planned to remake *A Guy Named Joe*. In *Poltergeist* (1982), Spielberg's earlier ghost movie, a clip from *Joe* plays on the television. During the 1980s, he commissioned a dozen scripts based on *Joe*, apparently for highly personal, emotional reasons. "But I was so touched by the idea, the concept of a romance like this. It had haunted me like Pete haunted Dorinda. Unlike Pete, it never released me" (Dollar 3). "This is the only remake I would really ever consider directing myself," he said (forgetting that he had already directed the remade "Kick the Can" for the *Twilight Zone* movie). "It's a story that touched my soul when I was fourteen years old and saw it on television. It was the second movie that ever made me cry that didn't have a deer in it" (Griffin 93). Evidently he is referring to *Bambi* (1942) and *The Yearling* (1946). He told other journalists that he saw *Joe* when he was twelve. Whatever Spielberg's exact age when he first viewed it, this fantasy appealed to his teary-eyed, romantic teenage side. He wanted to recuperate both his personal past and the cinematic past by remaking a movie which, when he first saw it, marked for him an adolescent rite of passage.

The psychiatrist Harvey Greenberg speculates that Spielberg was doing a conflicted homage to director Victor Fleming even as he engaged in an oedipal rivalry with him—a sort of anxiety of influence—and that is certainly possible, but difficult to prove (Greenberg, "Raiders"). Joseph

McBride speculates that *Always* emerged out of Spielberg's need to accept the loss and sense of failure represented by his parents' divorce and by his own divorce in 1989, and that is likelier (McBride 406). Spielberg has said of *A Guy Named Joe*, "I didn't understand why I cried. But I did. Pete [the hero of the movie] is powerless, unable to influence events, like a piece of furniture. As a child I was very frustrated and maybe I saw my own parents in it" (McBride 406). It is also possible that the disintegration of Spielberg's marriage recalled his helplessness at seeing his parents quarrel and separate.

Despite Spielberg's emotional attachment to the film, *A Guy Named Joe* was not a fantasy classic and not an obvious choice to remake: it received mixed reviews in 1943 and subsequent critics have never rated it highly.[1] *Always* was not acclaimed as a fantasy classic either; in fact, most reviews dismissed it as Spielberg's weakest film since *1941* (1979).[2] Pauline Kael sums up the critical response: "Was there no one among Steven Spielberg's associates with the intellectual stature to convince him that his having cried at *A Guy Named Joe* when he was twelve was not a good enough reason for him to remake it?" (Kael 92).

But aside from unconscious or emotional reasons, there may have been more pragmatic reasons why he was drawn to the project: this would be his first romantic film, and in the late 1980s, both Spielberg and the movie audience were growing older. In many respects, *Always* (1989) also has the earmarks of a typical Spielberg-directed film: McBride calls it "a smorgasbord of Spielbergian motifs and psychological hangups" (McBride 407). It features lavish cinematography, airplanes, a prankish ghost, comedy, adventure, separation and reunion, the spiritual element of death and rebirth, and a schmaltzy, operatic conclusion amplified by John Williams's score. Also like most Spielberg films, *Always* is upbeat. He says, "It's a reassuring story. It's about life and saying it while you're here and doing it while you can" (Griffin 93). The film is a character study of the growth of three characters: Pete, the hero who must learn how to love and how to say good-bye; Dorinda, the heroine who has to overcome her mourning for Pete; and Ted, who like Pete has to grow up.

Moreover, *Always* continues Spielberg's romance with old movies, which are his love and his religion. Whatever their ostensible subject matter, most of his films are about the power of the movies. *Always* is self-consciously metacinematic, not only a remake of a 1940s film but also a homage to Howard Hawks's *Only Angels Have Wings* (1939): the rapid, overlapping dialogue; the male-female sparring with wisecracks; and the camaraderie of male flyers (Denby 58). There are possible allusions to other films as well: *Red Skies of Montana* (1952), about forest-fire fighters, and *The Hellfighters* (1969), featuring John Wayne fighting oil fires (Graham 8). In addition, characters do impressions of Woody Woodpecker, John Wayne, James Cagney, and Clark Gable (Al calls Dorinda "Miss Scarlett" as he invites her to dance). Spielberg choreographs a dance hall sequence like a 1930s musical and casts Audrey Hepburn, a goddess of the old Hollywood, as an angel. When Pete signals the band to start playing his and Dorinda's song, he says, "It works in the movies." *Always* is filled with the sort of things that work in the movies, such as guardian angels and love at first sight. But while reprising old movie genres may succeed in escapist fantasies set in the past, such as the *Indiana Jones* films, it does not work as well in a supposedly contemporary romance. *Always* is too bathed in nostalgia, "a movie about a modern grown-up's warmly recalled childhood memories of watching Hollywood movies" (Brode 197).

For the movie to succeed, we would have to get out our hankies at the end. In Spielberg's words, it would have to touch the soul, like *E.T.*, *The Color Purple*, or *Schindler's List*. But although I enjoy the dazzling aerial cinematography, *Always* leaves me cold. It is a flawed film, and I feel detached from the characters.

Since Spielberg's attraction to the material was highly emotional, I want to consider *Always* as an unresolved, uncomfortable oedipal fable and speculate as to why I or other viewers might react against its characters and plot. *Always* is part of Spielberg's continuing cinematic autobiography, his attempt to grow up on film, and Pete is another typical Spielberg hero, a child-man. Previous Spielberg films were primarily about children separated from and searching for mothers (or, as in *Close Encounters*, a mothership), but *Indiana Jones and the Last Crusade* (1989) introduces oepidal concerns: conflict with a father, romance, and jealousy. *Always* continues these concerns, but its resolution is unsuccessful, I would argue, because viewer sympathies are split between the two heroes Pete and Ted. For comparison, I want to read *Always* against three similar but more psychologically satisfying films: *A Guy Named Joe*, *Casablanca* (1942), a film with a similar oedipal plot, and *Ghost* (1990), a romantic fantasy released about the same time as *Always*.

THE PLOT OF *A GUY NAMED JOE*

A Guy Named Joe concerns Pete (Spencer Tracy), a cocky, hotshot American bomber pilot in England during World War II, and Dorinda (Irene Dunne), his girlfriend, a pilot with the Air Ferrying Command. Pete wants Dorinda to stop flying; Dorinda, in turn, wants Pete to stop flying because he takes excessive risks. She threatens to get herself transferred to Australia unless he returns to the States as a flying instructor, in which case she'll go with him and take a desk job. Dorinda wants to marry, but Pete has been avoiding commitment. Under duress, Pete agrees to her deal, but later that day, while bombing a German ship, he is killed. He dies without ever having told Dorinda he loved her, and Dorinda feels as if part of her has died with him.

Pete finds himself in heaven, a sort of Air Force in the clouds, and returns to earth a ghost, with orders from his heavenly commanding general ("the Boss") to guide a nervous young trainee pilot, Ted Randall (Van Johnson). People aren't aware Pete is around, but they sense his thoughts as if they were their own. Under Pete's tutelage, Ted turns into a flying ace.

Once Ted is assigned to the Pacific, Pete reencounters his best friend Al and Dorinda. When Ted and Dorinda fall in love and get engaged, Pete grows jealous and prompts Ted to fly crazy stunts, at which point Pete is recalled to the clouds and the Boss delivers the film's patriotics wartime message: stop being jealous because they're all working together for a free world. Back on earth, Pete finally tells Dorinda that he loves her, but that it's all right for her to marry Ted and that he will protect him.

Nevertheless, Dorinda breaks off the engagement, saying she still loves Pete. But when Al says Ted is leaving on a dangerous mission to bomb a Japanese ammunition dump, she steals Ted's plane and flies the mission herself, despite Pete's objections. Rather improbably, she succeeds with Pete's guidance. After the explosions, on the calm flight back, Pete tells her how wonderful the rest of her life will be. When she lands, he tells her to go to Ted, that he is setting her free and saying good-bye. His last line is a paternalistic "That's my girl. And that's my boy," which is also the last line of *Always*. Pete disappears in a slow fade out, and the film ends as it began, with shots of clouds to the patriotic tune "Off We Go Into the Wild Blue Yonder."

A GUY NAMED JOE AS A BLEND OF 1940S MOVIE GENRES

Joe blends three popular 1940 film genres: the World War II adventure, the romantic tearjerker, and the ghost comedy (Basinger 288). Like *Casablanca*, which was released the previous year, it advocates subordinating oneself and one's romantic difficulties to the cause of the war: as Rick tells Ilsa, the woman he loves, as he lets her return to her husband, "The problems of two little people don't amount to a hill of beans in this crazy world." *Joe* came out in 1943, during the height of the war, the same year as other combat movies such as *Destination Tokyo*, *Air Force*, *Action in the North Atlantic*, and *Sahara*, all of which were meant to boost public morale for the fight. As a topical, patriotic adventure it served a need for its guaranteed audience: to reassure war widows and women with loved ones overseas that their sacrifices were worthwhile and that life would go on despite loss and to reassure men in uniform that they would somehow survive even after death to inspire others in the continuing struggle.[3]

As a woman's film, *Joe* also resembles weepies about the sufferings of a good woman such as *Christopher Strong* (1933; with Katherine Hepburn as a headstrong aviator), *Stella Dallas* (1937), and *Now, Voyager* (1942). Although Pete is the protagonist, Dorinda is a strong 1940s heroine whose romantic problems, mourning, and courage are central to the story. But even if *Joe* is a woman's film, it is not by today's standards a "feminist" film since the heroine will give up flying to please her man and only succeeds in her heroic action because her ghost boyfriend is backseat driving. *Always* will not satisfy feminist viewers either; in fact, Spielberg could even be accused of weakening Dorinda's character.

Finally, as fantasy, *Joe* also partakes of the conventions of a popular late 1930s and 1940s subgenre, the ghost comedy, which includes the *Topper* series (1937, 1939, and 1941), *Heaven Can Wait* (1941), *Here Comes Mr. Jordan* (1941), *It's a Wonderful Life* (1946), and *The Bishop's Wife* (1947), as well as the British films *Stairway to Heaven* (1945) and *Blithe Spirit* (1945).[4] In the traditional ghost comedies, the emphasis is not on the spooky but on ghosts as guardian angels and on sympathetic human beings given a second chance at life through supernatural intervention. During and immediately after World War II, ghost comedies also reassured the audience about survival after death.

PETE IN *A GUY NAMED JOE*

As portrayed by Spencer Tracy in *A Guy Named Joe*, Pete is a gruff, cocky guy, a daredevil pilot who takes heroic risks in combat. Before we meet him, he is called both "the best flyer in the whole world" by a hero-worshiping English kid and "a grandstanding windbag" by his commanding officer. Pete is both and needs to lose some of his egotism and arrogance. Nevertheless, he is made sympathetic by the lyrical speech about the joys of flying he delivers in the opening scene to a group of adoring kids.

Pete is at ease with kids because he's a typical American male, 1940s style, a loveable, overgrown boy. He's also comfortable with his sidekick Al (in *Joe*, unlike *Always*, Al is married and has a son—he's a mature foil to the boyish Pete and not a potential rival for Dorinda). Pete is adolescent in his relationships with women, whom he alternately denigrates and idealizes. He's emotionally immature, afraid of saying "I love you" and afraid of commitment. He seems attracted to Dorinda because she's a flyer too, one of the guys, but at the same time he wants her to give up flying because that's a man's job, and he tries to feminize her with a gift of "girl clothes" so he can put her on a pedestal. Once she changes from uniform to party dress, she's like Cinderella transformed at the ball and Pete becomes a worshipful boy who can only murmur "Gosh!" in admiration.

Pete grows up after he dies; he is forced into a paternal role as a guardian angel. In *Joe* heaven is patriarchal: it's all-male, another army.

As Pete turns into a father, we watch Ted grow up as Pete's son and his replacement. Ted duplicates Pete's confidence, ego, and flying ability, and even copies some of Pete's moves and lines. But Ted is not simply a double; he's an improved version of Pete — younger, taller, handsomer, with more money (four million dollars), more education (an advanced degree in engineering), and more charm—and thus a worthy replacement for Pete in Dorinda's affections. In contrast, Ted in *Always* is young and handsome, but a poor, dumb cluck. Pete's role as Ted's guardian conflicts with his sexual rivalry with him.

A GUY NAMED JOE AS OEDIPAL TALE

The film develops a classic oedipal triangle. As the only woman in the story, Dorinda is both lover and symbolic mother to the two men. Pete's being turned into a ghost substitutes for emasculation. Significantly, Pete dies right after he agrees to marry; his death could be seen as a way to rescue him from a relationship he both desires and fears. Pete then projects himself into the role of the father (but a father unable to touch the mother) and Ted replaces Pete in the son's position. But Pete's oedipal jealousy is now displaced onto his double Ted.

In the middle of *Joe*, Ted relates a lengthy tall tale he never finishes; it has no punchline and no apparent plot function but perhaps reveals the unconscious wish at the heart of the story. His seemingly pointless joke concerns a man who loses a big toe in a sawmill accident but grows a new one. Then he loses a foot, and the rumor is that he'll grow a new one. On the surface, *Joe* is about overcoming the fear of death by the fantasy of returning as a ghost; on another level, it's about overcoming the fear of emasculation by the fantasy of growing a replacement. Ted is that replacement.

DORINDA IN *A GUY NAMED JOE*

However, if we look at *Joe* as a woman's film, it is also the story of Dorinda, a woman competing in a male arena and struggling to overcome her mourning for Pete. Both problems are resolved in the final sequence. She sees Ted not only turning into Pete but about to share Pete's fate on a suicide mission. By flying the mission herself, she spares Ted and replays the original traumatic event, Pete's last flight, this time taking charge instead of helplessly standing by. Finally, Freud claimed that the mourner tries to resurrect the dead person by acting like him (Freud, *Standard Edition* XIV 243–58): Dorinda here mimics Pete as heroic, suicidal daredevil pilot.

THE CRITICS ON *A GUY NAMED JOE*

Reviewers were confused as to how to take *A Guy Named Joe*. Although they enjoyed the warmth and humor of the Pete-Dorinda relationship, they disliked the later portion with Pete as ghost, when the picture grew too serious (*Variety*). Perhaps because the movie spends so much time making us like Pete and Dorinda and developing their romance, some viewers may have been uncomfortable watching Dorinda's new romance. If they shared Pete's jealousy, it was not as pleasant or funny to watch anymore. Two reviewers mention the age difference between Dorinda and Ted (Tracy was then 43, Dunne 41, but Johnson only 27), a discrepancy which seems to make Dorinda a cradle-robber and unfortunately to highlight the movie's oedipal motif (*Variety* and *New York Times*). *Joe* also becomes sappy and moralistic toward the end, with too many long speeches (Corliss 258).

In the original ending, Dorinda dies and is reunited with Pete in heaven. When preview audiences balked—they preferred Dorinda alive and with a live lover—the producer ordered a new ending over the director's strenuous objections (Wakeman 356).

A GUY NAMED JOE AND *CASABLANCA*

Joe has many similarities to *Casablanca*. Both films are set during the war and involve a romantic triangle in which the heroine is torn between two men. In both, the hero solves the problem at the end by reaffirming his love for the heroine even as he selflessly renounces her to his rival for the sake of a higher cause, the war effort. The psychiatrist Harvey R. Greenberg sees *Casablanca* as an oedipal triangle in which Rick "gives up his claim upon his mother and identifies with his father" by returning Ilsa to her husband (Greenberg, *Movies on Your Mind* 100).

Why is *Casablanca* far more popular and memorable than *A Guy Named Joe?* Perhaps because *Casablanca* has truly evil villains whereas in *Joe* the enemy is faceless. Perhaps because Rick and Ilsa seem more *modern*—more complex, conflicted, "neurotic," and alienated—they appeal more to postwar audiences. Or perhaps because *Casablanca* keeps us guessing as to Rick's choice until the end; Pete is a ghost and it's a foregone conclusion that he'll have to renounce Dorinda. Perhaps Rick's gesture seems nobler because he's like a son yielding to a father whereas Pete's sacrifice is the reverse. Finally, perhaps it's because Victor Laszlo in *Casablanca* never really seems an *erotic* rival to Rick but Ted is one to Pete.

ALWAYS COMPARED TO *A GUY NAMED JOE*

Always is less successful than either *A Guy Named Joe* or *Casablanca*. *Always* has its good points: as in any Spielberg film, the craftsmanship is meticulous. Dynamic camera placement, mise en scene, and cutting energize the action. The dance hall scene flows well; it is choreographed like an old Hollywood musical. The cinematography makes the aerial stunts look thrilling, and the handheld shots of blazing forests add to the realism.[5] The lighting is carefully controlled, with the dominant contrast being between warm yellow exteriors, suggesting life, love, and safety, and cold blues, suggesting death, danger, or the spirit world. There are many memorable images: Al's horrified face pressed against the cockpit glass as he helplessly watches Pete's plane explode in midair; the wordless scene as Al informs Dorinda of Pete's death; and Dorinda in her party dress, dancing alone on the anniversary of Pete's death as the invisible Pete accompanies her. The final sequence is a series of striking images: Dorinda plunging into a blazing inferno; her plane shooting out of a wall of flames; a rift in the clouds opening to reveal a black night sky sprinkled with stars; a tiny plane crossing the starry immensity (like Elliott and E.T. on a bicycle, silhouetted against the moon); and Pete and Dorinda underwater, swimming up to the light. Spielberg emphasizes the four basic elements, so that there are impressive images of earth, air, fire, and water.[6]

Since it has the same plot as *A Guy Named Joe* and the advantage of color, why should *Always* be less satisfying? Some reviewers complained that the picture was visually and aurally overdone, compared to the relative simplicity of *A Guy Named Joe* (Greenberg, "Raiders" 143; Brode 197). Others complained about the loss of the World War II setting. I would add that the change in the interpretation of the three major characters makes them less likeable, and the film overemphasizes the voyeuristic and masochistic aspects of the story, Pete's guilt and pain.

As reviewers emphasized, *Joe* is a period piece, and by transferring the action from bomber pilots fighting World War II to contemporary pilots fighting forest fires, *Always* wrenches the events out of their original time and place, in which they made more sense, and loses the intensity of the wartime setting; there is simply less at stake (Ansen; Novak 14). The film unfortunately makes us aware of this loss of intensity with Al's speech to Pete:

> What this place reminds me of is the war in Europe. Which I personally was never at, but think about it. The beer is warm, the dance hall is a quonset. There's hotshot pilots outside, There's B-26s outside, there's an airstrip in the woods—it's England, man! Everything but Glenn Miller. Except we go to burning places and bomb them till they stop burning. You see, Pete, *there ain't no war here*. This is why they don't make movies called *Night Raid to Boise, Idaho* or *Fireman Strike at Dawn*. This is why you're not exactly a *hero* for taking these chances. You're more what I'd call a *dickhead*.

PETE IN *ALWAYS*

Although Pete may not be exactly a "dickhead," as played by Richard Dreyfuss he comes across as an obnoxious smart aleck. Spencer Tracy's

Pete was stocky and gruff, a confident, rugged, loveable, everyday "Joe." But Dreyfuss's Pete has the same edge as his Hooper in *Jaws* or many of his other performances: he's a bright, cocky, restless, and nervous wise guy. Reviewers found him unconvincing as a heroic pilot (Stack E12; Kael 92). And Dreyfuss is so close to Spielberg in age, Jewish upbringing, appearance, and personality that Spielberg is clearly using him as an alter ego.

For example, the opening displays Pete as a childish, competitive show-off. To impress the other pilots and Dorinda (he thinks it's her birthday), he takes unnecessary risks, runs out of fuel, and then makes a daring emergency landing to the cheers and applause of the crowd. In other words, the character resembles Spielberg as prankster and showman. But the director seems both to celebrate this Hardy Boys heroism and to criticize it as adolescent. As a result, from the opening scene Pete is obnoxious, unlike Tracy's version.

DORINDA AND TED IN *ALWAYS*

Dorinda's response to Pete's stunts is fear and anger. As dispatcher she is forced to watch him perform (this was not true of Dorinda in *Joe*). In the opening, her fear and anger build until they explode. She is so tense she twists a metal spoon into a pretzel; we get the impression she would like to do the same to Pete. She retaliates by flying dumb stunts herself to scare him, although she's not as good a pilot as Pete, not even as good as Dorinda in *Joe*. Holly Hunter's Dorinda comes across as more angry, reckless, competitive, and vindictive than Irene Dunne's Dorinda. The movie opens not with her tenderness and affection for Pete, but with her *rage* against him; thus it can never entirely convince us that these characters really love each other. Lester Friedman finds Dorinda "a mosaic of mixed messages. She is a tough-talking, clever-bantering Hawksian heroine. . . . Yet she is also a severe mother figure who . . . attempts to clip the wings of the main character . . ." (Friedman 16).

Except for Brad Johnson's bland Ted, the major characters in *Always* are angrier than their counterparts in *Joe,* as if Spielberg has raised the emotional thermostat too high in this melodrama. Pete and Dorinda bicker furiously, and Al explodes at his hapless trainees and even at Dorinda for mourning too long and too hard.

If Pete is played as obnoxious and Dorinda as angry, then Ted is turned into a bashful fool; Pete becomes adolescent wiseacre and Ted adolescent klutz. They are both manchildren; Pete must become Ted's father so that Ted, too, can grow up.

Like E.T., Pete as ghost resembles a boy's "imaginary companion." And like E.T. and Elliott, Pete and Ted are doubles who communicate by telepathy and gestural mimicry. But because they love the same woman, they are romantic rivals. Later, however, Ted begins to echo Pete's lines ("You're the reason I'm

Always: Pete and Dorinda. *Universal, 1989.*

here"), to laugh like a donkey as Pete did, to pluck his eyebrows nervously like Pete, and to fly like Pete (E.T. also taught Elliott to fly). When Dorinda is doodling Ted's name, she writes "PETED" and crosses out the "D." The merger of souls is complete and now Pete, like E.T., is almost ready to go home. Nevertheless, Ted's transformation into Pete is abrupt and unconvincing. Pauline Kael notes, "One moment, Brad Johnson is the goofus who can't follow orders; the next, he's the top flying ace. There's nothing in between" (93).

The romance between Dorinda and Ted is also mishandled. Since Ted is so dull, a scene has been added to give Dorinda a reason to love him: she watches Ted administer CPR to a school bus driver who has suffered a heart attack. Not only is Ted good with kids, but he brings a man back to life! This contrived scene compares unfavorably with the sweaty realism and black humor of the school bus scene in *Duel.*

THE SEARCH FOR THE MOTHER IN *ALWAYS*

Aside from changing the characters, Spielberg has also altered the focus of the film so that it resembles his previous films and symbolically concerns the separation and reunion of child and mother. When Pete's plane runs out of fuel, he pleads, "C'mon, mama, up and over. C'mon, mama, we're too cute to die." As Dorinda, Spielberg cast Holly Hunter, who is short and feisty, like Spielberg's own mother. He says, "This is somebody no taller than my mom, but on the screen she's overwhelming" (Mathews 32). When an interviewer suggested that there might be a connection between Spielberg's preference in heroines and his mother, he agreed: "I've always been attracted to forthright women who aren't afraid to lay it on the line . . . even if sometime that line goes right across our chests" (Griffin 93). Nancy Griffin also noted that Spielberg's "alter ego Dreyfuss . . . was far more interested in the mothership in *Close Encounters* than he was in his wife" (93).

Spielberg changed heaven from a patriarchal Air Force in the clouds into a fertile, matriarchal clearing in the forest and a wheat field. Hap, Pete's angelic guide, is described in the script by Jerry Belson and Ron Bass of April 21, 1989 as "a nice, good looking, elderly man with frank blue eyes and a good voice" ("Always" 46). But Spielberg instead cast Audrey Hepburn as Hap, again suggesting Pete's search for mother love; Spielberg said Audrey Hepburn "was closer to the maternal side of nature" (McBride 407).

Hap is dressed all in white, like Dorinda in the dance hall scene (the heroines in *Poltergeist*, *Raiders of the Lost Ark*, *Empire of the Sun*, and here dress all in white). David Denby writes of the moment when Dorinda in her white dress dances with all the men: "It's the most purely sexless moment in Spielberg's long, long career as a boy, and it made me realize to what extent sex in his movies is a matter of dreams and idealizations" (Denby 58). The goddess in white seems like the boy's romanticized view of the mother.

A few lines cut from the script also suggest the search for the mother. As Pete and Al watch Dorinda fly, they sing "Papa Loves to Mambo"; in the song, "Papa" is looking for "Mama," but she "is nowhere in sight" ("Always" 15). Instead, in the film Al is singing these same lines to himself when Pete finds him in the office. Finally, a deleted line from the script has Dorinda describe Pete as "This punk doing stunts to scare his mother" (96).

MALE BONDING IN *ALWAYS*

Always suggests two alternatives to the search for the mother or the feminine principle: male bonding and flying.

Even as Pete searches for Dorinda like a child seeking his lost mother, there is a suggestion that the only true, unconflicted love of his life is with his good buddy Al. The male bonding between Pete and Al is reminiscent of that between Hooper and Brody in *Jaws*. Al also loves Dorinda, but at a safe distance, first through Pete and then through Ted. Although Pete delights in playing pranks on Al, he loves him so much he dies saving his life. And Al tells Dorinda about Pete, "I miss him every day. I loved him like I never loved a guy. And I don't love guys," that last line sounding like defensive denial.

There are other hints of gender bending in *Always*; in the scene in which Al denies loving guys, we see Dan Aykroyd in a *Saturday Night Live* skit on TV in a dress, imitating Julia Child. And when Ted does his impression of John Wayne, Dorinda one-ups him by doing Wayne and also James Cagney.

THE ROMANCE OF FLYING IN *ALWAYS*

In *Always*, as in so many Spielberg films, flying is erotically charged. Spielberg says, "Romance and flight have a lot in common. I wanted this to be off the ground. When they flew and when they loved, they were off the ground" (Dollar 3). The film equates flying and firefighting with making love. As the script by Belson and Bass describes a scene: "Pete in the screaming plane diving. The fire in his face, glittering his eyes. He throws the switch that releases the juice" (6).

Flying is male competition in *Always*. There is ambiguity in the hero's name: is he the heavenly "Saint Peter" (his nickname as a pilot) or the sexually suggestive "Peter"? Al calls Pete a "dickhead" because of the way he flies, and Pete retaliates with a crude gesture indicating that Al is masturbating. Ted looks macho but he's a clumsy *shmuck* who gets lost flying and keeps spilling liquids at the wrong time. Later he turns into a confident stud both as pilot and lover. Women aren't allowed into the masculine competition; when Dorinda steals Ted's plane, Al tells her not to be "dickin' around with an airplane." The performance anxiety behind flying these big planes is suggested by the premature release of "the juice" ("a little premature," Al tells a trainee) and by the limp windsock.[7] The climactic scene in which Dorinda dives into the fire is the most passionate scene in the film, making the love scenes tame by comparison. After their exciting climax in the air, Pete and Dorinda are intimate in a kind of blissful, postcoital calm. Erotic imagery pervades this scene: as the clouds part to reveal the night sky, the image seems unmistakably vaginal. Next, as the tiny plane flies across the darkness, it reminds one of the "Mother Night" image in *E.T.*, with its suggestions of a return to the womb.

DEATH AND REBIRTH IN *ALWAYS*

The water in which Dorinda almost drowns suggests a return to an attractive and devouring womb. Both Pete and Dorinda have a suicidal streak—Pete in his recklessness and Dorinda in her mourning. When her plane fails, Pete tells her to head for the water: "the water is easy." And indeed, the lake looks particularly lovely at night as the plane glides down. But when Dorinda crashes, the plane sinks to the bottom and she is trapped in the cockpit as the water rises. (*A.I.* too has images of the protagonist underwater, first at the bottom of a swimming pool and later at the bottom of the ocean.) Dorinda tries to escape but then seems to resign herself to drowning until Pete rescues her; how exactly this works is unclear, since people aren't supposed to be able to see or touch him. As they swim upward toward the light, the image suggests both a near-death experience and rebirth, with Pete functioning as midwife giving new life to Dorinda.

Separation anxiety and the desire for fusion with a mother figure who is both attractive and devouring, life-giving and deadly are at the heart of many of Spielberg's films. In *Always* the hero overcomes separation anxiety by transforming himself from lost child into powerful parent (as in his parting line: "That's my girl. And that's my boy"). Like *A Guy Named Joe*, although the resolution seems at first to represent the hero's symbolically overcoming an oedipal crisis, the desire remains in circulation: Pete acts like the father, but Ted is a second Pete, his double and therefore no longer his rival. As Nigel Morris writes, Pete at the end "asserts patriarchal authority that the narrative simply contradicts" (Morris 174).

VOYEURISM IN *ALWAYS*

The voyeurism in *Always* bothered critics, who called it "ghoulishly voyeuristic" (Novak 15) and noted the "voyeuristic queasiness in the idea of playing cupid to the girl you love and lost, and fixing her up with the next guy" (Kael 93). J. Hoberman speculates that Dreyfuss as voyeur is stand-in for Spielberg as director (51).

Pete is a voyeur of Dorinda even while he is still alive. In an early scene, as Dorinda dances with the men, Pete is on a landing on the stairs, watching her proudly and possessively from above. As she dances, she waves gaily toward him; her arm stretches out but cannot reach him. This scene foreshadows Pete's later position as onlooker and ghostly guardian to Dorinda: aloof, voyeuristic, paternalistic, physically separate yet still emotionally connected. As a ghost, he cannot touch her physically, but he takes advantage of his invisibility to spy on her, to stay close to her, and to control her.

Pete *enjoys* the power of invisibility until Ted reveals Pete's physical impotence. The most unpleasant scene in the movie is Pete watching Ted and Dorinda's first kiss. Pete is near tears as he begs Hap to get him out of there; there is no such scene in *Joe*. I too wanted to get out of there; in its painful voyeurism, the scene is perhaps too close to undefended primal scene material. In *Always*, our sympathies are split between Pete and Ted, so when Ted begins to make love to Dorinda, we are caught in a bind. The film does not successfully defend against the jealousy and guilt it may arouse in the audience.

GHOST AND *ALWAYS*

Ghost (1990), a romantic fantasy with a similar premise, released the same year as *Always*, was more successful at the box office. *Ghost* is flawed—for example, the heroine is too passive, and the ridiculous demons at the end resemble those in a Disney cartoon—but a comparison with *Ghost* may highlight some of the problems of *Always*.

The plot of *Ghost* resembles that of *Always*: a man who is unable to say "I love you" is killed just when he finally decides to marry, and then he returns as a spirit to haunt his lover and to watch in anguish as another man woos her. But *Ghost* has sexier stars (Patrick Swayze and Demi Moore) and erotic scenes to convince us of their passion, better comedy (Whoopi Goldberg as a psychic), and the added interest of a murder mystery and a revenge plot. The hero, Sam, doesn't die in an accident but is murdered and must find his killer. Sam's bewilderment when he is suddenly thrust into the spirit world is convincing; in contrast, Pete takes the transition calmly. Pete is instantly provided with a guide, but Sam must struggle to understand what has happened. *Ghost* takes place in an urban jungle more bleak and threatening than the pastoral settings of *Always*: it has the compelling image of ghosts doomed to ride the New York City subways.

In *Ghost*, the hero needs to return not only to tell his woman that he loves her but also to protect her from the people who killed him and to gain revenge. Unlike *Always*, the audience's sympathies are not split. We can hate the man who tries to replace Sam in the heroine's affections: it is his false best friend who hired the murderers. Like Pete the ghost, Sam the ghost gets to dance with his woman one last time, but unlike Pete, he doesn't have to feel *guilty* about it. *Ghost* successfully combines various Hollywood genres—romantic fantasy, comedy, and murder mystery—without the painful emotional ambivalence of *Always*.

CONCLUSION

The end of *Always* has many of the same elements as the end of *E.T.*: a near death and a rebirth, a thrilling rescue, a flight across the skies, a reaffirmation of love, and a final separation from the loved one. These work in *E.T.* but fail here because I believe most of the audience cannot bond with the characters in *Always* and so remain insufficiently moved. David Ansen writes, "As romantic fantasies go, this one is oddly masochistic: do we really want to watch a ghostly Richard Dreyfuss watch Holly Hunter fall in love with a big, square-jawed hunk . . . ? It's like rooting for Christian over Cyrano in pursuit of Roxane" (Ansen 60). John Baxter believes that, "Given the sexual jealousy, impotence and isolation which pervade *Always*, it's more likely that Spielberg was replaying the last painful months of his marriage" (Baxter 353). Voyeurism, masochism, jealousy, impotence, and isolation make for a confusing and painful romance.

NOTES

1. For reviews when *A Guy Named Joe* first appeared, see Crowther, *Time*, and *Variety*. Crowther said *A Guy Named Joe* "just misses the boat" and the conclusion is "foolish." *Time* found it "highly romanticized and somewhat overlong" but "sincere." *Variety* also said it was too long and concluded that the picture should have stayed with its humor instead of going for "serious overtones" and "spiritual counseling." For more recent criticism of *Joe*, see Corliss, Maltin, and Scheuer (Maltin says "Good cast flounders in meandering fantasy"; both Maltin and Scheuer give it two and a half stars out of a possible four).

2. For representative reviews of *Always*, see Ansen, Denby, Ebert and Siskel, Graham, Kael, Novak, and Stack. Ansen, Denby, and Novak praised Spielberg's visual technique but Ansen said he had "picked the wrong movie to remake" and Denby called it "mysticism for softheads" (58). Novak said it was "mega-sentimental" and that "there is too much serious-toned posthumous love story, not enough wit or perspective" (14), echoing the *Variety* review of *A Guy Named Joe*. Spielberg should have read those old reviews! Ebert and Siskel called it "one of Spielberg's weakest movies since *1941*." Stack thought Dreyfuss was miscast as a daring aviator and said "hardly a moment rings true" (E1). According to J. Patrick Graham, "Spielberg's close encounter with adulthood looks more like a case of arrested development." I discuss Kael's review in the text.

3. Ansen writes, "Victor Fleming's movie was no gem, but in a nation of war widows it must have packed an inspirational punch." Shindler says the purpose of *Joe* "was to emphasize the need for self discipline" (76). Kael claims that the purpose of the film in 1943 was to suppress "the finality of death" (93).

4. A lot of the 1940s ghost comedies were remade in recent decades. *Topper* was remade for television in 1979, *Here Comes Mr. Jordan* was remade as *Heaven Can Wait* (1978) and as *Down to Earth* (2001) with an African-American hero, and *The Bishop's Wife* was remade as *The Preacher's Wife* (1996) with an African-American cast. The genre was also revived in the 1990s in films such as *Ghost* (1990) and *Ghost Dad* (1990). *Ghostbusters* (1984) does not really resemble the 1940s ghost comedies because it plays it for spectacle and slapstick and lacks the element of spiritual redemption.

5. "Flight buffs are probably the only folks who will find things to like about *Always*. . . . You sit there sweating as the planes scrape the burning treetops and some-

times explode when their fuel systems suck in a spark. There is a sense of intense realism certain to give a jolt to aviation fans . . ." (Stack E12). ". . . *Always*, at its peaks, is filled with the nostalgic romance of daredevil flying. . . . We're not meant to take the feats of derring-do—the preposterous rescues and show-off stunts—as literal truth. What's being celebrated is the pictorial excitement of flying, not the reality of flying. *Always* has the heady exuberance of an aerial-adventure film from the thirties, but with color and blazingly successful special effects added" (Denby 58).

6. The film opens and closes with images of fire and water. One possible way to read this repeated juxtaposition is that it suggests underlying urethral fantasies (the common fantasy of urinating on a fire to put it out, as in Swift's *Gulliver's Travels*).

7. One woman viewer of *Always* told me she interpreted the red chemical the firefighting planes dropped as menstrual; for her, it was not a masculine film. Similarly, two women told me they preferred to envision the truck driver in *Duel* (the antagonist whose identity is never revealed) as female rather than male. This suggests the ways different viewers transact films and make them into their own fantasies.

REFERENCES

A Guy Named Joe. MGM 1943. Director: Victor Fleming. Producer: Everett Riskin. Screenplay: Dalton Trumbo. Adaptation: Frederick Hazlitt Brennan. Story: Chandler Sprague and David Boehm. Starring: Spencer Tracy, Irene Dunne, Van Johnson, Ward Bond.

"Always." Production Draft, by Jerry Belson and Ron Bass. April 21, 1989 (w/Blue Rev: 4/28/89; w/Green Rev: 5/1/89; w/Pink Rev: 5/4/89).

Always. 1989. Director: Steven Spielberg. Producers: Steven Spielberg, Frank Marshall, and Kathleen Kennedy. Co-Producer: Richard Vane. Screenplay: Jerry Belson. Based on Dalton Trumbo's screenplay *A Guy Named Joe*. Director of Photography: Mikael Salomon. Editor: Michael Kahn. Music: John Williams. Starring: Richard Dreyfuss, Holly Hunter, Brad Johnson, John Goodman.

Ansen, David. "Air Spielberg Heads for Heaven." *Newsweek*, January 1, 1990, 60.

Basinger, Jeanine. *The WW II Combat Film: Anatomy of a Genre*. New York: Columbia University Press, 1986.

Baxter, John. *Steven Spielberg: The Unauthorised Biography*. London: HarperCollins, 1996.

Brode, Douglas. *The Films of Steven Spielberg*. New York: Citadel Press, 1995.

Casablanca. Warners. 1942 Director: Michael Curtiz. Screenplay: Julius J. Epstein, Philip G. Epstein, and Howard Koch. Based on *Everybody Comes to Rick's*, a play by Murray Burnett and Joan Alison. Starring: Humphrey Bogart, Ingrid Bergman, Paul Henreid.

Corliss, Richard. *Talking Pictures*. New York: Penguin, 1975.

Crowther, Bosley. Review of *A Guy Named Joe*. *New York Times*, December 24, 1943, 17:2.

Denby, David. "Flying Low." *New York*, January 8, 1990, 58-59.

Dollar, Steve. "You Can't Always Be a Boy Wonder." Cox News Service. *Gainesville, [FL.] Sun*, December 22, 1989, *Scene Magazine*, 3 and 21.

Ebert, Roger and Gene Siskel. Review of *Always*. CBS TV, December 24, 1989.

Friedman, Lester D. *Citizen Spielberg*. Urbana: University of Illinois Press, 2006.

Freud, Sigmund. "Mourning and Melancholia." *The Standard Edition of the Complete Psychological Works of Sigmund Freud*. Vol. XIV (1914–1916). Ed. James Strachey. London: Hogarth, 1957, 243–58.

Ghost. 1990. Director: Jerry Zucker. Script: Bruce Joel Rubin. Cast: Patrick Swayze, Demi Moore, Whoopi Goldberg, Tony Goldwyn.

Graham, J. Patrick. Review of *Always*. *1990 Motion Picture Guide Annual*, 8.

Greenberg, Harvey R. *The Movies on Your Mind*. New York: Dutton, 1975.

———. "Raiders of the Lost Text." *The Films of Steven Spielberg: Critical Essays*. Ed. Charles L. P. Silet. Lanham, MD: Scarecrow Press, 2002, 141–56.

Griffin, Nancy. "Manchild in the Promised Land." *Premiere*, June 1989, 86, 89, 90, 93–94.

Hoberman, J. "Sex, Lies, and Videodrones." *Premiere*, April 1990, 51 and 53.

Kael, Pauline. Review of *Always*. *New Yorker*, January 8, 1990, 92–93.

Maltin. Leonard, ed. *TV Movies, 1981–1982*, rev. ed. New York: Signet, 1982, 310.

Mathews, Jack. "No Southern Comfort." *American Film*. December 1989, 28–33.

McBride, Joseph. *Steven Spielberg: A Biography*. New York: Simon and Schuster, 1997.

Morris, Nigel. *The Cinema of Steven Spielberg: Empire of Light*. London: Wallflower Press, 2007.

Novak, Ralph. Review of *Always*. *People*, January 15, 1990, 13–15.

Scheuer, Steven H., ed. *Movies on TV*. 9th rev. ed. New York: Bantam, 1981, 280.

Shindler, Colin. *Hollywood Goes to War: Films and American Society, 1939–1952*. London: Routledge, 1979.

Stack, Peter. "Spielberg's 'Always' Makes Crash Landing." *San Francisco Chronicle*, December 22, 1989, E1 and E12.

Time. Review of *A Guy Named Joe*. January 10, 1944, 92 and 94.

Variety. Review of *A Guy Named Joe*. December 29, 1943.

Wakeman, John, ed. *World Film Directors*. Vol. I: 1890–1945. New York: H. W. Wilson, 1987.

10

Short Films

"Kick the Can"(1983) and "The Mission" (1986)

"KICK THE CAN": BACK TO CHILDHOOD

"Kick the Can" is a short segment Spielberg directed as one of four directors of the anthology film *Twilight Zone—The Movie* (1983). This remake
of a half-hour episode from the *Twilight Zone* television series concerns a
group of men and women in an old-age home who are offered the chance
to become children again by an old wizard named Mr. Bloom. It is sentimental and old-fashioned, suffused with a golden glow of nostalgia:
for Rod Serling's science fiction and fantasy television series; for the late
1950s and early 1960s, when the series was popular; and for Spielberg's
childhood, which the period and the series represent. In making the film,
Spielberg is attempting to recover his childhood, just like the characters in
the story. Similar material—old people discover a fountain of youth—is
better handled in *Cocoon* (1985). In fact, the original "Kick the Can" from
the television series is better than Spielberg's remake, which Pauline Kael
terms a "lump of ironclad whimsy" (Kael 20).

The story must have appealed to Spielberg since it involved themes
dear to him. Like *Close Encounters*, *E.T.*, and *Hook*, it deals with the joys
of childhood and the magical power of play. Like *Poltergeist*, it is about
overcoming the fear of aging and of death. Mr. Bloom is a kindly wizard who helps the characters' wishes come true, as Lacombe did for Roy
Neary in *Close Encounters*. And, also like *Close Encounters*, *E.T.*, or *A.I.*, it
is about overcoming separation anxiety. The old folks in Sunnyvale Rest
Home resemble children cast out by their families. The most poignant
moments in the episode involve parting, and the characters' most painful
memories are of the loss of a parent or a spouse. As in *Close Encounters*,

the solution to separation anxiety is a return to childhood—in this case, a literal return. But in the end, most of the characters reject this fantastic solution for the more rational one of growing old but keeping a "fresh young mind."

The Plot of "Kick the Can"

The rest home is introduced as a boring place where retirees sit in the lobby all day watching TV or listening to pep talks on vitamins. The dim, sepia tones of the interior contrast with the dazzling light outdoors, where children play kick the can. The symbolically named Mr. Bloom is a recent arrival who wants to make these old folks feel young again, although they already seem well advanced into a second childhood. Mr. Mute blows bubbles and plays with dolls, Mrs. Weinstein goes barefoot and recites jump rope rhymes with Mrs. Dempsey, and Mr. Weinstein calls Mr. Conroy "popsicle head." They're already childish; they don't really want their childhoods back, simply the physical ability they once had to run or dance or have sex. They're playful enough, but too stiff to play.

The spoilsport is Mr. Conroy, who is devastated at being left behind by the son and grandchildren who no longer want him. Every time they visit, he has his bags packed, ready to follow them home, and every time they leave him standing at the gate. Mr. Conroy is determined to make everyone as miserable as he is. So when Bloom starts talking like the messiah who can make them young again, Conroy objects. But the group has heard his pessimism too often and brushes him off like his family does.

Bloom's ascendancy over the group is shown by the change in his position and in the camera angles during the opening scene. He begins sitting in the background and ends standing on the stairs, viewed from a low angle, while the group are below him and shot from a high angle.

Bloom works his magic at night: yellow bulbs cast a golden glow over the backyard, and the tin can he polishes sparkles magically. As Nigel Morris says, "cans of magic for Spielberg mean one thing: film." To Morris, Spielberg's "twilight zone" is the movie theater, and Bloom is a director who motivates his cast (98).

In the film's most inventive moment, the rejuvenation of the old folks takes place offscreen. As they chant "Olley-olley-oxen-free!" we hear their voices suddenly change in pitch to those of children as we see a reaction shot of Conroy in bed as he mutters, "Damn kids." Their energetic play contrasts with his lying in bed. There follow some nice comic moments since the children look and sound like their adult selves and wear the same clothing, which is now laughably large. Even Mrs. Dempsey's cat has regressed to kittenhood. As the characters play, in contrast to the opening scene there is sprightly music, lots of movement, and rapid cutting.

But after their initial enthusiasm, the group returns to Bloom with second thoughts: being children means going back to school and having to watch loved ones die again, and there is no one to take care of them. They prefer the security of the old age home to the uncertainty of childhood. So Bloom offers to return them to their old bodies, still retaining some of the magic in the form of "fresh young minds." The kids enter Conroy's room and tease him, but when Conroy returns with the supervisor Miss Cox, the group are their old selves again.

The surprise is the Englishman, Mr. Agee, who leaps from under some blankets; he alone has chosen to remain a child. In his youth, the dashing Agee was a ladies' man, and now he can reexperience puberty and act out his romantic dream of being Douglas Fairbanks (typical of Spielberg, the fantasy is borrowed from a movie). Agee somersaults over a bed and springs out the window like Peter Pan.

Although the crestfallen Conroy pleads with Agee to take him along, Agee leaves him behind, just as Conroy's family had earlier, another painful scene of parting. The nurse draws the curtain, leaving Conroy literally behind the veil, but now the group gathers around him to console him.

The next morning, Conroy is kicking a can around the lawn, trying to recapture his lost youth, as the rest of the group goes out the gates on a picnic. While the nurse searches for the missing Agee, Bloom leaves for another rest home, where he will presumably once again dispense his magic. In the final shot, he points his walking stick like a magic wand at an old man leaning on a gate.

Spielberg's Version Compared to the Original

The original *Twilight Zone* teleplay by George Clayton Johnson was changed. The movie segment was scripted by Johnson, Richard Matheson (author of Spielberg's *Duel* and of many of the old *Twilight Zone* scripts), and "Josh Rogan," the nom de plume of Melissa Mathison, who wrote the screenplay for *E.T.* Neither Johnson nor Matheson were happy with the finished product (Baxter 264). In the teleplay, the protagonist is a white man, Charles Whitley, consigned to the rest home after his son refuses to take him in (like Conroy in Spielberg's version). In the movie, however, Bloom is a black man. Sunnyvale is not run by Miss Cox but by Mr. Cox; Spielberg has turned the rest home from a patriarchy into a matriarchy.

Spielberg's version lacks the dramatic urgency of the teleplay: Bloom is serene and comes and goes as he pleases, but Whitley is desperate, rejected by his family and afraid that if he doesn't get out of Sunnyvale he will die. Bloom, a recent arrival, doesn't know the residents and has nothing at stake in the outcome, but Whitley, who has been in Sunnyvale a long time, is arguing for his life before his friends, including his lifelong friend Conroy.

Bloom has no trouble persuading the residents to play, but Whitley has to struggle and plead: "Look! Think! Feel! [He hands them the tin can.] Here, hold it. Doesn't that wake some sleeping part of you? Listen, can't you hear it? Summer, grass, run, jump—youth! Wake up! Wake up! Oh, this is your last chance!" They only agree when he cries, *"I can't play kick-the-can alone!"* The eloquence and desperation of the hero and the life-and-death struggle are missing in the movie version.

In the teleplay, Whitley is no wizard; the magic happens because of the collective effort of the old people. But here Bloom is a miracle maker (Brode 131). David Ansen saw the magician Bloom as representing Spielberg as moviemaker and "his familiar compact with the movie audience: 'If you believe, I can make you all feel like children'" (Brode 133).

Spielberg also alters the story's ending. In the original, the entire group, including Whitley, changes into children and stay that way. They leave behind the lone sourpuss Conroy, who had refused to play. Marc Scott Zicree sees Johnson's teleplay as "not an escapist fantasy" but a story that emphasizes that youth means taking risks; his friends care enough about Whitley to risk looking foolish by playing kick the can (Zicree 263). Mott and Saunders speculate that Spielberg changed the ending to fit the times: it was no longer the youth-oriented sixties but the aging America of the 1980s (Mott and Saunders 130). Slade and Watson complain that the ending is confusing, since Spielberg seems to be trying to have it both ways: thinking young versus being young. "Indeed, Agee seems to have escaped into a Never Never Land, free from all the problems of growing up which so worried the others," as if Spielberg is conjuring up *Peter Pan* (78). Joseph McBride claims that "part of Spielberg could not surrender that dream of escapism, which he had inherited from his own father, a boyhood admirer of Fairbanks" (McBride 351).

Although Johnson's 1962 teleplay is a sentimental fantasy, it has certain resemblances to Ken Kesey's novel of that same year, *One Flew over the Cuckoo's Nest*. In both stories a man committed to an institution rebels against the rules, using imagination and play to bring the inmates back to life. By changing the hero from a rebel to a wizard, Spielberg dilutes some of the early 1960s nonconformity of Johnson's original story.

Stereotyping in "Kick the Can"

There are some contradictions in Spielberg's treatment of the material. For example, the rest home in Spielberg's version is integrated—Protestants, Catholics, Jews, and one black—but the characters are stereotyped. The old Jewish couple talk with comic Yiddish accents, and Mr. Bloom, played by the black actor Scatman Crothers, always grins heartily. To Pauline Kael, the smiling black hero suggested Disney's *Song of the South*, in which the kindly old slave Uncle Remus tells fables to entertain the white children on the plantation (Kael 20). Since Bloom is the lone African-American, unfortunately he functions as what director Spike Lee would term the "magical negro," seen in so many Hollywood movies, who uses his powers to serve the white characters (McDonough). The film also stereotypes the aged, trying to win laughs in the opening scene at the expense of a toothless old man smacking his dentures together, a senile man who blows bubbles, and an old lady who giggles at the mere mention of sex.

Conclusion

The positive note in the project is that for the first time a Spielberg film suggests that one might actually *prefer* to be a grownup; only one of the characters decides to remain a child. "It initially indulges a nostalgia for the past but then begins to question it" (Sinyard 104). It is possible to grow up and to grow old gracefully, so long as one continues to think young, which anticipates the discovery of the inner child in *Hook*. But it is unfortunate that Spielberg made a plea for "fresh young minds" with such stale material.

"THE MISSION" (1986): "STUCK IN MAMA'S BELLY"

Amazing Stories (1985–1986)

Spielberg fled the lockstep of episodic television directing in 1972 for the greater freedom of directing movies. But in 1985, he returned to television for the opportunity to use some of his short-film ideas in an anthology series akin to *Twilight Zone*. He called the series "my elephant burial ground for ideas that will never make it to the movie screen because they are just too short form" (Breskin 24). "I wouldn't have gotten back into TV unless there was a challenge for me: to try and bring back the anthology series that I used to love years and years ago" (Bianculli 18). And a television show could potentially reach over 25 million viewers in a half-hour. As he and Lucas had done in *Raiders*, Spielberg would be trying to revive an old genre. The *Amazing Stories* concept was amorphous: a series of science fiction and fantasy stories, whatever Spielberg considered "amazing." And it was risky: anthology series had gone out of fashion after the 1960s. Without a continuing story or familiar characters to follow from week to week, there was little to keep viewers watching.

Spielberg spent a lot of time developing *Amazing Stories*. He came up with story ideas for sixteen of the first twenty-two shows and directed two of them: "Ghost Train" (1985) and "The Mission" (1986). The old pros he invited to direct the first season included movie directors Clint Eastwood, Martin Scorsese, and Irvin Kershner. *Amazing Stories* also functioned like a film school, giving new talent a training ground; a third of the first-season directors were neophytes.

Amazing Stories and the Return to the Family

As with his films, Spielberg created a family on the set, with himself as gentle autocrat. *Amazing Stories* was Spielberg's way of returning to an imagined or wished-for past. First, it created the film school past he never had: "It really is like having a group of film students around, and we're having fun making a project together" (Bianculli 17). Second, it fulfilled his idealized conception of the Hollywood studio past, "which to me is very glamorous and romantic . . . the old days when Louis B. Mayer was head of MGM and they had a whole stable of contract actors and writers and directors and film composers and technicians" (Breskin 72). Third, it re-created the fantasy television series he loved as a boy, such as *Science Fiction Theater, The Outer Limits, One Step Beyond,* and *The Twilight Zone.* Finally, it was a return to the family closeness he experienced when he was a boy and his father was the official storyteller.

Spielberg spoke of the series in terms of family closeness, particularly the kind a child experiences at the age of four or five. Describing his relationship with the new young directors for *Amazing Stories,* he says, "It's kind of like when your mom and dad took you to school for the first time, you wanted them to take you the first day" (Breskin 70). Spielberg says the *Amazing Stories* "were the sort told to me when I was sitting on my father's knee at four or five years old" (Morrison): in other words, the good old days, before divorce and before the alienation between father and son. Spielberg harked back to an imaginary golden age when the short story was the center of family entertainment:

> Yes, parents would read to kids from a rocking chair, and families were very, very close. They used to gather around the reader, or the *seer,* of the household, and in the Twenties and the Thirties, usually it was the father. And then television replaced the father, and now it seems to be replacing both the father and the mother. (Breskin 24)

In a reverse of *Poltergeist,* he would enter the family through the new center of the American home, the television set, not to kidnap the children but to try to return the parents to their proper roles, particularly the once-dominant father. Like *Poltergeist, E.T., Indiana Jones and the Last Crusade,* or *Hook, Amazing Stories* was in part Spielberg's attempt to rectify the past, heal the broken family, and reinstate the absent father.

The Critics on *Amazing Stories*

The premiere episode of *Amazing Stories*, on September 28, 1985, was "Ghost Train," directed by Spielberg. The story concerned a grandfather who had survived a train accident as a boy; he tells his grandson that the train will return and carry him to the afterlife. The close relationship between the boy and the storytelling grandfather suggests parallels with Spielberg as a boy listening to stories at his father's knee. Late one night, the train crashes through the house, the grandfather boards, and the train departs. As in *Poltergeist*, the family is unhurt, but the home is wrecked. The episode ends on a comic note, with the mother wondering about insurance coverage. Mott and Saunders write, "'Ghost Train' is recognizably Spielberg with its fast-paced dialogue and action, bright backlighting, and score by John Williams. As with his 'Kick the Can' segment, Spielberg opts for 'nice'" (Mott and Saunders 150).

By the end of the first season, the critical judgment on *Amazing Stories* was that the high production values and special effects could not compensate for the uneven quality due to some apprentice directors and weak stories.[1] The series lasted two seasons but was not renewed.

Themes of "The Mission"

"The Mission" is a short film Spielberg directed in 1986 for *Amazing Stories*. Originally intended as a half-hour segment, it "was padded to fill an hour slot when his first cut clocked in eight minutes too long" (McBride 389). I consider it here because it became part of *Amazing Stories: The Movie* (1987), released theatrically outside the United States and later syndicated as a movie on American television. Menno Meyjes, screenwriter for Spielberg's *The Color Purple* (1985), wrote the teleplay based on a Spielberg story. It is a Spielberg epic in miniature, using some of the same crew as his feature productions and a cast of movie stars, not television actors. As in *Duel*, he relies on cinematography and editing to overcome the limitations of the made-for-TV movie, such as limited budget, less production time, shorter length, and smaller screen. But despite good suspense, which is aided by production values, direction, and acting, "The Mission" is a cliched nostalgia film reminiscent of many old Hollywood films about aerial combat in World War II, and its fantasy ending is incongruous and unconvincing after the sweaty realism. "The director staged the crash landing of a bomber with elaborate, often dazzling camerawork, but the story built to a ridiculous climax" (McBride 390).

The production values, as usual for Spielberg, are excellent. Exterior shots are limited since most of the action takes place inside a B-17 bomber. Spielberg daringly films the entire opening scene in a single, unbroken shot, moving the camera rather than cutting. In the tight interior of the plane, he sometimes relies on moving camera, but he also varies angles, uses deliberately shaky handheld camera for realism, and cuts frequently. The brief, intense battle scene is convincing through quick cuts, closeups of blazing guns, and a move in on the hero's panicked face as debris from an explosion seems about to hit him.

The material is familiar Spielberg: an American bomber crew flying a mission from England to Germany during World War II. The story continues his romance with flying and with the war, as in *1941*, *Raiders*, *The Last Crusade*, *Empire of the Sun*, *Always*, *Schindler's List*, and *Saving Private Ryan*. But the characters here are stereotypes, all-American flyboys who chew gum, play the harmonica, and whistle "Off We Go Into the Wild Blue Yonder": the protagonist Jonathan, the "Kid" from California, a belly turret gunner who is the group's mascot and lucky charm; the fatherly, cigar-chomping Captain Spark; Sergeant Static from Minnesota, a radio operator who plans to study engineering after the war; and Lamar the navigator, a Southern farmboy. Rounding out the crew are Jake, the gum-chewing copilot; Bullseye, the nose gunner; and Sam and Dave, twin door gunners who serve as comic relief. The twins worship the famous pinup picture of Betty Grable— like Jonathan, another lucky charm.

The themes of "The Mission" are close to the surface. First, it is about the power of the artistic imagination, and the hero Jonathan, a cartoonist, can be considered a stand-in for Spielberg as filmmaker. Spielberg views the imagination as a transcendent power and the artist as a magician who is both parent and child. Second, it is also about the central concern of most of Spielberg's films: separation anxiety. For most of the action, Jonathan is the "Kid" in danger of dying, and when the crew believes he is a goner, there are tearful and prolonged farewells milking the emotion, a typically Spielbergian scene. Third, "The Mission" can be considered the anxiety dream of an expectant parent (Spielberg and Amy Irving were expecting their first child when he came up with the story; Jonathan too is expecting his first child). Jonathan in his belly turret himself resembles a fetus in the womb. The plane is about to make a belly landing, with no landing gear; in other words, Jonathan is in danger of being aborted. The story evokes the child's desire to return to the womb, along with a fear that it will become a tomb, and the expectant parent's desire that the child be born, along with the fear (and the repressed desire) that it not be born. But whichever way we view it, the central conflict in the story involves separation versus fusion.

Spielberg's father Arnold served as a radio operator and flew several missions on a B-25 bomber squadron in Burma during World War II, and his stories inspired Spielberg's fascination with aviation and the war, to which he returns in movie after movie, most successfully in *Empire of the Sun*, which came out the year after "The Mission." Through "The Mission," Spielberg is paying homage to his father even as he expresses his own anxieties about becoming a father; Jonathan the expectant father plans to name his child "Arnold."

The Plot of "The Mission"

Let me briefly relate the plot. Like *Duel* or *Jaws*, "The Mission" creates suspense by putting an ordinary man under intense pressure and steadily increasing the peril until he rescues himself at the last minute. As it opens, the B-17 bomber crew is glum because the Captain refuses to allow Jonathan, their lucky charm, to fly with them again because of the superstition that any man's twenty-fourth mission is jinxed. But Jonathan shows up anyway, forcing the Captain to choose between "a green gunner or a jinxed one." The Captain gives his assent by rubbing Jonathan's head for luck, a signal for the crew to do the same, their traditional preflight ritual. The morning ground fog then clears, as if by magic.

Jonathan, we learn, is a talented artist who wants to become a Disney animator. He draws cartoons for each mission which the crew admiringly pin up. He is married to an Englishwoman who is expecting in four months; he wants his child to be born in California.

The bomber is attacked by several German fighters which the Americans successfully fight off. Jonathan destroys one plane, but the debris from the explosion penetrates the fuselage of the bomber. A heavy piece of wreckage—black and ominous, marked with a swastika and crackling with sparks—prevents Jonathan from exiting the belly turret until they can land and blowtorch him out. But Jonathan is not worried.

Then the Captain discovers that, in the attack, the landing gear was damaged. Jonathan can see the damage; in his exposed position, a crash landing would crush him. He starts to get scared but relies on the Captain to find a solution. The Captain tries but can't budge the debris; frantically he kicks and hammers at it until he burns his hand from an electric shock. Jonathan begins to panic.

The plane is now close to home, with two engines out, and running dangerously low on fuel and altitude. The crew try delivering Jonathan a parachute, but it rips going through the small hole, and the plane is too low for them to try again. Assuming he is a goner, all the men say good-bye by rubbing his head once again. Jonathan and his best friend Sergeant Static are in tears.

Officers on a tower anxiously await the plane's return as Jonathan's wife arrives to watch the landing. Father McKay, an Anglican priest, recites over the radio to the men verses from the Book of Revelations.

Lamar proposes a mercy killing, over Static's violent protest, but as time runs out, Static decides to do it with his own pistol. Meanwhile, in desperation, Jonathan tries his last chance: he draws a picture of the plane with huge balloon wheels and tells the Captain to try the landing gear again. It works, but what comes down are animated cartoon wheels.

After they land, the Captain and crew cannot believe their eyes. Jonathan is in a trance, and the Captain has him carefully cut out of the belly turret without waking him (suggesting a caesarean delivery). Once he is safely clear of the plane, they wake him, the wheels disappear, and the plane collapses, crushing the belly turret. His wife, the crew, and everyone else on the field gathers around Jonathan, gazing with amazement, like the observers of the mothership in *Close Encounters*. "How in God's name did he do that?" asks Static, suggesting it is a religious miracle. "Some guys have all the luck," replies the Captain. Once more, they rub Jonathan's head for luck.

Belly Turret as Womb and Tomb

The central image of the film is Jonathan trapped inside the belly turret, suggesting a fetus in a womb. (It also recalls the hero of *Duel* framed in the glass circle of the door of a clothes dryer or David in *A.I.* trapped underwater in the helicopter.)

In an introduction to his poem, "The Death of the Ball Turret Gunner," Randall Jarrell explains the symbolic position of this extremely vulnerable member of the bomber crew: "A ball turret was a plexiglass sphere set into the belly of a B-17 or B-24, and inhabited by two .50 caliber machine-guns and one man, a short small man. When this gunner tracked with his machine-guns a fighter attacking his bomber from below, he revolved with his turret; hunched upside down in his little sphere, he looked like the foetus in the womb" (Jarrell, *Selected Poems* xiii). Thus the first line of Jarrell's poem: "From my mother's sleep I fell into the State" (137). As Lamar tells Jonathan, "You're stuck in mama's belly. "

Aside from the womb symbolism of the turret, the film has several other references to babies. In the opening scene, Bullseye tells Lamar as he places the bombs in their racks, "Don't stack those babies so close!" The Captain has a pair of bronzed baby shoes dangling in the cockpit for good luck. And, of course, Jonathan and his wife are expecting a baby in four months.

Just as the bomb "babies" deliver death and destruction, so the ball turret or belly turret is a death-dealing womb. The film opens on a cartoon of an angry-looking B-17 chomping a cigar; the camera pulls back to reveal the cartoon pasted on the window of Jonathan's turret as the turret guns protrude. In John Irving's novel, *The World According to Garp* (1979), Garp's father is a ball turret gunner wounded in World War II. Irving describes the position of the gunner: "There were wooden handles with buttons on the tops to fire the guns; gripping these trigger sticks, the ball turret gunner looked like some dangerous fetus suspended in the bomber's absurdly exposed amniotic sac, intent on protecting his mother" (18). Jarrell's gunner speaks posthumously, after his horrible death; he was cannon fodder who died without ever really having a chance. And after he is shot in the head, Garp's father relapses for some time into babbling infancy before dying. Both Jarrell and Irving's ball turret gunners go directly from womb to tomb. The imagery suggested by the ball turret gunner is common in popular culture, although Jarrell uses the situation of the gunner for tragedy, Irving for black comedy, and Spielberg for melodrama and suspense.

Jonathan's womblike enclosure also threatens to become his tomb. As the crew threads the parachute through, Jonathan pleads frantically, "Feed it to me! Feed it to me!" When the chute tears, it is as if his lifeline or umbilical has been cut.

Jonathan as Child and Father

The film emphasizes Jonathan's childlike qualities: he is small, playful, loves to draw cartoons, and looks up to the Captain as a father who will indulge and protect him. The men call him "the Kid," and muss his hair fondly. As in *Raiders* and *Last Crusade*, the Nazis are evil father figures, symbolized by the black wreckage from the German plane which pierces the bomber, marked with a swastika, crackling as if alive, and threatening Jonathan's life.

At the same time that Jonathan resembles a child or even a fetus in the womb, he is a warrior who shoots down an enemy plane, and he is about to become a father. Thus he is simultaneously child and parent, and the baby he is expecting is also his double. In that respect, he is like other magician figures in Spielberg's films who seem simultaneously weak and powerful, young and old, playful and serious, child and parent, such as the aliens in *Close Encounters*, E.T., Tangina the dwarf in *Poltergeist*, Mr. Bloom in "Kick the Can," and Pete the ghost in *Always*. Jonathan is also the crew's "mascot," a word that derives from the French for "sorcerer."

Jonathan, however, is the magician as artist, and thus also a stand-in for the filmmaker. Roy Neary in *Close Encounters* is a similar man-child, both parent and boy, and also an artist of sorts, obsessed with sculpting his mountain ("Spielberg" translates from the German as "toy mountain" or "play mountain"). Roy's favorite movie is the Disney animated feature *Pinocchio*, and Jonathan aspires to be a Disney animator. Jonathan could be said to partake of Spielberg's self-image as father-to-be and as artist-magician who combines the best of both parent and child: the power and responsibility of the adult with the playfulness and imagination of the child. Static says, "Jonathan's got the old imagination. That and a penny and we'll all be working for him someday"—just as everyone involved in *Amazing Stories* was working for Spielberg. The imagination is valorized here as a transcendent, even magical power. Jonathan seems for a while as helpless, dependent, and apparently doomed as E.T., but like E.T., he proves to be a powerful figure who saves his own life. The teamwork and support of the crew are important, like the camaraderie of the kids in *E.T.*, but ultimately the crew and even the Captain, Jonathan's beloved father figure, can't rescue him, and Jonathan must rely on his inner powers. Through his talent, he saves himself and the men, the artist reborn through his imagination, becoming his own mother and father.

Intrusive Spirituality

The cloying spirituality inserted at the end of the film, however, emphasizes not the power of the artistic imagination but the power of Christianity. Perhaps Spielberg, who is Jewish, is trying to appeal to a mass audience by relying on the New Testament in his films. For example, in *Close Encounters*, the chaplain blesses the astronauts, saying "God has given his angels charge over you"; *E.T.* does not quote scripture but creates an implied parallel between the creature and Christ; and in *The Last Crusade*, everything depends upon the Holy Grail and the leap of faith. It is a cliche of airplane movies that the people in peril must pray. In "The Mission," Jonathan prays to God and the chaplain Father McKay quotes at length from "Revelations" in the New Testament:

> I saw new heavens and a new earth. The former heavens and the former earth had passed away and the sea was no longer. I also saw a new Jerusalem coming down out of heaven from God, beautiful as a bride prepared to meet her husband. I heard a loud voice from the throne ring out, 'This is God's dwelling among men. . . . He shall wash every tear from their eyes. . . . For the former world has passed away. . . .

The passage is filled with images of rebirth and promises of heavenly salvation; as he tries the landing gear for the last time, the Captain echoes the priest's line, "For the former world has passed away."

Just as the extraterrestrials in *Close Encounters* perform miracles for Roy Neary because he believes in them, the implication here is that Jonathan has a direct line to the Almighty. The miracles in both films resemble the transformative power of the cinematic apparatus: the overwhelming light and sound show of the mothership or the animated cartoon. Both suggest the power of the movies as substitute religion.

Conclusion

"The Mission" anticipates Spielberg's 1989 fantasy film about aviators, *Always*. Both are nostalgia films, retrieving the benevolent fantasies of World War II American popular culture. According to Lynette Carpenter, "wartime fantasy presented a vision of an ordered universe guided by the hand of a benign Providence or destiny. . . . Moreover, the powers that be took an active hand in the battle, as well as an active interest in the fates of individual American soldiers" (55). But such fantasies seemed out of date in the 1980s.

Despite its good cast and direction, high production values, and suspense, "The Mission" fails to satisfy for three reasons: the World War II material and the characters are cliched and dated; the spiritual element is jarring; and the last-minute fantastic twist is weak. Visions of a "new Jerusalem" do not gibe with cartoon balloon tires. Richard Matheson, the fantasy and science-fiction writer, author of the story and screenplay for *Duel* and a story consultant on *Amazing Stories*, told Spielberg, "they spent all this money on 'The Mission,' they had a great cast, and it was all based on this guy *drawing a wheel!*" (McBride 390).

NOTE

1. One reviewer wrote, "Spielberg's autocratic leadership and rose-colored world view just isn't good enough to pull it off. . . . In Spielberg's universe, there's always a happy ending. . . ." (Kaplan 37). Another wrote, "Viewers may not be sophisticated, but they can usually tell . . . when they are being pandered to or patronized. And that, frankly, is what *Amazing Stories*, with its folksy suburban homilies and absence of complex characters, consistently does" (Kelley 54).

REFERENCES

Baxter, John. *Steven Spielberg: The Unauthorised Biography*. London: HarperCollins, 1996.

Bianculli, David. "*Amazing Stories*: Interview with Steven Spielberg." *Starlog*, January 1986, 13–18, 23.

Breskin, David. "The *Rolling Stone* Interview: Steven Spielberg." *Rolling Stone*, October 24, 1985.

Brode, Douglas. *The Films of Steven Spielberg*. New York: Citadel Press, 1995.

Carpenter, Lynette. "Benevolent Fantasy and the Imagination in the Popular Literature and Films of the 1940s." *The Scope of the Fantastic: Culture, Biography, Themes, Children's Literature*. Ed. Robert A. Collins and Howard D. Pearce. Westport, CT: Greenwood, 1985, 51–57.

Irving, John. *The World According to Garp*. New York: Pocket Books, 1979.

Jarrell, Randall. *Selected Poems*. New York: Atheneum, 1966.

Kael, Pauline. *State of the Art*. New York: Dutton, 1985.

Kaplan, Michael. Review of *Amazing Stories*. *Cinefantastique*, May 1986, 37, 53.

Kelley, Bill. Review of *Amazing Stories*. *Cinefantastique*, May 1986, 36, 54.

"Kick the Can." Broadcast February 9, 1962, on Rod Serling's CBS series *The Twilight Zone*. Producer: Buck Houghton. Director: Lamont Johnson. Script: George

Clayton Johnson. Director of Photography: George T. Clemens. Music: stock. Cast: Ernest Truex (Charles Whitley), Russell Collins (Ben Conroy), John Marley (Mr. Cox), Barry Truex (David Whitley), Marjorie Bennett (Mrs. Summers), Earle Hodgins (Agee).

"Kick the Can." Segment Two of *Twilight Zone: The Movie*. Warner Bros., 1983. Director: Steven Spielberg. Producers: Steven Spielberg and John Landis. Executive Producer: Frank Marshall. Music: Jerry Goldsmith. Story: George Clayton Johnson. Screenplay: George Clayton Johnson, Richard Matheson, and Josh Rogan. Music: Jerry Goldsmith. Director of Photography: Allen Daviau. Editor: Michael Kahn. Cast: Scatman Crothers (Mr. Bloom), Bill Quinn (Mr. Conroy), Helen Shaw (Mrs. Dempsey), Murray Matheson (Mr. Agee), Selma Diamond (Mrs. Weinstein), Martin Garner (Mr. Weinstein).

"The Mission." Universal and Amblin Entertainment 1986. Executive Producer: Steven Spielberg. Production Executives: Kathleen Kennedy, Frank Marshall. Supervising Producers: Joshua Brand, John Falsey. Producer: David E. Vogel. Developed by: Steven Spielberg, Joshua Brand, John Falsey. Director: Steven Spielberg. Story: Steven Spielberg. Teleplay: Menno Meyjes. Director of Photography: John McPherson, ASC. Production Designer: Rick Carter. Story Editor: Mick Garris. Film Editor: Steven Kemper. Music: John Williams. Starring: Casey Siemazsko (Jonathan), Kevin Costner (Captain Spark), Keifer Sutherland (Sgt. Static).

McBride, Joseph. *Steven Spielberg: A Biography*. New York: Simon and Schuster, 1997.

McDonough, Kenneth. "The Mortar of Predictability: Brickmaker Tale Gets Stuck in the Familiar." *Newsday*, September 20, 2001, B31.

Morris, Nigel. *The Cinema of Steven Spielberg: Empire of Light*. London: Wallflower, 2007.

Morrison, M. Article on *Amazing Stories*. *Times-Picayune*, 6-23-85.

Mott, Donald R. and Cheryl McAllister Saunders. *Steven Spielberg*. Boston: Twayne, 1986.

Sinyard, Neil. *The Films of Steven Spielberg*. London: Bison Books, 1986.

Slade, Darren and Nigel Watson. *Supernatural Spielberg*. London: Valis Books, 1992.

Zicree, Marc Scott. *The Twilight Zone Companion*. New York: Bantam, 1982.

11

Hook (1991)

The Peter Pan Syndrome

PETER PAN, HOOK, AND MANHOOD

Like *Last Crusade* and *Always*, *Hook* (1991) continues Spielberg's concern with converting louts into "new age sensitive guys" who are fit to be fathers. *Hook*, yet another of Spielberg's moral fables about lost children and failed fathers, is his postmodern update on *Peter Pan*, the modern fairy tale that the critic Henry Sheehan argues has been "the central animating motif in his work" (Sheehan 68). Whereas Sir James Barrie's play *Peter Pan* (1904) and his novels about the character focused on the children, Spielberg's film focuses instead on the midlife crisis of a workaholic yuppie who must overcome his failures as husband and father by rediscovering and releasing his "inner child" or rather, his "inner Pan." Bob Hoskins, who plays Smee in the movie, explains: "*Peter Pan* is about lost childhood. *Hook* is about lost fatherhood. If you take the child's love away from him, Pan the father becomes impotent" (Taylor 140). *Hook* reflects both Spielberg's childhood anger at his father for neglecting him for work and his adult conflict about becoming a father—specifically, becoming like his own father. Spielberg says that when his son was born in 1985, "I suddenly became the spitting image of my own father, with all the parental cliches—all the things I swore I would never say to my own children" (Taylor 137).

Barrie never allowed his hero to grow up: "All children, except one, grow up" (Barrie, *Pan* 1). In a sequel to *Peter Pan* (1904), the playlet, *When Wendy Grew Up: An Afterthought* (1908) (Barrie, *When Wendy Grew Up*), Wendy is a grown woman who tells her little daughter Jane a bedtime story of how, as the years passed, Peter came once a year but then gradually forgot to come. Once Jane is asleep, Peter appears, asking Wendy to fly away with him, but she says she can't because she is no longer young. When Peter starts to cry, Jane wakes up, so he flies away with her instead. At the play's conclusion, Wendy tells the nursemaid Nana that this cycle will continue with subsequent generations, "for ever and ever, dear Nana, so long as children are young and innocent" (*Wendy* 32). Thus Barrie's Pan remains the *puer aeternus* (eternal child). In *Hook*, the same situation recurs, but with a different outcome. When Peter returns to find Wendy an old lady, he falls in love with her sleeping granddaughter Moira. Instead of flying off with Moira, however, he gives her a real kiss and chooses to abandon Neverland and to grow up. Subsequently, he suffers grownup problems.

As much as it takes off from *Peter Pan*, *Hook* is also a sentimental Christmas fable which resembles Dickens's *A Christmas Carol*: a greedy businessman who is isolated from his family learns a lesson on Christmas Eve through a fantastic intervention which temporarily returns him to his childhood and transforms him from a miser to a philanthropist with love in his heart. This model of a kinder, gentler capitalist recurs in *Jurassic Park* and *Schindler's List*.

Rather than being about children like *Peter Pan*, *Hook* is much more concerned with adult male identity and with the problems of contemporary American men (and of Spielberg) as businessmen, husbands, and fathers, so it is on those issues I wish to concentrate here. "Like all of Spielberg's films, *Hook* explores how men struggle to fulfill cultural expectations of generically masculine roles" (Friedman 22). *Hook*, like the Spielberg films which immediately precede and follow it—*Indiana Jones and the Last Crusade*, *Always*, *Jurassic Park*, and *Schindler's List*—is a New Age fable about a man who must learn to be more sensitive and caring, how to be a father or father figure. On the surface, *Hook* deals with the transformation of its hero's male identity through 1980s American pop psychological moralizing about workaholism, the Jungian men's movement, the "Peter Pan syndrome," and the "inner child." Underneath, however, it is concerned with deeper male anxieties: a fear of flying which may mask a fear of sexuality, of women, of impotence, and of homoeroticism.

BARRIE AND SPIELBERG

Spielberg is not only attracted to the Peter Pan myth but may also have some psychological affinities with Sir James Barrie, a man who suffered from a Peter Pan syndrome. *Peter Pan* emerged from the unconscious conflicts of the odd Barrie, who was both a spokesman for and a victim of the Edwardian cult of childhood. *Peter Pan* is a psychosexual minefield, as one critic notes, "a narrative whose whimsy veils but does not conceal a host of unspeakable, negative emotions: anger, frustration, guilt, envy, as well as forbidden desires of several sorts" (Hammer 173). *Hook* too ventures into that minefield and deals with forbidden desires.

Barrie was the youngest of nine children, and he never grew much beyond five feet tall. When Barrie was six, his thirteen-year-old brother David died in an accident, rendering his mother inconsolable and, for a long time, bed-ridden. Little James missed her so much that he tried to become a replace-ment child for his mother by imitating David, an act which may have made his personality inauthentic and rendered him incapable of fully attaining psychological adulthood. Ironically, it also gave him a lifelong connection to childhood which nourished his capacity for playacting and made him a writer. He was very close to his mother, to whom he wrote every day, and she slept with his latest letter under her pillow.[1] The deceased brother, who never grew up because he died at thirteen, may have inspired Peter Pan. A biographer calls Barrie's "prototypic story" an Oedipal situation. Barrie identified his mother "with the heroine of all his plays and novels," and she was "the object of his conscious rivalry with the dead brother"(Geduld 27). Children who enjoy *Peter Pan* "are not, of course, consciously aware of its psychological substructure, but its enduring popularity among young people may be attributed in part to the story's correspondence to their own ineffable Oedipal fantasies"(Geduld 58). As I will argue, *Hook* too has an oedipal substructure.

According to one critic, "Barrie's fantasy—of remaining always a boy, of inheriting a group of lost boys—came true after he had written it and then turned, in life, to tragedy and disillusion" (Wullschläger 111). Barrie had a childless marriage, neglected his wife, and attached himself to the attractive Llewelyn-Davies family because he loved their five young boys. To amuse the boys, Barrie invented and acted out stories about Peter Pan, with him-self playing his namesake Captain James Hook, and he photographed the boys as the Lost Boys or Peter Pan. When their parents died tragically young, Barrie became the boys' guardian, while his neglected wife had an affair and he divorced her, never to remarry. The boys did not lead happy lives. Two died young, one in World War I, a second by drowning (a possible suicide). A third, Peter, who was identified all his life as the original Peter Pan, felt that Barrie had ruined their lives by intruding into the family. When he was sixty, long after Barrie was gone, Peter killed himself.

There has been much speculation about Barrie's sexuality. "Barrie's im-potence was much rumored in his lifetime, some wag dubbing him 'the boy who wouldn't go up'" (Birkin 180). Some suspected him of perversion because of his attachment to the five Llewelyn-Davies boys, but the young-est, Nico, said, "I never heard one word or saw one glimmer of anything approaching homosexuality or paedophilia." Nico believed Barrie was completely asexual, erotically uninterested in either gender: "He was an in-nocent—which is why he could write *Peter Pan*" (Birkin 130). But in Barrie's novel in which he first introduced Peter Pan, *The Little White Bird*, the narrator talks about undressing a little boy and taking him to his bed. And in his last letter to George Llewelyn-Davies, Barrie writes that he is "more and more wishing you were a girl of twenty-one instead of a boy, so that I could say the things to you that are now always in my heart"(Wullschläger 137). Jacqueline Rose reads *Peter Pan* as a deeply closeted homosexual and pedophiliac fantasy. If that is so, then perhaps Barrie was no innocent, neither asexual nor presexual, but possessed fantasies he could neither consciously acknowledge nor act on. Later I will discuss the possible homoerotic subtext in both *Peter Pan* and *Hook*.

I do not mean to suggest that Spielberg is in any way as odd as Barrie—Spielberg has had two normal marriages and children of his own—merely that there are certain similarities in their personalities: both suffer from "the Peter Pan syndrome." Both artists are undersized. Spielberg has described himself as a boy as being "a wimp in a world of jocks. . . . I was skinny and unpopular. . . . I had friends who were all like me. Skinny wrists and glasses. We were all just trying to make it through the year without getting our faces pushed into the drinking fountain" (McBride 68). In addition, both adored their mothers and were alienated from their fathers, and both have vivid fantasy lives rooted in the stuff of childhood.

Perhaps the major difference between Barrie and Spielberg is that while the former's work is rooted in prepubescence, Spielberg's films venture into the adolescent. Barrie said, "Nothing that happens after we are twelve matters very much" (Wullschläger 112), and his works were sexless, or at least very sexually repressed. But a colleague says of Spielberg, "He has all the virtues—and defects—of a sixteen-year-old" (Baxter 7). The awkward, adolescent eroticism of *Hook* makes manifest the sexual undercurrents of Barrie's *Peter Pan*, although it also takes away some of the subtle charm of Barrie's work.

Barrie, moreover, was only aware years later that he had been writing about himself. In 1922, when he was sixty-two, he wrote, "It is as if long after writing *Peter Pan* its true meaning came to me—desperate attempt to grow up but can't" (Wullschläger 131). Spielberg, who has undergone psychotherapy, was well aware when he made *Hook* that it was in part a way of working through his own conflicts: that the son Jack is Spielberg as child, resenting his father's neglect of him, and that the protagonist Peter Banning is a composite of Spielberg's father and Spielberg as father. The film is self-consciously and self-reflexively psychoanalytic (Morris 184). When the adult Peter Banning first confronts Tinker Bell, he defends himself through psychobabble: "You're a complex Freudian hallucination, having something to do with my mother. . . ." Unfortunately, Spielberg's greater self-awareness than Barrie does not necessarily make *Hook* more psychologically resonant than *Peter Pan*. To the contrary: *Pan* remains powerful precisely due to the force of repression, to all that remains unstated, whereas *Hook*'s overt use of 1980s pop psychology makes it seem overly schematic.

1980s POP PSYCHOLOGY IN *HOOK*

Spielberg loads *Hook* with moral lessons derived from four trends in American pop psychology of the 1980s and early 1990s: workaholism, the Jungian men's movement (especially the influence of Robert Bly), the "Peter Pan syndrome," and the "inner child." By structuring this therapeutic comedy around these notions to help him understand and attempt to heal the dilemma of many contemporary middle-class American males, Spielberg also sheds some light on his personal dilemma as he struggled to grow up and to balance the conflicting demands of his roles as artist, adult (husband and recent father), and perpetual child.

The first term, "workaholic," came into vogue in 1971. In late twentieth-century America, the "addiction" model created new categories of behavorial disorder: suddenly, people were described as "addicted" to computers, video games, sex, or work. No doubt workaholism existed prior to 1971, but soon after the term was invented, it caught on. Suddenly, workaholism seemed epidemic, perhaps because the 1980s, the age of Reagan, was also the age of the "yuppie," when the children of the 1960s, now married and with children of their own, devoted themselves to careers and to making money, a trend that intensified with the economic boom of the 1990s. Workaholics are obsessive and driven by ambition. Narcissism and paranoia take over, and they become anxious when not working. The workaholic is "emotionally crippled and addicted to power and control in a compulsive drive to gain approval and success . . . they gradually become personally irresponsible and lose their capacity to be loving and intimate" (Killinger 6–7).

Peter Banning, the protagonist of *Hook*, is such a man. His cell phone, which is never off, ties him to work and interferes with his family time; even while watching his daughter in a school play, he feels compelled to answer its ring. His wife finally becomes so annoyed that she grabs the phone out of his hand and tosses it out the window.

Apart from its function in the plot, the portrait of the workaholic Peter Banning critiques some characteristics of Spielberg's father, Arnold Spielberg, and of Spielberg himself. An electronics engineer who worked his way up in the growing computer industry after World War II, Arnold Spielberg moved his family every few years from state to state—from Ohio to New Jersey to Arizona, and finally to California—as opportunities opened in the new field. "I always felt my father put his work before me," Steven Spielberg has said. "I always thought he loved me less than his work and I suffered as a result" (McBride 41). "He left home at 7 a.m. and sometimes didn't get home until 9 or 10 p.m. I missed him to the point of resenting him" (Baxter 18). Arnold Spielberg acknowledges that he did this when stressed, especially during the breakup of his marriage, when Steven Spielberg was a teenager: "I plunge deeper into work, to compensate." Consequently, Steven Spielberg experienced his father as a distant, aloof figure (McBride 42).

Like his father, Spielberg is extremely ambitious and work-oriented. He says, "My workaholism is a real weakness. Because I nourish it, and when I don't have to work, I do anyway. It's a problem, and I'm working on it. . . . It's not a disease, though: I love to make movies so much . . ." (Breskin 78). Ironically, he has to *work* at not working so much. Part of it is an avoidance of emotional intimacy, preferring his creative work to relating to people. When Amy Irving, later his wife, visited him on the set of *Close Encounters*, he said, "I wish she hadn't come. She keeps crying and I keep wanting to say, 'Don't you understand, I'm fucking my movie'" (McBride 296). When he saw the script for *Hook*, "I related to the main character, Peter Banning . . . a 'type A' personality. I think a lot of people today are . . . so self-involved with work and success and arriving at the next plateau that children and family almost become incidental. . . . I have even experienced it myself when I have been on a very tough shoot and I've not seen my kids except on weekends. . . . And I've been both guilty and wanting to do something about it" (Bahiana, 154).

The feminist critic Marleen Barr praises Spielberg as an "antipatriarchal fabulator" who "exemplifies Hollywood entrepreneurial manhood critiquing itself. . . . His enactment of manhood involves functioning as both a nurturer and a businessman" (Barr 113). She argues that *Hook*, although not a feminist narrative, is "a male-centered tale that critiques manhood" (122). By rejecting the workaholic notion of entrepreneurial manhood, Spielberg, she claims, opens up the possibility of "new master narratives about gender roles" (121).

In that regard, however, *Hook* seems to me not so much novel as trendy, reflecting the changing views of manhood of the American men's movement of the 1980s and 1990s and the more nurturing model of manhood, both new ways to shore up a crumbling patriarchy. Patricia Pace argues that the transformation of Peter Banning resembles "the series of 'awakenings' detailed in the books of the Jungian men's movement, and most often associated with Robert Bly, James Hillman, and John Rowan" (Pace 160). In his 1990 best-seller *Iron John*, Bly argues that contemporary men have an intense "father hunger" because of debased images of fathers in popular culture and the broken father-son bond. Younger men need initiation rituals led by older men, he claims, and "fairy stories, legends, myths, hearth stories" hold the clues to such ceremonies (Bly xi). Through participation in rituals, men can get in touch with archetypes of primal masculinity such as the "Wild Man," accessing the inner "warrior" and also becoming more nurturing. *Hook's* Peter Banning follows Robert Bly's formula: he finds the key to his manhood in the fairy story of *Peter Pan,* and by participating in rituals (not with older men but with the Lost Boys) he becomes both the warrior Pan and a more nurturing father.

Fred Pfeil calls 1991 "the year of living sensitively" and sees such transformed heroes in a series of films released the same year as *Hook,* including *City Slickers, Regarding Henry, The Doctor,* and *The Fisher King.* In fact, I believe that heroes who are transformed into "New Age sensitive guys" enter Hollywood films a year or two earlier, with Spielberg's *Always* (1989), *Pretty Woman* (1990), and *Dances with Wolves* (1990). But by 1991 the trend was clear. Pfeil speaks of a series of films "explicitly concerned with the conversion of their white male protagonists from one or another variant of closed-down, alienated boor to an opened-up, sensitive guy" (Pfeil 37). At the end of *Hook,* the patriarchy is restored and capitalism is redeemed, albeit with a more nurturing father in charge.

Aside from "workaholism" and the Jungian men's movement, *Hook* also relies on the pop psychological trend of the "Peter Pan" syndrome, a term coined in *The Peter Pan Syndrome: Men Who Have Never Grown Up* (1983), by Dan Kiley, which was influenced by feminist critiques about the supposed infantilism of many baby boomer men. The boomers, Spielberg's generation, grew up in an American youth culture that valued the qualities of childhood and adolescence, such as intensity, spontaneity, imagination, and the drive toward freedom and individuality. "Never trust anyone over thirty" was a slogan of 1960s youth. But once this generation was over thirty, clinging to adolescence could become a problem. Kiley blamed this perpetual adolescence on unhappy parents who spoiled their children, producing sons who were poorly adjusted to reality, feared growing up, and avoided adult responsibility and commitment. Kiley's argument resembles the conservative scolding of "permissive parenting" as the source of all of society's problems since the 1960s. Moreover, such childish men may have always existed, and he does not explain why the supposed syndrome affects men more than women. Although the "Peter Pan syndrome" has never been medically accepted, within the last twenty years the term has become deeply rooted in American pop psychology.[2]

In 1985, two years after the release of Kiley's book, Spielberg said, "I have always felt like Peter Pan. I still feel like Peter Pan. It has been very hard for me to grow up. . . . I'm a victim of the Peter Pan syndrome." Spielberg's mother, Leah Adler, explains, "We're all for immaturity in my family. The rule at home was, 'Just don't be an adult.' Who needs to be anything but ten?" Spielberg says, "We never grew up at home, because *she* never grew up" (McBride 42). This sentiment is reflected in *Hook.* When Granny Wendy greets Peter and Moira Banning's children Jack and Maggie, she says there is only one rule in her home: "No growing up. Stop this very instant," echoing Spielberg's mother. So Spielberg does seem partly to fit Kiley's "syndrome." For many years, Spielberg was also friends with Michael Jackson, who created his "Neverland" ranch as a private fantasy world dedicated to perpetual childhood so he would never have to grow up.

E.T. (1982) includes a scene in which the mother reads from Barrie's classic story to her little daughter. After E.T., there were rumors that Spielberg was going to film *Peter Pan*, a movie he seemed destined to make. In fact, Spielberg says the film was ready to go, a musical with nine songs by John Williams. But in 1985 he abandoned the project, after his son Max was born: "the last thing I wanted was to raise nine kids in London . . . instead of being with my own son, raising *him*. And I think I lost interest in the theme of the boy who refuses to grow up" (Taylor 70). Upon becoming a father, Spielberg felt he finally had to grow up. Yet five years later, he returned to the theme in *Hook*, perhaps to overcome the Peter Pan syndrome once and for all.

Banning's Peter Pan syndrome in *Hook* is reinforced by his workaholism because both are aspects of his narcissism and his flight from adult roles as husband and father. As Jeffrey Satinover writes about the *puer* or perpetually childish personality, "some *puers* are overworkers who are unable to stop working and enjoy the fruits of their labors" (Satinover 152).

The therapeutic concept of "the inner child" is the final pop psychological trend of the 1980s and 1990s on which *Hook* relies, elaborated in such books as *Reclaiming the Inner Child*, edited by Jeremiah Abrams (1990), and *Homecoming: Reclaiming and Championing Your Inner Child* by John Bradshaw (1992), which claim that psychologically wounded adults can only be healed by rediscovering and reintegrating their repressed, lost, or abused childhood selves. John Bradshaw was a consultant on the script of *Hook* and present on the set during filming. Spielberg cast Bradshaw's daughter in the film, and it was rumored that he was in analysis with Bradshaw (McBride 400).

Most of the "inner child" therapists depend on the psychoanalyst C. G. Jung's notion of the child archetype. As Jung writes, "The 'child' symbolizes the pre-conscious and the post-conscious essence of man" (Jung 29) and "if . . . the childhood state of the collective psyche is repressed to the point of total exclusion, the unconscious content overwhelms the conscious aim and inhibits, falsifies, even destroys its realization. Viable progress only comes from the cooperation of both" (Jung 28). The psychologist Nathaniel Branden summarizes the therapy that derived from Jung's notion of the child archetype: "The child-self is the internal representation of the child we once were . . . and that enjoys psychological immortality as a component of our total self. It is a *sub*self, a *sub*personality —a mind state that can be more or less dominant at any given time. . . ." But "when the child-self is left unconscious, or is disowned and repudiated, we are fragmented; we do not feel whole; in some measure we are self-alienated." The rejected child-self can turn into a "'troublemaker' that obstructs our evolution as well as our enjoyment of existence . . . we will at times exhibit harmfully childish behavior, or fall into patterns of inappropriate dependency, or become narcissistic. . . . On the other hand, recognized, accepted, embraced, and thereby integrated, a child-self can be a magnificent resource that enriches our lives, with its potential for spontaneity, playfulness, and imaginativeness" (Branden 243–44).

At the start of *Hook*, Peter Banning is a middle-aged man suffering total amnesia about his childhood before the age of twelve or thirteen, that is, before puberty—his apparent age when Granny Wendy arranged his adoption—and he has completely repressed his childhood identity as Pan. As "inner child" therapists such as Branden would describe it, he is self-alienated and narcissistic, cut off from his wife and children, emotionally irresponsible, and inappropriately dependent on work for his identity. He exhibits "harmfully childish behavior," such as playing a game of fast draw at his office with a cell phone when he should be attending his son's baseball game. The transformational moment comes when he glimpses his reflection in a pool in Neverland: staring back at him he sees his child-self, Peter Pan. From that moment on, he is able to access this repressed self and reintegrate it to heal his personality. As Spielberg says, Banning "rescued that memory of himself as a child and carried that best friend with him the rest of his life" (McBride 412). *Hook* depends upon the therapeutic logic of the "inner child" movement of the 1980s and 1990s for its moral lessons.

FEAR OF FLYING

It is not in its surface, pop psychology and didactic moralizing but in deep fears that the unconscious interests of the film lie. As we have seen, Spielberg's films frequently deal with his fears and phobias, acted out and overcome by his protagonists, such as David Mann's highway fears and paranoia in *Duel*, or Chief Brody's fear of water in *Jaws*, or Indiana Jones's snake phobia, or Peter Banning's fear of flying in *Hook*. As McBride says, "Spielberg often is mistakenly accused of having an overly sunny view of life, but the phobias he has wrestled with since childhood have deeply affected his work" (McBride 357).

Spielberg says what first attracted him to the Peter Pan myth was not the idea of perpetual youth but flying, although he has always been profoundly ambivalent about flight: "my first memory of anybody flying is in *Peter Pan*. . . . I am absolutely fascinated and terrified by flying. It is a big deal in my movies. All my movies have airplanes in them. . . . To me, flying is synonymous with freedom and unlimited imagination but, interestingly enough, I'm afraid to fly. . . . I'm only not afraid to fly in my dreams and in my movies, but in real life, I'm terrified of flying. Just like the Peter Banning character in the beginning of *Hook*. . . . I'm aware of the psychoanalytic implications of flight but, no, I have never been analyzed. . . . I think I need it, but I'm always afraid that if I get psychoanalyzed my movies will suffer because I'll become more intellectual about them" (Bahiana 153–54).

Spielberg is being disingenuous here because elsewhere he admits, "I saw a shrink—primarily to get out of the Army—when I was eighteen" (McBride 132). He would also have been suffering the effects of his parents' recent divorce when he was eighteen. In 1987, before his own divorce, he went again: "All my friends went to therapy and I thought that maybe I would learn something about myself, so I went for a year. . . . Everything I learned about myself I knew already or I'd guessed for myself" (400). McBride claims that Spielberg is so involved in his heroes' neuroses in *Indiana Jones and the Last Crusade* (1989), *Always* (1989), and *Hook* (1991)—the three films released immediately after his 1987 therapy and his 1989 divorce—that they resemble "cinematic Rorschach inkblots" (400).

When Spielberg mentions that he is "aware of the psychoanalytic implications of flight," he probably alludes to the well-known Freudian notion that dreams of flying have a thinly disguised erotic content. A fear of flying would therefore suggest a fear of sexuality. Freud believed that dreams of flying are related "to games involving movement, which are extraordinarily attractive to children. . . . It not uncommonly happens that these games of movement, though innocent in themselves, give rise to sexual feelings. Childish romping . . . is what is repeated in dreams of flying, falling, giddiness, and so on" (Freud, *Interpretations*, 428–29). Freud also mentions other theorists who believe that dreams of flying are dreams of erection (Freud 430).

"Childish romping," climaxing in dreamlike flying, describes *Hook*. When his children Jack and Maggie are captured by Captain Hook, Peter Banning is forced to return to Neverland to recover his former identity and long-dormant powers as Pan (to "fly, fight, and crow") through childish romping with the lost boys. However, there is too much heavy handed childish romping in the movie and too little flying.

Banning, who suffers from a phobia so intense that he grows white-knuckled in airplanes, achieves a breakthrough when he finally recovers his boyhood ability to fly. Banning flies across the sun as Pan, like Elliott soaring across the moon on his bicycle in *E.T.* Because of the hero's fear of flying and related problems with his masculine identity, the scenes of flight in *Hook* function as erotic release and rejuvenation: "Banning is virtually ejaculated into the air and catapulted off to confront Hook, whom he now calls 'old man'" (Pace 162).

MALE IDENTITY AND PHALLIC SYMBOLS IN *HOOK*

Fear of flying, as we have seen, has to do with problems of male identity. *Hook*, like so many Spielberg films, is about failed, impotent fathers and lost children and revolves around the displacement, loss, and final restoration of potency on the part of father and son. The problems of male identity of the two are connected: Jack rebels against his father not because his father is too masculine but because Banning is not man enough. Jack suffers from what Robert Bly calls the "father hunger." Not until Banning assumes his proper role as husband and father will Jack be comfortable as his son, and probably for that reason, *Hook* is filled with more phallic symbols—a baseball, a cell phone, watches and clocks, a hook, and a sword—than most Spielberg films.

Jack is associated with a baseball. Because his father failed to show up for the crucial last game, Jack is unnerved and strikes out. Later, aboard the plane to London, Jack rebels against his father by repeatedly bouncing the ball against the roof of the cabin. In London, Hook steals Jack's ball, but in Neverland, attempting to become Jack's surrogate father, he not only returns it but also stages a game so Jack can hit a home run to undo

Hook: A film about insecure male identity,
Hook is filled with phallic symbols. Columbia, 1991.

the damage caused by his father's absence at the previous game. The ball soars into the empyrean and disappears, a magical image of flight and of restored potency.

In the next scene, when the ball descends, it hits Banning in the head, a fortunate blow which leads directly to the recovery of his childhood memories and of his identity as Pan. The "happy thought" which finally enables Banning to fly again as Peter Pan is remembering the birth of his son, the moment he became a father. Thus the restoration of the son's potency also restores the father's.

In the movie's introductory scenes, Jack and his baseball are as inseparable as Banning and his phone, visually linked through match cutting: as Jack in the outfield stretches to catch the ball, his father at work catches the phone. While the children onstage sing "We want to be little Peter Pans, we don't want to grow up," Banning in the audience answers his phone, the image of everything odious about adulthood and the anti-Pan Banning has become. His wife eventually tosses his phone out the window because it threatens the family by taking him away from his role as husband and father and into his all-consuming role as businessman. Banning's constant use of the phone in front of his wife and children, like Jack's bouncing the baseball, is deliberately defiant. But there is also something guilty and shamefaced about the act, as if it is displaced masturbation. The phone is phallic: when it rings, he pulls out its extending antenna. He wears the phone on a holster on his hip, like a gun, and engages in a mock game of fast draw with his assistant Brad, which he wins, proving he is "the fastest phone in the West." Until he goes to Neverland, he puts Brad ahead of his family. So aside from its masturbatory implications, the phone calls represent a homoerotic bonding which also threatens the family.

Banning's masculine identity is also connected with his check book. When Hook and his men expect Banning to draw a gun, knife, or sword, he pulls out a checkbook, the weapon of a businessman, but Hook, quickly shooting a hole in it with his pistol, shows Banning's impotence in the pirate world.

Banning's watch is another image of potency. In London, trying to make amends for breaking his promise about the baseball game, he gives Jack the watch: "Jack, this is my very special watch, so you can keep track of the time." In Neverland, encouraged by Hook to rebel against his father, Jack smashes the watch.

Hook is paranoid about clocks and watches ever since Pan cut off Hook's right hand in a sword fight and fed it to a crocodile; the croc kept returning to devour the rest of the Captain, its presence signaled by the ticking clock it had swallowed. When Hook killed the huge reptile, he had it stuffed and mounted as a clock tower which tells faulty time. His fear of the croc has been replaced by a phobia about all clocks and watches, which he compulsively smashes. For Spielberg, the clock is a symbol of aging and mortality:

Hook: The homoerotic bond of Hook and Smee: the hook as fetish. Columbia, 1991.

"We are all afraid, like Hook, of that big clock in our lives. And when you have kids, the clock goes faster" (Taylor 139). But another way to see Hook is as a classic neurotic: all timepieces remind him of his traumatic loss.

Hook's prosthetic hand, his hook, is both a weapon and a sort of detachable phallus. The "missing hand and its steel replacement conflate both the fact and the threat of castration" (Morris 180). The hook stands for Hook and functions as a fetish with a life of its own, an object of worship. Before we first see Hook, we see his shiny hook being sharpened and then carried on a velvet cushion by his boatswain Smee, to the admiration of the pirates, who chant "Hook, hook, give us the hook!" suggesting both the Captain's name and his prosthesis. Smee helps the Captain put the hook on and off: with it on, Hook is triumphant; without it, he seems incomplete and helpless. According to Charles Rycroft, "Fetishists can be said to regard their fetish as being 'inhabited by a spirit,' since the fetish is clearly associated with a person without being one, and as having 'magical powers,' since its presence gives them the potency they otherwise lack" (Rycroft 51). When the Captain lets a prostitute touch his hook, she is thrilled. Banning, aided by the Lost Boys, attempts to steal the hook, as if stealing the Captain's potency. But he fails in the theft, unmanned when he sees that Hook has displaced him in Jack's affections.

If Banning the businessman is associated with the cell phone, the check-book, and the watch, then Pan is associated with the sword. A masculine contest ensues over this sword, which is first possessed by Rufio, the ado-lescent boy who in Peter's absence has become "the Pan," the leader of the Lost Boys. Rufio at first shows contempt for his old and weak rival, cutting Banning's belt with the sword so his pants fall down. When Banning finally recovers his ability to fly, he retaliates and does the same to Rufio. Rufio, with sword drawn, advances menacingly, only to kneel before Banning and relinquish it, acknowledging the supremacy of Banning as the Pan. The ear-lier shot of a reduced Banning framed between Rufio's legs is now matched by one of Rufio framed between Pan's legs, and Pan echoes Rufio's earlier action of drawing a line in the sand with the sword.

PETER AND HOOK AS DOUBLES

According to Henry Sheehan, Hook is "Peter's dark double. . . . Jack and Mag-gie are gone because Peter has wished them gone. Hook is merely the agent of Peter's most repressed desires, and as such is his mirror image" (Sheehan 70–71). There are many parallels between the two characters, aside from their

Hook: Hook as evil father tries to remake Jack in his image. Columbia, 1991.

rivalry for Jack's affection: both are crippled by phobias (fear of flying or fear of clocks); are narcissists (Hook preens before triple mirrors) who require the uncritical adoration of a band of followers (pirates or Lost Boys); are hypermasculine yet childish; and are child-haters. Hook is the cruel Captain of an all-male band of pirates which Maggie says is because he has no mother. Yet Smee is a kind of nursemaid who mothers Hook, coddling his master and intervening to prevent his ritual suicide attempts, ploys to attract Smee's attention. He also encourages Hook to play with a toy ship to distract him from his worries. The intimacy between the two is like that of mother and child. "I want to go beddy-bye," says Hook, and Smee helps him undress and sings him the lullaby "Rock a Bye, Baby." Despite his childishness, Hook is a kid-hater who kidnaps and mistreats Pan's children and intensely desires to kill Pan. Banning, like Hook, engages in hostile takeovers as a pirate in the male-dominated business world. Jack admires his father's role, using nautical metaphors, "When a big company is in trouble, Dad sails in, and if there's any resistance—any resistance, and he blows 'em out of the water." To which Granny Wendy says wryly, "Peter, you've become a pirate." Also like Hook, Banning is cruel to Jack and Maggie. At first he neglects them, but in Wendy's home he "pulls, pushes, yells at, and actively rejects his kids" (Sheehan 70).

If Banning and Hook are doubles, they are also rivals. "In Spielberg's metaphoric ceremony of manhood, Pan must defeat Hook, at once the rival father and the disturbing spectre of the feminized male" (Pace 162). When Hook constructs initiation ceremonies to make Jack his son—a classroom lesson, a ritual smashing of his father's clock/phallus, a (rigged) baseball game, and ultimately dressing him as Hook, Jr. before preparing to pierce his ear to make him a pirate—Banning, now transformed back into Pan, disrupts this final ritual to reclaim his son.

The hypermasculinity of Hook and Banning depends upon props—the hook or the cell phone—without which both feel impotent. Hook is also "feminized" through his hysteria about time and his histrionic suicide threats (Pace 162), just as Banning is feminized through his phobia and his humiliating early failure to rescue Jack and Maggie. The film suggests that these childish and insecure men are momma's boys: Peter Pan ran away from his mother only to be mothered by Tink, Wendy, and Moira; and Hook's last word before the crocodile swallows him is "Mommy!" Even more, they behave at times like closeted gays, as in Hook's intimacy with Smee or Banning's preference for Brad over Moira.

Marjorie Garber reads Barrie's play *Peter Pan* as a drag show because it carried on the traditions of the English pantomime, in which the Dame was played by a man and the Principal Boy by a woman. For a century, it has been traditional for Peter Pan to be played onstage by a woman. In addition, Hook shows many of the affectations of a stereotyped aging queen, including fastidiousness, vanity, dandy dress, and a wig. Hook, according to

Garber, "is as much a figure for (as well as of) cross dressing as Peter. . . . The hints that Peter is himself a version of Hook, or that he might become so, contribute to the sense that cross-gender representation is itself at stake in *Peter Pan*" (Garber 181). *Hook* also has some aspects of a drag show: Dustin Hoffman's version of Hook "resembles a female impersonator" (Pace 162). When Banning shows up dressed as Pan, Hook admires that the grown Pan can still "fit into those smashing tights," as if they were rival drag queens.

WOMEN IN *HOOK*

Moira, Wendy, and Tinker Bell, the three main women characters in *Hook*, all love Peter with a mix of romantic adoration and maternal scolding. They are male-created variations on the same figure: the woman as lover and mother, as sexual aggressor, and as superego figure and rescuer. Although Moira, Banning's wife, is devoted to her children, and a strong woman on whom he relies, mostly we see her scold him for neglecting the children. Their romance is limited to a kiss when they first meet as children and another when they reconcile at the end of the film.

Wendy is another strong mother figure, symbolic mother to hundreds of lost boys whose adoptions she arranged. Her relationship with Banning is a complicated, oedipal one. When they were children the same age, she felt unrequited love for Peter Pan, but he only loved her as a surrogate mother figure. As she grew older, Peter did not age, until she functioned literally as his stepmother, whom he calls "Granny Wendy," and he transferred his romantic desires to her granddaughter Moira. Perhaps because of their generationally confused relationship, Banning has grown alienated from Wendy and not seen her for ten years, the years in which he became a father. The most blatantly oedipal scene in the film occurs when Granny Wendy tells Banning the story of his life as she flirts with him. She touches his face and toys with his vest, pulling him toward her in her bed as the camera lingers in a painfully intimate two-shot, saying, "You know, when I was young, no other girl held your favor the way I did. I half expected you to alight on the church and forbid my vows on my wedding day. I wore a pink satin sash. But you didn't come." To see the ninety-year-old Wendy behave like a jilted lover toward the forty-year-old Banning makes both the hero and the audience uncomfortable.

Like Wendy, Tink is surrogate mother and unrequited lover of Peter who repeatedly mothers and rescues him only to lose him. Having brought him to Neverland when he was an infant and raised him, when she loses him to Moira she is crestfallen. When Peter is an adult, she flies him back to Neverland to be reborn, again swaddling him in a sheet like an infant (Pace 161). She saves him from Hook and the pirates, intercedes on his behalf with the Lost Boys, and acts as Banning's cheerleader to turn him back into the

Peter Pan she loved. Like Wendy, she is sexually aggressive toward the hero, the son whom she wants as lover. The painfully uncomfortable scene when Granny Wendy flirts with Banning in her bed is paralleled by the awkward scene when the tomboyish Tink, suddenly grown into a full-size woman and dressed in a beautiful gown, kisses Banning on the lips.[3]

In all the male-female relationships in *Hook*, the hero is passive while the women are an aggressive combination of lover and mother, as in the scene in which three beautiful mermaids rescue Banning, saving him from drowning by using kisses as mouth-to-mouth resuscitation.

The three main mother figures in *Hook*—Moira, Wendy, and Tink—are much stronger than the childish and insecure father figures, Hook and Banning, which is especially significant because of the absence of other fathers in the film. Wendy is a grandmother, but there is no mention of her husband. The only man in her household is the childish, senile Tootles, a Lost Boy she adopted. Hook wants Smee to function as his mother, and at the end he cries out for Mommy, not Daddy. The pirates grow misty-eyed when little Maggie sings a song about missing her mother. The Lost Boy Thud misses his mother but not his father, and Peter remembers his mother but not his father. Peter ran away as an infant so as not to grow up like his father, a judge; ironically, he becomes a lawyer. And we learn nothing about his American stepfather Hank Banning. Peter says he chose to grow up and stop being Pan so he could become a father, but it is no wonder he does such a poor job of it because he seems to have had no paternal role models. The strong mothers and weak fathers in the film may indirectly reflect Spielberg's situation growing up in a household filled with women—his mother and his three younger sisters—where the mother dominated and the father was usually absent.

CONCLUSION: THE CHILD AS FATHER TO THE MAN

Although *Hook* was a box office hit, most reviews were negative. A repeated complaint was that the film was overproduced: the expensive, cluttered sets of Neverland looked too much like stage sets, weighing down the fantasy. One review called it an abortive musical in which the big production numbers lack song and dance (Canby). Perhaps that was because Spielberg originally planned it as a musical, but only traces remain: the children in the school play sing a few lines about "We wanna be little Peter Pans; we don't wanna grow up"; the pirates briefly chant "Hook, hook, give us the hook"; and little Maggie sings the one full-length song. Other reviewers felt that scenes went on too long or over-relied on heavy-handed slapstick and that most of the scenes of Peter with the Lost Boys are unfunny. If it is perhaps amusing to see the adult burglars outsmarted by the boy hero in *Home Alone* (1990), it is embarrassing to see the adult hero humiliated by a group of boys in *Hook*, and even more embarrassing when he descends to their level with an exchange of gross insults and a food fight.[4] James Barrie's *Peter Pan* offers imaginative play, not simply fooling around.

While he was making it, Spielberg knew that *Hook* was not his best work: "For some reason this movie was such a dinosaur coming out of the gate. It dragged me along behind it. . . . Every day I came on to the set, I thought, Is this flying out of control?" (McBride 412). Ironically, for a director who fears flying, his film was "flying out of control." Spielberg had not expressed such negative feelings about a film since his overproduced slapstick farce *1941* (1979), to which some critics compared *Hook* (Hicks; Scheib).

The most significant failing of *Hook*, however, is that Spielberg had proved in films such as *E.T.*, *Poltergeist*, *The Color Purple*, or *Empire of the Sun* that he could tap sensitively into the joys and terrors of childhood, yet *Hook* "isn't for or even about children. *Hook* caters to those self-involved baby-boomers who are now parents and see movies like this as a chance to wax sentimental about their own childhood" (Hennessy). Another reviewer agrees: "But, honestly, who cares about Pan the man; it's the boy we want. Leave the problems of the grown-ups looking for lost childhoods to the pop psychologists forging theories of Peter Pan syndromes . . ." (Baumgarten). In sum, *Hook* was a misstep. Under the guise of updating *Peter Pan*, Spielberg constructed instead an uncomfortable psychodrama about his lost childhood and his midlife crisis as grownup and parent.

"The child" is not a fixed symbol; the idea of the child changes historically and culturally. *Peter Pan* was written in 1904, during the golden age of English children's literature, the Victorian and Edwardian age, which created a cult of childhood in which James Barrie participated. The Victorians and Edwardians romanticized and sentimentalized the child and saw children "as a symbol, in a prosperous, progressive society of hope and optimism" (Wullschläger 12). The child then symbolized the confidence, hope, and belief in their own moral innocence of the British empire prior to World War I. But in America in 1991, when *Hook* appeared, the child was called upon to perform a very different function: to be father to the man and to shore up a patriarchy in crisis and the troubled nuclear family in a shaky American empire. *Peter Pan* is about children, but *Hook* is about a father who wants to rediscover his "inner child," which is something else entirely, and not the stuff of great children's literature.

NOTES

1. See also Howard Kissel's discussion of Barrie's obsession with his mother.
2. Kiley coined another term inspired by J. M. Barrie in his book *The Wendy Dilemma*, but that term never caught on. More recently the supposed Peter Pan syndrome

was given a Jungian interpretation in Ann Yeoman and Marion Woodman's *Now or Neverland.*

3. Tink's transformation recalls similar scenes in *Raiders of the Lost Ark* and *Always* when the tomboy, pants-wearing heroine suddenly appears as a sexy woman in an evening gown, surprising and awing the boys. Such scenes seem like adolescent male fantasies.

4. For a sampling of negative reviews, see Baumgarten, Canby, Ebert, Hennessy, Hicks, Howe, and Scheib. Friedman finds the film artificial and overstuffed and says it "ultimately sinks under its own bloated weight" (Friedman 24–25). The movie is primarily about the adult Pan, yet it often tries to appeal to a much younger audience. Morris says such scenes as the food fight embarrass "adults excluded by the movie's mode of address" (Morris188).

REFERENCES

Abrams, Jeremiah, ed. *Reclaiming the Inner Child.* Los Angeles: Jeremy P. Tarcher, 1990.

Bahiana, Ana Maria. *"Hook." Steven Spielberg Interviews*, ed. Lester D. Friedman and Brent Notbohm. Jackson: University of Mississippi Press, 2000.

Barr, Marleen. *Lost in Space: Probing Feminist Science Fiction and Beyond.* Chapel Hill: University of North Carolina, 1993.

Barrie, J. M. *Peter Pan.* 1911; New York: Charles Scribner's Sons, 1980.

———. *When Wendy Grew Up: An Afterthought.* 1908; New York: Dutton, 1958.

Baumgarten, Marjorie. Review of *Hook. Austin Chronicle*, December 13, 1991.

Baxter, John. *Steven Spielberg.* London: HarperCollins, 1996.

Birkin, Andrew. *J. M. Barrie and the Lost Boys.* New Haven, CT: Yale University Press, 2003.

Bly, Robert. *Iron John: A Book About Men.* New York: Addison-Wesley, 1990.

Bradshaw, John. *Homecoming: Reclaiming and Championing Your Inner Child.* New York: Bantam, 1992.

Branden, Nathaniel. "Integrating the Younger Self." Ed. Jeremiah Abrams. *Reclaiming the Inner Child.* Los Angeles: Jeremy P. Tarcher, 1990, 242–47.

Breskin, David. "The *Rolling Stone* Interview: Steven Spielberg." *Rolling Stone*, October 24, 1985.

Canby, Vincent. "Peter as a Middle-Aged Master of the Universe." *New York Times*, December 1991.

Ebert, Roger. Review of *Hook. Chicago Sun-Times*, December 11, 1991. www.suntimes .com/ebert/ebert reviews/1991/12/684934.html

Friedman, Lester D. *Citizen Spielberg.* Urbana: University of Illinois Press, 2006.

Freud, Sigmund. *The Interpretation of Dreams.* Trans. James Strachey. 1900; New York: Avon, 1965.

Garber, Marjorie. *Vested Interests: Cross-Dressing and Cultural Anxiety.* New York: Routledge, 1992.

Geduld, Harry M. *Sir James Barrie.* New York: Twayne, 1971.

Hammer, Stephanie Barbé. "Nasty Boys, Feminine Longing, and Mourning the Mother in J. M. Barrie's *Peter Pan* and Anne Rice's *The Witching Hour." Nursery Realms: Chil-*

dren in the World of Science Fiction, Fantasy, and Horror. Ed. Gary Westfahl and George Slusser. Athens: The University of Georgia Press, 1999, 171–84.

Hennessy, Doug. Review of *Hook*. filmcritic.com 2003. www.filmcritic.com/misc/ emporium.nsf/84dbbfa4d710144986256c290016f76e/50fd0a4ca6dc77f288256d 99000a2b1e?OpenDocument&Highlight=0,Hook

Hicks, Chris. Review of *Hook. Deseret Morning News*, December 11, 1991. http:// deseretnews.com/movies/print/1,4194,'1418',00.html?curTitle=Peter+Pan

Howe, Desson. *Washington Post*, December 13, 1991. n.49.

Jung, C.G. "The Psychology of the Child Archetype." *Reclaiming the Inner Child*. Jeremiah Abrams, ed. Los Angeles: Jeremy P. Tarcher, 1990, 24–30.

Kiley, Dan. *The Peter Pan Syndrome: Men Who Have Never Grown Up*. New York: Dodd Mead, 1983.

———. *The Wendy Dilemma : When Women Stop Mothering Their Men*. New York: Random House, 1986.

Killinger, Barbara. *Workaholics: The Respectable Addicts*. Richmond Hills, Ont.: Firefly Books, 1997.

Kissel, Howard. "Peter Pan." *Horizon* 22 (December 1970): 19–24.

McBride, Joseph. *Steven Spielberg: A Biography*. New York: Simon and Schuster, 1997.

Morris, Nigel. *The Cinema of Steven Spielberg: Empire of Light*. London: Wallflower, 2007.

Pace, Patricia. "Robert Bly Does Peter Pan: The Inner Child as Father to the Man in Steven Spielberg's *Hook*." *The Films of Steven Spielberg: Critical Essays*. Ed. Charles L. P. Silet. Lanham, MD: Scarecrow Press, 2002, 159–67.

Pfeil, Fred. *White Guys: Studies in Postmodern Domination and Difference*. New York: Verso, 1995.

Rose, Jacqueline. *The Case of Peter Pan: Of the Impossibility of Children's Fiction*. London: Macmillan, 1984.

Rycroft, Charles. *A Dictionary of Psychoanalysis*. Totowa, NJ: Littlefield, Adams, 1973.

Satinover, Jeffrey. "The Childhood Self and the Origins of Puer Psychology." *Reclaiming the Inner Child*. Ed. Jeremiah Abrams. Los Angeles: Jeremy P. Tarcher, 1990, 144–55.

Scheib, Richard. Review of *Hook*. 1991. wysiwig://16http://members.fortunecity .com/roogulator/fantasy/hook.html

Sheehan, Henry. "Spielberg II." *Film Comment* 28.4 (July–August 1992): 66–71.

Taylor, Philip. *Steven Spielberg: The Man, His Movies and Their Meaning*. 3rd edition. New York: Continuum, 1999.

Wullschläger, Jackie. *Inventing Wonderland: The Lives and Fantasies of Lewis Carroll, Edward Lear, J. M. Barrie, Kenneth Grahame and A. A. Milne*. New York: Free Press, 1995.

Yeoman, Ann and Marion Woodman. *Now or Neverland: Peter Pan and the Myth of Eternal Youth: A Psychological Perspective on a Cultural Icon*. New York: Inner City Books, 1999.

12

Jurassic Park (1993) and *The Lost World: Jurassic Park* (1997)

Jaws on Land

JURASSIC PARK

Spielberg says, "I have no embarrassment in saying that with *Jurassic* I was really just trying to make a good sequel to *Jaws*. On land." (McBride 418). Like *Duel* and *Jaws*, *Jurassic Park* is a creature feature, an action adventure with elements of thriller and horror movie which unleashes monsters from the id and deals in primitive, sadistic fantasies.[1] The truck in *Duel* and the shark in *Jaws*, with their giant size and power and predatory cunning, prefigure the t-rex and the raptors of *Jurassic Park*.

But is *Jurassic Park* really "a good sequel to *Jaws*"? Although I appreciate the film as a spectacular technical exercise and find in it moments of wonder and terror, the human characters leave me cold. Its real stars are the dinosaurs. People came to see the special effects and to watch the characters being chased and eaten by rampaging prehistoric carnivores. I can identify and become emotionally involved with David Mann in *Duel*, Chief Brody in *Jaws*, Roy Neary in *Close Encounters*, or Elliott in *E.T.* because they seem to have inner lives and inner conflicts, but the characters in *Jurassic Park* strike me as formulaic and flat. Many reviewers agreed.[2] Peter Biskind argues, "the *Jaws* script featured three male leads that were vividly individuated, and it was fleshed out by three strong actors . . . who more than held their own with the shark. *Jurassic* failed the *Jaws* test miserably, perhaps a victim of '90s-style make-nice filmmaking, in which the characters' rough edges are rubbed smooth. . . . The characters, and the actors who played them, were simply overwhelmed by the dinos" (Biskind 199). Even the screenwriter David Koepp admits, "In writing *Jurassic Park*, I threw out a lot of detail about the characters, because whenever

Jurassic Park: Spielberg directs *Jurassic Park.* Universal, 1993.

they started talking about their personal lives, you couldn't care less. You wanted them to shut up and go stand on a hill where you could see the dinosaurs" (Biskind 199).

The Opening Scene

The opening scene of *Jurassic Park* resembles but is not as memorable as the opening of *Jaws*. Like *Jaws*, it opens at night. The first shots of *Jurassic Park* establish a mood of mystery and suspense, teasing the audience about what we are going to see. "Spielberg is adept at manipulating the spectator's expectations" (Buckland 182). There is a rustling in the jungle as the treetops sway, and we hear a loud crunching, as of something enormous and powerful crashing through the underbrush. In a clearing, a group of uniformed men nervously stand guard, rifles at the ready. As in the opening of *Close Encounters*, Spielberg fakes out the audience because we cannot see what is approaching and might assume from the noise and motion that the men are hunting a giant dinosaur which is on the loose in the jungle. Instead—surprise—what emerges into the clearing is a machine, a forklift carrying aloft a large metal crate. Some violent, unseen creature is about to be transferred from this cage into a large concrete pen.

As Robert Baird notes, "The devilish genius of *Jurassic Park* is in the way it activates offscreen space" (Baird 96), so that the menacing dinosaurs "were fully revealed onscreen for about 6 percent of the film but were suggestively presented for about 21 percent of the time" (Baird 95), leaving a great deal to the viewer's imagination. Of course, this activation of offscreen space is a device Spielberg mastered in *Jaws*.

The rest of the opening scene reprises the opening of *Jaws*: in a scene of sudden, shocking, but bloodless violence, a man-eating predator captures and devours an innocent person who is fighting to survive. As in *Jaws*, we cannot see most of the attack or the creature; it is left largely to our imaginations, which makes it worse. And, as in *Jaws*, we sometimes share the animal's viewpoint—we don't see it at first, but a few shots show its view through the slats of the cage—so that we may even identify with it.

What happens is that the gatekeeper, a nameless park employee, ascends the cage and lifts the door to let the dinosaur enter the pen. The creature slams forward, forcing the cage backward, the man falls into the gap, and he is pulled into the cage from the feet to the waist. We cannot see what horrible things are happening to him below the waist (shades of castration anxiety!), just as in the shark attack in *Jaws*, where we see the head and shoulders of the woman, not what is happening to her below the surface of the water. The man grabs hold of a bar on the outside of the cage, and Muldoon, the hunter in charge of the transfer of the animal, holds onto the man. Just as the woman in *Jaws* is pulled across the water in a terrifying fashion, in the grip of something monstrous below, so the man is pulled, not horizontally but vertically, until he is lifted several feet into the air, suggesting the enormous power of this unseen creature.

Eloquent, repeated shots of *hands* and *eyes* during the attack evoke the shower scene in *Psycho* (Morris 194). The man's hand, grasping first the bar of the cage and then Muldoon, represents his last hold on life, and the closeup of the hand losing its grip and slipping away means his death, just as it meant the death of the woman in *Psycho*. The tough eyes of Muldoon are juxtaposed with the cold, reptilian eyes of the dinosaur (a velociraptor, we later learn), setting up a comparison and a competition between them, which ultimately leads to Muldoon's death.

As in *Psycho*, or in *Jaws*, which was influenced by Hitchcock, the attack on the innocent victim is also an assault on the viewer through shock cutting. As Baird notes, the attack on the gatekeeper "totals only forty-five seconds. In that time the viewer is assaulted with twenty-three different shots, numerous rapid visual movements, and disturbingly loud sounds, a *Jurassic Psycho* shower scene" (Baird 95).

Nevertheless, despite its impressive technique, the opening of *Jurassic Park* is not as memorable as either the shower scene in *Psycho* or the opening of *Jaws*. For one thing, Spielberg seems here to be echoing *Jaws*. For another, the scene lacks a character with whom to identify. In *Psycho*, the heroine is suddenly killed after we are well into the movie and feel strongly about her. And even though the woman in *Jaws* is killed in the opening scene, we know a bit about her: she has a few lines of dialogue, a name, Chrissy, and an appealing personality (and body). Chrissy is flirtatious and a little daring from drink, runs down the beach flinging off her clothes, and goes skinny-dipping by moonlight. The attack on her is unexpected and shocking; she screams in pain and cries for help, but none comes, which makes her death poignant. In contrast, the gatekeeper in *Jurassic Park* is nameless and anonymous and has no dialogue, so it is harder to care about him. Moreover, he is an employee in a hazardous occupation who deals with dangerous predators every day, for pay, so his death, while shocking, is not as unexpected. He never says a word or cries out. Help comes from Muldoon and the guards, but it is too late. And, although it may be uncomfortable to admit, the victims in both the shower scene in *Psycho* and the opening of *Jaws* are beautiful, naked white women, prized characters in American culture, whereas the gatekeeper is an anonymous Costa Rican man, a Latino, which makes him—at least for a white American audience—more disposable.

So whom can we identify with in the opening: the great white hunter Muldoon? or the unseen raptor? Muldoon shows steely determination, going to the man's rescue and yelling at the guards, "Shoot her!" But he shows absolutely no fear. Later, Muldoon never mentions the death of this man, for which he may have been partly responsible by not taking enough precautions (we later learn that he knows about the cunning of raptors). There is not enough of a complex, conflicted human being here with whom to identify; the raptor, a caged predator that wants its freedom and the chance to hunt, is really the most interesting character in the opening scene. As I argue, *Jurassic Park* works well on the spectacular and technical level but is not sufficiently absorbing as human drama.[3]

Jurassic Park: From Novel to Movie

Michael Crichton's novel, on which the movie is based, was strong on science and thrills but weak on characters, primarily interested in selling the idea of genetically engineered dinosaurs. Crichton wanted to warn about the dangers of "the commercialization of genetic engineering" (Shay 4) and sold his far-fetched premise by grounding the story in believable science and

Jurassic Park: Yet another Spielbergian endorsement of fatherhood and the nuclear family. The hierarchy is clear in the arrangement of characters. Universal, 1993.

realistic-seeming dinosaurs, not realistic-seeming people. "So the first thing was to make compelling dinosaurs. . . . That was my overriding concern" (41). For Crichton, "the theme park idea had to do with how to pay for such a project. . . . The fact that these dinosaurs are made for a park, it seemed to me, emphasized rather nicely the idea that all this amazing technology is being used for essentially commercial and frivolous purposes" (4).

The novel is darker and much more pessimistic than the movie, and the characters largely unappealing or uninteresting. The screenwriters, closely guided by Spielberg—first Crichton, then Malia Scotch Marmo, and finally David Koepp—tried to humanize the characters. David Koepp says, "There was a general feeling that Grant and Ellie weren't interesting enough personally and that we ought to think about how this experience was going to affect them as people, not just as scientists" (Shay 56). Spielberg wanted a mass audience, a family audience, so the solution was to create a sort of family unit consisting of Dr. Allan Grant, the paleontologist hero; Dr. Ellie Sattler, the paleobotanist; and Hammond's young grandchildren, Tim and Alexis (Lex), whose parents are divorcing. In the novel, Grant is much older than Ellie, his student, who is engaged to another man. In the film, however, they are closer in age and given a romantic connection to increase audience interest. In the novel, "Grant liked kids—it was impossible not to like any group so openly enthusiastic about dinosaurs" (Crichton 115). But in the film he is, rather improbably and arbitrarily, turned into a kid-hater, to which Ellie objects because she wants to have children. David Koepp notes, "we found ourselves turning back to our central theme, which is that life will find a way. With Grant as our lead and his being totally unequipped to deal with kids, we could use the presence of the kids to educate him about his own life and to show him the real value of children and the optimism they bring for the future" (Shay 57). Grant's rescuing the children from the rampaging dinosaurs and leading them safely through the park then becomes his rite of passage to prepare him for marriage and fatherhood.

Thus, like most Spielberg films, *Jurassic Park* is about the contemporary American family. Nevertheless, Spielberg's concern with fatherhood seems awkwardly grafted onto Crichton's original premise, which was to create believable dinosaurs and then let them run amok to warn about the commercialization of genetic engineering. Crichton's theme becomes lost as the film turns into yet another Spielbergian endorsement of fatherhood and the nuclear family. As Stephen Jay Gould writes, "Unfortunately, the plot line for the human actors reduces to pap and romantic drivel of the worst kind, the very antithesis of the book's serious themes" (Gould 181).

Another problem with *Jurassic Park* is that Spielberg's preaching of "family values" does not sit well with the film's appeal as violent spectacle. Audiences came to see realistic-looking dinosaurs chase and eat people, not to receive lessons about how to raise children. The sentimental element thus seemed a way to make the audience feel less guilty about enjoying the violence. As W. J. T. Mitchell notes, "a family cannot be brought together by a film that is too violent for the children in it to see. Spielberg thought that the film would be too frightening for his own children" (Mitchell 225).

Duel and *Jaws* are also violent spectacles, but neither preaches family values, although their protagonists are fathers. Rather, those films are about men who must prove their manhood by getting away from their wives and children and killing a powerful, evil enemy in a one-on-one showdown, the pattern of the classic Western. Even Roy Neary in *Close Encounters*, who does not want to kill the aliens but just to meet them, succeeds in his quest only after abandoning home and family. It is only in Spielberg's films of the late 1980s and 1990s, after Spielberg became a father, that his protagonists must grow up and learn how to be fathers, as in *Indiana Jones and the Last Crusade, Always, Hook, Jurassic Park, Schindler's List,* and *The Lost World.* Spielberg is dealing with personal concerns and also connecting to contemporary American cultural concerns (King, *Spectacular* 61). Nevertheless, sometimes, as in *Jurassic Park,* his obsession with families seems forced on the material.

The Greedy Villains

Crichton's critique of the commercial exploitation of science and technology remains in one scene in the film, but it is undermined because the film itself is caught up in the same commercialism. The scientist Ian Malcolm, who in the novel is Crichton's mouthpiece, in the film accuses John Hammond of abusing genetic discoveries for profit: "you've patented it and packaged it and slipped it on a plastic lunch box, and now, you're selling it!" But David Koepp, the screenwriter for *Jurassic Park,* says, "Here I was writing about these greedy people who are creating a fabulous theme park just so they can exploit all these dinosaurs and make silly little films and sell stupid plastic plates and things. And I'm writing it for a company that's eventually going to put this in their theme parks and make these silly little films and sell stupid plastic plates. I was really chasing my tail there for a while trying to figure out who was virtuous in this whole scenario—and eventually gave up" (Shay 56). *Jurassic Park* cost $100 million and had "an unprecedented marketing campaign (including a tie-in with McDonald's), with more than a thousand products being licensed officially" (Taylor 141). Ironically, this movie about a theme park led to a popular ride based on the movie at Universal Studios theme park (King, *Spectacler* 42). Thus *Jurassic Park*'s critique of the exploitation of technology in the interest of commercial greed seems uncomfortably self-reflexive and even hypocritical. Constance Balides argues that what is on display in the movie's flaunting of merchandise is the spectacle or "lustre of capital itself" (Balides 160). Spielberg says, self-mockingly, "I liken myself to the hunters that go after the animals [in *The Lost World,* the sequel to *Jurassic Park*]. They'll do anything for money, and so will we" (Biskind 201).

Jurassic Park: A cheerful Frankenstein, John Hammond behaves
like a jovial grandfather to the creatures he creates.
He oversees all the births. Universal, 1993.

In the novel the chief villain is John Hammond, the entrepreneur who creates the park, a greedy egomaniac. Hammond brings his grandchildren to the island to keep the park open, but he has no love for them or anyone else and little concern for anything other than money. In the end, he injures himself in an accident and is killed by scavenging dinosaurs, an appropriate fate.

In the film, though, the character of Hammond is softened, perhaps because Spielberg identified with him, and he is changed from a greedy villain into a kindly, jolly, grandfatherly eccentric, a showman who started with a flea circus and whose main concern is not money but pleasing the public. He loves his grandchildren and loves his dinosaurs so much that he is present at all their births as a sort of male midwife. Since he is portrayed so sympathetically, he survives in the film.

As I have mentioned, Spielberg often introduces a character into his films who serves as a surrogate self, such as the scientist Lacombe (played by the director Francois Truffaut) in *Close Encounters*, or Schindler in *Schindler's List*, who directs a company and is a showman concerned not with the product but with "the presentation." In *Jurassic Park*, John Hammond (played by the director Richard Attenborough) serves in a way as Spielberg's alter ego. As in *Close Encounters*, Spielberg's casting of a fellow director in a central role underscores the similarities between himself and the movie character. Just as Spielberg admired Truffaut, so he has called Attenborough "a director's director" (Spielberg 12). Both Hammond and Spielberg are entrepreneurs and showmen supremely concerned with pleasing an audience. Spielberg has admitted that "he could not help identifying with Hammond's blinkered obsession with showmanship" (McBride 421–22). Hammond creates a spectacular theme park, sparing no expense, trying to give the world real dinosaurs, and Spielberg creates the spectacular film *Jurassic Park*, sparing no expense, trying to give the world the illusion of real dinosaurs. Hammond says, "I wanted to show them something that wasn't an illusion, something that was real, something they could see and touch," and Spielberg says that the reaction he wanted from the audience was, "'Gee, this is the first time I've really seen a dinosaur. This isn't *Gorgo*, this isn't *Godzilla* [1950s dinosaur movies], this is really a movie I think is really happening as I'm watching it.'" In his concern to make the dinosaurs seem real, Spielberg says, "I initially wanted to make all the dinosaurs full size," echoing John Hammond (*Making of Jurassic Park* DVD).

Because Hammond in the film is now a good guy—misguided but not evil—his villainy is displaced onto two greedy, foul, stereotyped characters: the computer nerd Nedry and the lawyer Gennaro. The two suffer the most humiliating deaths in the film, and we are meant to applaud their demise. Just as in the novel, Nedry is a treacherous, greedy, fat slob who sabotages the park and is killed and eaten by a dilophosaur. The lawyer Gennaro is not a villain and survives in Crichton's novel. In the film, however, he is portrayed as a greedy, craven coward who abandons the children when the tyrannosaur attacks the car, and then hides in the bathroom, where the t-rex devours him.

Nedry is first introduced as he sits alone, stuffing his face at a restaurant. There he is met by Dodgson, a representative of a rival company, who offers him a satchel filled with cash, with more to follow if Nedry delivers stolen dinosaur fetuses. Nedry, a Judas who betrays his employer because he believes Hammond has not paid him enough, gleefully embraces the bag. When the check for Nedry's meal arrives, he insists that the other man pay: "Don't get cheap on me, Dodgson. That was Hammond's mistake."

In addition to his insatiable greed, Nedry is a destructive slob. When Dodgson gives him an aerosol can of shaving cream with a false bottom to transport the stolen fetuses, Nedry presses the nozzle to see if the can actually contains shaving cream. Then he does something disgusting: he wipes the shaving suds onto a slice of pie on an adjoining table, where some hapless diner may mistake it for whip cream. Nedry also makes a mess at work, constantly eating and drinking and strewing garbage.

The ultimate mess Nedry creates is the destruction of Jurassic Park. Significantly, Nedry has attached to his computer monitor a photo of J. Robert Oppenheimer, creator of the atomic bomb, with a cartoon of a mushroom cloud and the caption, "The beginning of the baby boom." Jurassic Park is thereby compared to the Manhattan Project—both products of advanced science that lead to destruction—but the evil is displaced onto Nedry, the admirer of Oppenheimer, rather than where it logically belongs: with Hammond, the park's creator.

When Nedry is killed by a dinosaur, it seems poetic justice: the man of outsize greed is himself eaten. In the last shot in the scene, the can containing the stolen fetuses is buried in mud in the rain—reduced to waste.

Gennaro, like Nedry, is caricatured as greedy and dirty, obsessed with "filthy lucre." In his first scene in the film, which seems to conjure up a symbolic descent into the bowels, Gennaro goes into a tunnel where men are mining precious lumps of prehistoric amber. When he first sees a living dinosaur, Gennaro, in contrast to the awestruck scientists, exclaims, "We're gonna make a fortune with this place!" Later, he says, "We can charge anything we want: $2,000 a day, $10,000 a day. And people will pay it. And then there is the merchandising—" Hammond counters with the desire not to overcharge but to make the park accessible to children, and he calls Gennaro "a bloodsucking lawyer," equating him with the mosquitoes who fed on the blood of the dinosaurs.

Nedry is a slob who leaves waste behind him, and the greedy Gennaro begins with a symbolic descent into the bowels and ends literally sitting on a toilet as he is devoured by the t-rex, a macabre yet comic scene. Although this is as grotesque as when Quint is eaten by the shark in *Jaws*, it is not as horrible because we dislike Gennaro and he suffers a humiliating fate. W. J. T. Mitchell notes that this scene parodies *King Kong*, with the blonde virgin tied to the altar as a sacrifice to the great ape being replaced by the lawyer on the john as a sacrifice to the dinosaur. "The ritual sacrifice of purification is parodied in a hilarious and horrible spectacle of ritual consummation/contamination in which the differences between eating and shitting, the altar and the toilet, the pure victim and the bloodthirsty monster, are systematically eliminated" (Mitchell 223).

Melanie Klein on Greed and Envy

If we look at the peculiar combination of greed and waste, oral and anal sadism of Nedry and Gennaro, through the theories of the psychoanalyst Melanie Klein, we can see the possible sources of these emotions in childhood anxieties. From her analysis of children and adults, Klein posited the earliest phase in development as the "paranoid-schizoid position," and suggested that infants feel persecutory anxiety, greed and envy toward the first object, the mother's body, which they attack in fantasy. "In the very first months of the baby's existence it has sadistic impulses directed, not only against the mother's breast, but against the inside of her body: scooping it out, devouring the contents, destroying it by every means which sadism can suggest." Klein writes, "in the phantasied attack on the mother's body a considerable part is played by the urethral and anal sadism which is very soon added to the oral and muscular sadism. . . . The excreta are equated with poisonous substances" (Klein 96). These fantasied attacks lead in turn to the child's fear of retaliation by "persecutors who it fears will devour it, scoop out the inside of its body, cut it to pieces, poison it—in short, compassing its destruction by all the means which sadism can devise" (Klein 116). The death of Nedry, who is killed by a dinosaur which blinds him by spitting poison in his eyes and then attacks and devours him, and the death of Gennaro, who is eaten while sitting on the toilet, seem to enact oral and anal sadistic fantasies.

Nedry and Gennaro are greedy characters, and Klein sees greed and envy as originating in oral and anal sadism: "At the unconscious level, greed aims primarily at scooping out, sucking dry, and devouring the breast . . . whereas envy not only aims at robbing in this way, but also at putting badness, primarily bad excrement and bad parts of the self, into the mother—first of all into her breast—in order to spoil and destroy her . . ." (Klein 213). Nedry suffers from both insatiable greed and destructive envy. His spoiling the pie with shaving cream could symbolize an excremental attack on the mother, and his sabotaging Jurassic Park an attack on a father figure. When he argues about salary with the unsympathetic Hammond, Nedry mutters sarcastically, "Thanks, Dad!"

The oral and anal sadism of Nedry and Gennnaro pervade the film, expressed by the dinosaurs, which can be considered monstrous surrogates acting out repressed human wishes and fears, whether of the characters, the filmmakers, or the audience. "Like beast fables of any kind, dinosaur stories are really about human beings. . . . As erect bipeds, they resemble us; as reptiles, they are the 'other'" (Mitchell 32).

The oral sadism of the predatory carnivores hardly needs commentary. The t-rex, like the shark in *Jaws*, is characterized by its enormous mouth and sharp, gigantic teeth. So are the vicious raptors, which hunt in packs and kill for sport. One critic noted the anal qualities of the dinosaurs, remarking on "*Jurassic Park*'s mudlust . . . its loving splats of paralyzing venom and benign sprays of Brachiosaurus snot" (Stephens 13). These effects are sometimes played for comedy, as when the brachiosaurus sneezes on Lex, or when Ellie (played by Laura Dern) tries to diagnose a triceratop's illness by examining a huge heap of its droppings, which Ian Malcolm wryly calls "one big pile of shit." The critic notes that we see "the fragrant immediacy of Laura Dern's long arms . . . plunging deep into a fertile mound of dino-dung" (Stephens 13). But anality can also add to the terror, as when the dilophosaur spits its venom on Nedry, or when the raptors stalk the children in the kitchen, a particularly creepy scene due to the contrast between the clean, shiny, reflective surfaces of the metal kitchen counters and the vile reptiles.

The Character of the Hero

Ironically, the hero Grant shares some of the oral and anal sadism of the villains Nedry and Gennaro and of the dinosaurs. His cruel streak shows when he admires the ferocious raptors, imitating one as he uses a raptor claw to frighten a child, saying, "And he slashes at you with this—six-inch retractable claw, like a razor, on the middle toe. He doesn't bother to bite your jugular like a lion. He slashes at you here or here. Maybe across the belly, spilling your intestines. The point is: you are alive when they start to eat you. So, you know, try to show a little respect." Nigel Morris notes: "The castrating, sickle-shaped claw, together with his attitudes . . . confirms him as another Hook" (Morris 205). As he speaks, Grant demonstrates the attack by passing the claw across the boy's belly, combining orally sadistic fantasies—being eaten alive—with anal ones: the spilled intestines. Yet, strangely, he claims his dislike of children is based on disgust; he tells Ellie that kids are "messy" and that "they smell."

The critic Henry Sheehan notes that although Grant's attack on the boy sets us up for the later attacks by the raptors, it is both improbable and excessive. First, it is improbable that a lone boy is on a dinosaur dig among professionals. Second, Grant is too cruel toward the child, enacting "child-murder fantasies," so that "the rest of the film is a ritualistic enactment of Grant's penance" for his sadistic streak (Sheehan 10). As Peter Wollen says, "*Jurassic Park* seems to represent displaced, stylized child molesting." Like Disney, Spielberg "both seeks to nurture children and at the same time often threatens to terrify them" (Wollen 9). The child-murder fantasy is simply there in the film, imposed on the material, another expression of Spielberg's "dark, almost morbid streak" and obsession with coupling children and death: "often it's a case of the father or father figure trying to rescue a child just before it undergoes the death the father has unwittingly devised for it," as in *Jaws, Temple of Doom, The Last Crusade, Hook,* or *Schindler's List* (Sheehan 10).

The nameless child in this scene is odd in another way: aside from there being no explanation for his presence, he is funny-looking and androgynous, as well as fat and obnoxious, so that he resembles the greedy Nedry, as if to justify the sadism of Grant's attack.

Later, after Grant has rescued the two children, Tim and his older sister Lex, sheltering them in a tree, he drops the raptor claw he has been carrying, symbolically relinquishing his hostility toward kids (King, *Spectacular* 62). Nevertheless, his cruel streak remains. After they narrowly escape a stampeding herd of gallimimus, Grant lingers to watch the t-rex devour one of the hapless creatures, although logically the characters should escape as soon as possible, while the t-rex is still absorbed in eating his prey. Even though Lex is appalled and twice asks to leave, Grant stays, showing a morbid fascination with the (offscreen) carnage, saying, "Look how it eats!" and "I bet you never look at birds the same way again." Later he plays a practical joke on Tim and Lex, pretending to suffer an electric shock when he grasps an electrified fence whose power is off. Lex, who has been terrified too often, does not find the joke funny. Tim does, although he will be shocked for real and almost killed when, as he climbs the fence, the power is turned back on. Again, it is as though Grant's fantasies of violent death are acted out on the children.

Grant resembles Muldoon, the great white hunter of the park: both admire and identify with the dinosaurs. Muldoon in turn resembles Quint, the Ahab-like shark hunter in *Jaws* who became like a shark in his obsession. Both Quint and Muldoon die at the hands of the monster they hunt, although Muldoon is not as obsessive as Quint, nor is his death shown in the same gruesome detail. The cuts in the opening scene of *Jurassic Park* from closeups of the raptor's cold, reptilian eyes to Muldoon's eyes suggest the similarity between the two. Later there are similar closeups of Grant's eyes. When the raptor attacks Muldoon, the hunter who has finally met his match, with his last words Muldoon admires the animal: "Clever girl!"

The Fascination with Dinosaurs

Spielberg has disavowed expressing any personal desires through *Jurassic Park*, saying, "I have my own secret desires, and I might make another kind of movie to express those, but I really think of the audience when I think of a *Jurassic Park* or a *Lost World* or the entire *Indiana Jones* series" (*Making of The Lost World* DVD).

Yet Spielberg may be disingenuous in denying that the film expresses any of his secret desires. He admits to a lifelong fascination with dinosaurs, about whom he has made two movies: "And I became fascinated as a kid, as all kids do, because I think they're bigger than us, and they were something that doesn't exist today. . . . I think even though it has the pull and seduction of mythology, it also has its roots in reality" (*Making of Jurassic Park* DVD). Language like "fascinated" and "pull and seduction" suggests that, for Spielberg, dinosaurs are sexy beasts.

Why people are fascinated by dinosaurs remains an open question. These prehistoric creatures were only discovered in the nineteenth century, and all we know or think we know about them is based on fossil traces and guesswork. We can reconstruct their skeletal remains, but how we flesh them out and bring them to life, and what meanings we ascribe to them, is up to our individual unconscious fears and desires and to our sometimes feverish cultural imaginations. Stephen Jay Gould mentions a psychologist who said the fascination with dinosaurs exists because the creatures are "'big, fierce, and extinct'—in other words, alluringly scary, but basically safe" (Gould

173). Yet Gould says that does not explain the periodic cycles of dinomania, which he posits are fads, the result of commercial exploitation (174).

A common psychological explanation is that, in their overwhelming size and power, dinosaurs represent "the infant's fantasies of the primal scene, of terrifying parents," which would help explain their fascination for young children. Peter Wollen speculates that even though the dinosaurs in Jurassic Park were originally programmed to be female, nevertheless we see the carnivorous dinosaurs in the film as "demented father figures" and the herbivorous dinosaurs as "beneficent mothers" (Wollen 8). This notion corresponds to the familiar equation of the "male with devourer and female with devoured" (Lévi-Strauss 106).

W. J. T. Mitchell gives an anthropological explanation, claiming that we have adopted the dinosaur as a cultural icon, "the totem animal of modernity" (Mitchell 77). Dinosaurs were discovered in modern times, yet they ruled the earth for millions of years, an extinct race of giants, and thus are our predecessors. "Traditional totem animals were the object of ritual sacrifices and spectacular feasts. The modern totem is brought back to life by means of a spectacle in which human sacrifice plays a central role. What is consumed in the dinosaur sacrifice is the spectacle of consumption itself. We love to watch them eat . . . us" (81). For Mitchell, *Jurassic Park* constitutes a kind of spectacular totem feast which expresses our ambivalence toward consumerism: we pay good money to watch a greedy lawyer eaten by a t-rex.

Conclusion

Jurassic Park was a blockbuster hit because it derived from a popular novel which exploited the popular fascination with dinosaurs and because it delivered the most realistic movie dinosaurs yet by taking the next step in digital imagery, seamlessly integrating mechanical and electronic effects with live action. The movie has a visceral power in its star attraction—the earth-shaking, ear-shattering, insatiably hungry t-rex—as well as in its insidious co-stars, the vicious and cunning raptors. Audiences worldwide craved the thrilling, violent spectacle of dinosaurs chasing and eating people. As Mitchell says, "Dinosaurs are tailor-made for the link-up of the disaster film and the action-adventure flick. Thus they epitomize . . . an aesthetics of spectacle, shock, mass consumption, and mass violence" (Mitchell 62).

But *Jurassic Park* is not all violence. In fact, most of the violence is bloodless, partially blocked from view, or occurs offscreen, devices Spielberg perfected in *Jaws* and other movies. Moreover, many subtle moments create suspense: a distant pounding, the rear-view mirror shaking, and the water vibrating in a cup, all suggesting the imminent arrival of the t-rex (much like the effects Spielberg uses to herald the approaching German tanks in the final battle of *Saving Private Ryan*). There are also moments of comedy amid the horror: a cowardly lawyer snatched from the john by a dinosaur, or the t-rex, as it chases a jeep, glimpsed in a side-view mirror which has printed on it: OBJECTS IN MIRROR ARE CLOSER THAN THEY APPEAR. And after this chase, Ian Malcolm quips, "Think they'll have that on the tour?" There are moments of wonder as well, like the characters' first sight of the splendid, towering brachiosaur stretching to nibble the treetops; the dinosaurs moving in herds; a baby raptor breaking out of its shell; a sick triceratops lying on its side, breathing heavily; or the brachiosaurs in the jungle at night, softly bellowing to one another, images in which Spielberg uses some of the techniques of the wildlife documentary to gain verisimilitude (Baird 92).

Only the family values seem to me awkwardly grafted onto the film because the thinness of the characters and the anarchic violence do not adequately support such sentiment. Blockbusters, argues Robert Baird, "exercise and explore the bodily-kinesthetic, the visio-spatial, and the most archaic of intra- and interpersonal expressions. There is a way in which blockbusters and threat scenes remind us that no one can ever really put away childish, archaic, and anarchic things" (Baird 97). *Jurassic Park* is powerful on this visceral level, indulging primitive fantasies about oral and anal sadism and child murder, but less convincing when it tries to counter these violent, archaic fantasies with compensatory grownup fantasies about the importance of love and the nuclear family.

THE LOST WORLD: JURASSIC PARK

If *Jurassic Park* reprises *Jaws*, then *The Lost World* (1997) reprises *Jurassic Park*. The dinosaurs are even more lifelike, due to four years of advances in animatronics and computer animation, and the film is darker and scarier than *Jurassic Park*. It was a big box-office hit in the summer of 1997, yet the critical consensus was that *Lost World* is less coherent than *Jurassic Park*, poorly structured, a series of spectacular action set pieces loosely tied together.[4] Reviewers sensed that Spielberg was disengaged; the adjective that most often cropped up in the reviews was "perfunctory."[5] Friedman calls it "a copy of a copy, a pale imitation" (Friedman 150). Spielberg admitted that while he was making *Lost World* he grew angry at himself for directing a sequel to *Jurassic Park*, a film that he considered "not even in the top five" of his best works, but one that was enormously popular. "I was just serving the audience a banquet, but I wasn't serving myself anything challenging" (Biskind 198, 206).

The Lost World is a disappointing sequel which offers much the same violent plot and pat moralizing as *Jurassic Park*: when an arrogant, greedy corporation creates a dinosaur theme park, disaster strikes and many people die. There are more scenes with sketchy characters threatened by many more carnivorous dinosaurs. Dr. Ian Malcolm steps into the role occupied by Dr. Alan Grant in the first movie, of the kid-hating scientist who must learn how to parent, and his girlfriend Dr. Sarah Harding fills the role of Dr. Ellie Sattler, the brave woman scientist who helps the hero (Friedman 149). The two kids of *Jurassic Park* are replaced by Malcolm's teenage daughter Kelly. Aside from similar characters, the sequel rehashes several scenes from the first movie. In *Jurassic Park*, a t-rex attacks a jeep and pushes it over a concrete embankment; in *Lost World*, two t-rexes attack a trailer and push it over a cliff. In both movies, raptors attack people inside a building, children are imperiled by man-eating dinosaurs, and the victims are villains or disposable minor characters. There are a few new, memorable images: the heroine suspended over an abyss on a pane of cracking glass; the raptors attacking in the tall grass; a stream of blood flowing down a creek after a man has been killed by a pack of tiny scavenging dinosaurs; and another stream of blood flowing down a waterfall after a man has been killed by a t-rex. But many scenes in the sequel simply repeat images from *Jurassic Park*: an impact tremor in a puddle or a silhouette signals the approach of a dinosaur, an angry t-rex peers at people through a car window, a t-rex sniffs but fails to see people who remain frozen in terror, and a raptor smashes through a glass window. The film's final sequence—the t-rex on the rampage in a city—repeats not *Jurassic Park* but *King Kong* (1933) and *Godzilla* (1956). It too lacks novelty.

The Lost World: Novel vs. Movie

Lost World has little in common with the best-selling 1995 novel of the same title by Michael Crichton, although this does not account for the weakness of the film, since films must be judged on their own merits and have no obligation to be faithful to their sources. Crichton's novel is in part a homage to Arthur Conan Doyle's novel *The Lost World* (1912); Spielberg's film is instead more of an homage to safari films like *Hatari* (1962) and to monster movies like *King Kong* and *Godzilla*.

Crichton wrote the foreword to the Modern Library edition of Doyle's *The Lost World*. In Doyle's novel, an imperialist fable, an English expedition sets out to explore an isolated Amazonian plateau in which time has stood still and dinosaurs have survived into the twentieth century. Crichton changes the setting to an isolated Pacific island off the coast of Costa Rica but borrows the title and the names of some of Doyle's characters (John Roxton and Challenger). Both Doyle and Crichton are concerned with the Darwinian theme of evolution and extinction, and Crichton's scientists often argue about these topics. Spielberg's film instead carries an ecological message about the supposed

The Lost World: Jurassic Park: Learning dinosaur family values. Universal, 1993.

need for human beings to allow dinosaurs to roam free on the isolated island. Reviewers found the environmentalist sentiments in the film unconvincing because of the ecological heroes' foolish and reckless behavior, which seems to value dinosaurs over humans and causes the violent deaths of many people.[6]

Both the novel and the movie take place four years after the events of *Jurassic Park* and are set mostly on Isla Sorna, a Costa Rican island which was "Site B," where the Ingen Corporation manufactured its dinosaurs. After being abandoned, the island has reverted to a wild, primitive realm where dinosaurs rule. Starting from that common basis, the film deviates from the novel, inventing many new characters and a new plot. In fact, the film uses only one of Crichton's action sequences: the characters bring an injured baby t-rex to the trailer and the mother and father t-rex attack the trailer.

In both novel and movie, the protagonists are Ian Malcolm, the mathematician and chaos theorist, and his sometime girlfriend, Sarah Harding, a field biologist who studies carnivores such as lions and hyenas in the wild. The film makes Malcolm far more heroic and Harding far less so than in the novel. In the film she is a damsel in distress who makes many foolish moves and frequently requires rescue by Malcolm, whereas in the novel Harding is tougher than the men and does most of the rescuing.

Dinosaur Family Values

Like *Jurassic Park, Lost World* is changed from Crichton's novel to reflect Spielberg's obsession with troubled contemporary families. In the film

The Lost World: Jurassic Park: Damsel in distress. Universal, 1993.

Jurassic Park, a hero who dislikes kids bonds with kids when he rescues them from dinosaurs. In the film *Lost World,* a hero who neglects his young daughter bonds with her when he rescues her from dinosaurs. The screenwriter David Koepp says, "On one level, this story evolved into one about parenthood and the instinct to protect your young. That idea ran through the human *and* the animal characters. . . .I liked the fact that both *Jurassic Park* movies were about families" (Duncan 18).

Nevertheless, the human families in *Lost World* are all dysfunctional; the ideal family is the mother and father t-rex and their baby. The movie's ostensible message is: "Dinos do it right; we don't" (Stamets). *Lost World* "is a veritable hymn in praise of dinosaur family values" (Mitchell 80). Most of the action involves the t-rex parents searching for and defending their offspring. Sarah Harding is on the island studying the child-rearing habits of dinosaurs. She says, "Dinosaurs were characterized very early on as vicious lizards. There's a great deal of resistance to the idea of them as nurturing parents." The Field Museum in Chicago opened an exhibit on "Dinosaur Families" to coincide with the opening of *Lost World,* with a press release reading: "Find out what family values meant some 80 million years ago"(Stamets).

Crichton's novel features two children: Kelly, a thirteen-year-old white girl, and Arby, an eleven-year-old black boy, who stow away but are unrelated to the members of the expedition. To emphasize the family theme, the film has only one child stowaway, Kelly, a thirteen-year-old black girl who is now Ian Malcolm's neglected daughter. "Obviously here only to appeal to demographics (both of age and race), she adds nothing to the story . . ." (Wright).

Lost World blames unhappy parents and broken marriages for putting children at risk. Like Tim and Lex in *Jurassic Park*, Kelly Malcolm is a child of divorce. When her father is about to leave on yet another expedition, she accuses him, "I'm your daughter all the time, you know. You can't just abandon me whenever opportunity knocks. . . . You like to have kids but you just don't want to be with them, do you?" Malcolm replies, "I'm not the one who dumped you here and then split for Paris. So don't take it out on me." When both her mother and father abandon her, it is not surprising that Kelly stows away.

Malcolm is presented as not only a neglectful father but also a neglectful boyfriend. Like Kelly, Sarah accuses him of never being there for her. She also suggests that Malcolm is as predatory as the dinosaurs, saying, "I've worked around predators since I was 20: lions, jackals, hyenas, you."

Aside from the rather pro forma conflict among Malcolm and his daughter and girlfriend, there are three other unhappy families in the film. *Lost World* opens as an extremely rich British family—mother, father, and a daughter who looks to be between eight and ten years old—picnic on the beach of the isolated Costa Rican island Isla Sorna, served champagne by their yacht crew. The mother stands, but the father lies on a lounge chair, isolated from them. Immediately the couple start quarreling because the daughter wants to explore the beach on her own; the mother is fearful there may be snakes. The father is annoyed with his wife, saying, "For God's sake, leave her alone, Dierdre. . . . There aren't any snakes on the beach. Just let her enjoy herself for once." This is not a happy family; it sounds like an old squabble over their differing styles of child care. The father wins, and the daughter scampers off down the beach, but the mother's fears prove justified. The girl is attacked, not by snakes, but by a horde of little scavenger dinosaurs called compys. The parents and the crew run to her aid, but the scene ends with the mother screaming.

This scene derives from an early chapter in Crichton's novel *Jurassic Park*, but there the family were middle-class American tourists on the mainland of Costa Rica. In the film, to explain the family's presence on a remote, unpopulated island, they are turned into wealthy Brits vacationing on a yacht. Thus an American audience is predisposed to dislike these super-rich, spoiled snobs who don't know how to raise their daughter. Even though Hammond later says that the little girl is all right, a vicious attack on a child seems a cruel way to open the movie.

From the shot of the mother screaming, ending the first scene, there is a match cut to Malcolm yawning. This is a trick shot because the mother is on a tropical island and there are tropical palms behind Malcolm, so that they seem to be in the same location. But when Malcolm moves, we see that he has been standing in front of an advertisement on a New York City subway platform. The gag establishes a visual link from one unsatisfactory parent to another.

Late in the film we are introduced to a third unhappy family. The male t-rex, on a rampage in San Diego, stops to drink from a suburban swimming pool. A little boy wakes up, sees the t-rex outside his bedroom window, and calmly wakes his parents: "There's a dinosaur in our backyard." As in a sitcom, the parents immediately start to bicker about who is to blame for the boy's fantasies—until they witness the t-rex, which has just swallowed the family dog, and they scream. Thus ends the scene. Although it is played for laughs, the scene is a sick joke because the dog is killed, and we never find out what happens to the family. In *Close Encounters* or *E.T.*, such a scene would evoke wonder; in *Poltergeist*, terror. But in *Lost World* it is a sight gag, tossed in for comic relief, as if Spielberg were reverting to the slapstick humor of his farce *1941* or simply parodying himself.

The most unnatural family in the film is John Hammond's. Peter Ludlow, Hammond's nephew, has usurped the company, like a rebellious son. Ludlow is introduced in Hammond's mansion as he seemingly takes over not only the old man's business but also his home. The film's chief villain, Ludlow is caricatured as a spoiled, ultra-rich British snob, just like the yachting couple. When Malcolm grabs his arm, Ludlow sneers, "Careful. This suit costs more than your education." Because Ludlow has the male t-rex and its baby captured and taken to San Diego for display in a zoo, it is meant to be poetic justice that, in the climax, Ludlow is captured and killed by the two dinosaurs as papa t-rex teaches his pride and joy how to hunt.

Conclusion: Hard to Swallow

Lost World implies that bickering or divorcing parents put their children at risk and so deserve to be punished by having themselves and their children threatened with death by dinosaur. At the same time, it showcases the t-rex family, which dismembers and eats numerous people, as its ideal family. But man-eating predators are hardly role models to inculcate lessons about human child care. As in *Jurassic Park*, because of the violence it is hard to take seriously the film's message about family values. And in *Lost World*, the self-mocking humor also undermines any serious themes the film attempts to present, whether about family or ecology.

The level on which the movie is most persuasive is not the moral but the visceral: reviewers who praised it called it "primal sensation" (Howe) and "a sheer adrenalin spike to the brain stem" (Hunter). As in *Jurassic Park*, beneath the surface concerns about family values lie primitive, anarchic fantasies about oral devouring and child murder. The movie flounders in this contradiction between its manifest and latent content. *Lost World* ends up being, as the saying goes, "hard to swallow."

NOTES

1. The critic Kim Newman has enumerated some of the similarities between *Jurassic* and previous Spielberg films: "The paring down of a monster best-seller into a suspense machine (*Jaws*); the tackling of a popular-science childhood sense of wonder perennial with state-of-the art effects that reimagine 1950s B-science fiction (*Close Encounters of the Third Kind*); the all-action jungle adventure littered with incredible perils and gruesome deaths (*Raiders of the Lost Ark*); and big-eyed creatures who range from beatifically benevolent to toothily murderous (*Gremlins, E.T.*)" (Baxter 373).

2. See, for example, Roger Ebert, Review of *Jurassic Park*: "The human characters are a ragtag bunch of half-realized, sketched-in personalities, who exist primarily to scream, utter dire warnings, and outwit the monsters."

3. Geoff King, Lester D. Friedman, and Warren Buckland all argue for the narrative coherence and interest of *Jurassic Park*. For example, Buckland writes that "Spielberg managed to balance the wonders of Industrial Light and Magic's digital dinosaurs with the audience's need for a good story" (Buckland 176). Although I admit that successful Hollywood blockbusters must also have narrative appeal, some stories are better than others, and sometimes, as in *Jurassic Park*, the thinness of the characters plus the intensity of the spectacle contradict the narrative's ostensible themes.

4. See, for example, reviews by Holden, LaSalle, O'Brien, and Stamets.

5. See, for example, Bill Stamets: "There's perfunctory romantic friction between Sarah and Malcolm, perfunctory parent-child friction between Malcolm and Kelly, and perfunctory corporate intrigue"; James Berardinelli mentions "how perfunctory and unimaginative Steven Spielberg's direction often is"; Roger Ebert claims that *Lost World* is "even more perfunctory" than *Jurassic Park*.

6. See, for example, reviews by Begg, LaSalle, and O'Brien.

REFERENCES

Baird, Robert. "Animalizing *Jurassic Park*'s Dinosaurs: Blockbuster Schemata and Cross-Cultural Cognition in the Threat Scene." *Cinema Journal* 37.4 (Summer 1998): 82–103.

Balides, Constance. "Jurassic Post-Fordism: Tall Tales of Economics in the Theme Park." *Screen* 42.2 (Summer 2000): 139–60.

Baxter, John. *Steven Spielberg: The Unauthorised Biography*. London: HarperCollins Publishers, 1996.

Begg, Ken. "Ten Things I Hate (and a whole lot more) about *The Lost World: Jurassic Park*." Online review, 1997. www.jabootu.com/lostworldnugget.htm

Berardinelli, James. Review of *The Lost World: Jurassic Park*. Online review, 1997. http://movie-reviews.colossus.net/movies/j/jurassic2.html

Biskind, Peter. "A 'World' Apart." *Steven Spielberg: Interviews*. Ed. Lester D. Friedman and Brent Notbohm. Jackson: University Press of Mississippi, 2000, 193–206.

Buckland, Warren. *Directed by Steven Spielberg: Poetics of the Contemporary Hollywood Blockbuster*. New York: Continuum, 2006.

Crichton, Michael. *Jurassic Park*. 1990; rpt. New York: Ballantine Books, 1991.

———. *The Lost World*. New York: Alfred Knopf, 1995.

Doyle, Arthur Conan. *The Lost World*. Introduction by Michael Crichton. 1912; rpt. New York: Modern Library, 2003.

Duncan, Jody. *The Making of The Lost World: Jurassic Park*. New York: Ballantine Books, 1997.

Ebert, Roger. Review of *Jurassic Park*. *Chicago Sun-Times*, June 11, 1993. www .suntimes.com/ebert/ebert reviews/1993/06/862231.html

———. Review of *The Lost World: Jurassic Park*. *Chicago Sun-Times*, June 6, 1997. www.suntimes.com/ebert/ebert reviews/1997/06/060601.html

Edelstein, David. "Museum of Jurassic Technology." *Slate*, May 25, 1997. http:// slate.msn.com/id/3220

Friedman, Lester D. *Citizen Spielberg*. Urbana: University of Illinois Press, 2006.

Gould, Stephen Jay. "Dinomania." *The Films of Steven Spielberg: Critical Essays*, ed. Charles L. P. Silet. Lanham, MD: Scarecrow Press, 2002, 171–88.

Holden, Stephen. Review of *The Lost World: Jurassic Park*. *New York Times*, May 23, 1997. www.nytimes.com/library/film/lost/html

Howe, Desson. "*Lost World*: Dino Might." *Washington Post*, May 23, 1997. www.washingtonpost.c...term/movies/review97/lostworldhowe.htm

Hunter, Stephen. "Sic Semper Tyrannosaurus." *Washington Post*, May 23, 1997. www.washingtonpost.c...term/movies/review97/lostworldhunter.htm

Jurassic Park. 1993. Director: Steven Spielberg. Screenplay: Michael Crichton and David Koepp, based on the novel by Michael Crichton. Cinematographer: Dean Cundey. Editor: Michael Kahn. Music: John Williams. Producers: Kathleen Kennedy, Gerald R. Molen. Stars: Sam Neill, Laura Dern, Jeff Goldblum, Richard Attenborough.

King, Geoff. *Spectacular Narratives: Hollywood in the Age of the Blockbuster*. London: I. B. Tauris Publishers, 2000.

King, Stephen. *Danse Macabre*. New York: Everest House, 1981.

Klein, Melanie. *The Selected Melanie Klein*, ed. Juliet Mitchell. New York: Free Press, 1986.

LaSalle, Mick. "Dinosaur Diner." *San Francisco Chronicle*. May 23, 1997. www .sfgate.com/article.cgi?file=/c/a/1997/05/23/DD5037.DTL

Lévi-Strauss, Claude. *The Savage Mind*. Trans. George Weidenfeld. 1962; Chicago: University of Chicago Press, 1966.

The Lost World: Jurassic Park. 1997. Director: Steven Spielberg. Screenplay: David Koepp, based on the novel by Michael Crichton. Cinematographer: Janusz Kaminski. Editor: Michael Kahn. Music: John Williams. Producers: Kathleen Kennedy, Gerald R. Molen, Colin Wilson. Stars: Jeff Goldblum, Julianne Moore, Vanessa Lee Chester, Vince Vaughn, Pete Postlethwaite, Arliss Howard, Richard Attenborough.

Making of Jurassic Park DVD.

Making of The Lost World: Jurassic Park DVD.

McBride, Joseph. *Steven Spielberg: A Biography*. New York: Simon and Schuster, 1997.

Mitchell, W. J. T. *The Last Dinosaur Book: The Life and Times of a Cultural Icon*. Chicago: University of Chicago Press, 1998.

Morris, Nigel. *The Cinema of Steven Spielberg: Empire of Light.* London: Wallflower, 2007.

O'Brien, Harvey. Review of *The Lost World: Jurassic Park.* 1997. http://indigo. ie/~obrienh/lwr.htm

Shay, Don and Jody Duncan. *The Making of Jurassic Park.* New York: Ballantine Books, 1993.

Sheehan, Henry. "The Fear of Children." *Sight and Sound* 3.7 (1993): 10.

Spielberg, Steven. "Introduction." *The Actor's Director: Richard Attenborough Behind the Camera.* ed., Andy Dougan. Edinburgh: Mainstream, 1994, 11–12.

Stamets, Bill. "Heavy on Its Feet." Review of *The Lost World: Jurassic Park. Chicago Reader,* May 1997. www.chireader.com/movies/archives/0597/05307.html

Stephens, Chuck. "Spielberg's *Lost World*: Franchise, Fatherhood, a World without Dung." *Film Comment* 33.4 (July–August 1997): 12–14.

Taylor, Philip M. *Steven Spielberg: The Man, the Movies, and Their Meaning.* 1992; rev. New York: Continuum, 1994.

Wollen, Peter. "Theme Park and Variations." *Sight and Sound* 3.7 (1993): 6–9.

Wright, Brian. "*The Lost World: Jurassic Park*: The wrong kid was mauled." Online review, 1997. www.geocities.com/tyrannorabbit/lostworld.html

13

A.I. (Artificial Intelligence) (2001)

Separation Anxiety

> I felt that Stanley really hadn't died, that he was with me for the three
> and a half months it took me to write the screenplay and then the three
> and a half months it took me to shoot the movie. I felt Stanley with me
> every moment.
>
> —Steven Spielberg (Cagle)

A.I. AS HOMAGE TO KUBRICK

A.I. (Artificial Intelligence) (2001) is an inherited project, Spielberg's collaboration with and homage to a dead director. *A.I.* was a story Stanley Kubrick toyed with for thirty years and left unfinished when he died. In 1969,
a brief magazine story by the English science-fiction writer Brian Aldiss,
"Supertoys Last All Summer Long," about a robot boy adopted by a human
family, attracted Kubrick's attention. It seemed an extension of the theme of
man-machine interaction which Kubrick had explored in the relationship
between the computer HAL and the astronauts in his film *2001* (1968).
Kubrick worked with Aldiss to develop the story into a screenplay, as he
had collaborated with Arthur C. Clarke to build one of Clarke's stories into
2001. Later he gave it to another SF writer, Ian Watson, who wrote a draft,
and he commissioned hundreds of drawings for a production. Kubrick
worked much too slowly to use a child actor, so he looked into the possibility of constructing a robot boy, but the difficulties were insuperable. After
Jurassic Park (1993) animated dinosaurs convincingly through computer
graphics, Kubrick spoke with his friend and fellow director Spielberg about
creating a robot boy electronically and integrating him with human actors.

In 1994, he offered the project to Spielberg to direct, feeling it was more in line with Spielberg's sensibilities, but Spielberg declined. When Kubrick died in 1999, his widow Christine and her brother, Kubrick's producer Jan Harlan, wanted Spielberg to complete *A.I.*, and this time he accepted.

Spielberg had long admired Kubrick, who was nineteen years older. He was influenced by his style, and included homages to Kubrick in his films, such as casting Slim Pickens from Kubrick's *Dr. Strangelove* in his *1941* (1979). The two met in 1979 and became friends. Spielberg considered Kubrick the best film artist of the last several decades. He says, "He's a master of concept lighting and composition and bravura subject matter," and he is also impressed by "the sheer variety in his films." He calls *Strangelove* a "visionary film" that "will live as a nearly perfect example of moviemaking." When he met Kubrick, he admired him as a surrogate Jewish father, saying "he's such a *mensch*" (Hodenfield 81–82). In 2001, Spielberg funded a sound stage at the University of Southern California film school and insisted that it be named after Kubrick (Lyman). The film is thus a collaboration between two *auteur* filmmakers, one living and one dead.

Spielberg, whose father was distant when he was growing up, has often been attracted to older Jewish men, movie moguls who function for him as father figures: Sidney Sheinberg, president of MCA/Universal, who signed Spielberg to his first contract to direct television in 1969 and brought the novel *Schindler's List* to his attention in 1982; Michael Ovitz, the superagent who headed CAA and for a while was Spielberg's agent; and Steve Ross, who founded Time-Warner and died in 1992. Spielberg dedicated *Schindler's List* (1993) to Ross and told Liam Neeson to model his portrayal of Schindler on his home movies of Ross (Richardson 70). Kubrick, another older Jewish man, is also one of Spielberg's mentors and surrogate fathers. Just as *Schindler* was a tribute to the late Steve Ross and a way to re-create Ross through the figure of Schindler, so *A.I.* is Spielberg's tribute to Kubrick and his way of mourning the older director.

A.I., MOURNING, AND SIMULACRA

It is not unusual for artists to use their works as, among other things, a way to overcome loss. What interests me about *A.I.* is that it is not only Spielberg's way of mourning Kubrick by completing his work, in a sense channeling Kubrick—"I felt that Stanley really hadn't died, that he was with me. . . ."—but also a film about separation anxiety, mourning, and the attempt to re-create the lost object by bringing back the dead, creating a simulacrum. Many of the characters rely on simulacra: the robot boy David is a replacement child for the scientist Dr. Hobby, who created him in the semblance of his dead son David; David is also a replacement for Monica's son Martin, who has been in a coma for years; the robot creatures in the last sequence mourn the death of humanity, who are, symbolically, their parents, and they create short-lived clones using the DNA of the dead; and finally, at the end, David mourns the loss of his adoptive human "mother" Monica by interacting briefly with her cloned simulacrum (Kreider 34).

A.I. is a profoundly sad film about lost objects which one cannot recover except through simulacra or dreams. It is only in dreams—or in death—that David can reunite with the lost mother. Ultimately, *A.I.* mourns not simply the mother but also the lost objects of "the human" and "the real," categories that become increasingly problematic and elusive in our postmodern, posthuman world. J. P. Telotte argues that what is always at stake in science fiction films about robots is "our humanness" (Telotte 3). We measure ourselves against the robot, trying to define what makes us human, fearing that even as we become more robotic, our creations become more human and may ultimately surpass or replace us. Thus *A.I.* ends with David, a robot, lying next to the dead simulacra of his human "mother" Monica, and neither is really "human" or "real." The film closes: "So David went to sleep too. And for the first time in his life, he went to that place where dreams are born." A robot has become "human" by attaining the ability to dream, yet dreams of the human are all that is left of humanity. As Baudrillard writes, "paradoxically, it is the real that has become our true utopia—but a utopia that is no longer in the realm of the possible, that can only be dreamt of as one would dream of a lost object" (Baudrillard, *Simulacra* 123).

Viewing *A.I.* can be a moving yet painful experience, perhaps because it reminds us of our own painful personal losses, like the reviewer who said it would "invade your dreams, as it has mine since I saw it." He concluded his review by remembering his lost brother George, with whom he used to go to the movies when they were children, and saying, "I only wish George were still alive to see and appreciate how deeply Mr. Spielberg has plunged into this forbidden cavity of the unconscious" (Sarris).

THE DIVIDED CRITICAL RECEPTION

The movie divided the critics, who either hated it as a meandering mess or loved it as a profound and moving meditation on such science-fictional ideas as the relation between the human and the machine, what it means to be human, and the nature of the real. A few fell in the middle, calling it "a fascinating wreck" (Travers). Many saw *A.I.* as a schizoid blending of two seemingly diametrically opposed sensibilities: Kubrick, who was often considered a cold, cerebral, pessimistic director, uninterested in pleasing audiences; and Spielberg, who is considered a warm, un-intellectual, optimistic director who loves to please. One reviewer writes: "Imagine the personals ad Kubrick might have taken out: 'YOU LIKE: sweetness & light, happy endings, "When You Wish Upon a Star." I LIKE: a hope-free environment, leering homicidal teens, pitilessly ambiguous *Götterdämmerungen*, icy Gyorgi Ligeti melodies. . . . LET'S MEET FOR A MOVIE!'" (Apello 44). Some attacked the film as a dysfunctional marriage which brought out the worst of both directors: "*A.I.* winds up with Kubrick's empathy and Spielberg's intellectual muscle. It's a lethal combination" (Bradshaw). Or "we end up with the structureless, meandering, slow-motion endlessness of Kubrick combined with the fuzzy, cuddly mindlessness of Spielberg" (LaSalle). Yet others praised it as a successful merger: "*A.I.* effectively combines the moody indeterminacy of Kubrick, especially the Kubrick of *2001*, and the addiction to happily-ever-aftering of Spielberg" (Apello 45). Many criticized the ending as "too facile and sentimental," and thus typical Spielberg (Ebert). Yet others confessed that the ending made them cry (Naremore).

Despite relatively weak box-office returns, at least in comparison to the usual Spielberg picture, Spielberg was satisfied with *A.I.* He says, "I realized I had succeeded when I saw what a Kubrickian reaction the film was getting. It was given exactly the same reception that every other Kubrick film has always gotten" (Svetkey 36). In other words, he had accomplished his main goal in making the film, which was to resurrect Kubrick.

Although Spielberg wrote the screenplay, Kubrick provided the plot structure, including that supposedly sentimental Spielberg ending. Kubrick originally called the project *Pinocchio* and wanted it to be "sentimental, dreamlike" (Argent 51). And there was a pattern of mutual admiration and mutual influence in the careers of Spielberg and Kubrick. *2001* was one of the films Spielberg screened several times while filming *Close Encounters*. Nigel Morris sees elements of *2001*—the "mystic light show" and "the magical resurrection"—in *Close Encounters* and other Spielberg films (Morris 300–301). And Kubrick was inspired to begin *A.I.* because of Spielberg's success with *E.T.* (Hoberman 17).

Moreover, I believe that neither Kubrick is as chilly as he is often portrayed nor Spielberg as sunny as many critics like to believe. Kubrick's films are filled with sly humor, albeit often ironic or black humor, and Kubrick laments the almost universal dehumanization that he portrays. And Spielberg has his dark side. Spielberg's obsessive topic has been lost children, especially lost boys in peril, seeking to reunite with mother, from *Sugarland Express* through *Close Encounters*, *Poltergeist*, *E.T.*, *The Color Purple*, *Empire of the Sun*, *Hook*, *Saving Private Ryan*, and *Catch Me If You Can*. Think of the little boy hiding in the latrine from the Nazis in *Schindler's List*, up to his neck in feces. It is an image of total abjection.

A.I. AND *EMPIRE OF THE SUN*

Empire of the Sun (1987), to which many critics compared *A.I.* (Sarris; S.E.; Travers; Taylor), greatly resembles *A.I.* in both storyline and dark tone. *Empire* is a harrowing odyssey of loss about Jim, a privileged, nine-year-old English boy who becomes separated from his parents in the chaos of Shanghai during World War II. Jim is forced to live on the streets, witnesses great brutality, and is in peril of his life from the Japanese occupying forces. He tries to survive by clinging to Basie, an unscrupulous drifter. Later he is interned with other English civilians in a Japanese P.O.W. camp. He alternates between terror, manic elation, and deep depression. At the end of the war, now thirteen, he is finally reunited with his parents. In the last scene, as his mother embraces him, he closes his eyes. One can see the similarities to *A.I.*: David, a perpetual ten-year-old robot boy, is exiled from his comfortable home when Monica, his adoptive mother, abandons him in the woods. He wanders, forced to survive in a cruel world that hates robots, witnesses great brutality, and is imprisoned and in peril of his life at the Flesh Fair. He tries to survive by clinging to Gigolo Joe, an amoral love-robot on the lam from the law. He alternates between terror, manic rage, and suicidal depression. In the end, he is reunited with his mother, or at least with a simulacra of her, and he finally closes his eyes. I called *Empire* "a boy's dream of war" (Gordon), and critics have called *A.I.* "a child's dreams" (Buckland 228) and "a troubling dream" (Apello 45). Kubrick gave Spielberg a chance to revisit familiar material through a science fictional lens. I consider both films—*Empire* and *A.I.*—to be thoughtful, carefully crafted, visually lavish, and psychologically profound.

The two movies are also linked by the theme of mourning. Since Jim is separated from his parents for the four years of the war and does not know if they are alive or dead, he is caught in suspension. He wants to mourn them but never knows if his mourning is warranted. Both films feature a lullaby. In *Empire*, it is the Welsh hymn "Suo Gan," which translates as:

Sleep, child, on my breast,
Warm and secure it is here.
Your mother's arms are round about you,
A mother's love is in my breast.

In *A.I.*, a robot nanny tries to comfort David when they are captured and being brought to the Flesh Fair where robots are destroyed. She holds him and says, "Don't be afraid, David," and sings a French lullaby which translates:

Sleep, sleep, the baby will go to sleep right away.

In both films, the separation from the mother induces in the boy a state
of unresolved mourning and a wish to return to infancy and to sleep in the
mother's arms, which is how both heroes end.

ROBOT EMOTIONS

In *A.I.*, however, the mourning is qualified by the element of the fantastic,
which renders it grotesque or uncanny. The nanny, after all, is not a human
being but a machine programmed to perform a function. And David too,
is not human but a robot designed to love. So the emotions expressed in
the scene, although they may evoke a sense of poignancy in the viewer, are
simulated emotions enacted by programmed machines, so that we don't
know how much to identify or invest in these emotions. We are moved by
David's plight yet distanced from him. As a reviewer notes, "the film keeps
confusing and undercutting our responses. . . . *A.I.* keeps us nicely off balance, our hearts continually pitted against our heads, Spielbergian images
pumped full of Kubrickian ironies" (Cooper).

David's dilemma is that he was created to fulfill a human need but trapped
by the programming that humans have inserted in him. His status is liminal,
between that of a human being and that of a doll. As Dr. Hobby says in the
opening, "Ours will be a perfect child caught in a freeze frame, always loving,
never ill, never changing. With all the childless couples . . . our little mecha
will not only open up a completely new market—it will fill a great human
need." ("Mecha" means robotic, as opposed to "orga" or organic.)

THE FIGURE OF THE SCIENTIST

Later we learn that, in addition to his scientific and entrepreneurial goals,
Dr. Hobby created David, the first robot who can love, for a very personal
reason, for David bears the name, image, and personality of his son, who
died at the age of ten. David is thus his surrogate son. Yet the Doctor is
trying not only to overcome his mourning but also to profit from it, for
soon his Cybertronics company will mass produce and market a stream of
"Davids" and their female equivalent, "Darlene," boxed like dolls or toys.
He has lost a son but compensated by creating a horde of identical robot
children. In creating the boy, Dr. Hobby acts not like a father but like an
arrogant god. In answer to a question about the responsibility of a person
toward the robot who loves him, he says, "But in the beginning, didn't
God create Adam to love him?" Dr. Hobby's motives in creating David are
mixed: to overcome his mourning by memorializing his son; to advance
science; to make a profit; and to play god.

He sometimes behaves like the cruel Dr. Frankenstein. In the opening scene, to prove a point to his students, he casually stabs a woman in the hand. Only after that do we learn she is a robot. He treats her like a slave and orders her to undress. And he says of her, "We are rightly proud of it, but what does it amount to? A sensory toy. . . ." This scene is echoed later when David is surrounded by a crowd of taunting boys, one of whom threatens him with a knife, claiming, "I'm not going to hurt you."

DAVID'S POSITION IN A HUMAN FAMILY

In contrast to Dr. Hobby's mixed motives, Monica's reason for adopting David is clear: her sick son Martin has been in cryogenic storage for five years. The physician warns her husband Henry, "She's in the most difficult position of feeling she should mourn the death of her son." Martin's condition may be incurable, but because his status is simply "pending," "All her grief goes undigested." This seems to be the central problem facing many of the film's characters: a grief which cannot be processed or digested and which requires the creation of a substitute for the lost object, a simulacrum.

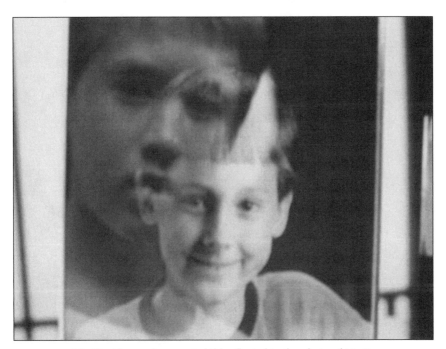

A.I.: David as replacement child reflected in the photo of Martin: ghostly doubles. Warner Bros./Dreamworks, 2001.

That David is intended as a replacement child is clear from his introduction into the Swinton household. David looks at a series of family photos, first a picture of the three of them: Henry, Monica, and Martin. David's face is reflected in the glass of the picture frame, as if he were a shadow member of the family. Next, David's face is reflected and superimposed on a photo of Martin.

The notion of David as a ghost double who does not really fit in the family is reinforced by repeated visual motifs of his separation from Monica and Henry: shots are deliberately distorted or seen through distorting glass, or he is isolated from them within the frame, or, as in the scene mentioned above, his image is doubled through reflections in glass, polished surfaces, or mirrors. To mention a few examples: in his introduction, David is first seen in a distorted fashion by Monica, "backlit to look like the tall, spindly extraterrestrials in *Close Encounters*" (Appelo 44). He also resembles an alien when his image is reflected in the kitchen counter, making him look as if he has four eyes (Morris 303). In the first dinner table scene, David is isolated from the couple, shot from above so that his image is framed within a round overhead lamp. When Monica is upset with David, she puts him in a closet behind a glass door. When she abandons him in the woods, he pounds on the glass of the car window separating them. Finally, as she drives off, his

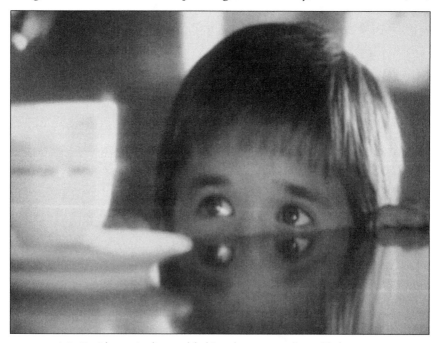

A.I.: David seen in distorted fashion, here as an alien with four eyes.
Warner Bros./Dreamworks, 2001.

image in her rear-view mirror dwindles, echoing an earlier pullback shot of David as he dwindled, left at the bottom of the swimming pool.

THE PROBLEM OF THE REPLACEMENT CHILD

One way to explain all these visually distorting shots is to see David as a replacement child. Two key elements of the psychological phenomenon of the replacement child are incomplete mourning and identity disturbance. Because the replacement child is introduced into the household before his predecessor has been completely mourned, there is a "distortion of the mourning process, a pseudo-resolution of mourning" (Cain 452). The substitute child is treated "more as an embodiment of a memory than as a person in its own right" (Sabbadini 530). The child is permanently haunted by its ghostly double and unconsciously feels guilty for the death of the previous child.

One can see this phenomenon, for example, in Art Spiegelman's memoir in comic book form, *Maus* and *Maus II*: Spiegelman's older brother died in the Holocaust before Art was born, and he must live in the shadow of this ghost brother. The brother is enshrined in a photo in his parents' bedroom, where there are no photos of Art. As he says, "It's spooky, having sibling rivalry with a snapshot" (Spiegelman, *Maus II* 15). At the end of the tale, his aged father mistakenly calls Art by his dead brother's name.

A.I. uses the fact that David is a machine, not a human being, as a metaphor for the circumstances of the replacement child, who is a surrogate object and not treated as "a person in its own right." The many shots in the first third of the movie which deliberately alienate, distort, or diminish David's image underscore his status as a thing, an object rather than a person in the Swinton household. In the scene just before Monica finally decides to keep David, she dresses him in pajamas and tucks him into his bed (which was formerly Martin's bed). As she gazes down fondly at the robot boy, she flashes back to images of Martin sleeping in his cryogenic chamber (images of present and past linked by blue light), a memory which makes her frown and weep and look again at David. In the next scene, she goes through the imprinting ceremony with David to insure his undying love for her, and, for the first time, David calls her "Mommy." This confirms his status as the replacement child for Martin.

But David's status in the household is always questionable. Is he a person, a son, or merely an object? The father Henry resents his presence: although using the robot boy was at first his idea, he soon finds the boy creepy and intrusive between him and Monica. Monica considers David "a child," but Henry rejects him as a mere "toy." Martin's recovery and return to the household follow soon after Monica imprints David, as if David's coming has miraculously resurrected Martin.

This pattern of death and resurrection is often repeated in the film. Later, as if playing out his guilty fate as replacement child, David mimics Martin's condition, trapped in cryogenic suspension in an amphibicopter under the frozen sea until he is brought back to life after 2,000 years. And Monica too returns from the grave in cloned form, albeit only for a day.

Once Martin returns, David's days in the Swinton family are numbered, for Martin is a monster child, manipulative and nasty, who sees David as a rival who must be eliminated. David is first marginalized and next expelled from the family, abandoned in the woods like Hansel in the Grimm brothers' fairy tale. Once the "real" son is restored, the replacement child, whose reality is lesser because it is merely a copy, a simulacrum of the original, then becomes superfluous.

THE LOST CHILD

David undergoes the ultimate Dickensian nightmare of the Spielberg child hero: he is orphaned and cast out into the world to wander and to fend for himself. As the boy Jim is told in *Empire of the Sun*: "Nobody wants you. You're worth nothing."

Because they are children under extreme stress, it is not surprising that both David and Jim resort to irrational fantasies. David fixates on the story of Pinocchio, pleading with Monica, "If Pinocchio became a real boy and I become a real boy, can I come home?"

"That's just a story,"she replies.

"Stories tell what happens," David says.

"Stories are not real," she says.

Yet the film questions the category of "the real." Martin says, "I'm real," differentiating himself from David, but Martin survived for years inside a machine and, even as he speaks, walks with the aid of a mechanical prosthesis (Stone). Later, we see the moon rise, only to realize it is not the real moon but a machine, a balloon whose crew hunt down stray robots.

The difficulty with David's quest is that we know from the start it is futile (LaSalle). Unlike Pinocchio, he does not exist in a fairy tale and we know he can never turn into a real boy. We also know Monica will never love him, for, as Gigolo Joe tells David, "She loves what you do for her, as my customers love what it is I do for them. But she doesn't love you, David. She cannot love you. You are neither flesh nor blood. . . . You were designed and built specific like the rest of us. You are alone now because they tired of you." Like Joe, David is a mechanical prostitute selling love to human customers.

Jim's quest in *Empire of the Sun* has some hope of fulfillment—he survives the war and he is reunited with his parents. He is four years older and deeply traumatized, but he can recover. David has no such hope, nor can he grow like Jim. Although David does grow more human on his journey—in the sense that he acquires the ability to experience a range of emotions, to be self-motivated, and to dream—he can never grow up. His programming fixes him forever at the mental age of a ten-year-old. Spielberg dealt with the Peter Pan syndrome in "Kick the Can" and *Hook*, but only *A.I.* shows the true horror of being unable to grow up.

David prizes the quality he believes distinguishes him and makes him worthy of Monica's love: "I'm special and unique. Because there's never been anyone like me before—ever." When he gets to Dr. Hobby's laboratory, though, and meets his double, he flies into a rage and destroys the other robot because it threatens his identity by taking away his uniqueness. Dr. Hobby's attempts to comfort him only make things worse. David says, "I thought I was one of a kind," and Hobby says, "My son was one of a kind. You are the first of a kind." To this, David says, "My brain is falling out." Once again, he is merely a replacement child, a dispensable copy.

When he then confronts a roomful of mass-produced, boxed Davids, he falls into suicidal despair and plunges into the sea, crying "Mommy," as if the oceanic fusion will reunite him with the lost mother. And in a sense it does: undersea he finds a statue of the Blue Fairy, which by now has become identified with the mother.

Since David's quest to become a real boy and to be reunited with Monica is unrealistic and hopeless, and since he is limited in his psychological development because he can never grow up, the ending gives us a fantasy that provides some amelioration for the poor child and a resolution of sorts to the film's central problem of unresolved and undigested grief.

THE FILM'S THREE ACTS

The film moves through three acts that are progressively more and more fantastic and distinguished as well by three radically differing cinematic styles. First is the opening act in the Swinton home, which is domestic melodrama and the closest to realism, shot mostly in daylight in a hermetically sealed suburban home, with subtle action and muted colors—mostly black, white, and grey. The middle act takes place at the Flesh Fair and Rouge City, and is dystopian satire, played broadly, shot at night with lots of violent action and lurid colors. The third and final act returns to the Swinton home, now transformed by fantasy, with the lighting and color scheme changed and "suffused with the gauzy, golden light of nostalgia" (Naremore). These tonal shifts are typical of Kubrick, as in *2001*, and are a deliberate part of the film's structure. "Stanley had this idea of mode jerking," says production designer Rick Carter. "You're in one place, one mode.

Then suddenly you're jerked out of it. That's the road map he laid out. And Steven did his best to realize it" (Daly, 30).

THE ENDING

Many critics hated the ending, seeing it as a typically saccharine Spielberg ending, a cop-out after all that had come before, a blatantly oedipal wish fulfillment. For example, one reviewer says "the romantic finale when he is reunited with his mommy; well, that is frankly unwholesome and tells me more about Steven Spielberg than I ever wished to know" (Bradshaw). A second says, "The sequence, bathed in morgueish blue light, borders on necrophilia, but Spielberg's treacly piety drains it of even that enjoyment" (Stone). And a third writes, "the most vicious parodist of Spielberg could not devise anything more precious, more shallow or more patently ridiculous" (LaSalle).

I believe that they misread the complex, fundamentally ambiguous tone of the ending. Recall that earlier scene in which the robot nanny croons a lullaby to the frightened David. Our awareness that these two are robots simulating emotion imbues the scene with the uncanny and qualifies our sentimental response. The ending evokes similar mixed emotions. Unlike the ending of *E.T.*, for example, Spielberg here undercuts his own sentimentality. We are always aware that the mother-and-child reunion in *A.I.* is an elaborate fake, a play stage managed by benevolent super robots who have constructed the set, which is only a simulacrum of the Swinton home, and that the robots are observing the play all the time. This stage set recalls the weird re-creation of a human room created by the unseen aliens in *2001* to observe the astronaut David Bowman (Morris 313). In addition, "the oversaturated colors and grainy stock emphasize this reconstruction's cinematic artificiality" (Morris 310). We are also aware that David is playing a role, concealing the truth from Monica. Moreover, we know that this is not the real Monica but a clone, a simulacrum, conveniently edited so that, as the voice-over narrator says, "All the problems seemed to have disappeared from his mommy's mind. There was no Henry, there was no Martin, there was no grief. There was only David." The voice-over narration distances us from the scene and reminds us of its problematic nature. The film is well aware that only in fantasy can one erase grief. And what Monica tells him— that she has always loved him—we know to be a lie because this is not the real Monica, who never loved him and abandoned him in the woods. Each event in this carefully scripted day between David and Monica rewrites a disaster in their actual life together (Kreider 38). "Spielberg's redemptive impulse is there, but muted and restrained, while Kubrick's own lurking misanthropy gets brightened, or lightened, into somberness. What results is the best of both temperaments—dark, but not heartless" (Cooper).

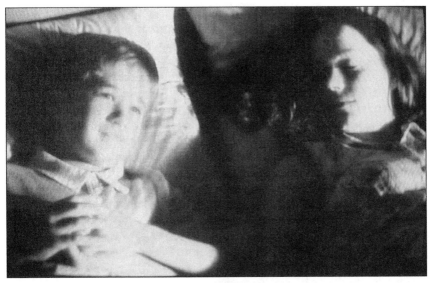

A.I.: The sleep and dream into which David falls at the end is ambiguous.
Warner Bros./Dreamworks, 2001.

The added poignancy of this final little stage play is that there are no
human beings in it. David is a robot and Monica is a clone, a simulacrum
which will fade in a day. Like *2001*, the film pushes "into ever stranger territory, ultimately leaving the human world altogether" (Scott). Human beings created David and are responsible for his dilemma, his alienation and
his grief, and it is only the disappearance of the humans that can resolve
it. The human race is over, but the robots carry on the best of the human
spirit. We know that there is no Blue Fairy granting David's wish but that
the robots have created one out of David's imagination. As Dr. Hobby tells
David, "The Blue Fairy is part of the great human flaw: to wish for things
that don't exist. Or to the greatest single human gift: the ability to chase
down our dreams." The paradox is that our greatest flaw is also our greatest
gift. Believing in the imaginary may trap us in the irrational, but it is also
the basis of art and makes us human.

Both *Close Encounters* and *A.I.* meditate on the modern fairy tale of Pinocchio, but *A.I.* is far more mature and bittersweet in its use of Collodi's fantasy.
In *Close Encounters*, Spielberg seems to wholly identify with his adult hero's
regressive fantasies; in *A.I.*, however, he takes a compassionate but objective
view of a child's fantasies. Roy Neary wants his kids to see the Disney film
Pinocchio so they will believe in magic, but they refuse. Roy chases after the
mothership as obsessively as David seeks the Blue Fairy. When Roy ascends
into the mothership, his wish upon a star is granted and he is symbolically
reborn. As Spielberg says, Roy "becomes a real person. He loses his strings, his

wooden joints . . ." (McBride 283). David too gets his wish granted to become a "real" boy, yet his fulfillment is brief and phantasmatic, sad and not triumphant like Roy's. Although David has taken on human qualities, he will never attain the love he desires, for there are no humans left to return it.

The sleep and dream into which David falls at the end is ambiguous, because he lies beside the dead Monica, and we wonder, now that his wish has been granted through this playlet, what is left for him except death. The film implies that there are some lost objects which will never return and that there is some mourning which can never be resolved except through dreams or death. Writes A. O. Scott, "the very end somehow fuses the cathartic comfort of wish fulfillment—the dream that the first perfect love we experience as the fall from Eden might be restored—with a feeling almost too terrible to acknowledge or name. Refusing to cuddle us or lull us into easy sleep, Mr. Spielberg locates the unspoken moral of all our fairy tales. To be real is to be mortal; to be human is to love, to dream and to perish."

Or as Wallace Stevens puts it in his poem "Sunday Morning":

Death is the mother of beauty; hence from her,
Alone shall come fulfillment to our dreams
And our desires. . . .

REFERENCES

Appelo, Tim. "Virtual Pinocchio." *The Nation*, July 23/30, 2001, 44–45.

Argent, Daniel. "Steven Spielberg as Writer: From *Close Encounters of the Third Kind* to *A.I.*" *Creative Screenwriting* 8.3 (May/June 2001): 49–53.

Baudrillard, Jean. *Simulacra and Simulation*. Trans. Sheila Faria Glaser. Ann Arbor: University of Michigan Press, 1994.

Bradshaw, Peter. Review of *A.I. The Guardian*. September 21, 2001. http://film.guardian.co.uk/Print/0,3858,4261392.00/html

Buckland, Warren. *Directed by Steven Spielberg: Poetics of the Contemporary Hollywood Blockbuster*. New York: Continuum, 2006.

Cagle, Seth. "Real Intelligence." Interview with Steven Spielberg. *Time*, June 17, 2001. http://www.time.com/sampler/article/0,8599,130934.00.html

Cain, Albert C. and Barbara S. Cain. "On Replacing a Child." *Journal of the American Academy of Child Psychiatry* 3 (1964): 443–56.

Cooper, Rand Richards. "Pinocchio Redux." *Commonweal*, August 17, 2001. http://www.findarticles.com/cf_0/m1252/14_128/78804065/p1/article.jhtml?term=A.I.+%2B+Spielberg+%2B+Kubrick

Daly, Steve. "Human Nature." *Entertainment Weekly*, July 13, 2001, 24–30.

Ebert, Roger. Review of *A.I. Chicago Sun-Times*, June 29, 2001. www.suntimes.com/ebert/ebert_reviews/2001/06/062901.html

Gordon, Andrew. "Steven Spielberg's *Empire of the Sun*: A Boy's Dream of War." *Literature/Film Quarterly* 19.4 (1991): 210–21.

Hoberman, J. "The Dreamlife of Androids." *Sight and Sound* 11.9 (September 2001): 16–18.

Hodenfield, Chris. "*1941*: Bombs Away!" *Steven Spielberg Interviews.* Eds. Lester D. Friedman and Brent Notbohm. Jackson: University Press of Mississippi, 2000, 70–83.

Kreider, Tim. Review of *A.I. Film Quarterly* 56.2 (2003): 32–39.

LaSalle, Mick. *San Francisco Chronicle,* June 29, 2001. http://www.sfgate.com/cgi-b

Lyman, Rick. "A Director's Journey Into a Darkness of the Heart." *New York Times,* June 24, 2001, Section 2, 1, 24.

McBride, Joseph. *Steven Spielberg: A Biography.* New York: Simon and Schuster, 1997.

Morris, Nigel. *The Cinema of Steven Spielberg: Empire of Light.* London: Wallflower, 2007.

Naremore, James. Lecture at the University of Florida, April 1, 2002.

Richardson, John H. "Steven's Choice." *Premiere,* January 1994, 66–72, 92–93.

Sabbadini, Andrea. "The Replacement Child." *Contemporary Psychoanalysis* 4 (1988): 528–47.

Sarris, Andrew. Review of *A.I. New York Observer,* June 25, 2001. www.findarticles .com/cf_0/m0ICQ/2001_June_25/81474644/p1/article.jhtml?term=A.I.+%2B+S pielberg+%2B+Kubrick

Scott, A.O. "Do Androids Long for Mom?" *New York Times,* June 29, 2001. www .nytimes.com/2001/06/29/arts/29ARTI.html

S.E. "All Grown Up." *Los Angeles Magazine.* September 2001. www.findarticles.com ...p1/article.jhtml?term=A.I.+%2B+Spielberg

Spiegelman, Art. *Maus: A Survivor's Tale.* New York: Pantheon, 1986.

———. *Maus II: A Survivor's Tale: And Here My Troubles Began.* New York: Pantheon, 1991.

Stevens, Wallace. *Poems by Wallace Stevens.* Ed. Samuel French Morse. New York: Vintage, 1950.

Stone, Laurie. "Freaks Are Us." *Tikkun* November-December 2001. www.tikkun.org /magazine/index.cfm/action/tikkun/issue/tik0111/article/011153.html

Svetkey, Benjamin. "Tom Cruise Reboots." *Entertainment Weekly,* June 14, 2002, 30–39.

Taylor, Charles. Review of *A.I. Salon.com,* June 29, 2001. www.salon.com/ent /mo...al_intelligence/index.html?CP+IMD&DN=110

Telotte, J. P. *Replications: A Robotic History of the Science Fiction Film.* Urbana: University of Illinois Press, 1995.

Travers, Peter. Review of *A.I. Rolling Stone* 873, July 19, 2001. www.rollingstone .com/mv_reviews/review.asp?mid=2042269&afl=imdb

14

Minority Report (2002)

Oedipus Redux

Minority Report (2002), based on Philip K. Dick's 1956 short story, is a thoughtful, visually enthralling science fiction film noir propelled by an oedipal plot. In the film, Chief John Anderton heads a "Precrime" squad that uses precognitive seers to stop murders before they occur. When these mutants predict that Anderton himself is about to commit murder, he flees. The "precogs" function like the divine oracle in Sophocles' play *Oedipus Rex*, and Anderton becomes Oedipus, the King who seeks a murderer only to discover he himself is the murderer. Also like Oedipus, Anderton voluntarily undergoes blindness. Finally, Anderton's real enemy, the man he must destroy, proves at the end to be his elderly boss, who had been like a father to him. The oedipal implications might have been latent in Dick's story, but Spielberg's screenwriters make them manifest. Because Spielberg deals in melodrama—adventure stories or fairy tales—his film is not Sophoclean tragedy. Unlike Oedipus, Spielberg's hero regains his sight, kills no one, and is finally exonerated.

Dick finished "The Minority Report" in December 1954; it was published in *Fantastic Universe* in January 1956. In the early 1950s, as he first tried to make a living writing SF, he churned out over twenty stories a year because the SF pulp magazines paid so poorly. But unlike the usual hack writer, Dick dealt with serious themes. His fiction has one central concern: the unstable nature of reality, which makes his protagonists paranoid. In "The Minority Report," Dick employs the devices of pulp fiction—a murder story filled with violent action and plot twists—to construct an existential science fiction thriller. According to Brian Aldiss, "Between life and death lie the many shadow lands of Dick, places of hallucination, illusion, artificial reality, dim half life, paranoid states" (Aldiss 310). As Douglas A. Mackey writes, "Dick's stories both reflect and comment upon the paranoiac temperament of the 1950s" (7). "The Minority Report" reflects and comments upon the Cold War paranoia of the early 1950s, of the Korean War and the McCarthy era. Spielberg's film instead reflects the paranoia of the American surveillance state of the George W. Bush era. According to one review, the film concerns "a kind of Ashcroftian security state in which individuals are literally imprisoned within their own heads, for crimes they haven't (yet) committed" (O'Hehir).

DICK'S "THE MINORITY REPORT"

The protagonist of Dick's story is John Anderton, the aging Commissioner of Precrime, a police division that relies on the predictions of precognitives. Thirty years before, Anderton had worked out the theory for Precrime, and he has headed the organization ever since. The precognitives are three deformed idiots with hyperdeveloped psychic abilities who can see up to a week or two ahead in time. Called "monkeys," they are kept imprisoned and their babbling analyzed and decoded to reveal future crimes, so that potential perpetrators can be arrested before the crime. There hasn't been a murder in five years. "In our society we have no major crimes,'" says Anderton. "'But we do have a detention camp full of would-be criminals'" (Dick 72).

The story opens as Anderton meets Ed Witwer, assigned as his assistant and eventual replacement upon his retirement. Anderton instantly dislikes Witwer because the young man makes him feel "Bald and fat and old" (71). No sooner does he meet Witwer than a card appears, announcing that within the week Anderton is going to kill a man. He conceals the card and becomes jealous and suspicious when his "slim and attractive young wife, Lisa" (75), his former secretary, is friendly to Witwer. Privately, Anderton tells her "'I'm being framed—deliberately and maliciously. This creature is out to get my job. The Senate is getting at me *through* him'" (76). He is even suspicious of Lisa, who says he is acting paranoid. She tells him to look again at the card: his supposed victim is not Ed Witwer but Leopold Kaplan, someone of whom he has never even heard.

Anderton goes home to pack and flee, but he is stopped by a thug with a gun, who takes him to Kaplan, who turns out to be a retired "General of the Army of the Federated Westbloc Alliance" (79). The Army gets duplicates of the Precrime data, and Kaplan has been informed. Anderton insists he is being framed, but Kaplan instructs his men to turn him over to the police. The radio announces that Anderton is now a wanted man. On the way to the police station, the car crashes and Anderton is rescued from the crash by a stranger named Fleming, who claims he's from "'a sort of police force that watches the police'" (83). Fleming tells him he is indeed being framed by Witwer and Lisa, and he gives him fake identification cards. Anderton hides out in a cheap hotel in the slums.

He persuades a technician, Wally Page, to let him in to Precrime headquarters to remove the data tapes for one of the "monkeys," Jerry, whose vision is out of phase with the other two precogs. This is "the minority report" he believes will prove his innocence.

Lisa discovers him there but helps him escape in an airship. She tells him there is no conspiracy and the majority report was no fake. Because the minority report will discredit the police, she urges him to turn himself in so that Precrime will survive. He refuses, saying, "'If the system can survive only by imprisoning innocent people, then it deserves to be destroyed'"(90). Lisa then pulls a gun on him. But Lisa is overpowered by Fleming, who has stowed away on the airship. Fleming claims that Kaplan, Witwer, and Lisa are all part of the plot against him. But when Fleming tries to strangle Lisa, Anderton knocks him out. Fleming is revealed to be an Army Major and an agent of Kaplan.

Anderton goes to Witwer, explaining it has all been an Army conspiracy to discredit Precrime and return to power. Wally Page has been feeding information to Kaplan. When Anderton examines all the data tapes, he discovers there is no majority report; the three precogs predicted three different scenarios. Kaplan too now has the precog reports and announces a rally to publicly discredit Precrime. Anderton tells Witwer he is going to kill Kaplan to protect the agency. Anderton goes to the rally and shoots Kaplan dead. But Witwer gains him clemency: exile for him and his wife to a colony planet.

In the end, as he prepares to leave for exile, Anderton explains that each of the reports was accurate, but foretold a different reality because they were out of phase. Anderton's behavior kept changing as he gained new information, so the outcome kept shifting. He killed Kaplan, but it was a free choice, based on his knowledge of all three predictions and of what was best both for himself and for the preservation of the balance of power. His situation was unique because Anderton was the first accused criminal with access to all the data. With a grin, he tells Witwer, "'It could happen again—but only to the next Police Commissioner. So watch your step'" (101).

At the beginning, the aging Anderton is insecure about his job and his marriage. Once he is accused, he falls into a nightmare world. He loses everything and begins to suspect everyone: the Senate, the Army, his wife, his assistant, even the police agency he had headed for decades. Nothing is certain; his conception of the nature of the reality around him keeps shifting. Dick's story is a paranoid fantasy of the McCarthy era, a time when no one was safe, when the system could turn against its own, when even powerful people could be accused of Communist sympathies and be ruined. The happy ending of Dick's story, in which the hero keeps his wife and retires into exile rather than prison, is ironic: Anderton is a murderer, and the system of Precrime, which gives the state preternatural power, is preserved.

The oedipal undertones in Dick's story reside in Anderton's jealousy of the younger man Witwer, whom he sees as a rival for his job and his wife. However, the pervasive paranoia of the story, in which Anderton imagines that Witwer is his persecutor, suggests instead that Anderton is repressing homosexual desires, if we accept Freud's explanation that "what lies at the core of the conflict in cases of paranoia is a homosexual wish phantasy of loving a man" (Freud 32).

SPIELBERG'S VERSION COMPARED TO DICK'S STORY

Spielberg's film retains Dick's premise: John Anderton, Chief of Precrime, discovers he is about to kill a total stranger. Sure that he has been framed by Witwer, he flees and hides in the slums. Later he returns to headquarters to steal the minority report to prove his innocence. Aside from those elements, however, the plot of the film differs completely because it lacks Dick's paranoia, in which Anderton even doubts his wife and the nature of the reality keeps twisting. It also lacks Dick's moral ambivalence. In the film, the hero kills no one, and Precrime is not preserved but shut down and the prisoners pardoned and released.

The hero in the film is a very different man from the protagonist of Dick's story, both younger and more sympathetic. Anderton here is not on the verge of retirement but a young man, played by Tom Cruise, so that he can engage in the physical action demanded by a cinematic thriller.

Minority Report: The hero on the run. The film turns Dick's Anderton into a young man so he can engage in the physical action of a film thriller. Twentieth Century Fox/Dreamworks, 2002.

Anderton is also wracked with grief and guilt: six years earlier, while Anderton and his little boy Sean were at a public swimming pool, Sean was
abducted and is presumed dead. In the wake of this trauma, his marriage
dissolved. Now he suffers from numerous addictions: to his work, which
prevents murders and so assuages his guilt over the loss of his son; to watching hologrammed tapes of happy scenes from his family life, when Sean
was alive and he was still with his wife; and to the addictive drug neuroin.
The film concerns "addiction, grief and addiction to grief . . . with addiction
to images as the primary metaphor" (James 13). *Minority Report* becomes
the story of the recovery of a fallen man who needs to get over his grief and
to return to his wife; losing his job leads to his redemption. His motive for
murder is now personal: not to preserve the system but to gain revenge for
the loss of his son. This reflects Spielberg's repeated concern with broken
families: lost children or the parents who seek them (as in *Close Encounters,
Poltergeist, The Color Purple, Empire of the Sun, Hook, A.I.,* and *Catch Me If You
Can*). David in *A.I.* grieves inconsolably for his lost mother, and Anderton
is inconsolable over the loss of his son.

Although Anderton is still the chief cop, the creator of Precrime and head
of the bureau is Lamar Burgess, Anderton's boss and his surrogate father.
In Dick's story, Anderton is ready for retirement; now it is his superior,
Burgess. Spielberg is following the conventions of film noir, in which the
detective is the underdog, often fighting a corrupt system controlled by the
killer, a situation which is inherently an oedipal, son-father conflict. Thus
Dick's elderly villain, General Kaplan, has been turned into the elderly
Burgess. Kaplan wanted to return the Army to power and so manipulated
Anderton; Burgess wants to conceal his crime to maintain power, so he sets
up Anderton and kills two more people. "Anderton does not realize until
long after we do that Burgess (Max von Sydow), his fatherly superior—following in the footsteps of hundreds of duplicitous Hollywood judges and
police commissioners before him—is perhaps not worthy of his undying
trust" (O'Hehir).

MINORITY REPORT AND *OEDIPUS REX*

In adapting Dick's story, Spielberg's screenwriters Tom Cohen and Scott
Frank, whether intentionally or not, highlighted the plot's oedipal nature.
The "precogs" are now turned into divine oracles and Anderton is like
Oedipus, the detective who discovers that the murderer is himself and pun-
ishes himself with self-blinding. Finally, Anderton's real enemy, whom he
ultimately must destroy, is Burgess, his fatherly superior.

Oedipus Rex is a murder mystery: who killed King Laius? Until the killer is
brought to justice, the state rests on shaky ground and the people will suffer.

In the film, the mystery is who killed Ann Lively, who turns out to be the mother of the precog Agatha. The murder of Ann Lively is the original sin on which the Precrime system was founded, and the system is corrupt and the state will suffer until the killer is revealed and punished. There is also another murder, or attempted murder, years before the action of *Oedipus Rex*: because of a prophecy, King Laius and Queen Jocasta had their infant Oedipus bound at the ankles and cast out on the mountainside to die. The corresponding event in the film is the abduction of Anderton's son Sean, who is missing and presumed dead.

Dick's story does not have a spiritual dimension, but the film does, which constitutes yet another parallel to the Sophoclean drama. Witwer, who in the film is a former divinity student, emphasizes the theological nature of the enterprise: the tank which holds the precogs is called "the Temple," and the public worships them as quasi-divine beings, like the oracles in Greek myth. One of Anderton's men says, "We're more like clergy than cops."

The theme of sight and blindness, both metaphoric and literal, also connects the film with *Oedipus Rex*. Dick's story ends with Anderton advising Witwer, "'Better keep your eyes open'" (102). One of the film's screenwriters, Tom Cohen, says, "One of the themes is about seeing, looking into the future. For me, that was the great insight about shaping the story into a script. . . . I found my theme: sight, eyes; what do you see, what does the hero see; what do the precogs see?" (*Minority* DVD). Burgess tells Anderton, "Remember the eyes—the eyes of the nation are on us now." Images of eyes are omnipresent in the film, as in the repeated closeups of the all-seeing eyes of the precog Agatha as she foresees murders. Anderton's job involves sight and insight: as detective, he takes the fragmentary visions of the precogs and, like a film editor, weaves the images together into a coherent narrative. But from the striking opening scene, a murder scene given us out of context and in a barrage of distorted and seemingly disconnected shots, images are often uncertain and subject to interpretation and reinterpretation. The film "raises crucial questions about the complexities of spectatorship, the shifting truth of images, and the inherent subjectivity of visual information" (Friedman 53). Agatha grabs Anderton and pleads with him, "Can you see?" Much later, when Anderton finally realizes that the murdered Ann Lively was Agatha's mother, he says to his wife, "How could I not have seen this?"

In an ironic scene in the opening, an unfaithful wife tells her husband, "You know how blind you are without your glasses." Meanwhile, their son is making a Lincoln mask for school: wielding a scissors, he cuts out the eyes. Such repeated images of blindness foreshadow Anderton's lack of insight and, later, the actual loss of his eyes. In an early scene, Anderton meets his drug connection in the dark, nighttime sprawl of the city. This narcotics peddler is a blind man, and when he removes his dark glasses, his eye sockets, horrifyingly, are empty pits. He tells Anderton, "In the land of the blind, the one-eyed man is king." This man resembles Tieresias (Friedman 55), the blind seer who taunts Oedipus: "You have eyes, but see not where in evil you are. . . . You who now see straight shall then be blind." The blind peddler foreshadows Anderton's physical condition later in the film.

When Anderton is on the run, he goes for advice to Dr. Hineman, a scientist who helped develop Precrime. She is a wise woman but also a kind of witch who breeds poisonous plants which nearly kill Anderton. Because the society tracks citizens through omnipresent retinal scans, she advises Anderton that his best hope is an illegal operation to replace his eyes. She tells him, "Sometimes in order to see the light, you have to risk the darkness." As Anderton leaves, the elderly doctor plants a big kiss directly on his lips, an inappropriate gesture for a woman old enough to be his mother. She is the film's Jocasta.

The eye operation is the most horrifying scene. It initiates a series of sadistic jokes at Anderton's expense, as if he must be punished for his crime (a crime he has not yet committed). The operation takes place in a filthy tenement, and is performed by a sleazy surgeon with a runny nose, a man Anderton once sent to prison for mutilating his patients. Now he has Anderton drugged and at his mercy. As he clamps on a device to hold Anderton's eyes open for surgery, he comments sarcastically, "Confinement was an education, a real eye opener." We fear that this doctor means to permanently blind him. After the operation, Anderton has his eyes bandaged and is left alone and told not to expose them to light for twelve hours or risk permanent blindness. Blindfolded, he stumbles about the apartment, where the creepy doctor has arranged some cruel jokes, such as planting rotten food in the refrigerator. Soon the police, searching for Anderton, unleash robot spiders. He submerges in a bath of ice water to evade them, but the robots find him and probe under the bandages with laser light. Later, in a comically gruesome scene, Anderton drops his old eyeballs and chases them as they roll down a corridor. The grisly notion of losing one's eyeballs plays on castration anxiety. Just as Oedipus gouged out his eyes to punish his crimes, Anderton must risk blindness to gain insight.

AGATHA AND ANDERTON

The central role played by Agatha in the film humanizes and softens the story, turning it from the tragic to the melodramatic. In Dick's story, the precogs are "three gibbering, fumbling creatures with their enlarged heads and wasted bodies. . . . All day long the idiots babbled, imprisoned in their special high-backed chairs, held in one rigid position by metal bands, and bundles of wiring, clamps. Their physical needs were taken care of automatically. They had no spiritual needs. Vegetable-like, they muttered and dozed and existed. Their minds were dull, confused, lost in shadows" (Dick 73). The description makes us pity these poor creatures, called "monkeys," who are imprisoned and exploited, yet in the story they are not freed.

In the film, however, the three precogs are three handsome young people, playfully named after writers of detective fiction: Dashiell, Arthur, and Agatha. Instead of being imprisoned in chairs, they lie drugged and floating in a pool, like embryos in amniotic fluid, their sleep periodically troubled by grotesque nightmares, repeated images of future murders. Wires attached to their shaven heads capture their visions on TV screens. Anderton says, "It's better if you don't think of them as human." They are cared for by a creepy attendant with a possessive love for his comatose wards, especially Agatha.

Because the precogs are humanized, the narrative creates the need to free them from their slavery. So instead of stealing the data tapes, as in Dick's story, in the film Anderton rescues Agatha and takes her with him to download the "minority report" which her mind contains. In the process, he discovers that they are both victims of Burgess, who not only set up Anderton but also, years before, to maintain Precrime killed Agatha's mother. Out of mutual victimization and need, the two become friends. Agatha helps him escape with her precognitive abilities and acts as Anderton's conscience, stopping him from killing his intended victim and helping him reconcile with his wife.

In many ways, Agatha resembles E.T. Spielberg says that Agatha "gets a chance to experience the world for the first time when she emerges from the liquid tank. She's embryonic" (Kennedy 112). Samantha Morton, who plays Agatha, says, "She's a child. . . . She has a wisdom far beyond her years. . . . She's an oracle. . . . She feels people's pain and suffering" (*Minority* DVD). Spielberg's cinematographer Janus Kaminski says of Agatha, "She has this angelic quality. . . . I wanted to reflect that quality in lighting" (*Minority* DVD). These are also attributes of E.T., who is embryonic—he even resembles a fetus—innocent and childlike and experiencing this world for the first time. E.T. is a seemingly helpless child who is also angelic and messianic, possessed of paranormal powers and able telepathically to feel people's pain and suffering.

Agatha and Anderton are like twins, a pair of lost children who rescue each other. Agatha is an orphan whose mother was murdered; because of her gifts, she is a slave to the Precrime system. Anderton too has lost his family and lost his way. Just as E.T. and Elliott are psychologically twinned, and E.T. heals Elliott's broken family while the boy helps the alien return home, so Agatha and Anderton are linked: Agatha heals Anderton's broken family while Anderton helps her find a home. Nigel Morris notes "a shot modeled from *Persona*, as Agatha and Anderton form a Janus-faced image, suggestive of merging of identity or personalities" (Morris 325).

Minority Report: Anderton and Agatha as twins. Twentieth Century
Fox/Dreamworks, 2002.

Warren Buckland, however, sees Agatha and Anderton not as twins but
as a potential daughter-father unit, especially since Anderton kidnaps her
from her pool just as his son was kidnaped from a swimming pool. "But
the script does not take this possible road." Instead, in the happy ending,
Anderton is reunited with his wife and they are expecting another child.
Precrime has been shut down and the precogs freed and transferred to a
remote island where they can live in peace. Buckland finds this ending
"forced and unsatisfactory" (Buckland 207). Morris too calls it a "sickly
sentimental Hollywood ending" (Morris 327).

CONCLUSION

Spielberg says of *Minority Report:* "I wanted to make the ugliest, dirtiest
movie I've ever made. I want this movie to be dark and grainy and the world
to be really cold. This is a rather rough and tumble and gritty world of film
noir, which I'd never really done film noir before" (*Minority* DVD). The film
is indeed dark and disturbing, both visually and thematically. It borrows

some of Dick's paranoid vision and it even skirts the darkest edge of all, the realm of *Oedipus Rex.*

Yet Spielberg's fundamental sweetness and light only let him skirt but not enter the tragic. Oedipus has no choice in his destiny; it has all been predetermined. Anderton is shown his destiny, yet Agatha tells him, "You can choose." He chooses not to kill and thus averts the fate of Oedipus. The ending steers the film out of the darkness and into the light. Anderton becomes not like Oedipus but more like Saint Paul, who persecuted Christians until he was blinded by the light of God.

REFERENCES

Aldiss, Brian. *Billion Year Spree: The True History of Science Fiction.* New York: Shocken, 1974.

Buckland, Warren. *Directed by Steven Spielberg: Poetics of the Contemporary Hollywood Blockbuster.* New York: Continuum, 2006.

Cook, Albert. *Oedipus Rex: A Mirror for Greek Drama.* Belmont, CA: Wadsworth, 1964.

Dick, Philip K. "The Minority Report," *The Minority Report and Other Classic Stories.* New York: Kensington, 2002, 71–102.

Friedman, Lester D. *Citizen Spielberg.* Urbana: University of Illinois Press, 2006.

Freud, Sigmund. "On the Mechanism of Paranoia (1911)." *General Psychological Theory.* Rpt. New York: Crowell-Collier, 1963, 29–48.

James, Nick. "An Eye for an Eye." *Sight and Sound* 12.8 (August 2002): 13–15.

Kennedy, Lisa. "Spielberg in the Twilight Zone." *Wired*, June 2002, 106–13, 146.

Mackey, Douglas A. *Philip K. Dick.* Boston, MA: G. K. Hall, 1988.

Minority Report DVD. 2002. Director: Steven Spielberg.

Morris, Nigel. *The Cinema of Steven Spielberg: Empire of Light.* London: Wallflower, 2007.

O'Hehir, Andrew. "Meet Steven Spielberg, hardboiled cynic," Salon.com, June 21, 2002. http//:dir.salon.com/ent/movies/reviews/2002/06/21/minority_report/print.html

15

War of the Worlds (2005) and Trauma Culture

THE TRAUMA OF 9/11

Speaking of his 2005 film version of *The War of the Worlds*, Spielberg mentions "the image of everybody in Manhattan fleeing across the Brooklyn Bridge in the shadow of 9/11, which is something that is a searing image that I haven't been able to get out of my head. This [the movie] is partially about the American refugee experience, because it's certainly about Americans fleeing for their lives after being attacked for no reason, having no idea why they're being attacked and who is attacking them" (Interview).

As E. Ann Kaplan observes, "visual media like cinema become the mechanisms through which a culture can unconsciously address its traumatic hauntings." Cinema can "allow spectators to register what they (and the culture at large) do not want to consciously 'know'"(Kaplan 69). But politics intervenes in managing cultural trauma. Kaplan questions, "May cinema in its classical and dominant Hollywood form, 'translate' an event for a culture, unconsciously colluding with dominant political forces?" (66). Apart from docudramas like *United 93* (2006) and *World Trade Center* (2006), echoes of 9/11 have begun to creep into American fiction films, with *War of the Worlds* being a blatant example. My question is whether, by translating the events of 9/11 into the context of a fictional horror story, Spielberg is helping the culture to overcome the trauma, or "unconsciously colluding with dominant political forces," or simply exploiting the horror of real events.

According to Kaja Silverman, historical trauma is what "interrupts or even deconstitutes what a society assumes to be its master narratives" (55). An injury to the American body politic, 9/11 was a historical rupture, a moment of collective trauma that we still have not worked through. With drastic suddenness, it interrupted such American master narratives as the notions of American innocence, American exceptionalism, and American invulnerability. Such an event shatters the sense of national identity. No attack on American soil by a foreign power had taken place for sixty years, since Pearl Harbor in 1941. The destruction of the World Trade Center came out of the clear blue sky, not during wartime, and the victims were civilians. The television, newspaper, and magazine images of 9/11 shocked the world and continue to haunt the American imagination. Millions witnessed the plane crashes, the catastrophic fall of the towers, and the death of thousands on live television, as the events happened. Even those who did not lose friends or loved ones or who were not in New York that day experienced secondary or vicarious trauma via the media. "Given trauma's visuality as a psychic disorder, this event seemed to feed trauma by being so highly visual in its happening. The images haunted one waking and dreaming. American culture was visually haunted by the repeated still unbelievable shots of a huge plane full of people plunging into a seemingly impenetrable tower, and bursting into fabulous orange flames" (Kaplan 13).

The United States is still wounded by 9/11. It is, in fact, to the advantage of the government to make 9/11 the code for a permanent state of emergency, "deployed in the telescoping of an entire worldwide threat into the living rooms of each and all of us" (Simpson 17). Hal Foster wonders whether, in the wake of 9/11, we are now living in WTC: "World Trauma Center," a trauma that results in endless, nightmarish fear and perpetual war across the globe (Foster). In other words, we all may now be undergoing *The War of the Worlds*.

Cathy Caruth defines post-traumatic stress disorder as

> a response, sometimes delayed, to an overwhelming event or events, which takes the form of repeated, intrusive hallucinations, dreams, thoughts or behaviors stemming from the event, along with numbing that may have begun during or after the experience. . . . The event is not assimilated or experienced fully at the time, but only belatedly. . . . To be traumatized is precisely to be possessed by an event. . . . The traumatized, we might say, carry an impossible history within them, or they become themselves the symptom of a history that they cannot entirely possess (4–5).

American society, then, can be said to still be possessed by the impossible history or rupture in our historical narratives represented by 9/11.

H. G. WELLS'S *THE WAR OF THE WORLDS*

That may help in part to explain Spielberg's attraction to *The War of the Worlds*. H. G. Wells's *The War of the Worlds* (1898) is a paradigmatic text which has been reworked in various iterations for over a century. Wells invented many of the tropes of science fiction, and this novel, the very first alien invasion story, seems to have particular resonance for the shocks of modernity. When it appeared in 1898, it reflected popular apocalyptic, fin de siècle fears about the impact of science and technology. Wells was doing a variation on a popular subgenre of the time, the tale of invasion, novels such as Chesney's *The Battle of Dorking* (1871), fictions which seemed to anticipate the total, technological wars of the twentieth century (McConnell 131–33). In addition, *War of the Worlds* includes Wells's critique of British imperialism. The narrator says of the invading Martians, "And before we judge of them too harshly we must remember what ruthless and utter destruction our own species has wrought, not only upon animals, such as the vanished bison and the dodo, but upon its own inferior species. The Tasmanians, in spite of their human likeness, were entirely swept out of existence in a war of extermination waged by European immigrants, in the space of fifty years. Are we such apostles of mercy as to complain if the Martians warred in the same spirit?" (Wells, 4).

War of the Worlds is a scare story, a tale of horror that has always been associated with moments of historical trauma. Forty years after the novel, less than a year before the beginning of the massive slaughter of World War II, when Americans feared rising fascism and imminent war in Europe and Japan, Orson Welles's famous radio dramatization created widespread panic among jittery Americans who mistook it for the real thing. In 1953, the Hollywood version, produced by George Pal, played on Cold War fears of Communist invasion and the atomic bomb. And in 2005, Steven Spielberg's version, which pays homage to all its predecessors—the novel, the radio adaptation, and the 1953 film—is a horror movie which depends upon the fear of terrorism in the wake of the trauma of 9/11 and the Iraq War.

To begin with, Wells's novel recounts the invasion of England by Martians, who land in capsules and then construct giant tripods, huge fighting machines which lay waste to the populace and the landscape with heat rays and poisonous black smoke. The British army and its weapons are quickly destroyed by the overwhelming power of the Martian machines, and terrified refugees flee the towns and cities in search of safety. "It was a stampede—stampede gigantic and terrible—without order and without a goal, six million people, unarmed and unprovisioned, driving headlong. It was the beginning of the rout of civilization, of the massacre of mankind" (Wells, 171). The story is told in vivid and horrific detail by an unnamed first-person narrator, a writer who witnesses events as he wanders the countryside, struggling to survive and to get back to his wife. We also get a third-person account of his brother's escape from London and journey to the coast to catch a ship. Along the way, the narrator is trapped in a house with a cowardly curate who goes insane, until the narrator knocks him out to silence his raving because it may attract the invaders. A Martian probe enters the house and drags the curate to his doom. The narrator later briefly joins forces with an artilleryman who has concocted a bizarre plan to fight the invaders from underground.

The Martians are hideous monsters, physically repulsive and utterly ruthless. To them, human beings are beasts for slaughter or insects they trample underfoot. The artilleryman tells the narrator, "'This isn't a war. . . . It never was a war, any more than there's a war between men and ants'" (254). Those the Martians do not exterminate, they harvest, seizing people whom they imprison in baskets hanging from the tripods. For the Martians "took the fresh, living blood of other creatures and injected it into their own veins. . . . Blood obtained from a still living animal, in most cases from a human being, was run directly by means of a little pipette into the recipient canal" (208). Bram Stoker's incredibly popular *Dracula* appeared only a year before *War of the Worlds*. Wells, always commercially canny, adds to the aliens' monstrosity by making them vampires.

In the end, the Martians appear to have won. In a suicidal mood, the narrator enters London, seeking out the invaders, only to discover them dying. He and the rest of humanity is saved not because of the military but because the Martians have no resistance to Earth's bacteria. He returns home and is reunited with his wife.

ORSON WELLES AND GEORGE PAL DO
THE WAR OF THE WORLDS

Orson Welles's 1938 radio broadcast opens and closes with his narration, straight from the opening and closing chapters of the novel. But he restructures the story for radio, updating it to 1938, transposing the events from England to New Jersey, and brilliantly turning it into a simulated real broadcast, live music periodically interrupted by increasingly alarming news bulletins. There are interviews with scientists, military officers, and bystanders, and eyewitness accounts by breathless reporters. A curious mob surrounds the pit containing the Martian cylinder until it opens and the broadcast abruptly breaks off. Finally the growing catastrophe preempts all other programming. This technique gives the drama tremendous immediacy and poignancy, as if the crisis were occurring while you are listening. As the tripods wade across the Hudson, they shoot down a fleet of bomber planes with heat rays. A reporter atop a skyscraper describes New York being taken over as he awaits his doom. The news reports finally end in an ominous silence. The second half of the program is the journal of a scientist named Pierson, also voiced by Orson Welles. Like the narrator in the novel, he wanders the blighted landscape and meets a man with a plan, a dangerous crank who echoes a lot of the dialogue of the artilleryman. The radio broadcast ends like the novel, with mankind saved by bacteria.

The 1953 George Pal film, directed by Byron Haskin, incorporates elements of both the novel and the radio show. It retains the opening and closing voice-over narration and also the reporters broadcasting on location. The film updates the events to the early 1950s and sets them in southern California but expands the action through montages to suggest that the invasion is occurring simultaneously around the world. The hero is once again a scientist, but now he is a Hollywood handsome young man who spends most of the movie repeatedly saving his new love interest, the damsel in distress. A long sequence in which they are trapped in a farmhouse surrounded by Martians is the only one which repeats a scene from the novel. The other major plot line concerns the military's attempts to coordinate their defenses, culminating in the dropping of an atomic bomb on a nest of alien ships in the southern California hills. The military officers are shown in a positive light, as strong, efficient leaders who do their best, even though all their efforts prove futile since the Martian ships are equipped with impenetrable force fields. These aliens are even more unstoppable than in Wells's novel.

The 1953 film is fast moving and features fine visual and sound effects. The Martian ships in particular look and sound truly evil (Warren 157). They are not tripods but resemble floating manta rays with cobra heads which shoot out green death rays, vaporizing everything they touch. Kim Newman calls it "an erotic apocalypse. With its pretty colors, flashing lights, and unearthly zapping noises, *War of the Worlds* discovers the pornography of the Bomb" (Newman 122).

But the film is marred by an intrusive religiosity: a minister advances on the Martian ships, holding up a Bible and reciting the twenty-third psalm, only to get zapped; in the final scenes, several churches are blasted. In the end, the hero and heroine are reunited in a church, and saved as if by a miracle. Mark Jancovich argues that the heroine "embodies the Christian values which the film promotes, and which the hero eventually must learn to embrace" (Jancovich 56). Science and technology will not save them, but prayer will. The implication is that the invading Martians, who stand in here for the Communists, are defeated because they are godless. At the time, the United States was engaged in a war against the Communists in Korea, which also explains the film's pro-military stance, despite the fact that the army is ineffective against the invasion.

According to Jancovich, the film, which opens in a small town in southern California, celebrates small-town America. In the towns, people are "warm and supportive," but when the action shifts to Los Angeles, we see urban riots (56). Panicked mobs fleeing the city knock the hero down and steal his truck. As John J. Smith claims, in 1950s science fiction film, "the

usual remedy for alien invasion is almost invariably regression to a paternalistic, hierarchical system," here represented by Christianity and small-
town, family values (Smith 90).

SPIELBERG'S VERSION

Spielberg's film pays homage to over a hundred years of different versions
of *War of the Worlds*, incorporating elements of the novel, the radio broadcast, and the 1953 film. Once again, it is updated to the present day in
the United States, opening not in California as in the previous film but in
New Jersey, as in the radio show. The origin of the invaders is unspecified;
today we know too much to call them "Martians." The tripods resemble the
machines described by H. G. Wells, but they are nearly invulnerable due to
protective force fields, as in the 1953 film. And the aliens are vampires, as
in the novel. The hero is beaten up and his car stolen by a panicked mob,
as in the film. Later he meets a loony survivalist who tries to recruit him
to the resistance, as in the novel and the radio show. There is an extended
sequence with the characters trapped in a farmhouse, surrounded by aliens,
until an alien probe searches them out, as in the novel and the film. And,
like all the versions of the story, the aliens are destroyed at the end not by
military force but by bacteria. Finally, in homage to the 1953 version, he
includes the stars of that film, Gene Barry and Anne Robinson, in a cameo
appearance as the children's grandparents in the final scene.

Spielberg says that although he admires the 1953 film, "I just thought
that we could make a version a little closer and darker toward the original
novel"(Interview). His version is intense, almost unremittingly grim and
scary. Reviewers saw it as the opposite of the sweetness and light of *Close
Encounters* or *E.T.*, with their gentle aliens, but compared it instead to other,
more horrific Spielberg science fiction and fantasy films, such as *Duel*, *Jaws*,
Jurassic Park, and *A.I.* And they saw as well parallels with his early film
about a squabbling couple on the road, *The Sugarland Express*. Finally, they
likened it to his previous war films: *Empire of the Sun*, *Saving Private Ryan*,
and *Schindler's List*. Spielberg says, referring to alien invasion films, such
as the 1953 *War of the Worlds* and *Independence Day* (1996), "It could have
been much more about the army vs. the extraterrestrials. I didn't want to
go there. I wanted this, in a strange way, to be a little more of a cousin to
Saving Private Ryan in the genre of science fiction. It's more of a story told
in a first person point of view" (Interview).

This time the hero is not a writer or a scientist but a working-class guy.
Ray Ferrier is a typical Spielberg hero, an ordinary man in extraordinary
circumstances, pushed to his limits and beyond. One reviewer writes that
"the 1953 version dramatized the collective efforts of Americans and their

overseas allies to resist the invasion through the same kind of alliance that defeated Nazism. . . . By contrast, Tom Cruise as anti-hero seeks only to take the next step out of harm's way" (Review).

Like the radio program and the George Pal film, this *War of the Worlds* sets up the action in a prelude using voice-over narration. In an arresting visual, the opening shot shows swarming bacteria, pulling back to reveal paramecium, until finally we see that all this activity is happening in a single drop of water on a leaf. The round drop then changes into the planet Earth seen from space, mirroring the narration about humanity being studied coldly by alien beings, as if we were bacteria under a microscope. The microscopic organisms in the opening also foreshadow the defeat of the aliens, so that the film returns to the same images in the end.

The opening scene shows the New York skyline from across the Hudson. On the New Jersey docks, a huge crane unloads cargo. The camera closes in to introduce Ray Ferrier, a stevedore high atop the crane, working the controls to move huge metal containers. His operation of an enormous machine is mimicked later by the killer tripods, which are also controlled by operators at the top. We almost anticipate a scene later on in which Ray takes control of one of the alien machines to use it against them, but since this never happens there is no payoff to the opening scene.

If the 1953 movie promoted family values through a boy-meets-girl plot, Spielberg's film turns into a melodrama about a dysfunctional family bonding through crisis.

War of the Worlds: Father and daughter face the unknown. Paramount, 2005.

As in M. Night Shyamalan's film *Signs* (2002), an alien invasion is viewed through the eyes of a family, and the entire global catastrophe seems designed simply to bring one family together. Spielberg has obsessively worked and reworked the absentee dad and the imperiled family in his science fiction and fantasy films: in *Hook* (1991), a workaholic dad must rescue his kidnapped children from Captain Hook by accessing his inner Pan; in *Jurassic Park* (1993), a kid-hating scientist must shepherd two children to safety across a park filled with rampaging dinosaurs; in *The Lost World: Jurassic Park II* (1997), a neglectful dad must rescue his daughter, again from dinosaurs.

Typical of Spielberg's films, Ray is a defective father, an overgrown adolescent who must learn responsibility for his kids. Ray lives in a working-class neighborhood near the Bayonne bridge, in a messy town home with a partially disassembled V-8 engine in the living room. He is divorced and alienated from his kids, ten-year-old Rachel and sixteen-year-old Robbie, who are left with him for the weekend while his wife Mary Ann visits her parents in Boston. The remarried Mary Ann is now pregnant. Working-class Ray resents her yuppie husband Tim and his expensive new SUV, and also resents Tim's affectionate relationship with the children. But Ray has not prepared for the children's visit. He arrives a half-hour late, has an empty refrigerator, goes to bed and tells his daughter to order out for a meal.

Rachel at least gives him a hug, but the sullen Robbie refuses to speak to him. When Ray tries male bonding via an aggressive game of catch, Robbie participates reluctantly and then walks away, saying, "You're an asshole. I hate coming here." This family is uniformly unlikeable—the childish father, the sullen teenage son, the spoiled and wise-beyond-her years daughter— and their squabbling quickly grows tiresome because it is overly familiar from a hundred American melodramas and comedies, both in the movies and on television.

Thankfully, the meat and potatoes of the film soon takes over: pure, terrifying, run-for-your-life spectacle, raw, visceral, and extremely shocking, although some of it is horrifically beautiful, even haunting: a gathering storm and shattering blasts of lightning; the first eruption of a gigantic alien tripod from beneath a Newark street; the fragments of a fallen jetliner strewn across a suburban neighborhood; a host of dead bodies glimpsed by a little girl as they float down a river; a panicked mob seizing the family's car and ejecting the family; a railway train speeding past a crossing, every car ablaze; a tripod rising like Leviathan out of the Hudson River to overturn a ferry.

PARALLELS TO 9/11

Blatant parallels to 9/11 meant to disturb or scare us begin early and continue throughout the film. First, the catastrophic event erupts without warning on the city streets on an ordinary fall day during peacetime, striking civilians who are totally unprepared and unprotected. After the giant tripod bursts out of the street, it begins incinerating everyone in sight with heat rays. The victims are instantly reduced to ash, which covers the fleeing Ray, like the survivors coated in white powder as they struggled through clouds of dust in lower Manhattan after the fall of the towers.

As in 9/11, the attack comes out of nowhere, and no one knows who is responsible or what their goals are:

ROBBIE: "Is it terrorists?"

RAY: "These came from someplace else."

ROBBIE: "You mean, like Europe?"

RAY: "No, Robbie—not like Europe!"

The family takes shelter in the mother's new home in the suburbs. But during the night, it is struck by a downed airliner. As during 9/11, there seems to be no safe place. In the morning, Ray walks amid the debris of the crashed jet, yet another echo of the traumatic event. Seeing the wreckage, the enraged young Robbie is eager for revenge, and he tries twice to run away and join the army, like many patriotic American teenagers after 9/11.

After they lose the car to a panicked mob, they join the exodus crossing a bridge on foot. This procession of refugees is Spielberg's recalling "the im-

War of the Worlds: Fascinated and horrified spectators watch alien tripods erupt from the ground. This evokes the witnesses in Manhattan on 9/11. Paramount, 2005.

age of everybody in Manhattan fleeing across the Brooklyn Bridge." People hold up posters with pictures of missing persons, and the signboards at the ferry dock are thick with such homemade signs, like the streets of lower Manhattan in the days after 9/11.

Another echo of 9/11 is the haunting image of the family fleeing through the woods under a rain of falling fragments of clothing, the only remnants of the vaporized dead. This is reminiscent not only of the debris from the destroyed buildings which drifted across New York after the disaster but also of the black ash falling across Krakow from the sky from the bonfires of dead bodies in *Schindler's List*.

Spielberg's *War of the Worlds* is a profoundly dark and disturbing film, made even scarier because it replays fearful images of a recent, real catastrophe. Perhaps the parallels are justified because, as David Simpson says, the events of 9/11 looked "like the work of agents so unfamiliar as to seem almost like aliens" (Simpson 6). Kai Erikson notes that, in trauma, "Something alien breaks in on you, smashing through whatever barriers your mind has set up as line of defense. It invades you, takes you over, becomes a dominating feature of your interior landscape . . . and in the process threatens to drain you and leave you empty" (183). That could serve as an excellent summary of Spielberg's film, including the revelation that these aliens feed on human blood and drain you dry.

PARALLELS TO THE IRAQ WAR

There is also a subtext in the film related not only to 9/11 but also to the Iraq War. Early in the film, his mother mentions that Robbie must complete a homework assignment on the French occupation of Algeria. And Harlan Ogilvy, the loony survivalist, says: "We're the resistance, Ray. They can't occupy this country. Occupations always fail. History's taught us that a thousand times." "You can read our movie several ways," says screenwriter David Koepp. "It could be straight 9/11 paranoia. Or it could be about how U.S. military interventionism abroad is doomed by insurgency, just the way an alien invasion might be" (Barboza). Lester Friedman says, "As Wells's novel transformed England into a nation whose people are subjugated or massacred, so Spielberg shows Americans as refugees in their own country, forced to abandon their homes and suffering under direct siege from a superior military force" (Friedman 159). In other words, Spielberg's film forces Americans to experience what the Iraqis must have felt during the American "shock and awe" and subsequent occupation.

Nevertheless, if it intends such a critique, then the film is inconsistent because Ogilvy, the only spokesman for the resistance, is both wrong about history and insane. As mentioned, the aliens are not destroyed by an insurgency but by bacteria. Spielberg also tries to recuperate the otherwise helpless U.S. military near the end by showing the army bring down a tripod by firing bazookas, but the scene is superfluous because the aliens are already dying.

Moreover, the film cannot be about both the 9/11 attacks on America and the American occupation of Iraq because the two are fundamentally different events: in the former, the Americans were the victims, but in the latter, the aggressors. If the film is intended to support both readings, as David Koepp suggests, then it is confused and self-contradictory. H. G. Wells's novel may have been intended as a critique of European colonialism, but Spielberg's film finally contains no coherent political message (Villareal). Writes one reviewer: "*War of the Worlds* is an old-fashioned monster movie—one that, despite some pretensions, ultimately has nothing more profound to say than 'mass death and destruction are bad'" (Noah).

THE ENDING

By showing a family that survives and is strengthened and a cruel enemy that is ultimately defeated, Spielberg seems to be trying to leave us with an upbeat ending. Yet the message audiences take away contradicts that optimism. Because the veneer of civilization in the film breaks down so quickly, and groups act mostly as panicked mobs, selfishly and violently, one reviewer suggests that the real message is that "humanity exists in a Hobbesian state" (Review). And I wondered what will become of Ray's little daughter Rachel, who screams throughout the film as she repeatedly witnesses mass death and destruction, narrowly escapes death, and is traumatized a dozen times over.

Like little Rachel, the film works us over and leaves us exhausted, not redeemed. It is too long and spasmodic in structure. The 1953 film moved briskly, but this version drags, and the farmhouse sequence—trapped in the basement with a madman—weighs it down.

Despite the length of the film, the happy ending feels rushed and unearned. Boston is surprisingly untouched by the catastrophe. Robbie's survival is improbable and unexplained since the last time we saw him he was on a hillside that was enveloped in flames. The presence of Gene Barry and Anne Robinson from the 1953 film doing a cameo as the grandparents suddenly yanks us out of the narrative and reminds us we are only watching a movie, robbing the audience of some of the potential catharsis of the ending. Furthermore, although the father and son finally hug, Ray is left out in the middle of the street as the rest stand on the porch above him. No one invites him in. It is an awkward moment: his wife is pregnant with another man's child, his in-laws still reject him, and there is no place for him in the family structure.

SPIELBERG'S FILM AND NATIONAL TRAUMA

Given the film's general bleakness, does it perform any healing function for an American audience traumatized by 9/11 and kept in a state of permanent crisis and fear by the government? Communal trauma, according to Kai Erikson, can take two forms: "damage to the tissues that hold human groups intact, and the creation of social climates, communal moods, that come to dominate a group's spirit" (Erikson 190). 9/11 and its aftermath seems to have done both kinds of damage to the American body politic. A few reviewers were genuinely offended by the film's persistent analogies between horrible, real-life events and fantasy, such as Stephanie Zacharek, who says "I suspect Spielberg wants to cover all the bases: 'War of the Worlds' can be a political movie for those who want to see it as such, and a mindless entertainment for everyone else" (Zacharek). And Timothy Noah writes indignantly, "Because *War of the Worlds* has nothing to say about 9/11, its appropriation of 9/11 imagery can only be described as pornographic. . . . He borrowed from a real-world tragedy—one about which feelings are still fairly raw" (Noah). It is surprising that Spielberg, who showed such sensitivity to Holocaust survivors in *Schindler's List*, might exploit recent mass trauma simply to scare us with a horror movie.

So maybe the film retraumatizes the audience, reopens the wound of 9/11 for no good reason. Or perhaps it is more symptom of trauma than therapy, a replay of the events, for, "above all, trauma involves a continual reliving of some wounding experience in daydreams and nightmares, flashbacks and hallucinations, and in compulsive seeking out of similar circumstances. . . . Our memory repeats to us what we haven't yet come to terms with, with what still haunts us" (Erikson 184). Spielberg too may be possessed by the images of 9/11, compelled to replay but not yet able to master them.

REFERENCES

Barboza, Craig. "Imagination is infinite." *USA Weekend*, June 19, 2005. www .usaweekend.com/05_issues/050619/050619spielberg.html

Caruth, Cathy, ed. *Trauma: Explorations in Memory*. Baltimore, MD: Johns Hopkins University Press, 1995.

Erikson, Kai. "Notes on Trauma and Community." *Trauma: Explorations in Memory*. Ed. Cathy Caruth, Baltimore, MD: Johns Hopkins University Press, 1995: 183–99.

Foster, Hal. "In New York." *London Review of Books*, March 20, 2003.

Friedman, Lester D. *Citizen Spielberg*. Urbana: University of Illinois Press, 2006.

Interview with Steven Spielberg. www.cinecon.com/news.php?id=0506281

Jancovich, Mark. *Rational Fears: American Horror in the 1950s*. Manchester: Manchester University Press, 1996.

Kaplan, E. Ann. *Trauma Culture: The Politics of Terror and Loss in Media and Literature.* New Brunswick, NJ: Rutgers University Press, 2005.

McConnell, Frank. *The Science Fiction of H. G. Wells.* New York: Oxford University Press, 1981.

Newman, Kim. *Apocalypse Movies: End of the World Cinema.* New York: St. Martin's, 1999.

Noah, Timothy. "9/11 Was No Summer Movie." Slate.com, July 19, 2005. www.slate .com/id/2123008/

Review of *The War of the Worlds* posted to www.marxmail.org on July 5, 2005. www.columbia.edu/~lnp3/mydocs/culture/WaroftheWorlds.htm

Silverman, Kaja. *Male Subjectivity at the Margins.* New York and London: Routledge, 1992.

Simpson, David. *9/11: The Culture of Commemoration.* Chicago: University of Chicago Press, 2006.

Smith, John J. *Men of the Cold War: Warrior Ethos and Domesticity in 1950s America.* Dissertation, University of Florida, Gainesville, FL, 2002.

Villareal, Phil. "Spielberg Wows Us." Tucson, *Arizona Daily Star*, June 29, 2005. www.aztarnet.com/dailystar/printSN/81810.php

The War of the Worlds (Paramount, 1953). Producer: George Pal. Director: Byron Haskin. Screenplay: Barré Lyndon. Starring: Gene Barry, Ann Robinson, Les Tremayne.

War of the Worlds (Dreamworks and Paramount, 2005). Producers: Kathleen Kennedy, Colin Wilson. Director: Steven Spielberg. Screenplay: Josh Friedman, David Koepp. Starring: Tom Cruise, Dakota Fanning, Miranda Otto, Tim Robbins.

Warren, Bill. *Keep Watching the Skies: American Science Fiction Movies of the Fifties,* Volume I: 1950–1957. Jefferson, NC: McFarland, 1982.

Wells, H. G. *The War of the Worlds.* 1898; rpt. New York: Simon and Schuster, 2005.

Zacharek, Stephanie. Review of *War of the Worlds.* Salon.com, June 29, 2005. http://dir.salon.com/story/ent/movies/review/2005/06/29/war/index .html?CP=IMD&DN=110

Conclusion

Moving Toward the Light

SEPARATION AND ABANDONMENT

Whether they are SF, fantasy, or more "realistic" genres, Spielberg's films deal with certain repeated situations: kidnaping or imprisonment, invasion by monsters or aliens, and the stranger-in-a-strange-land facing problems of adaptation and communication.

Certain plot devices—separation and abandonment, the quest of the parent for the lost child or of the lost child for the parent, and the last-minute rescue—occur in almost every Spielberg movie, and he often makes films about broken homes, families in trouble, and children in peril. Spielberg's suburban trilogy—domestic fantasies, cinematic fairy tales about loss, separation, and abandonment, culminating in mother-and-child reunions—are his signature films, in which he forged his characteristic style and subject matter. As I argue, in some ways *Close Encounters*, *E.T.*, and *Poltergeist* are so closely linked that they might be considered three versions of the same film, which re-create Spielberg's boyhood home in suburbia and attempt to overcome the shattering of that idyllic existence caused by his parents' divorce. He says, "*E.T.* is a film that was inside me for many years and could only come out after a lot of suburban psychodrama" (Sragow 108). Elsewhere, he says, "The whole thing about separation is something that runs very deep in anyone exposed to divorce. All of us [his entire family] are still suffering the repercussions of a divorce that had to happen. But the whole idea of being taken away from your parents and forced to adapt to a new routine—I'm *not* good with change, personally speaking" (Forsberg 129). Although these films may stem from his personal trauma, they also speak to the concerns of an increasingly rootless postwar America, with its rising divorce rate.

He has made many other films about "being taken away from your parents": either the parents seek the little child lost or the child searches for the lost parents. Even *Saving Private Ryan* is about a search for a lost boy, Mrs. Ryan's sole surviving son. His films often end with joyful reunions or tearful, prolonged farewells: the lost child has been returned to the family or the family must reluctantly part with a loved one. *Close Encounters, E.T., Schindler, A.I.,* and *The Terminal* combine the family reunion with the protracted farewell, blending the sweet and the sad. Spielberg altered the true story to give Oskar Schindler a more melodramatic final parting from his Jewish "family."

Behind the suburban trilogy, *Empire of the Sun,* and many other Spielberg films, including *Schindler,* is a child's fear of being separated from family, driven from home, in peril of his life. They are animated by a deep desire for rescue. The little child lost in a nightmare world is a story Spielberg tells over and over, a tale of sentiment and horror, a fairy-tale journey through anxiety and depression into the elation of last-minute rescue. The fear in his films is often counterbalanced by wonder; indeed, the wonder may be a defense against the anxiety.

CHILDREN IN PERIL: TWO SCENES

I want to look at two scenes concerning children in peril—one from *Close Encounters* and another from *Schindler's List*—which epitomize the spectrum of Spielberg's work, from wonder to terror, from dream to nightmare.

The first, from *Close Encounters,* is the third scene in the movie, a quintessentially cinematic moment without dialogue, just the play of light and sound. The first two scenes—in the Mexican desert and in the Indianapolis Air Traffic Control Center—establish a buildup of strange events worldwide involving UFOs, but the third scene moves the action from the large, public world into an intimate closeup on the domestic uncanny, as aliens invade a typical American household, and it gives us a child's-eye view of the event. Four-year-old Barry Guiler, a blonde-haired, pug-nosed little boy, awakens in his bed in an ordinary midwestern home in Muncie, Indiana, in the middle of the night to unexpected noise and commotion: battery-operated toys suddenly animating themselves. A monkey clangs cymbals, as if heralding something, and Frankenstein's pants fall down (a strange contradiction—a harmless, comic monster). While toy police cars, with sirens blaring and lights blinking, crash into toy planes, suggesting an emergency, a phonograph turns itself on and plays a children's song, telling him to "Look with care for the shape of a square," suggesting a quest. Wearing a Boston University t-shirt and pajama bottoms with booties (Spielberg carefully grounds his fantasies in such contemporary American details), little Barry goes downstairs to investigate. So the opening images of the scene suggest a monstrous disturbance, an intrusion of the chaotic, the inexplicable, and the uncanny into the everyday, domestic scene, and these mysterious, unseen alien invaders constitute an emergency. There is something monstrous about them—yet at the same time a contrary suggestion of something appealingly childlike and comic, so that the little boy is curious rather than fearful.

Downstairs, Barry finds the front door open, and then the screen door suddenly swings shut. Yet he can't find anyone. In the kitchen, there is chaos: the refrigerator wide open, drawers pulled out, Coke spilling from a tipped-over can, a trail of cans, carrots, packages of meat, and broken eggs strewn across the floor, the dog door rapidly banging back and forth, as if someone—or something—has just made a midnight raid. (Later in the movie, the boy will be abducted by unseen aliens through that same door.) Barry walks into the kitchen and looks down at the mess.

When he looks up, there is a long, sustained closeup on his face. In the background, tree shadows flicker on the walls. He gazes at some unspecified thing or things offscreen, at his eye level, something moving and making noises. We hear a tinkling sound and a rattle like a can rolling across the floor. He stands and stares with the totally absorbed, rapturous gaze of a little boy. His head turns back and forth. We never see what he is looking at, but the camera stays in a closeup on his face for what seems an extraordinarily long stretch of screen time as he registers first curiosity, then astonishment, and finally sheer delight. His eyes widen, his mouth drops open, and then a big smile breaks across his face at the antics of something strange and amusing that we now wish devotedly to see.[1] We must wait till the end of the film to witness what Barry was looking at.

This scene opens with elements of mystery and danger: unseen, alien intruders, a household invaded and turned upside down, and a child alone and in peril. These elements are repeated in the other two films of Spielberg's suburban trilogy, *E.T.* and *Poltergeist*. Usually the scenes balance between fear and wonder, although in *Poltergeist*, the unseen alien intruders are horror-movie monsters. In this scene from *Close Encounters*, the alien invasion and the mess are resolved as benign through a child's grin. Barry's wonder balances the adults' fear, and allows us for a moment to gaze at the world afresh, through the eyes of a child, puzzled, astonished, and delighted at wonderful things we have never seen before.

The other scene occurs midway through *Schindler's List*. *Close Encounters* is in vivid color, but this scene is stark black and white. A selection is taking place in a Nazi labor camp in Poland: Jewish prisoners too old, ill, or young to work are being selected for the death camps. A skinny little boy only a few years older than Barry, wearing laced boots with no socks, shorts, a shirt, and a cap, is among a crowd of children being herded onto trucks.

The loudspeaker plays a soothing recording of a woman singing a German children's song. Most of the children march happily onto the trucks, shepherded to their doom by the Nazi Pied Piper. But the boy is wary and glances around, sensing something wrong. He sees his chance, breaks from the crowd, and runs away.

He heads for the barracks, but his frantic search quickly reveals that every hiding place, even under the floorboards, has already been taken by other children, who tell him, "There's no room for you here!" He is like a little cartoon mouse scurrying to find a hole (Farrell 192–93). So he runs into the latrines, and, without hesitation, tosses in his cap and lowers himself down a hole. He lands with a splash that spatters his face with excrement, and he stands in the foul stew up to his armpits. But, surprise! A group of children are clustered together in a circle of light under the next hole. They glare at him, and the oldest boy whispers angrily, "Get out! This is our place! Get out!" The happy German nursery song is still playing. With shit-smeared face, the little boy glances up at the light and trembles. Up above, the lambs are being led to slaughter. There is no place left for him to go.

The scene in the camp has some of the same elements as the one in *Close Encounters*: a child in peril, alien invasion, chaos and disruption, monsters on the loose, even a recording of a woman singing a children's song. *Schindler's List* occasionally takes the point of view of the child, but the effect is not like *Close Encounters* but more like *Poltergeist*: to heighten the terror. In *Schindler*, however, the evil is far worse than in *Poltergeist* because it is human and historically real. The mess in *Schindler* is not comic, as in *Close Encounters* or *E.T.*, or disturbing, as in *Poltergeist*, but shocking and appalling. This is a child's nightmare, a descent into hell.

Barry is unafraid, but the boy in *Schindler* knows only fear. He resembles the boy Jim in *Empire of the Sun*, the extraterrestrial in the opening scene of *E.T.*, or the robot boy David in *A.I.*: a little innocent hunted by sinister adults, desperate for a hiding place so that he may survive. The look on the little boy's face in *Schindler* as he glances upward from the latrine is reminiscent of Jim's panic when he loses his parents in the mob in wartime Shanghai, or *E.T.*'s despair as the mothership leaves the planet without him, or David's hysteria when his mother abandons him by the roadside. This Jewish boy is the ultimate outcast, the lowest of the low, unwanted even in the worst place imaginable.

CHILD AND FATHER

Beginning with *Close Encounters*, another major concern in Spielberg's films is the difficulty of growing up: his heroes are often child-men who suffer from a Peter Pan syndrome. Spielberg sees his childhood as the source of his creativity and is reluctant to give it up; this is reflected in the conflict in his characters between the rational adult self and the irrational child. Spielberg often appeals to children or to the "inner child" in adult viewers, the side that is playful, prankish, and imaginative, but cries easily and gets fearful about being separated from mother, and his films offer what the child wants: a chance to triumph over the adult world and nevertheless to be lifted up and embraced. Thus Roy Neary or E.T. rise up into the heavens in their motherships, or Jim at the conclusion of *Empire of the Sun* is hugged by his long-lost mother, while the robot boy David gets his wish granted from "The Blue Fairy" to be reunited with his human mother, if only for a day. Spielberg's films also successfully overcome what the child fears: growing up and losing the ability to play (as in *Close Encounters*, the "Kick the Can" episode, and *Hook*), being separated from mother (as in so many of his works), or the obverse—being swallowed alive, as if returning to the womb (as in all his horror films).

Spielberg usually shies away from depicting adult romance, and his films, like many fairy tales, rarely venture very far into that realm. The criminal protagonist of *Catch Me If You Can*, for example, is a con artist who thrives on imposture and deception and so cannot sustain a relationship; Oscar Schindler is a compulsive philanderer who, for most of the film, is alienated from his wife; and the romance of the hero of *The Terminal* is never consummated. *Always* (1989), his only romantic film, most critics consider an awkward failure. He says, "I've always been embarrassed by screen sexuality" (Ebert and Siskel, 54). His action films, such as the *Indiana Jones* series or *Jurassic Park* and its sequel, allow little time amid the adventures to develop anything more than cursory relationships between a hero and a girlfriend. Rather than concentrate on male-female relationships, Spielberg prefers to focus on mother-child or father-child situations.

However, in his films after 1987, after Spielberg married and became a father, the story of the lost child changes into the story of a man who must learn how to become a father: from *The Last Crusade* (1989) through *War of the Worlds* (2005), most of the films are conversion narratives about reluctant fathers or father figures forced through adversity to recognize their responsibility to their children (or, in Schindler's case, to the Jews he has "adopted").

Spielberg's collaboration with George Lucas in the three *Indiana Jones* films combine the preoccupations of Spielberg with those of Lucas. Whereas Spielberg is concerned with the development of the child, Lucas addresses the rebellious adolescent. Spielberg is interested in mothers, and fathers in his films are often weak, withdrawn, or absent, whereas Lucas concentrates instead on tyrannical fathers. Lucas's heroes rebel against the oppressive system or the oppressive father, which become equivalent, and his films are not so much fairy tales as oedipal myths. The *Indiana Jones* films share many of the mythic and structural elements of the *Star Wars* trilogy. The first in the series, *Raiders of the Lost Ark*, recapitulates the tale of initiation of the hero told in *Star Wars*. The second, *Indiana Jones and the Temple of Doom*, is mostly a return to the womb, more suggestive of Spielberg. And the last, *Indiana Jones and the Last Crusade*, deals with the hero's confrontation and ultimate reconciliation with a tyrannical father, as in *Return of the Jedi* (1983).

THE PSYCHOLOGICAL DIMENSIONS OF SPIELBERG'S FILMS

One of the interesting aspects of Spielberg's work is that he is equally skilled at sentiment and at horror. *E.T.* is a masterpiece of sentimental melodrama that tugs the heartstrings. Yet he also plays expertly on an audience's fears: the fear of being singled out at random and killed at any moment by monsters in his horror movies, or by monstrous Nazis in *Schindler*. He also explores the more subtle, internal realms of fear. First there is paranoia, most notably in *Duel* but also in many of his other films: the saucer chasers in *Close Encounters* behave like paranoids who suspect a government conspiracy (which proves true), *1941* makes fun of mass hysteria, the hero on the run in *Minority Report* never knows whom to trust, nor does the Israeli agent by the end of *Munich*. Second is phobia: fear of highway driving in *Duel*, fear of the ocean in *Jaws*, fear of snakes in *Raiders of the Lost Ark*, and fear of flying in *Hook*.

One way to account for both the sentiment and the horror in his work is to say that the primary psychological axis of Spielberg's films involves questions of separation versus fusion with the mother. On the one hand, the films about the lost child often express profound separation anxiety and an anxious depression; on the other hand, the ambivalence toward fusion leads either to the ecstasy of union with a benign and loving other, as in *Close Encounters*, *E.T.*, and *A.I.*, or the terror of being devoured by a monster, as in his horror movies. The positive feeling may derive from overcoming separation anxiety through ecstatic union, the horror from the fear of engulfment.

Mania and depression also seem Spielberg's characteristic cinematic territory: think of Roy's alternation between these two states in *Close Encounters* or Frank's mood swings in *Catch Me If You Can*. His most emotionally profound films, such as *E.T.*, *Empire of the Sun*, *Schindler's List*, or *A.I.*, move between depression, terror, and elation. His weakest lack one or more of these emotions: the out-of-control farce *1941* (1979) is unmitigated mania, and there is no real terror in "Kick the Can," in *Always*, or in *Hook*.

The two emotions—ecstasy and terror—are closely linked in his work and are often evoked in the same movie, indeed even within the same scene. There is a characteristically Spielbergian mix of feelings toward the unknown: for example, in *Close Encounters*, the child associates the extraterrestrials with toys and ice cream and chases after them as beloved playmates, but the mother screams in anguish when her child is abducted from her house by the aliens. In *Poltergeist*, the mother jumps with joy like a cheerleader as she shows off the supernatural phenomena beginning to happen in her house, the little daughter yawns (she's already bored with this game), but the father is terrified. Later, all three feel terror and despair when the daughter is kidnaped by these malicious spirits.

THE DREAM SCREEN

When Gene Siskel asked Spielberg for one "master image" that could sum up his pictures, Spielberg said, "I think it's the little boy in *Close Encounters* opening the door and standing in that beautiful yet awful light, just like fire coming through the doorway. And he's very small, and it's a very large door, and there's a lot of promise or danger outside that door." Siskel then asked if that was Spielberg's "symbol of the human condition," and Spielberg replied:

> That we don't know what's out there, and yet we should discover what's out there. We should be afraid of not knowing. And we should take a step toward what we don't understand and what we don't know about and what scares us. We shouldn't be self-destructive about it, but we should go toward that kind of proverbial light and see what's out there for us. (Ebert and Siskel 72)

The image of the very little boy standing in the very large doorway, looking toward the "beautiful yet awful light" is a rich and evocative image central both to *Close Encounters* and to all of Spielberg's work. It is dreamlike and begs for interpretation. In the opening scene of *Close Encounters*, a Mexican policeman uses similar words to describes the alien light he saw the night before in the skies : "Una luz muy bonita pero muy espantosa"—"A very beautiful but a very frightening light." Such a blinding light suggests the divine or the afterlife; it is what many report after near-death experiences. It is such a light against which the parents in *Poltergeist* caution their little daughter when she is trapped in the spirit world.

Film is painting with light. And the ecstasy and terror of the unknown, that overpowering, blinding light which could be divine or demonic, and the need to move toward the strange light, to embrace what could transform us and to confront what scares us, is at the core of the appeal of the SF, fantasy, and horror films of Steven Spielberg.

But the image from *Close Encounters* is suggestive in other ways as well. The image of the boy in the doorway contains a series of oppositions characteristic of much of Spielberg's work: small versus large, inside versus out-side, and dark versus light. Nigel Morris mentions how often Spielberg uses beams of light to suggest both "the desires and fantasies of characters" as well as the beams of a movie projector flashed across the darkened theater onto the screen (Morris 6–7). The doorway in this particular shot creates a frame within the frame, and the boy is small, like a spectator in a movie theater enthralled by images cast by the light upon a giant screen.

Moreover, the boy stands on the threshold, in a liminal space, neither wholly inside nor wholly outside. As the child psychiatrist D. W. Winnicott writes, play takes place neither inside nor outside: "play is in fact neither a matter of inner psychic reality nor a matter of external reality" (Winnicott 96). "The place where cultural experience is located is in the *potential space* between the individual and the environment (originally the object). The same can be said of playing. Cultural experience begins with creative living first manifested in play" (100). So Spielberg returns us to the child at play, the child on the threshold, first discovering this transitional or potential space which is the origin of all cultural experience, both of moviemaking and of movie viewing.

Finally, to return to an idea I mentioned in the introduction, Robert T. Eberwein compares viewing film to dreaming. "Films in general seem both real and dreamlike because they appear to us in a way that activates the re-gressive experience of watching dreams on our psychic dream screens. The actual screen in the theater functions as a psychic prosthesis of our dream screen, a structure constituted by the mother and breast, or a surrogate for it, or by our own ego" (Eberwein 192).

And as I mentioned in regard to *Close Encounters*, the psychoanalyst Christopher Bollas speaks of "the transformational object": a memory from early object relations, when the mother "continually transforms the infant's internal and external environment." In later life, we may "search for an object that is identified with the metamorphosis of the self." In aesthetic experiences, for example, we may feel "an uncanny fusion with the object" which derives from the return of something strangely familiar, "something never cognitively apprehended but existentially known" (Bollas 16), perhaps a recollection of fusion with the maternal "transformational object." All this is also suggested by the image from *Close Encounters*: that the boy is viewing an image on his own internal dream screen, just as we do when viewing a movie, and that the boy is searching for fusion with a transformational object.

I have unpacked the image to suggest a cluster of connected ideas: a child at play, a spectator at a movie theater, the quest for the alien or the divine or the afterlife, and the quest for the transformational object. Spielberg's films concern all these activities, which are ultimately versions of the same thing: play, watching movies, searching for the alien or the divine, and pursuing

Close Encounters: Facing the dream screen. Columbia, 1980.

the transcendent object which will change our lives. His films are not only projected on our own dream screens; they also take us to that place where dreams are born.

NOTE

1. In an interview with me in 1993, Cary Guffey, the actor who played Barry in *Close Encounters*, said that what he was looking at was a man in a monkey suit. Spielberg placed the man off camera and had him jump up and down to make the boy smile.

REFERENCES

Bollas, Christopher. *The Shadow of the Object: Psychoanalysis of the Unthought Known.* New York: Columbia, 1987.

Ebert, Roger and Gene Siskel. *The Future of the Movies: Interview with Martin Scorsese, Steven Spielberg, and George Lucas.* Kansas City, MO: Andrews and McMeel, 1991.

Eberwein, Robert T. *Film and the Dream Screen: A Sleep and a Forgetting*. Princeton, NJ: Princeton University Press, 1984.

Farrell, Kirby, "The Economies of *Schindler's List.*" *The Films of Steven Spielberg: Critical Essays*. Ed. Charles L. P. Silet. Lanham, MD: Scarecrow Press, 2002, 191–214.

Forsberg, Myra. "Spielberg at 40: The Man and the Child." *Steven Spielberg: Interviews*. Eds. Lester D. Friedman and Brent Notbohm. Jackson: University Press of Mississippi, 2000, 126–32.

Morris, Nigel. *The Cinema of Steven Spielberg: Empire of Light*. London: Wallflower, 2007.

Sragow, Michael. "A Conversation with Steven Spielberg." *Steven Spielberg: Interviews*. Eds. Lester D. Friedman and Brent Notbohm. Jackson: University Press of Mississippi, 2000, 107–19.

Winnicott, D. W. *Playing and Reality*. New York: Basic Books, 1971.

Index

Note: *Page numbers in italics refer to photographs.*

Abraham, Karl, 27n5
Abrams, Jeremiah, 190
Action in the North Atlantic (film), 154
The Adventures of Don Juan (film), 114
Affron, Charles, 8
A.I. (Spielberg), 227–40, *233*, *234*, *236*;
  and childhood experience, 236–38;
  critical response to, 229–30, 238;
  emotional impact of, 2; *Empire of the
  Sun* and, 231–32; ending of, 238–
  40; family in, 233–35; Kubrick and,
  227–30, 237–39; and mourning,
  228–29, 231–33, 235; and *Pinocchio*,
  239; replacement child in, 235–36;
  robot emotions in, 232; scientist
  in, 232–33; separation anxiety in,
  169; Spielberg on, 230; three acts of,
  237–38
Air Force (film), 154
airplanes. *See* flying
Aldiss, Brian, 4, 16, 17, 18, 21, 227,
  243
Alice in Wonderland (Carroll), 8
Alien (film), 34, 35
aliens: in *Close Encounters*, 65–68, 103;
  in *E.T.*, 79–80; in *Poltergeist*, 68, 103.
  See also monsters

Allen, Karen, 68
alter ego, E.T. as, 86–87
Always (Spielberg), 151–65, *160*, 179,
  192; cinematography of, 157–58;
  critical response to, 152, 165n2;
  death and rebirth in, 162–63;
  Dorinda and Ted in, 159; emotional
  impact of, 2, 153; fathers in, 184;
  flying in, 62, 162; *Ghost* and, 164;
  A Guy Named Joe and, 151–52, 154,
  157–60; male bonding in, 161–62;
  manhood in, 189; "The Mission"
  and, 180; mothers in, 161; movie
  influences on, 152–53; Pete in,
  158–59; sexuality in, 162; voyeurism
  in, 163–64
Amazing Stories (television series),
  173–75
Amazing Stories: The Movie, 175
American monomyth, 29
Amis, Martin, 90
anal sadism, 25, 213–14
Ansen, David, 165, 172
anxiety, horror films and, 30–31
anxiety dreams, 19, 47
Appelo, Tim, 230, 231, 234
art, 60

Attenborough, Richard, 71, 210
Auty, Chris, 49, 103

Bach, S., 86
Baird, Robert, 205, 217
Balides, Constance, 209
Bambi (film), 151
Bambi Meets Godzilla (cartoon), 17, 80
Barr, Marleen, 188
Barrie, J. M., 76, 183–86, 200
Barry, Gene, 258, 263
Baskin-Robbins, 57
Bass, Ron, 161, 162
The Battle of Dorking (Chesney), 255
Baudrillard, Jean, 229
Baxter, John, 76, 122n1, 165
Beatles, 86
belief: *Close Encounters of the Third Kind*
    and, 64; *Indiana Jones and the Last
    Crusade* and, 143; Lucas films and,
    143; Spielberg films and, 143
Belson, Jerry, 161, 162
Benchley, Peter, 32, 38
Beowulf, 29
Bettelheim, Bruno, 10, 77–78, 87–88,
    125
Bible, 29
The Birds (Hitchcock), 15
The Bishop's Wife (film), 155
Biskind, Peter, 38, 46, 140, 141, 145,
    146, 148n2, 203
blackboard screech, 44
The Black Stallion (film), 76, 89
Blithe Spirit (film), 155
blockbusters, 217
Bly, Robert, 187–89, 193
Boam, Jeffrey, 137
Bogart, Humphrey, 114
Bollas, Christopher, 60, 66, 274
Bradshaw, John, 190
Branden, Nathaniel, 190–91
breast imagery: in *Close Encounters*,
    65–66; in *Indiana Jones and
    the Temple of Doom*, 129–32; in
    Poltergeist, 104
Britton, Andrew, 4, 46, 51
Brode, Douglas, 19, 89, 120, 122n1, 134

Brody, Ellen, 39
Brophy, Philip, 30–31
Brown, David, 39
Buckland, Warren, 32, 41, 62, 93,
    122n1, 204, 223 n3, 231, 251
buddy films: *Indiana Jones and the Last
    Crusade* and, 146–47; *Jaws* and, 45
Budweiser, 57
Bush, George H. W., 148n3
Bush, George W., 244
Butler, Bill, 34

Cain, Albert C., 235
Cain, Barbara S., 235
Cagney, James, 152
Calabrese, Omar, 110
Calvin and Hobbes (Watterson), 86
Campbell, Joseph, 111, 138
Canby, Vincent, 147–48
Capra, Frank, 9
Caputi, Jane E., 50
Carpenter, Lynette, 180
Carroll, Lewis, 7
Carroll, Noel, 31, 110
Carter, Rick, 237
Caruth, Cathy, 254
Casablanca (film), 154, 157–58
castration anxiety: *E.T.* and, 88; *Jaws*
    and, 38, 45, 49–51, 51n2
Catch Me If You Can (Spielberg), 247,
    271, 272
Chaplin, Charlie, 9, 75
childhood experience: *A.I.* and, 236–
    38; breasts and, 66; *Close Encounters*
    and, 61–62, 64, 268–69; death and,
    214; *E.T.* and, 9, 64, 76, 81–82,
    84, 89; film and, 6–8; historical
    interpretations of, 200; *Hook* and,
    64, 169, 173, 183, 189–91, 200;
    inner child and, 190–91; "Kick the
    Can" and, 64, 169–73; *Peter Pan*
    and, 184–85; *Poltergeist* and, 102–3;
    and relationship to parents, 37, 50,
    56–57; *Schindler's List* and, 268–69;
    sexuality and, 37, 50; in Spielberg's
    films, 1, 5–6, 56, 58, 230, 268–72.
    See also fairy tales; regression

child-murder fantasy, 214
Christianity, 180
A Christmas Carol (Dickens), 184
Christopher Strong (film), 154
Cinderella (film), 89
cinematography: in *Always*, 157–58; in *Close Encounters*, 61; in *E.T.*, 6, 75, 76, 78–79; in *Jaws*, 34–35; in "The Mission," 175–76; in *Raiders of the Lost Ark*, 110; in Spielberg's films, 1, 5
City Slickers (film), 189
Clarke, Arthur C., 227
clocks, 194–95
Close Encounters of the Third Kind (Spielberg), 2, 55–73, 60, 72, 179, 209; aliens in, 65–68, 103; breast imagery in, 65–66; and childhood experience, 61–62, 64, 169, 268–69; cinematography of, 61; critical response to, 5–6; as cult movie, 72, 75–76; emotional impact of, 2; *E.T.* and *Poltergeist* compared to, 55–58, 78, 94–95; as fairy tale, 72–73; family in, 63–64, 69–70; fathers in, 70–71; as horror film, 67; iconic image from, 273–74, 275n1; mass culture in, 57; opening scene of, 61–63; and *Pinocchio*, 239; pranksters in, 68–69; regression in, 60–61, 70–71, 88; and religion, 58–59, 61, 72, 73n1, 180; Roy Neary in, 63–65; science in, 83; sexuality in, 65; special effects in, 59; and suburbia, 4, 55–58, 63, 98, 267; *2001: A Space Odyssey* and, 230
Cocoon (film), 169
Cohen, Tom, 247, 248
Cold War, 244, 255
The Color Purple (Spielberg), 2, 6, 9
comic books, 121n1
Commander Cody (serial), 109
Conan Doyle, Arthur, 218
Connery, Sean, 138, 139, 147
consumerism, 209–10, 216
Corliss, Richard, 77

Crawley, Tony, 4, 14, 27, 33, 37, 80, 110, 112–14
Creature from the Black Lagoon (film), 31
Crichton, Michael, 4, 206–9, 218–21
Crothers, Scatman, 172
Cruise, Tom, 246, 259
cultural trauma. *See* national trauma

Dances with Wolves (film), 189
The Day The Earth Stood Still (film), 90n3
Dead of Night (film), 106
death, 99, 240
"The Death of the Ball Turret Gunner" (Jarrell), 178
Denby, David, 161
Dern, Laura, 213
Destination Tokyo (film), 154
Deutsch, Phyllis, 87
Dick, Philip K., 4, 243–46, 252
Dickens, Charles, 6, 184
Die Hard films, 110
dinosaurs, fascination with, 215
Disney, Walt, 1, 4
divorce: in *Close Encounters*, 58; *Poltergeist* and, 98–100, 105, 106; Spielberg's, 152; of Spielberg's parents, 56–57, 75, 99, 105, 152, 192, 267
The Doctor (film), 189
domestic realm, as foil for fantastic, 42, 57–58, 268–69. *See also* suburbia
Don Winslow of the Navy (serial), 109
double, E.T. as psychological, 86–87
Dracula (Stoker), 256
drag show, *Hook* as, 197
dreams: anxiety, 19, 47; *Duel* and, 19; film and, 6–7, 274–75; humanity and, 229; Spielberg's films and, 1–2, 10. *See also* nightmares
Dreyfuss, Richard, 30, 39, 76, 158–59, 161, 163
Dr. Strangelove (Kubrick), 228
Duel (Spielberg), 13–27, 18, 106; dialogue in, 15; family in, 22; and the fantastic, 15–17; history of,

13–14; and homosexuality, 21; as horror, 16; *Jaws* and, 47–48; merits of, 14–15; and paranoia, 2, 13, 18–21, 24–25; *Poltergeist* compared to, 96; pranksters in, 68; as science fiction, 16; themes in, 16–17; as thriller, 14–16; truck as character in, 26; women in, 21–24, 27
Dunne, Irene, 153, 159

Eastwood, Clint, 174
eating. *See* food imagery
Ebert, Roger, 230, 271, 273
Eberwein, Robert T., 6, 274
emotion: appeal of Spielberg's films to, 1–2, 8–9, 272–73; fear of, 8; film and, 8; horror films and, 30–31; robots and, 232; special effects and, 59
Empire of the Sun (Spielberg), 2, 6, 62, 134, 176, 231–32, 236–37, 272
The Empire Strikes Back (Lucas), 84
L'Enfant Sauvage (*The Wild Child*; Truffaut), 71
Erikson, Kai, 262, 264
E.T. (Spielberg), 6, 75–90, 106, 179; aliens in, 79–80; and childhood experience, 9, 64, 76, 81–82, 84, 89, 169; cinematography of, 6, 75, 76, 78–79; *Close Encounters* and *Poltergeist* compared to, 55–58, 78, 94–96; critical response to, 90n2; as cult movie, 75–76; *The Day The Earth Stood Still* and, 90n3; Elliott in, 85–88; emotional impact of, 2, 9, 75–77, 88–90; E.T. in, 83–88; as fairy tale, 4, 76–78, 84, 89–90; family in, 85, 87; fathers in, 82–83, 87; "The Frog King" and, 77; Kubrick and, 230; mass culture in, 57–58; as masterpiece, 75; the maternal in, 81; men in, 80, 83; *Minority Report* and, 250; opening scene of, 78–81; and Peter Pan, 190; and regression, 7; and religion, 58, 80, 84, 84–85, 180; science in, 82, 83; sexuality in, 87–88; Spielberg

on, 75, 86, 95, 267; and suburbia, 55–58, 78, 95, 267
Evans, Christopher, 72

Fairbanks, Douglas, 171, 172
fairy tales: *Close Encounters* and, 72–73; emotional appeal of, 10; *E.T.* and, 76–78, 85, 89–90; psychological truths of, 77–78
familiarity. *See* domestic realm; uncanny
family: in *A.I.*, 233–35; *Amazing Stories* and, 174; in *Close Encounters*, 63–64, 69–70; in *Duel*, 22; in *E.T.*, 85, 87; in *Hook*, 193–96; idealization of, 174; in *Indiana Jones and the Temple of Doom*, 132, *133*; in *Jaws*, 29, 39–40, 42–43; in *Jurassic Park*, 207, 208–9; in *The Lost World*, 220–22; in *Minority Report*, 247; in *Poltergeist*, 97, *98*, 98–100, 106; Spielberg's, 89, 199; in Spielberg's films, 247, 260, 267–68; in *The War of the Worlds*, 260, 263. *See also* divorce; fathers; mothers and the maternal
Fantasia (film), 81
fantastic: domestic realm as foil for, 42, 57–58, 268–69; *Duel* and, 15–17; as genre, 16
fantasy films: critical bias against, 6–8; revolution of 1970s in, 3–4, 10n4; Spielberg and, 2–10. *See also* fairy tales
Farber, Stephen, 60
Farrell, Kirby, 270
fathers: in *Always*, 184; in *Close Encounters*, 70–71; in *E.T.*, 82–83, 87; in *Hook*, 183; in *Indiana Jones and the Last Crusade*, 137–48, 184; in *Indiana Jones and the Temple of Doom*, 131; in *Jaws*, 44, 45, 50; in *Jurassic Park*, 184, 208–9; men's movement and, 188; in *Raiders of the Lost Ark*, 120; in *Schindler's List*, 184; in Spielberg's films, 271; in *The War of the Worlds*, 260. *See also* oedipal themes

Fenichel, Otto, 27 n5
Field Museum, Chicago, 220
film: dreams and, 6, 274–75; emotional appeal of, 8–9; manipulative nature of, 9; regressive nature of, 7–8
film noir, 247, 251
The Fisher King (film), 189
Fleming, Victor, 151
Flight of the Navigator (film), 83
flying: in *Always*, 162; in *Hook*, 192; and sexuality, 162, 192; Spielberg's attitude toward, 191–92; in Spielberg's films, 62, 176, 191
Flynn, Errol, 114
food imagery: in *Close Encounters*, 65, 102; in *E.T.*, 102; in *Indiana Jones and the Temple of Doom*, 125–26, 128–31, 129; in *Jurassic Park*, 211; in *Poltergeist*, 102
Ford, Harrison, 110, 114, 138, 139, 146
Ford, John, 9, 17, 137, 138
Foster, Hal, 254
Frank, Scott, 247
Freud, Anna, 86
Freud, Sigmund: and flying dreams, 88, 192; and ghosts, 102; and mourning, 156; and paranoia, 21, 24, 246; and phobia, 49; and primal horde, 45; and sacrifice, 121; and taboos, 111–12, 115; and totem object, 119; and the uncanny, 57
Friday the Thirteenth movies, 34
Friedman, Lester D., 4, 18, 73n1, 110, 159, 184, 201, 217, 248, 262
"The Frog King," 4, 77, 87–88

Gable, Clark, 152
Garber, Marjorie, 197
Geduld, Harry M., 185
gender bending, 162
Genelli, Lyn Davis, 106
Genelli, Tom, 106
Ghost (film), 164
ghost comedies, 155, 165n4
"Ghost Train" (Spielberg), 174, 175
Giles, Dennis, 36

Godzilla, 218
Goldberg, Whoopi, 164
Goldenberg, Billy, 14
good/bad dichotomy: in *Indiana Jones and the Last Crusade*, 141, 144, 146; in *Indiana Jones and the Temple of Doom*, 130–32; in *Indiana Jones* films, 143; Klein on, 128; in *Poltergeist*, 100
The Goonies (film), 125–26
Gordon, Andrew M., 2, 73n2, 76, 11, 231
Gottlieb, Carl, 38, 39, 41
Gould, Stephen Jay, 208, 215–16
Greenberg, Harvey, 23, 34, 35, 151, 157
Gremlins (film), 103
Grenier, Richard, 90n2
Griffin, Nancy, 137, 161
Griffith, D. W., 75
Grimm brothers, 77, 131
Guffey, Cary, 275n1
Gunga Din (film), 127
A Guy Named Joe (film), 165n1
A Guy Named Joe (Fleming), 151–57

"Hansel and Gretel," 4, 73, 100, 131
Harlan, Jan, 228
Harwood, Sarah, 88
Haskin, Byron, 257
Hatari (film), 218
Hawks, Howard, 29, 93, 152
Heath, Stephen, 36
Heaven Can Wait (film), 155
heimlich. *See* uncanny
The Hellfighters, 152
Hepburn, Audrey, 153, 161
Hepburn, Katherine, 154
Here Comes Mr. Jordan (film), 155
The Hero with a Thousand Faces (Campbell), 111
Herrmann, Bernard, 14
Heung, Marina, 87
High Noon (film), 40
Hillman, James, 7, 188
Hitchcock, Alfred: *Duel* and, 15–16; emotional appeal of, 9; on plot, 121; *Psycho*, 14, 30, 31, 32–35, 37–38,

104, 205–6; subversiveness of, 100; thrillers of, 13; *Vertigo*, 48
Hitler, Adolf, 145
Hoberman, J., 163
Holy Grail: in *Indiana Jones and the Last Crusade*, 140, 142–46; Lucas on, 138
Home Alone (film), 199
Homecoming (Bradshaw), 190
homoeroticism, 47, 186
homosexuality: Barrie and, 185–86; in *Duel*, 21; in *Hook*, 194, 197–98; in *Jaws*, 47; paranoia and, 21, 246
Hook (Spielberg), 183–200, *196*; and childhood experience, 64, 169, 173, 183, 189–91, 200; critical response to, 199; family in, 260; fathers in, 183; flying in, 192; and homosexuality, 194, 197–98; manhood in, 184, 188, 193–97; men in, 196–98; phallic imagery in, *193*, 193–96; pop psychology in, 187–91; sexuality in, 186, 198–99; Spielberg on, 200; themes in, 77; women in, 198–99
Hooper, Tobe, 10n3, 93–94, *94*, *95*
horror films: appeal of, 30–31, 33; *Close Encounters* and, 67; creatures in, 35; critical bias against, 6–8; cruel, 34; *E.T.* and, 95; in 1970s–1980s, 29; *Poltergeist* and, 95–100, 106; psychoanalysis and, 31; *Raiders of the Lost Ark* and, 115; Spielberg and, 2–10
Hoskins, Bob, 183
Hunter, Holly, 159, 161
Huston, John, 111, 113
Huyck, Willard, 125–26

imaginary companions, 86
Independence Day (film), 258
Indiana Jones and the Last Crusade (Spielberg and Lucas), 137–48, 192; as buddy film, 146–47; critique of, 147; Elsa in, 144–46, *145*; fathers in, 137–48, 184; movie influences on, 139; opening sequence of, 139–42; and religion, 180

Indiana Jones and the Temple of Doom (Spielberg and Lucas), 125–34; critical response to, 126; family in, 132, *133*; fathers in, 131; food imagery in, 125–26, 128–31, *129*; Kleinian reading of, 127–28; opening sequence of, 128–29; racism in, 127; sexism in, 126–27; Spielberg on, 126, 127, 131, 134; underground in, 131–32
Indiana Jones films: hats in, 141; interrelationship of, 110–11; as Lucas-Spielberg partnership, 109, 271–72; mythic nature of, 109, 111; and religion, 143; taboos in, 115. *See also Indiana Jones and the Last Crusade*; *Indiana Jones and the Temple of Doom*; *Raiders of the Lost Ark*
inner child, 190–91
Iraq War, 262–63
Irving, Amy, 176, 188
Irving, John, 178
It Came from Outer Space (film), 62
It's a Wonderful Life (film), 155

Jackson, Michael, 190
James, Nick, 247
James Bond films, 110, 114, 122n4, 138
Jameson, Fredric, 29, 51n1, 122n2
Jameson, Richard, 79
Jancovich, Mark, 257
Jarrell, Randall, 178–79
Jaws (Benchley), 32
Jaws (Spielberg), 3, 26, 29–51, *30*, *32*, *42*, *46*, 106, 126; Brody, Hooper, and Quint in, 45–47; Brody in, 39–43; cinematography of, 34–35; critical response to, 29, 35–37; cruelty in, 34; depth psychology and, 30; *Duel* and, 47–48; emotional impact of, 2, 33–34; family in, 29, 39–40, 42–43; men in, 32, 38–47, 50; opening sequence of, 31–38; and phobia, 39, 47–50; *Poltergeist* compared to, 96; pranksters in, 68; psychological power of, 51; Quint in, 43–45; seen/unseen theme in,

31, 35–36, 51; sexuality in, 32–33, 35, 37–38, 50, 65; shark as monster in, 35; Spielberg on, 33–34, 37, 51; subjective camera in, 31, 48; women in, 49–50

Joannides, Paul, 76, 87

Johnson, Brad, 159

Johnson, George Clayton, 171–72

Johnson, Van, 154

Jones, Chuck, 4, 17

Jung, C. G., 190

Jungian men's movement, 188–89

Jurassic Park (Crichton), 206–9, 221

Jurassic Park (Spielberg), 26, 71, 126, 184, 203–17, *204*, *209*; anal sadism in, 213–14; and commercial exploitation, 209–10; critical response to, 203; family in, *207*, 208–9, 260; fathers in, 208–9; hero in, 214; novel as basis for, 206–9; opening scene of, 204–6; oral sadism in, 213–14; pranksters in, 68; Spielberg on, 203; villains in, 211–12

Kael, Pauline, 78, 87, 106, 128, 131–32, 147, 160, 169, 172

Kaminski, Janus, 250

Kaplan, E. Ann, 253, 254

Kasdan, Lawrence, 110

Katz, Gloria, 125–26

Kellner, Douglas, 49–50, 99

Kershner, Irvin, 174

Kesey, Ken, 172

"Kick the Can" (Spielberg), 169–73, 179; and childhood experience, 64, 169–73; original version versus, 171–72; plot of, 170; as remake, 151; stereotyping in, 172–73; themes of, 169

Kiley, Dan, 189

King, Stephen, 2, 16, 26, 106

King Kong (film), 35, 212, 218

King Solomon's Mines (film), 110

Klein, Melanie, 27n5: and good and bad object representations, 128, 131; on greed and envy, 212–13; and

paranoia, 24; and paranoid-schizoid position, 127–28, 130, 212; and sexual fantasies, 37, 50

Koepp, David, 203, 208, 209, 220, 262

Kolker, Robert Philip, 6, 9, 29, 45, 48, 61–62, 70

Kris, Ernst, 7

Kubrick, Christine, 228

Kubrick, Stanley: and *A.I.*, 227–30, 238–39; *Dr. Strangelove*, 228; *The Shining*, 106; *2001: A Space Odyssey*, 3, 83, 227, 230, 237, 239

Lasch, Christopher, 3

Lawrence of Arabia (film), 62

Leayman, Charles D., 139, 146

Lee, Spike, 173

Le Guin, Ursula, 7

Lethal Weapon films, 110

Lewin, Bertram D., 36–37, 49, 50

light, symbol of, 273–74

"Little Girl Lost" (Matheson), 96

The Little White Bird (Barrie), 186

The Lost World (Conan Doyle), 218

The Lost World (Crichton), 218–20

The Lost World (Spielberg), 26, 126, 217–22, *219*; critical response to, 217; family in, 220–22, 260; novel as basis for, 218–20; Spielberg on, 209, 217

Lucas, George: emotional appeal of films of, 6–7; *The Empire Strikes Back*, 84; and father-son relationship, 134, 137–38; and *Indiana Jones* films, 109–11, 125–27, 134, 137, 141, 271; influence of, 3–4; *Return of the Jedi*, 102; *Star Wars*, 2, 112, 137–39, 146; *THX 1138*, 16

macaque monkeys, 44

"MacGuffin" (Hitchcock's term), 121

Mackey, Douglas A., 243–44

made-for-TV movies, 27n1

"magical negro," 173

magician figures, 179

male identity. *See* manhood

The Maltese Falcon (Huston), 111

Manhattan Project, 211

manhood: in *Close Encounters*, 88; in
  Duel, 15, 27; in *Hook*, 184, 188,
  193–97; in *Indiana Jones and the Last
  Crusade*, 138, 141–42; in *Jaws*, 39–
  40, 42–44, 50; 1990s films and, 189

manipulation, Spielberg's films
  criticized for, 9

The Man Who Knew Too Much
  (Hitchcock), 15

The Man Who Shot Liberty Valance
  (Ford), 17

Marcus, Greil, 121n1

Marmo, Malia Scotch, 208

Marshall, Frank, 93

masculinity. *See* manhood

Masked Marvel (serial), 109

mass culture, 57–58

Matheson, Richard, 4, 14, 16, 96, 171,
  181

Mathis, Johnny, 57, 68

Mathison, Melissa, 76–77, 171

Maus (Spiegelman), 235

Maus II (Spiegelman), 235

Mavissakalian, Matig, 49

Mayer, Louis B., 174

McBride, Joseph, 8, 25, 26, 125, 126,
  132, 134n1, 134n3, 148, 151–52,
  172, 191, 192

McCarthy era, 244, 245

McDermott, John F., Jr., 87

McDonald's, 57, 209

Meissner, W.W., 26

men: bonding among, 43, 45–47,
  161–62; in *E.T.*, 80, 83; impotence
  of, 32; in *Jaws*, 32, 38–47, 50; in
  Poltergeist, 104; pop psychology of
  1980s and, 187–90. *See also* fathers;
  homosexuality

men's movement, 188–89

Metz, Christian, 7

Meyjes, Menno, 175

MGM, 174

Michelangelo, 84

Milius, John, 38

"The Minority Report" (Dick), 243–47,
  249–50

Minority Report (Spielberg), 243–52,
  246, 250; Agatha in, 249–51; *E.T.*
  and, 250; family in, 247; "The
  Minority Report" and, 246–47;
  oedipal themes in, 243, 247–49;
  seen/unseen theme in, 248–49;
  Spielberg on, 250

"The Mission" (Spielberg), 174–81;
  cinematography of, 175–76; flying
  in, 62; plot of, 177–78; and religion,
  180; themes in, 176–77

Mitchell, W. J. T., 208, 212, 216

Moby Dick (Melville), 29, 35

monsters, 33–36. *See also* aliens

Moore, Demi, 164

Morris, Nigel, 10n1, 15, 20, 26, 27, 32,
  80, 90, 128, 163, 170, 186, 205,
  214, 230, 251, 274

Morton, Samantha, 250

mothers and the maternal: in *Always*,
  161; in *E.T.*, 81

Mott, Donald R., 25, 35, 172, 175

mourning, *A.I.* and, 228–29, 231–33,
  235

Munich (Spielberg), 272

musical scores, 8, 14, 31

Myers, Wayne A., 86

Myles, Lynda, 18, 21, 51n2

mysticism, 3, 58, 76

myth, *Indiana Jones* films as, 109, 111–12

Naremore, James, 230, 237

narrative: emotional/visceral appeal of,
  1; fantasy nature of, 6

national trauma, 253–54, 264

Neale, Stephen, 6

Neeson, Liam, 228

Neustadter, Roger, 83

"Neverland" ranch, 190

Newman, Kim, 257

night, 81

Nightmare on Elm Street movies, 34

nightmares, 26, 30

9/11 terrorist attacks, 253–54, 260–62,
  264

1941 (Spielberg), 2, 13, 62, 68, 129,
  152, 200, 222

1930s popular media, 127
Noah, Timothy, 264
North by Northwest (Hitchcock), 15
Now, Voyager (film), 154
La Nuit Americaine (*Day for Night*;
 Truffaut), 71
Nyby, Christian, 93

object relations, 60. *See also*
 transformational objects
oedipal themes: Barrie and, 185; in
 Casablanca, 157; in *Close Encounters*,
 70–71; in *E.T.*, 88; in *A Guy Named
 Joe*, 156–57; in *Hook*, 198; in *Indiana
 Jones* films, 134, 138–39, 144–46; in
 "The Minority Report" (Dick), 246;
 in *Minority Report* (Spielberg), 243,
 248–49; in *Raiders of the Lost Ark*,
 111–12; Spielberg and, 151; in *Star
 Wars* films, 112; taboo and, 111–12,
 115
Oedipus Rex (Sophocles), 243, 247–49,
 252
offscreen space, activation of, 205
Old Yeller (film), 89
One Flew Over the Cuckoo's Nest (Kesey),
 172
One Step Beyond (television series), 174
Only Angels Have Wings (Hawks), 152
Oppenheimer, J. Robert, 211
oral sadism: *Jaws* and, 36–37, 49;
 Jurassic Park and, 213–14; *Poltergeist*
 and, 102
The Outer Limits (television series), 174
Ovitz, Michael, 228

Pace, Patricia, 188, 192, 197, 198
Pal, George, 255, 257
Palmer, Jerry, 18–19
paranoia: anal sadism and, 25; *Duel*
 and, 2, 13, 18–21, 24–25; "The
 Minority Report" (Dick) and, 246;
 Minority Report (Spielberg) and,
 244, 252; mother and, 23; repressed
 homosexuality and, 21, 246; thrillers
 and, 18–19
paranoid-schizoid position, 127–28, 212

Paul, Saint, 252
Peanuts (Schulz), 86
Perrault, Charles, 131
Persona (Bergman), 250
Peter Pan (Barrie), 4, 76–77, 172, 183–
 87, 190, 200
Peter Pan syndrome, 189–90, 237
Pfeil, Fred, 189
phallic imagery: in *Duel*, 25; in *E.T.*,
 80, 81, 83, 86–88; in *Hook*, 193;
 imaginary companions and, 86; in
 Indiana Jones and the Last Crusade,
 140; in *Indiana Jones and the Temple
 of Doom*, 132; in *Poltergeist*, 104; in
 Raiders of the Lost Ark, 113
phobia: *Jaws* and, 39, 47–50; nature of,
 48–49
Pickens, Slim, 228
Pinocchio (Collodi), 73, 236–37, 239
Pinocchio (film), 4, 10, 63–64, 179, 239
Pinocchio, as Kubrick's name for *A.I.*,
 230
play, 274
Poltergeist (Spielberg), 2, 93–106, *95*,
 134, 179; aliens in, 68, 103; and
 childhood experience, 102–3; *Close
 Encounters* and *E.T.* compared to,
 55–58, 78, 94–96; controversy over
 directorship of, 10n3, 93–94; critical
 response to, 96–97; critique of, 106;
 and death, 99, 169; and divorce,
 98–100, 105, 106; family in, *97, 98*,
 98–100, 106; as horror film, 95–100,
 106; mass culture in, 58; men in,
 104; opening scene of, 100–101; and
 oral aggression, 102; pranksters in,
 68, 102–3; regression in, 88; and
 religion, 58; sexuality in, 104–5;
 special effects in, 96–97; Spielberg
 on, 95, 103; and suburbia, 4, 55–58,
 95, 97–100, 103, 267
pop psychology, 187–91
popular culture, 57–58
Porter, Cole, 128
Postone, Moishe, 126–27
post-traumatic stress disorder, 254
pranksters: in *Close Encounters*,

68–69; in *Poltergeist*, 68, 102–3; in Spielberg's films, 68–69

Pretty Woman (film), 189

primal scene: in *Always*, 163–64; in *Close Encounters*, 65; dinosaurs and, 216; in *Indiana Jones and the Last Crusade*, 140; in *Jaws*, 45; in *Poltergeist*, 104

Psycho (Hitchcock): cruelty in, 34; emotional impact of, 30; musical score of, 14; sexuality in, 32; shower scene in, 31, 34, 37–38, 104, 205–6; subjective camera in, 31; suspense in, 33, 35

psychoanalysis, 31

puer, 190

Pye, Michael, 18, 21, 51n2

The Quiet Man (film), 87

racism, 127

Raiders of the Lost Ark (Spielberg and Lucas), 3, 109–21, *112*, *118*; Ark in, 111, 117–21; Belloq in, 116–17; cinematography of, 110; and comics, 121n1; fathers in, 120; filming of, 68; as horror film, 115; Indiana Jones in, 114–17; light and fire in, 120–21; Marion in, 117–20; moral ambiguity in, 114, 116; movie influences on, 110, 122n1; mythic nature of, 111–12; oedipal conflict in, 111–12; opening sequence of, 112–16; and serials, 109–10, 121n1; Spielberg on, 110, 112–14; taboo in, 114–16, 118–21; and the uncanny, 121

Rambo films, 110, 139

realism, 2, 6

rebirth imagery: in *Always*, 163; "The Mission" and, 180; in *Poltergeist*, 105

Reclaiming the Inner Child (Abrams), 190

Red Skies of Montana (film), 152

Regarding Henry (film), 189

regression: art and, 7; in *Close Encounters*, 60–61, 70–71, 88; in *Poltergeist*, 88; in Spielberg's films,

57. See also childhood experience

religion: *Close Encounters* and, 58–59, 61, 72, 73n1, 180; *E.T.* and, 80, 84, 84–85, 180; *Indiana Jones* films and, 143, 180; Lucas's films and, 143; "The Mission" and, 180; movies as substitute, 180; Spielberg's films and, 58, 143, 147; in *The War of the Worlds* (Pal), 257

remote control, 102–3

replacement child, in *A.I.*, 235–36

Return of the Jedi (Lucas), 102

"Road Runner" cartoons, 17

Robinson, Anne, 258, 263

robots, 229

romantic films, 154–55; *Always* and, 152; *Close Encounters* and, 67–68; Spielberg and, 271

Rose, Jacqueline, 186

Ross, Steve, 228

Rowan, John, 188

Ruppersberg, Hugh, 84

Ryan, Michael, 49–50

Rycroft, Charles, 195

Sabbadini, Andrew, 235

Sackler, Howard, 38

sadism: anal, 25; in *Jaws*, 37–38; oral, 37, 49

Sahara (film), 154

Sarris, Andrew, 88, 90n2, 102, 229

Satinover, Jeffrey, 190

Saunders, Cheryl McAllister, 19, 25, 35, 172, 175

Savage (Spielberg), 13

Saving Private Ryan (Spielberg), 217, 258, 268

Scheider, Roy, *30*

Schindler's List (Keneally), 228

Schindler's List (Spielberg), 68, 184, 210, 228, 230, 262, 264, 268–69

science: in *A.I.*, 232–33; child contrasted with, 83; in *E.T.*, 83

science fiction (SF) films: critical bias against, 6–8; revolution of 1970s in, 3–4, 10n4; special effects in, 59; Spielberg and, 2–10

Science Fiction Theater (television series), 174
scores. *See* musical scores
Scorsese, Martin, 174
Scott, A. O., 240
seen/unseen theme: in *Jaws*, 31, 34–36, 51; in *Minority Report*, 248–49
separation anxiety: in *Always*, 163; in *Close Encounters*, 68–70; in *E.T.*, 89; in *Indiana Jones and the Temple of Doom*, 134; in "Kick the Can," 169–70; in "The Mission," 176; in Spielberg's films, 56, 98, 134, 272
serials, 109–10, 121n1
Serling, Rod, 16, 169
sexism, 126–27, 145
sexuality: in *Always*, 162; Barrie's, 185–86; in *Close Encounters*, 65; in *E.T.*, 87–88; flying and, 162, 192; "The Frog King" and, 87–88; in *Hook*, 186, 198–99; in *Indiana Jones and the Last Crusade*, 146; in *Jaws*, 32–33, 34, 37–38, 50, 65; in *Poltergeist*, 104–5; pre-pubertal period versus, 65; in Spielberg's films, 104, 161. *See also* homosexuality; primal scene
Shakespeare, William, 99
Shaw, Robert, 39
Sheehan, Henry, 183, 196, 214
Sheinberg, Sidney, 228
Shell, 57
The Shining (King), 106
The Shining (Kubrick), 106
Shyamalan, M. Night, 260
Signs (Shyamalan), 260
Silverman, Kaja, 253
Simpson, David, 262
simulacra, *A.I.* and, 228–29
Singer, Jerome, 86
Sinyard, Neil, 95
Siskel, Gene, 273
Slade, Darren, 172
"Sleeping Beauty," 131
Smith, Howard K., 57
Smith, John J., 257–58
Snow White (film), 89
Snyder, Thomas Lee, 17, 18

Sobchack, Vivian, 2, 59, 78, 88
Something Evil (Spielberg), 13, 96
Song of the South (film), 172–73
Sophocles, 243
special effects: in *Close Encounters*, 59; emotional impact of, 59; in *Poltergeist*, 96–97
Spiegelman, Art, 235
Spielberg, Steven, 30, 94, 95, 204; on *A.I.*, 230; alter egos of, 159, 163, 210–11; and *Amazing Stories*, 173–75; Barrie and, 184–86; childhood movie experiences of, 109; and dinosaurs, 215; divorce of, 152; and divorce of parents, 56–57, 75, 99, 105, 152, 192, 267; as Eagle Scout, 139; ego ideal of, 71; on *E.T.*, 75, 86, 95, 267; family of, 89, 199; as father, 176–77, 183, 209; father figures for, 228; father of, 176–77, 183, 187–88, 228; and father theme, 137–38; fears and phobias of, 191; as filmmaker, 68–69, 163, 172, 176, 179; and flying, 191–92; on *Hook*, 200; on *Indiana Jones and the Temple of Doom*, 126, 127, 131, 134; on *Jaws*, 32–34, 37, 51; on *Jurassic Park*, 203; and Kubrick, 227–28, 230; life changes for, 148; on *The Lost World*, 209, 217; on *Minority Report*, 250; mother of, 129, 161, 189; and *Peter Pan* musical, 190; and Peter Pan syndrome, 189–90; on *Poltergeist*, 95, 103; professional start of, 13; and psychotherapy, 186, 192; on *Raiders of the Lost Ark*, 110, 112, 114; on *The War of the Worlds*, 258; and women, 161; workaholism of, 188; youthful influences on, 3, 151–52. *See also* Spielberg, Steven, films of
Spielberg, Steven, films of: *A.I.*, 2, 227–40; *Always*, 2, 62, 151–65, 179, 189, 192; autobiographical nature of, 153; characteristics of, 1–3; and childhood experience, 1, 5–6, 56, 58, 230, 268–72; *Close Encounters of the Third Kind*, 2, 3, 5–6, 55–73, 78, 83,

88, 169, 179, 209, 230, 267, 268–69, 273, 275n1; *The Color Purple*, 2, 6, 9; critical response to, 1, 5–10; *Duel*, 2, 13–27, 31, 68, 96, 106; emotional appeal of, 1–2, 6–9, 272–73; *Empire of the Sun*, 2, 6, 62, 134, 176, 231–32, 236–37; *E.T.*, 2, 4, 5, 6–7, 9, 31, 55–58, 64, 75–90, 94–95, 106, 169, 179, 190, 230, 250, 267; family in, 247, 260, 267–68; fathers in, 271; flying in, 62, 176, 191; "Ghost Train," 175; Hitchcock's films compared to, 15, 32–35, 37–38, 48, 100; *Hook*, 64, 77, 173, 183–200, 260; *Indiana Jones and the Last Crusade*, 137–48, 192; *Indiana Jones and the Temple of Doom*, 125–34, 126; influence of, 3–4, 10n4; influences on, 5; *Jaws*, 2, 3, 26, 29–51, 68, 96, 106, 126; *Jurassic Park*, 26, 68, 71, 126, 184, 203–17, 260; "Kick the Can," 64, 151, 169–73, 179; *The Lost World*, 26, 126, 217–22, 260; mass culture in, 57–58; "The Mission," 62, 174–81; moralizing in, 147; movie influences on, 152; *1941*, 2, 13, 62, 68, 129, 152, 200, 222; *Poltergeist*, 2, 4, 10, 55–58, 68, 78, 88, 93–106, 94–95, 134, 169, 179, 267; pranksters in, 68–69; psychological dimensions of, 272; *Raiders of the Lost Ark*, 3, 68, 109–21; romance in, 271; *Savage*, 13; *Saving Private Ryan*, 217, 258, 268; *Schindler's List*, 68, 184, 210, 228, 230, 262, 264, 268, 268–69; separation anxiety in, 272; sexuality in, 161; and SF/fantasy/ horror genres, 2–10; *Something Evil*, 13, 96; *Sugarland Express*, 68, 134; television in, 57; themes in, 267–68; *The War of the Worlds*, 253–64
splitting, psychological defense of, 86–88, 100, 127–28, 130
Spy Smasher (serial), 109
Stairway to Heaven (film), 155
Star Wars (Lucas), 2, 57, 112, 137–39, 146
Stella Dallas (film), 154

Stephens, Chuck, 213
Sterritt, David, 98
Stevens, Wallace, 240
Stoker, Bram, 256
storytelling. *See* narrative
Stoves, Richard, 89
St. Paul, 59
subjective camera, 31, 48, 80
suburbia: *Close Encounters* and, 4, 55–58, 63, 98, 267; *Duel* and, 16; *E.T.* and, 55–58, 78, 95, 98, 267; *Poltergeist* and, 55–58, 95, 97–100, 103, 267; Spielberg's films and, 4, 55–58. *See also* domestic realm
Sugarland Express (Spielberg), 68, 134
"Sunday Morning" (Stevens), 240
Superman, 113
Swayze, Patrick, 164

taboo: Freud on, 111–12, 115; *Raiders of the Lost Ark* and, 114–16, 118–21; touching and, 115–16
Tailspin Tommy (serial), 109
Tales of the Gold Monkey (television show), 110
television: in *Close Encounters*, 101; cultural attitudes toward, 101, 174; in *Poltergeist*, 100–101; in Spielberg's films, 57
Telotte, J. P., 229
The Ten Commandments (DeMille), 57, 58
Terminal, The (Spielberg), 268
The Texas Chainsaw Massacre (Hooper), 93
Them (film), 62
The Thing from Another World (film), 93
The Thirty-Nine Steps (Hitchcock), 15
Thomson, David, 38, 45, 93
thrillers: *Duel* and, 14–16; of Hitchcock, 13; paranoia as theme in, 18–19
"Through Channels" (Matheson), 96
THX 1138 (Lucas), 16
Tiger, Lionel, 43, 45
Todorov, Tzvetan, 16
Tomasulo, Frank P., 111

Tom Sawyer (Twain), 139
Topper films, 155
totem, 119, 216
Totem and Taboo (Freud), 111–12, 120
Touch of Evil (Welles), 15
Tracy, Spencer, 153, 155, 158
transformational objects, 60–61, 274
transitional objects, 86
Traube, Elisabeth, 126–27
trauma. *See* national trauma
The Treasure of the Sierra Madre
  (Bogart), 114
Truffaut, François, 71, 210
Trumbull, Douglas, 66
The Twilight Zone (television series), 16,
  96, 171, 174
Twilight Zone: The Movie, 151, 169
2001: A Space Odyssey (Kubrick), 2, 83,
  227, 230, 237–39

uncanny: *A.I.* and, 232, 238; *Raiders of
  the Lost Ark* and, 121; in Spielberg's
  films, 57–58
United 93 (film), 253
Universal Studios, 13
Universal Studios theme park, 209

Variety (magazine), 94
Vertigo (Hitchcock), 48
visual style. *See* cinematography; special
  effects
Von Sydow, Max, 247

The War of the Worlds (Pal), 255, 257,
  258
The War of the Worlds (Spielberg),
  253–64, *259*, *261*; ending of, 263;
  family in, 260, 263; Iraq War and,
  262–63; and national trauma, 264;
  9/11 parallels in, 260–62; previous
  versions and, 258–59; Spielberg on,
  258

The War of the Worlds (Welles), 255–57
The War of the Worlds (Wells), 254–56,
  263
Warren, Bill, 93
Watson, Ian, 227
Watson, Nigel, 172
Wayne, John, 87, 152
Weaver, Dennis, 15
Welles, Orson, 15, 255–57
Wells, H. G., 4, 254–56, 263
Westerns: *Duel* and, 17; *Jaws* and, 51n4;
  realism and, 6
When Wendy Grew Up (Barrie), 183–84
white, symbolic value of, 161
White, Armond, 148n2, n3
Williams, John, 31, 152, 175, 190
Winnicott, D. W., 274
The Wizard of Oz (film), 4, 90
Wollen, Peter, 214, 216
womb imagery: in *Always*, 162; in *Close
  Encounters*, 61, 65; in *E.T.*, 88; in
  Jaws, 37, 49; in "The Mission," 176,
  178–79; in *Poltergeist*, 102
women: in *Duel*, 21–24; fear/hatred of,
  21–24; in *Hook*, 198–99; in *Jaws*,
  49–50; and sexism, 126–27, 145.
  See also mothers and the maternal
Wood, Robin, 6, 8
Woody Woodpecker, 152
workaholism, 187–88
The World According to Garp (Irving),
  178–79
World Trade Center (film), 253
World War II adventure films, 154
Wright, Will, 6
Wullschläger, Jackie, 185, 200

The Yearling (film), 89, 151

Zacharek, Stephanie, 264
Zanuck, Richard, 39
Zicree, Marc Scott, 172

About the Author

Andrew M. Gordon teaches in the Department of English at the University of Florida and directs the Institute for the Psychological Study of the Arts. His B.A. is from Rutgers University and his M.A. and Ph.D. from the University of California, Berkeley. He served as a Fulbright Lecturer in American Literature in Spain, Portugal, and Serbia and as a visiting professor in Hungary and Russia, and he taught in the University of Florida programs in Rome and Paris. He is the author of *An American Dreamer: A Psychoanalytic Study of the Fiction of Norman Mailer*, coeditor with Peter Rudnytsky of *Psychoanalyses/Feminisms*, and coauthor with Hernán Vera of *Screen Saviors: Hollywood Fictions of Whiteness*. In addition, he has written many articles on contemporary American fiction and on science fiction film, especially the films of the directors George Lucas, Robert Zemeckis, and the Wachowski brothers, and served as editorial consultant on science fiction film for the journal *Science Fiction Studies*. He is a member of the Science Fiction Research Association.